Crawford Howell Toy

Advanced Praise for *Crawford Howell Toy*

Mikeal Parsons puts a sharp pin to our mythic balloons regarding brilliant C. H. Toy, the nineteenth century "heretic" at Southern Seminary who went on to international fame at Harvard Divinity School. Toy, far ahead of his times in biblical scholarship, has at last found a careful, wise, and talented biographer in Parsons who has gone back in time to correct the story. Exceedingly well-written and stunningly well-researched, this is a very important book on many levels.

—*Walter B. Shurden*, minister at large, Mercer University

A brilliant, definitive biography. A masterpiece exhaustively researched and documented and engagingly written, this study will be the standard reference for all future studies not only of Toy's life and career at The Southern Baptist Theological Seminary and Harvard University but also of the evolution of American linguistic and biblical studies during the late-nineteenth and early-twentieth centuries.

—*E. Glenn Hinson*, professor emeritus,
Baptist Theological Seminary at Richmond

Deeply learned and richly textured, this fully-orbed analysis of one of Southern Seminary's most storied figures adds to the scholarship about C.H. Toy and corrects many assumptions about his "heretical" theology. Parsons narrates how a scholar who gets out of provincial Southern Baptist consensus is treated. Had Toy been allowed to remain at Southern he could have helped fashion a more balanced approach to biblical studies, reconciling keen intellect with vibrant spirituality.

—*Molly T. Marshall*, president and professor of
Theology and Spiritual Formation,
Central Baptist Theological Seminary

In spite of C.H. Toy's significance as a topic of study, many conclusions about Toy rest on secondary accounts and speculations. Mikeal Parsons' meticulous work through primary documents, some of which had never been examined, yields a major contribution to understanding Toy's professional and personal life, unearthing new facts and creating revised (and more accurate) understandings of already known facts. Whether exploring his relationship with missionary Lottie Moon, his conflict and camaraderie with fellow academics at Southern Seminary, or his post-Southern Baptist life at Cambridge, Parsons' biography expands our base of knowledge and analysis of Toy. The study will be required reading for Baptist history.

—*Merrill Hawkins*, professor of Religion,
Carson-Newman College

Generations of Southern Seminary students heard the story, but only part of the story. Mikeal Parsons has filled a gap in Baptist history with this definitive biography. What happened to Crawford Toy after he left Southern Seminary? And what was his relationship with Lottie Moon? Meticulously researched and delivered in lively prose, this book brings Toy out of the mists of the past for lovers of biographies, Baptists interested in their heritage, the Harvard community, and historians now and for generations to come.

—*R. Alan Culpepper,* former dean and
professor emeritus, McAfee School
of Theology, Mercer University

Mikeal Parsons has given us an extraordinary narrative, telling the story of C.H. Toy, a generally misunderstood and often vilified nineteenth-century Baptist seminary professor, and untangling the half-truths and myths that have continued to surround Toy's life and legacy. The inclusion of lengthy excerpts from Toy's correspondence, much of which has never been published, offers readers insight into the layered complexity of his spiritual development, intellectual interests, and personal relationships. Parsons moves past the popularly accepted disparaging and romanticized accounts of Toy's life and instead relies on primary sources, church records, and letters that present a much more complete picture. Parsons' excellent research, his engaging writing style, and his even-handed analysis also make this a much-needed resource for Baptist scholars and Baptist laity alike.

—*Pam Durso,* executive director,
Baptist Women in Ministry

PERSPECTIVES ON BAPTIST IDENTITIES

The National Association of Baptist Professors of Religion is proud to join with Mercer University Press in the creation of a new academic series. *Perspectives on Baptist Identities* will explore the rapidly evolving questions of identity that press upon those who call themselves Baptist in the twenty-first century: What does it mean to be Baptist? What does the future hold for Baptists? How does the Baptist tradition relate to the global Church and other ecclesial traditions? How does Baptist identity impact Scripture reading and Christian practice? The series hopes to generate significant scholarly research and engender fruitful and lively conversation among various types of Baptists and non-Baptists.

Dr. Adam C. English
Professor of Theology and Philosophy
Department of Christian Studies, Campbell University

Dr. Alicia Myers
Associate Professor of New Testament and Greek
Divinity School, Campbell University

Crawford Howell Toy

THE MAN, THE SCHOLAR, THE TEACHER

Mikeal C. Parsons

*To Bunt,
& in friendship,
Mikeal*

MERCER UNIVERSITY PRESS
Macon, Georgia
1979–2019
40 Years of Publishing Excellence

MUP/ P593

© 2019 by Mercer University Press
Published by Mercer University Press
1501 Mercer University Drive
Macon, Georgia 31207
All rights reserved

9 8 7 6 5 4 3 2 1

Books published by Mercer University Press are printed on acid-free paper
that meets the requirements of the American National Standard for
Information Sciences—Permanence of Paper for Printed Library Materials.

Printed and bound in the United States.

Book cover design by Burt&Burt.
This book is set in Adobe Caslon Pro.

ISBN   978-0-88146-725-3
Cataloging-in-Publication Data is available from the Library of Congress

For C. Douglas Weaver

Faithful friend through four decades,

Baptist champion of religious liberty and

freedom of conscience extraordinaire

Contents

FOREWORD

In 1879, Crawford Howell Toy (1836–1919) resigned his decade-long position as Professor of Old Testament and Oriental Languages at the Southern Baptist Theological Seminary, Louisville, Kentucky, in response, among other things, to concerns related to his leftward views of biblical inspiration. An editorial published shortly thereafter in the local *Louisville Courier Journal* and republished in the *Western Recorder*, a Kentucky Baptist periodical, opined, "We are assured that the resignation has been accepted with undiminished kind feeling on the part of all concerned. Dr. Toy is a man of signal ability, extraordinary learning and very noble character."[1] Almost a century later, another Baptist professor would observe, "Never was a heretic more beloved by his accusers."[2]

It wouldn't last. Toy's acceptance of an invitation to become Hancock Professor of Hebrew and other Oriental Languages at Harvard University in 1880 confirmed for later generations of conservative Southern Baptists that he was a brilliant but far from benign wolf-in-sheep's-clothing whose removal was essential to the preservation of Christian orthodoxy in Baptist theological education. Indeed, in 2018 the online summary of "Our History" at the Southern Baptist Theological Seminary (SBTS) included this description of "Controversy 1878–1889":

> Toy initially professed firm belief in biblical truth, declaring in his inaugural address that without the Bible, man is "on a boundless ocean, wrapped in darkness." But Toy embraced Darwinian evolution and naturalistic "higher criticism" of the Old Testament. He became convinced that Scripture contained error, science trumped Scripture's plain meaning, and conscience was the test of truth. The orthodoxy Toy claimed stood in stark contrast to the false interpretations he believed.[3]

Crawford Toy was perhaps the first in a rather substantial line of liberal, progressive, and/or non-fundamentalist professors at multiple Southern Bap-

---

[1] *Western Recorder*, May 22, 1879.

[2] John Powell Clayton, "Crawford Howell Toy of Virginia," *Baptist Quarterly* 24 (1971): 50.

[3] "Our Story," The Southern Baptist Theological Seminary, http://archives.sbts.edu/the-history-of-the-sbts/our-story/controversy-1878-1889/.

tist-related educational institutions who "had to go" in the nineteenth, twentieth, and twenty-first centuries because of their beliefs, their publications, or even their gender. (But that's another story.)

Suffice it to say that from the time of his departure from Southern Baptists' first seminary, Crawford Toy's life and thought never lacked for examination, analysis, and debate in multiple investigations circulated through articles, textbooks, doctoral dissertations, scholarly inquiries, and populist rhetoric, each offering varying degrees of explanation, affirmation, or condemnation. In *Crawford Howell Toy—From Southern Seminary to Harvard University*, Mikeal C. Parsons, professor and Macon Chair of Religion at Baylor University, provides an exceptional study that offers a breadth and depth of research, documentation, and complexity for understanding Toy's life and times as well as his place in American higher education. That Parsons should have undertaken such a biographical analysis is not surprising given that he too is a celebrated specialist in biblical studies, a prolific writer, and an ordained Baptist minister with a PhD from the Southern Baptist Theological Seminary where Crawford Toy was both student and professor. In 2018, his two sons were Harvard undergraduates. Parsons's superb volume, published in the centennial year of Toy's death, is important for numerous reasons.

First, as professor, researcher, and author, Crawford Howell Toy made significant contributions to American higher education, particularly in religious studies, at some six schools, with his longest tenure at the Southern Baptist Theological Seminary and Harvard Divinity School during the decades immediately following the Civil War. A master linguist, Toy taught Hebrew and Hebrew Bible classes at two schools that spanned the theological spectrum, while also tutoring students at both institutions in a variety of ancient Middle Eastern languages. At Harvard, he encouraged and contributed to the study of "comparative religion," anticipating modern university programs that investigate diverse religious traditions and the nature of religion itself. Crawford Toy is worth studying for who he was and what he meant to American higher education.

Second, Toy's life as teacher/scholar represents something of a bridge between regional, cultural, and academic disciplines, methodologies, and ideologies—South and North—in the post-Civil War era. A Virginia native, Toy graduated from the University of Virginia in 1856. While there, he experienced Christian conversion during a local revival meeting, receiving baptism through a congregation affiliated with the Southern Baptist Convention, a denomination established in 1845 because of Baptist differences regarding chattel slavery. When war came, Toy served as a chaplain in the Confederate

Army, strongly supporting the Southern cause. Although he apparently never owned slaves, Toy became the fifth faculty member at SBTS, a school at which his four faculty colleagues were known slaveholders, a reality that continues to compromise their claims of Christian orthodoxy.

The depth of Toy's Southern heritage and Confederate sentiments makes even more striking the decision of President Charles William Eliot and the Harvard faculty to offer him a distinguished professorship merely fifteen years after the war's end. Parsons's study carefully documents the various ways that Toy responded to life "up East" and the multiple contributions he brought to his academic research and classroom teaching at Harvard University, bridging broken cultures in post-Civil War America.

Third, Professor Parsons's meticulous documentation of the details of Toy's life is yet another reason why his research is so significant. One of the book's most outstanding contributions involves the way in which it clarifies, and in several cases challenges, the historicity of earlier claims regarding Toy's personal story. Indeed, Parsons has discovered numerous sources that provide new insights on a variety of "myths" related to Toy's beliefs, relationships, and activities. These findings compel a reexamination of certain assertions made in earlier studies.

Fourth, the book offers fascinating details of Toy's varied personal relationships with religionists, academics, politicians, and other public figures nationally and internationally. We learn of his friendships with the movers and shakers of the Southern Baptist Convention, including John A. Broadus, his early academic and pastoral mentor at the University of Virginia and Southern Baptist Seminary; James P. Boyce, president of the seminary; and William H. Whitsitt, the school's second president, himself sent packing in 1899. Parsons documents the dynamics of these interactions, sometimes deep and exalted, sometimes troubled and petty.

Parsons's study explores Toy's relationship with certain females, including Lottie Moon, the iconic Baptist missionary to China to whom he was allegedly engaged for a time, and Nancy Inge Saunders, whom he married in 1888 and who was a resourceful individual with her own creative approaches to modernity. Her friendships with public figures such as President Woodrow Wilson and his two spouses, Edith and Ellen Wilson, are yet another fascinating element of the book. Both Nancy and Crawford Toy forged important bonds with well-known Harvard-related academics such as philosopher George Santayana, psychologist William James, and President Charles Eliot. Parsons's discussion of the academic and personal connections between Toy and David Lyon illustrates Toy's role as colleague and mentor in bringing

Lyon, his student at Southern Baptist Seminary, to the Harvard Divinity School faculty. At Harvard, Lyon made his own significant contribution to biblical studies and higher education.

Finally, Mikeal Parsons documents the fact that Crawford Toy's academic and religious experiences anticipated explosive theological divisions that descended on American Christian institutions over questions of science, biblical and ecclesiastical authority, the use of confessional documents, and the nature of orthodoxy itself. Toy's sense of Christian spirituality was clearly shaped by the conversion-oriented experientialism of the Believers' Church tradition, within and beyond his experience at the Southern Baptist Theological Seminary. Yet his engagement with modern historical-critical methods of biblical and theological studies set him on a collision course with the confessional identity of the seminary and its parent denomination. The events of the now infamous "Toy Controversy," however, occurred at a time in American religious history when neither liberalism nor its reactive fundamentalism had acquired the fiery intensity that would explode across the theological landscape in the "controversy of the 1920s" and beyond.

Crawford Toy was but the first of a rather substantial group of individuals nurtured in the Southern Baptist Convention who were unable to remain due to multiple theological, ecclesiastical, and cultural disputes. Some, like Toy, left or were forced out because the denomination was too conservative; others, like fundamentalist J. Frank Norris, because it was not conservative enough. Still others, on both right and left, remained connected to the denomination, their views tolerated, if not accepted, at specific moments in Southern Baptist history.

Professor Parsons revisits, indeed revises, various aspects of the life and work of Crawford Howell Toy, with implications for theological issues and disputes that continue to fracture American religious institutions and faith communities. In the end, Parsons reminds his readers that Crawford Toy, the man and "the controversy," emerged not only with the rise of theological liberalism but also in a denomination born in defense of chattel slavery in the United States of America. Those twin realities temper claims of orthodoxy— North and South, left and right, then and now.

Bill J. Leonard
Dunn Professor of Baptist Studies Emeritus
Wake Forest University

PREFACE

The path that led a New Testament professor to write a biography on a scholar of Hebrew and Oriental languages is a bit circuitous. In the spring semester of 2017, my spouse, Heidi Hornik, and I were Visiting Scholars at Harvard Divinity School. Our time there was gratifying both personally and professionally. We were able to visit regularly with our sons, Mikeal Joseph and Matthew, who were both Harvard undergraduates. I was working on a book, *Ancient Rhetoric and the New Testament*, and Heidi was finishing a book, *The Art of Christian Reflection*, both of which are now published.[4] As it happened, the divinity school was celebrating its 200th anniversary while we were there, and I often stopped to read the associated exhibits that lined the walls between our office and the Andover-Harvard Theological Library. One exhibit on the Hebrew Bible and Jewish Studies at Harvard featured Crawford Howell Toy. The placard read:

> Study of the Hebrew Bible, revered by Harvard's Puritan founders, had a secure place in the curriculum long before the founding of the Divinity School. Ability to read the Old Testament in the original languages, Hebrew and Aramaic, joined the knowledge of Latin and Greek as a foundation of the learned ministry. The Hancock Professor of Hebrew and Other Oriental Languages was Harvard's third endowed chair, established in 1764. The Hancock Professor was required to publicly "declare himself to be of the Protestant reformed religion as it is now professed and practiced by the churches in New England."
>
> President Eliot turned first to the Hancock Professorship when he reached beyond the Unitarian faith and the New England region to establish the academic preeminence of the Divinity School faculty in 1880. Determined to demonstrate scholarly rigor as well as intellectual independence from the churches, he offered the post to W. Robertson Smith, the British advocate of higher criticism then on trial for heresy in Scotland. Believing incorrectly that he had been acquitted, Smith declined.
>
> Eliot then offered the position to Crawford Howell Toy, professor of Old Testament at Southern Baptist Seminary in Louisville, Kentucky, who had studied in Germany. Toy was forced to resign his Southern Baptist post when he taught that writers of the New Testament misinterpreted the Old

---

[4] Heidi J. Hornik, *The Art of Christian Reflection: Imagination, Interpretation, and Ethics* (Waco, TX: Baylor University Press, 2018); Mikeal C. Parsons and Michael Wade Martin, *Ancient Rhetoric and the New Testament: The Influence of Elementary Greek Composition* (Waco, TX: Baylor University Press, 2018).

Testament when they viewed it through a Christological lens. Adoption of the higher criticism ended not only Toy's job, but also his hopes for marriage to his former Hebrew student, Southern Baptist icon Lottie Moon, who severed their engagement. After eight years at Harvard, Toy foiled Eliot's original intent by joining a Unitarian church.[5]

This description, I later discovered, contains several misstatements, or half-truths, that have contributed to the ongoing Toy saga. Toy's views on the interpretation of the OT in the NT were not part of the original concerns expressed about his teaching and scholarship at Southern Seminary, though they did play a role at the very end. Nor is there conclusive evidence that Moon broke an engagement with Toy (if there was one) over differences in theology (in fact, an engagement announcement was published in a denominational paper in 1882, nearly three years after Toy's departure from Southern and after his second year at Harvard). Finally, it is imprecise to say that Toy "joined" the Unitarian church. He did, in fact, leave the Old Cambridge Baptist Church (under his own volition, and with OCBC's commendation that he was of "good Christian character," contrary to another version of the myth) and attended the First Parish Unitarian Church in Cambridge, but there is no record that he ever joined there (and the membership records of First Parish during this time are very complete). These points, and many more, are addressed in this book.

I thought I knew Toy's story—or part of it, at least—from a course on Baptist history that I took with Dr. Walter "Buddy" Shurden at Southern Seminary in the fall semester of 1981. The account of Toy's rise and fall among the luminaries at Southern Seminary was fascinating to me at that time, and seeing his image, along with a brief description of his life at Harvard, renewed my interest.[6] What happened to Toy after he left Louisville, I wondered. Thus began a quest to learn more about the life of Crawford Howell Toy. That search led me first to the libraries and archives at Harvard and Boston College and later to research trips to Southern Seminary in Louisville, Kentucky; the Virginia Baptist Historical Society in Richmond, Virginia; the Southern Baptist Historical Library and Archives in Nashville, Tennessee; the University of Texas in Austin; and the Woman's Missionary Union Archives in Birmingham, Alabama, as well as to correspondence with archivists and

---

[5] The exhibit was on display for most of spring semester 2017.

[6] Below the placard quoted above were pictures of three professors who had held the Hancock professorship: Toy, Frank Moore Cross, and Peter Machinist. About Toy was written, "At Harvard Toy (1836–1919) taught Arabic as well as Hebrew and Aramaic, and was a founder of the Semitic Museum and the Department of Semitic Languages (now, Near Eastern Languages and Civilizations)."

librarians at Furman University, the University of Virginia, the University of North Carolina Chapel Hill, the Historical Society of Norfolk, Virginia, the (now defunct) Andover-Newton Theological Seminary, the International Missions Board Archives, and the University of South Carolina. For all the wonderful resources and assistance rendered by those personnel, I am truly grateful (for archival abbreviations, see Bibliography). Dr. Cody Sanders, pastor of Old Cambridge Baptist Church, opened the church's archives to me, and Cody and the OCBC congregation provided a church home for me during my research leave. Adam Winter at Southern Baptist Theological Seminary in Louisville; Fred Anderson, Nathan Taylor, and Darlene Herod at the Virginia Baptist Historical Society and the University of Richmond Archives; and Taffey Hall of the Southern Baptist Historical Library and Archives in Nashville were especially helpful. Adam sent numerous pdfs upon request and fulfilled my every bibliographic request during my return to my alma mater in the summer of 2017, and Taffey Hall provided a Lynn E. May, Jr. Study Grant that facilitated my visit to Nashville, where I was able to consult various denominational papers. I am not by training a historian of American religion, so I am grateful to these librarians and archivists for lending their expertise.

I discovered along the way that with regard to citing primary documents, historians seem to fall into one of two camps: those who prefer relatively shorter quotations with more interpretation and those who prefer (or at least tolerate) longer citations of primary material to allow the sources to speak for themselves (though with requisite historical context and interpretation). I had intended to focus only on Toy's Harvard career, given its neglect in existing scholarship. But in my research I found documents that had been underused (Toy's "Sketch of My Religious Life") or previously unavailable (W. H. Whitsitt's diary), in addition to Toy's scattered correspondence preserved in the libraries and archives listed above. Therefore, I have definitely followed the approach of providing extensive citations from primary sources, especially because many of the long quotations from Toy's formative period and later Harvard career are previously unpublished and not always easily accessible. There are also the remarkable and rare glimpses into the interactions of a late-nineteenth/early twentieth-century woman of letters with men of power and influence provided by the correspondence between Nancy Saunders Toy (Crawford's spouse) and President Woodrow Wilson as well as philosopher and litterateur George Santayana. Thus, I hope by providing generous quotations in terms of number and length to invite others to (re-)engage the interpretation of the life and work of Crawford Toy, though I do not expect this explanation to thwart those (especially reviewers) who prefer more minimal citations.

I should single out several colleagues at Baylor and beyond who read all or parts of the manuscript drafts, many of them trained historians who kept me from making serious interpretative missteps (as always, those that remain are solely of my own doing). Thanks to Catherine B. Allen, Carol Ann Vaughn Cross, Alan Culpepper, Betsy Flowers, Joseph Greene, Barry Hankins, Barry Harvey, Bruce Longenecker, Peter der Manuelian, Mandy McMichael, Chris Moore, Scott Moore, and Doug Weaver, to whom the work is dedicated. My appreciation for Doug's friendship over the years (going back to our days together at SBTS) is beyond words. Special thanks to Bill Leonard, who deserves a double portion of gratitude for offering to write the foreword to the book. Portions of chapter 2 and the Toy-Moon Excursus were presented at the National Association of Baptist Professors of Religion; appreciation is expressed to all those who offered encouragement and critique, often simultaneously!

Bill Bellinger, my departmental chair, provided support and necessary resources for research and writing. I am grateful to Alicia Myers and Adam English for accepting the manuscript in the Perspectives on Baptist Identities Series and to Marc Jolley and his staff at Mercer University Press for publishing it. A number of graduate students helped prepare the manuscript for publication, and I wish publicly to acknowledge my gratitude to Greg Barnhill, Rebecca Hays, Samuel Otwell, Marcus Jerkins, and Josiah Hall, who prepared the index. Nathan Hays's work on Toy's published writings (and their critical reception) was done so well that I invited him to serve as a co-author of that section of chapter 5. As always, Heidi Hornik has enriched my life, personally and professionally, beyond measure.

After hours and hours of searching for and then poring over correspondence to and from Crawford Howell Toy located in Cambridge, Massachusetts, and across the Southeast, as well as the body of secondary literature produced on Toy, I think that I have come to understand a bit better this brilliant scholar, but I cannot claim to have fully understood his complex personality. I am pleased to share what I have learned about this remarkable man as a commemoration marking the centennial of his death in 1919.

Mikeal Parsons
Department of Religion
Baylor University

LIST OF FIGURES

INTRODUCTION

1

Hero or Heretic?

In a January 11, 2010, editorial for *EthicsDaily.com* titled "Lottie Moon and Crawford Toy: Two Baptist Heroes," Tony Cartledge asserts: "I have also come to admire Crawford Toy, who was no less devoted to Christ, and who was willing to suffer rejection by Southern Baptists rather than surrender to the narrow-minded demand that he forgo scholarship and limit his teaching to popularly accepted notions. There's more than one way to be a hero."[1]

In a response to the column, Al Mohler, president of Southern Seminary, called the essay "deeply disturbing." He argued:

> After his resignation from Southern Seminary, Crawford Toy acepted a professorship at Harvard University, where he taught for many years and established a reputation for scholarship. By all accounts, Toy was an esteemed member of the faculty. Nevertheless, Toy's theological trajectory did indeed take him not only out of the Southern Baptist fellowship, but out of the Christian faith altogether. During his time at Harvard, Toy eventually became a Unitarian—a faith that denies the deity of Christ and the doctrine of the Trinity. He also accepted an evolutionary understanding of religion which accepted religion as a purely natural phenomenon. In other words, Toy became what Christians throughout all the centuries of church history and in all the major traditions of the Christian Church would rightly identify as a heretic. He abandoned faith in the deity of Christ and abandoned the Christian faith. Yet, moderates in the SBC controversy often celebrated Crawford Toy as a hero and as a theological martyr for academic scholarship. Tony Cartledge continues this tradition by expressing his admiration for Crawford Toy, going so far as to claim that he "was no less devoted to Christ" than Lottie Moon.[2]

---

[1] Tony Cartledge, "Lottie Moon and Crawford Toy: Two Baptist Heroes," http://www.ethicsdaily.com/news.php?viewStory=15446. The editorial was prompted by an announcement at the time by Paige Patterson, President of Southwestern Baptist Theological Seminary, that the seminary was in receipt of some of Lottie Moon's furniture from her time as a missionary to China.

[2] Albert Mohler, "Heresy Is Not Heroic—Is Crawford Howell Toy a Baptist Hero?" January 13, 2010, https://albertmohler.com/2010/01/13/heresy-is-not-heroic-is-crawford-howell-toy-a-baptist-hero/; see also S. Craig Sanders, "Making a Heretic," *Towers*

This renewed conflict occurred 130 years after the so-called "Toy controversy" culminated in Toy's forced resignation from the faculty of Southern Seminary. In fact, over the years the Toy episode has fired the imagination and fueled the controversies between Baptists of various stripes. During the so-called "Elliott controversy" in which Midwestern Baptist Seminary Professor Ralph Elliott was ultimately fired for theological views expressed in his Genesis commentary,[3] the North Carolina *Biblical Recorder* printed a critical commentary, comparing the Elliott affair with the Toy controversy (and also with a controversy involving W. H. Whitsitt): "It's a trite saying, but it's amazing how history repeats itself as Midwestern Seminary trustees this week discuss the fate of Dr. Ralph Elliott who has Southern Baptist history against him in defending his book on Genesis. ...in both instances [Toy and Whitsitt] the men involved stepped aside, thus avoiding a serious split in the convention."[4]

During the height of the conservative takeover of the Southern Baptist Convention, W. A. Criswell, pastor of the First Baptist Church, Dallas, gave a now famous sermon, "Whether We Live or Die," to the SBC Pastor's Conference in which Criswell asserted "the virus of higher criticism destroyed his [Toy's] spiritual life and work." He concluded that portion of his sermon by asserting that "we must wage a war against the disease that, more than any other, will ruin our missionary, evangelistic, and soul-winning commitment."[5] According to Jerry Sutton, Criswell claimed this sermon was the most important he ever preached.[6]

Despite the fact that the story of Crawford Howell Toy clearly continues to have currency, it is striking that he has never been the subject of a full-length published study. In fact, aside from one unpublished 1965 SBTS dissertation,[7] scholars have tended to focus on one specific period—indeed on just a few days in Toy's career that culminated in his forced resignation from the faculty of The Southern Baptist Theological Seminary in May 1879. They

---

14/7 (2016), http://equip.sbts.edu/publications/towers/making-a-heretic-crawford-toys-tragic-path-from-star-student-to-false-teacher/.

[3] See Walter Shurden, *Not a Silent People: Controversies That Have Shaped Southern Baptists* (Macon, GA: Smyth & Helwys, 1995) 69–92.

[4] "Trite but True: History Repeats Itself with Southern Baptists," *Biblical Recorder*, September 29, 1962. In fact, Elliott was dismissed for insubordination.

[5] "Whether We Live or Die," *W. A. Criswell Sermon Library*, June 10, 1985, https://www.wacriswell.com/sermons/1985/whether-we-live-or-die-sbc/; see also Jerry Sutton, *The Baptist Reformation: The Conservative Resurgence in the Southern Baptist Convention* (Nashville: Broadman and Holman, 2000) 147.

[6] Sutton, *The Baptist Reformation*, 147.

[7] Billy G. Hurt, "Crawford Howell Toy: Old Testament Interpreter" (Ph.D. diss., The Southern Baptist Theological Seminary), 1965.

have attended to what preceded the "Toy controversy" as mostly prelude and largely ignored what followed. This monograph attempts to fill that lacuna. Sandwiched between this introduction and a conclusion are seven chapters arranged in two parts. The first part deals with Toy's life from birth (1836) through the controversy and its aftermath (1881). These chapters basically follow a chronological arrangement. The second part deals with Toy's career at Harvard through his retirement years (1880–1919). These chapters have a more topical arrangement. The topics are determined by the kind of criteria typically used to judge a professor's accomplishments (publications, university and community service, and interpersonal relationships). Two chapters deal with Toy's professional life at Harvard (and beyond); two chapters deal with Toy's personal relationships with two key figures, David Gordon Lyon and his spouse, Nancy Saunders Toy. The conclusion attempts to move beyond judging whether Toy is a hero or heretic in order to understand his place in the modern American religious landscape, as well as his role in the development of modern Baptist identity.

In 1880, Professor Ezra Abbot of Harvard University, presumably upon the request of President Charles Eliot, wrote John A. Broadus to inquire about the suitability of Crawford Howell Toy as a possible replacement for Professor Edward J. Young, who had recently resigned his post as Hancock Professor of Hebrew and other Oriental Languages. Abbot wrote, "As you have been associated with Professor C.H. Toy, I venture to ask you to give me frankly and somewhat fully your opinion of him as a man, a scholar, and a teacher."[8] We do not have Broadus's reply to Abbot, but apparently he gave a strong recommendation, and that, combined with President Eliot's personal interview of Toy, led to the appointment of Crawford Howell Toy as the sixth Hancock Professor at Harvard University. Toy's path to Harvard was winding and often turbulent; his life in Cambridge was more settled, but not without adventure! Crawford Howell Toy is a figure whose life as a man, scholar, and teacher is deserving of nothing less than a "frank and somewhat full account." By the book's end, dear reader, I hope you will agree.

---

[8] Ezra Abbot to John A. Broadus, February 12, 1880, Archives and Special Collections, James P. Boyce Centennial Library, The Southern Baptist Theological Seminary, Louisville, KY (ASC, SBTS).

PART 1.
LIFE BEFORE 1880

FORMATIVE YEARS THROUGH SBTS AND (SLIGHTLY) BEYOND (1836–1881)

2

The Formative Years (1836–1869)

In 1866 Crawford Howell Toy boarded a steamer bound for Europe, where he would continue his studies in Germany. The path to this moment in his life was, as we shall see, circuitous with delays and side trips and cul-de-sacs. Always a devoted student, he had decided in college to pursue language studies in Europe. A stirring sermon by John Broadus led him to commit his life to missionary service; the Civil War prevented him from fulfilling that call. A Confederate Chaplain, he was taken as a prisoner of war at the Battle of Gettysburg. After a year's imprisonment at Fort McHenry, he had teaching stints at the University of Alabama and the University of Virginia. He also returned to the Albemarle Female Institute where he had previously taught for three years. During that time, he made the decision to return to his college dream of further studies in Europe. On the night before Crawford Toy left Charlottesville on his way to his trans-Atlantic voyage, he composed a farewell address for the students he had been teaching at the Albemarle Female Institute.

New York, June 16th, 1866

My dear pupils,

On the eve of my departure for Europe, I cannot leave without once more saying goodbye, and assuring you of my affectionate solicitude for your welfare. Our intercourse as Teacher and Pupil has been very pleasant and profitable to me, and I trust not altogether useless to you. I have not time now to say what my anxiety for you would suggest to me, and I can only beg you to carry out faithfully the principle of study and of life which it has been our aim to impress on you. I believe that you set up for yourselves a high standard, and that your aims will be noble. Do not suffer the cares, perplexities, and failures, of life, to divert you from your purposes, and never forget that our weaknesses must be supplemented by the Divine Strength which is promised us. Wherever I may be, I shall hear with exceeding interest all that concerns you, shall rejoice in your happiness, and sorrow in your mourning, and be thankful for all that you effect for the glory of God and the good of man.

I shall always pray that the Triune blessing may accompany you. I do not know that we shall ever again meet in this world; we may all cherish the hope of sympathy in our aims and efforts in this world, and through the grace of God, reunion in the world to come.

May all mercies, temporal and spiritual, be with you. May I not ask for myself a place in your prayers, which may preserve me in many a moment of temptation and weakness.

Your affectionate friend and teacher,

C.H. Toy[1]

The letter reveals a compassionate and thoughtful teacher, concerned for the intellectual and moral development of students in his care. Barely thirty years old himself, Crawford Toy was already an experienced classroom teacher. The adventure he was about to take in Germany would, in many ways, define the trajectory of his own intellectual and spiritual development and shape the style and substance of his pedagogy and scholarship for the rest of his life. But to narrate that story, it is best to begin at the beginning.

Crawford Howell Toy was born on March 23, 1836, in Norfolk, Virginia, to Thomas Dallam Toy and Amelia Rogers Toy.[2] Crawford was the oldest of nine children (four boys and five girls). His father attended school until the age of thirteen and then was apprenticed to a Dr. Santos, who managed the largest drug store in Norfolk. At the age of twenty-one Thomas Dallam Toy became a member of the firm. Except for two periods (1838–1840 in Nashville and 1862–1866 in Baltimore), the Toys lived in Norfolk, and he was a successful druggist.[3]

Mr. Toy was also an amateur linguist.[4] His nephew, Morton Howell, Jr., shared this family reminiscence about Thomas Dallam's blossoming interest in languages during his apprenticeship:

The boy soon observed that Dr. Santos, being of Portuguese birth and Portuguese being his native language, had all the trade of Portuguese war and private vessels that came into the port. Sometimes a customer [who did not speak English] would call when the doctor was out, and then there would be no one to attend him. Thereupon he quietly procured the necessary books and studying at night with the aid of a good knowledge

---

[1] Crawford H. Toy, "Letter to the Students of the Albemarle Female Institute," June 16, 1866, ASC, SBTS.

[2] Amelia Ann Rogers was the granddaughter of a Revolutionary officer. For more on the Toy family, see Morton B. Howell, "The Howells and the Toys," Appendix B in John Lipscomb Johnson, *Autobiographical Notes* (n.p., 1958), 359–66.

[3] Howell, "The Howells and the Toys," 365–66. Howell was Crawford Toy's first cousin and a frequent correspondent during Toy's years at UVA.

[4] Howell, 364.

of Latin, he soon acquired a respectable knowledge of the Portuguese language. In a few months he was able to assist Dr. Santos in supplying and holding the trade of Portugal.[5]

In addition to Latin, Portuguese, and French, Thomas Dallam Toy also studied Hebrew, Italian, Spanish, and German.[6] His knowledge of modern foreign languages especially was an asset in dealing with sailors looking for medicines while in port.[7] Mr. Toy would pass his love for and facility in ancient and modern languages to his son, Crawford.

His granddaughter, Jessie Johnson Harris, preserved this family memory about Thomas Dallam Toy: "Grandpa Toy was a prosperous druggist in Norfolk, wholesale and retail. He was a man of fine intellect, well read and a student of the languages. He was also a man of strong religious convictions. He almost put his religion before his business."[8] The Toys were founding members of the Freemason Street Baptist Church in 1848 and were active in all aspects of the church's ministries. Harris reports, "At one time it is said he [T. D. Toy] mortgaged his home to buy a pipe organ for the beautiful Freemason Street Church. His name is on one side of the stained glass window back of the pulpit."[9] By all available accounts, the Toys were a pious family characterized by daily prayers and family Bible readings.[10]

Crawford Toy recalled his childhood in an essay titled "Sketch of My Religious Life":

My boyhood passed quietly. A trip to Nashville, when I was about 3 years old, and a sojourn there of a year, was the event of that period of my life.

---

[5] Howell, 364–365. Howell also reports that Mr. Toy acquired a "fluent, speaking knowledge" of French to accommodate sailors on French trade vessels (365).

[6] Reuben Jones, *A History of the Virginia Portsmouth Baptist Association* (Raleigh, NC: Edwards, Broughton & Company, 1881), 280; Hurt, "Toy," 12.

[7] Hurt, "Toy," 11; Ella Marshall Thomas, *History of the Freemason Street Baptist Church* (Norfolk, VA: Hampton Roads Paper Company, Inc., 1917), 16.

[8] Jessie Johnson Harris, "My Mother, Julia Ann Toy Johnson," Appendix A in *Autobiographical Notes*, 347. These notes were written by John Johnson at the request of his grandchildren and begun in March 1910 in anticipation of his and Julia Ann Toy's fiftieth wedding anniversary. Howell, "The Howells and the Toys," 365–66, adds: "I heard him [T. D. Toy] say to my father in 1852 that his net income from the store averaged $10,000 a year. But he never saved any money. He and Mr. Dey, a rich retired tailor, whose son afterwards married Toy's oldest daughter, paid the pastor's salary and all the expenses of the Freemason Street Baptist Church in Norfolk, and this cost him nearly $4,000 annually."

[9] Harris, "My Mother," 347. Thomas Toy also directed the choir at Freemason Baptist Church for a period (Thomas, *History of Freemason Street Baptist Church*, 237).

[10] Thomas, *History of Freemason Street Baptist Church*, 16; David G. Lyon, "Crawford Howell Toy," *Harvard Theological Review* 13 (1920): 2.

I grew up, as most town boys do, learnt to read early, when I was about 4 years old, and was mostly occupied with books. All the while my religious education was carefully attended to. My father's ideas of observance of the Sabbath, and similar things, were string. I was never allowed to go to the circus or theatre, and was expected to be regular in attendance at the Sunday School. Sunday afternoon, just after dinner, we children used to recite a lesson to my father, from a Scripton Question Book, or from the Bible, or Biblical Antiquities, or with the youngest, he would read or tell them Scripture stories, on which he would afterwards question them. This Sunday afternoon exercise, kept up for many years, and graduated to our capacity, we found and find very profitable. It not only kept us from idleness between dinner and the prayer meeting, but stored our minds with knowledge of Bible-facts and -doctrines. I learnt many texts and passages of Scripture, came to be familiar with the order of books, and experience now the advantage of that training.[11]

Despite this intense religious training, Toy found it difficult to achieve a satisfying religious stance: "At one time, when I was 11 or 12 years old, I set myself seriously to mend my ways. I retired for prayer and reading the Bible. I read diligently a little book called 'A Guide to the Saviour.' I was anxious to be good, but my evil temper would triumph over my good resolutions, fortified, though these were by reading and prayer, and I gave up the attempt." When he was about thirteen, the newly established Freemason Street Church held revival services. Toy recounts,

During the meeting I became interested, went forward and asked the prayer of the church, and finally professed conversion, more, however, by [evangelist] Mr. R[eynoldson]'s persuasion than by my own conviction. My feelings had not been deeply stirred, as, indeed, my temperament, did not admit. It was, throughout, conviction of duty that urged me on. As I had no overpowering sense of sin, so there was no burst of light and joy. I cannot well describe my state of mind at the time. I wish I could recall it. But, I took stand as a professor of religion—took part in

---

[11] Crawford H. Toy, "Sketch of My Religious Life," May 24, 1860, in T. T. Eaton's Papers, ASC, SBTS. See Appendix 1. The purpose of this essay is unclear, as is why it was found in Eaton's papers. At the end of the document is a note indicating the handwritten document was transcribed by Jason Fowler on January 27, 2003. The note suggests, "This document appears to be in Toy's own hand. The document may have been a prerequisite to his ordination or his examination by the Foreign Mission Board." As such, the sketch contains features typical of a conventional "conversion" narrative including expressions of self-doubt and unworthiness. Thus, the genre of Toy's description of his childhood and youth needs to be accounted for when assessing its historical value. Nonetheless, there seems no need to doubt the broad contours of the narrative.

prayer meeting, was regular in my devotions, etc., but did not offer myself for baptism. Gradually my interest abated, my hope, never very bright, grew less and less, till a year or so from my profession, I had a conversation with [pastor] Mr. Jones, and we agreed that it would not be well for me to ask for baptism. After this, I gave up my religious profession. Looking back now, I can see that I acted precipitately in the first case; I was not sufficiently cared for. But I do not know whether my conversion was real or not. I fell into sin afterwards, but so have many Christians. I lost sight of Christ, and was utterly without religious hope, or enjoyment. I continued to be outwardly respectful to religion, and even devout. I was always a regular attendant on the prayermeetings of the church, where my father commonly led, and I joined in the hymns with as much zeal as anyone. I was not happy. My conscience continually urged on me the claims of religion, and I quaked inwardly at many a sermon, and hoped vaguely that I should be a Christian at some time.[12]

Toy's intense religious introspection and reflection would accompany him throughout his life.

After completing preparatory studies at Norfolk Academy,[13] Crawford Toy entered the University of Virginia in 1852, at the age of sixteen. Toy reminisced about his arrival at college: "I was nothing but a boy, had never been away from home, and was thrown alone into the temptations of a great university. It was the University of Va to which I went. But here my previous education, which had provided me with fixed principles, and my temperament, which was not excitable, proved, under Providence, my safeguard. At college I was a regular in the discharge of religious duties, went to church, prayer meeting, and S. School, and towards the close of the session, I again experienced a hope that my sin was forgiven."[14]

Correspondence between Toy and his cousin, Morton "Mote" Howell (son of pastor, R. B. C. Howell), provide glimpses into his life at an institution of higher learning, a context (of varying expressions) in which he would spend the better part of the next six decades.[15] Toy wrote to his cousin "Mote" on October 11, 1852, just days after arriving on the campus of the University of

---

[12] Toy, "Sketch of My Religious Life."

[13] Lyon, "Toy," 2, reports that upon graduation from the Norfolk Academy, Toy received a copy of Shakespeare's works "for excellence."

[14] Toy, "Sketch of My Religious Life."

[15] The Howell family were great advocates of letter-writing; see Harriet Chappell Owsley, "The Morton B. Howell Papers," *Tennessee Historical Quarterly* 25/3 (1966): 287–309. Owsley comments, "The children of the minister and his wife were urged to write good letters and were reproached for any neglect of this duty" (287).

Virginia. This is the earliest extant piece of writing that can be securely attributed to Toy. His opening line reveals a certain coyness: "I think we differ in our opinions as to which should commence a correspondence, the one who goes away or the one that remains. You maintain the latter, and you should, therefore open, but I think it my duty to write first, and I commence by telling what you probably don't know, that I arrived here safely, more than a week ago."[16] This light-hearted introit soon gives way to the anxiety and uncertainty experienced by many university students on their first extended stay away from home: "I felt rather queerly at first among so many strangers, but have gotten over that in great measure & now feel very much at home. I am very much [?] the homesick; to be sure I do feel a rise in my throat when I think much of home."[17] Still, Toy has little time for self-pity: "I have no time to think, except in bed before I get to sleep. They keep me going pretty straight, & I have not yet commenced two classes that I intend taking." He tells Howell he is enrolled in intermediate and senior Math, Junior and Senior Natural Philosophy, and Chemistry. He observes that his new professor of Chemistry, Dr. Lawrence Smith, had not yet arrived on campus. Toy notes that Smith is "said to be a very distinguished man, and to have made twenty-five discoverys in Chem. and Geology;" then wryly adds, "He is a smarter man, I hope, than his predecessor."[18] Toy's characteristic discernment and wit are already evident at age sixteen!

Not all of Toy's first year was consumed with study, however, his comment above notwithstanding. In a letter to Morton Howell, dated November 11, 1852, he recounts how some of the "fellows had a very nice frolic…in celebration of [U.S. President] Pierce's election." "They were all drunk, of course," and built a bonfire on the college lawn and dragged an engine onto the Rotunda porch. No injuries were reported by Toy other than a cut hand in an attempted stabbing. Toy also notes that while the college had voted for the Whig candidate, Winfield Scott, the returns from across the state showed a "tremendous beat" in favor of Pierce. Toy reveals his own political leanings, calling the democratic victory "a shameful thing," noting that even his hometown of Norfolk had voted with the democratic majority (though Richmond, he says, remained Whig).[19]

One of the first persons Toy met in Charlottesville was John A. Broadus,

---

[16] Crawford H. Toy to Morton B. Howell, October 11, 1852, in biographical note, genealogical data on Howell-Toy families, and letters of Crawford H. Toy, 185201907, ASC, SBTS. There are in this collection sixteen letters from Toy to Howell between 1852 and 1859.

[17] Toy to Howell, October 11, 1852.

[18] Ibid.

[19] Toy to Howell, November 11, 1852, ASC, SBTS.

then Greek tutor in UVA, soon to be pastor of the Baptist church there, and later Toy's teacher, colleague, and mentor at Southern Seminary. Toy later recalled:

> When I went to the University of Virginia, in 1852, he [Broadus] was tutor in Greek, and was regarded as an admirable Greek scholar. He was very kind to me personally (I had a letter of introduction to him), but he left the University before I entered the school of ancient languages, and I did not at that time come under his teaching. His acceptance of the charge of the Charlottesville Baptist Church was greatly regretted in University circles; it was believed that if he had remained there as teacher he would have become an eminent Greek scholar (and, as it happened, this is what he did become).[20]

In his letter of March 8, 1853, Toy claims "an abundance of excuses to offer for my long silence," the most pressing of which is his preoccupation with intermediate examinations which "are now in full play." Despite the workload, Toy reports that he has deemed it "more than fair for me to indulge myself in a small holiday" to venture to downtown Charlottesville to view the "great painting of Rossiter, 'The Captive Israelites' and the accompanying celebrated artistes."[21] Thomas Prichard Rossiter (1818–1871) was a well-known American artist. *The Captive Israelites* (or *Jews in Captivity*) was part of a traveling show making its way around Virginia.[22] Toy expressed regret at not having yet seen it, remarking that "it is undoubtedly a fine thing, and an honor to American art." From this early age (despite his self-described deprivation of exposure to the fine arts because of his father's religious convictions), Toy demonstrated appreciation and knowledge of the fine arts—art, music, even dancing (see below). Still, his experiences as a college student were far from unique, even in comparison with today's students. In the same letter, he bemoans the fact that "my purse is in a very weak state, from an empty stomach."[23]

In the next extant letter to Morton Howell (April 6, 1853), Crawford Toy regales his cousin with a story of a shooting that had "roused" the student body from its "stagnation." Toy tells the particulars of a shooting in which a

[20] Quoted in Archibald T. Robertson, *Life and Letters of John Albert Broadus* (Philadelphia: American Baptist Publication Society, 1909), 111–112.
[21] Toy to Howell, March 8, 1853, ASC, SBTS.
[22] The Richmond *Daily Dispatch*, February 22, 1853.
[23] In this same letter (March 8, 1853) he goes on to observe, "I think that a few figs that I ate the other night makes me sick. I've been feeling horribly for two or three days, not quite sick enough to go to bed, but unable to read or study with any pleasure."

fellow student, "Moseby," had shot a medical student, "Turpin," over something Turpin had said at a party. Toy recounts,

> the number of witnesses was very great, and the testimony very interesting, and so far against Moseby as to decide them to refuse his bail.... It was a very cowardly trick in Moseby; he went, armed, and with two friends, when he knew that the other fellow had no weapons, and was alone.... When the former [Turpin] refused to make an apology, Moseby held the pistol within three inches of his face, and fired, burning him very much: the ball grazed his shirt-collar, passed under his cheek, round the neck, in which it lodged, and where it still remains: it severed a few veins, which, of course, bled freely, this was the only bad effect, except the usual danger of mortification.... The case is laid over to be taken up by the Superior court.[24]

The perpetrator of the crime was John Singleton Mosby (1833–1916), who went on to serve as a colonel in the Confederate army and led an elite guerilla unit known as "Mosby's Rangers."[25] He was subsequently convicted of the nonfatal shooting of George Turpin and expelled from school. He was given a year's prison sentence but was pardoned in December 1853. As a result of this incident, Mosby studied and practiced law in Albemarle County from 1855–1858. He returned to his law practice after the Civil War, and in his later years served as U.S. Consul in Hong Kong (1878–1885) and as a lawyer for the Southern Pacific Railroad (a position secured for him by U. S. Grant, who had befriended Mosby after the war). In 1901 President McKinley appointed him to the General Land office in the U.S. Interior Department.[26]

At the close of this letter, Toy remarks on a topic to which he will return during his collegiate correspondence with Howell: "I can't say that I think visiting the ladies a very bad habit. I have not indulged in it to any extent myself this session; I intend to make up for lost time, during the vacation."[27]

---

[24] Toy to Howell, April 6, 1853, ASC, SBTS. This is actually a rather famous story in the lore of the University of Virginia, telling of an event that occurred on March 29, 1853. Turpin was described as a "bully" and had threatened to eat Mosby [sic] "blood raw." Turpin survived the gunshot wound, but he died in Newbern, Alabama, in 1858 at the age of twenty-five (see https://uvastudents.wordpress.com/2014/03/06/george-r-turpin-13-aug-1832-6-aug-1858/).

[25] See John W. Munson, *Reminiscences of a Mosby Guerrilla* (New York: Moffat, Yard, and Co., 1906).

[26] For this information on Mosby, see Ruth Ann Coski, "John Singleton Mosby (1833–1916)," https://www.encyclopediavirginia.org/Mosby_John_Singleton_1833-1916#start_entry.

[27] Crawford H. Toy to Morton B. Howell, April 6, 1853, ASC, SBTS.

Toy is found true to his word in his letter to Morton over summer vacation, indulging in two "bad habits." In addition to reading novels ("which bad habit I intend to drop sometime during the last week in September"), Toy confesses to "another bad habit I have contracted (isn't it a bad one?)" which is "visiting the girls. I am however very moderate and therefore feel no bad effect from it. I shall drop it too, mostly."[28]

By the time Toy began his second year at UVA in fall 1853, he was feeling much more comfortable on the campus: "I arrived here safely, and with a great deal more of pleasure than at a similar time last year. I met a good many familiar faces, and I was even glad to look at the old buildings in college again."[29] Part of his more general satisfaction with his present circumstances no doubt had to do with his new living arrangements: "I am very well situated in No. 27 Western Lawn, with a nice crowd, and at a first-rate boarding house, the best in college. I think I eat more dinner than I ever did before in my life…. We had two large cakes, four jars of preserves and pickles, a good deal of cheese, a bag of crackers, and two bags of small cakes, all of which have long ago disappeared." He reassured Howell that such consumption "does not affect my health in the least."[30]

His studies turned toward languages, a harbinger of his future expertise and career path; his courses included Latin, Greek, Italian, German, and Anglo Saxon.[31] He was also enrolled in Political Economy, of which he observes, "I like exceedingly." The last course was taught by Dr. William Holmes McGuffey (1800–1873), who had already achieved fame for the McGuffey reader, the first series of textbooks for elementary school children in America.[32] Having previously served as president of Cincinnati College (1836–1839) and Ohio University in Athens, Ohio (1839–1943), McGuffey joined the UVA faculty as chair of moral philosophy in 1843, a position he held until his death. Toy praises McGuffey:

> I don't believe that more general information and more correct views of
> things can be obtained anywhere, than by an attendance on Dr.

---

[28] Toy to Howell, July 29, 1853.

[29] Toy to Howell, November 9, 1853.

[30] Ibid.

[31] Ibid. Toy's interest in general philology is evinced later in the letter when he asks Howell if he had seen the new book on comparative philology by Dr. Schele, a UVA professor (see M. Schele de Vere, *Outlines of Comparative Philology, with a Sketch of the Languages of Europe, Arranged upon Philologic Principles; and a Brief History of the Art of Writing* [New York: G.P. Putnam & Co., 1853]).

[32] The readers were published between 1836 and 1879. See "William Holmes McGuffey: American Educator," *Online Britannica*, https://www.britannica.com/biography/William-Holmes-McGuffey.

McGuffey's lectures on Moral and Political [philosophy]. He makes you apply all the knowledge you have to practical affairs, & teaches you how to use it. He has a private class of…in which the members debate, write essays, and criticize books and each other's essays—I intend to take it next session if possible.[33]

For the first time, Toy turns his attention to the religious atmosphere on campus. He explains that two ministers had held services in the chapel and "had a very good effect. From all appearances there is a serious feeling throughout the college—the Sunday afternoon prayer meetings are very well attended; so is the morning chapel. Eight or nine have professed religion this session, & there are about twenty who intend to study for the ministry. Dr. [Benjamin Holt] Rice [1782–1856, Presbyterian minister of Hamden-Sydney] lectured this to the members of the church on the call to the ministry & the duty of young men to devote themselves to it. He is a very clear old fellow."[34] During the revival, Toy himself made a profession of faith and was baptized by John A. Broadus, who had become pastor of Charlottesville Baptist Church.[35]

Several years later, Toy recalls his own religious experience within the context of that spring's revival:

About April, 1854, there commenced a season of revival in college. It was very quiet. There were sermons in the Chapel Sunday, and part of the time, special meetings in the Presbyterian and Baptist Churches in Charlottesville, about a mile from which the University is situated. Dr. Hoge and others preached in the former, and Dr. Jeter and Cumberland George in the latter. The students held quiet prayermeetings among themselves, and Dr. Rice, of the Presbyterian Ch. did much good by the conversations which he held with them in private. Many interesting cases of conversion occurred. After much doubt and trouble, I offered myself to the ch in Charlottesville for baptism, and was received. After this, for months, I was subject to the most harassing doubts. Bro. J. A. Broadus was my advisor and guide throughout this period. I often wished myself out of the church, felt that I was acting the hypocrite, and had little peace of mind. By bro. B's advice, I retained my place as a church-member. In a case of alternating doubt and hope, when one is conscious of sincerity

---

[33] Toy to Howell, November 9, 1853.
[34] Toy to Howell, April 18, 1854. Toy goes on to ask Howell about the other minister: "Have you ever heard Mr. Hoge preach? He is one of the prettiest speakers I ever listened to." Toy does not, at this point, indicate that he himself was admitted as a candidate for baptism during the revival.
[35] See William Cathcart, ed., "Toy, Crawford H.," *The Baptist Encyclopedia* 2:1159–1161; cited by Hurt, "Toy," 19.

of intention, it is no hypocrisy to stand before the world a professed Christian. For a long time every public act that involved a profession of religion cut like a dagger into my soul. But gradually my faith and hope became steadier. I took part in the public worship more freely. And I have been enabled to maintain my profession ever since, often with much trembling, sometimes almost in despair, but never for a long time unable to look to Christ as my salvation.[36]

Once again, Toy's self-examination of his religious convictions results in often agonizing confessions of despair, but ultimate hope.[37]

In a letter dated June 1, 1854, Toy indicates his understanding that Howell planned to enroll in law school in the next session (fall 1854) and provides needed details for his transition (classes offered and their times, cost of courses, necessary "fixings" to carry to college [e.g., a workbag but not a "towel and silver fork"]). Thus, there is no further correspondence from Toy to Howell for nearly two years (March 6, 1856). By now, Toy is a senior about to graduate from UVA, and he tells Howell in passing that he had attended a "choir-meeting." Music was a lifelong passion, and Toy later gained some local notoriety for his singing abilities.[38] By the time Toy graduated from the university with an A.M. degree in June 1856, he had studied with a number of eminent professors; in addition to McGuffey and J. Lawrence Smith, there were also Gessner Harrison in Greek and Latin and William B. Rogers in Physics. Besides the various courses in ancient and modern languages, Toy had a class in constitutional and international law with Professor Minor and engaged in a study of medicine.[39]

After graduation, Toy took a teaching position at the newly established Albemarle Female Institute in Charlottesville in fall 1856.[40] The Institute was

---

[36] Toy, "Sketch of My Religious Life."

[37] This language is, again, reminiscent of the genre and language of traditional conversion narratives. It was important to Toy to communicate to those reading his account, presumably officials at the SBC Foreign Mission Board in charge of his missionary appointment, concerning the seriousness with which he took such issues of faith.

[38] W. H. Whitsitt to Florence Wallace, February 2, 1876, in Mary Whitsitt Whitehead, ed., *"Hold the Mirror Up": Letters of William Heth Whitsitt to Florence Wallace*, unpublished manuscript, VBHS, 119 (henceforth, this book is referred to as *Mirror*).

[39] Lyon, "Toy," 3; George F. Moore, "An Appreciation of Professor Toy," *AJSL* 36/1 (1919): 1.

[40] *Religious Herald*, August 28, 1856. See Garnet Ryland, *The Baptists of Virginia* (Richmond, VA: The Virginia Baptist Board of Missions and Education, 1955), 292; cited by Hurt, "Toy," 21. At least one denominational paper referred to Toy as "Professor of Mathematics" (North Carolina *Biblical Recorder*, January 17, 1877). Toy's next extant letter to Howell, April 10, 1857, was a hurried note (7 lines), indicating he was prepared to meet Howell, "convey him to my sanctum," and that "I will reserve what news I have till I see

begun during John Broadus's pastorate and "organized largely under his influ-ence, the Albemarle Female Institute, the very first school…to put the Eng-lish language on a footing of parity with the ancient classics and the cultured tongues of modern Europe. More of credit for this bold innovation is, per-haps, due to the principal, Prof. John Hart, and his assistant, Crawford H. Toy, but it was not made without consultation of the trustees."[41]

The curriculum consisted of ancient and modern languages, natural sci-ences, English literature and composition, mathematics, moral philosophy, and history.[42] Charlotte "Lottie" Moon was a member of the second class who entered in 1857. At this time, Moon would have been a student of Toy's. Moon was, by all accounts, an outstanding student. One of her Albemarle instructors, unnamed, made this tribute in the *Biblical Recorder*:

> Miss Moon came to the school at Charlottesville with very good prepa-ration as to attainments, and with unusual preparation as to natural abil-ities. Thus her career as a student was marked by distinguished success. She never failed to pass every examination that she attempted, and usu-ally she was highest in the class. It would be hard to say in what studies she most excelled. The writer, who had the pleasure of reading many of her examination papers, remembers her superlatively fine work in Latin, history, literature, and moral philosophy. He thinks that her strength lay especially in the direction of the languages and Belles Lettres studies. The Greek language was not included in the graduating course; but Miss Moon, entering on the work with her usual industry and intelligence, became a very good Greek scholar. Since that day, the writer has not heard young ladies read with fluency and appreciation the plays of Eu-ripides and Sophocles…. It is not insidious to say that, in the judgment of many who had opportunity to know, she was the most scholarly of all the graduates of that school.[43]

Some have been inclined, not without good reason, to attribute this quo-tation and other accolades like it to Crawford H. Toy.[44] Earlier biographers even suggested that there was a developing romance between Toy and Moon

---

you." The only indication in this letter that Toy is no longer a student at UVA is the change of address from the "University" to "Charlottesville."

[41] H. H. Harris, *Religious Herald*, March 21, 1895; quoted in Robertson, *Life and Letters*, 121, and Hurt, "Toy," 21. Harris was an early faculty member of the Institute and would later be president of the SBC Foreign Mission Board (Catherine B. Allen, *The New Lottie Moon Story* [Nashville: Broadman Press, 1980] 32).

[42] Allen, *New Lottie Moon*, 32.

[43] North Carolina *Biblical Recorder*, January 17, 1877; cf. Allen, *New Lottie Moon*, 33.

[44] Allen, *New Lottie Moon*, 33.

that resulted in a rejected marriage proposal in 1861.[45] There is, however, no evidence of such a relationship in this period.[46] Of course, it "was not unheard of for Albemarle Female Institute's professors to show attentions to young women," and girls "were known to develop serious crushes on the eligible Professor Toy."[47] Sarah Ann Strickler [Fife] wrote in her diary about meeting Toy for the first time, as a student at AFI (during Toy's second stint at AFI): "I was presented today, to my most worshipful masters Rev. H. H. Harris and Rev. C. H. Toy (an unmarried man); both said to be very smart, especially the latter who is so extremely dignified and exquisite that the girls stand in awe of him."[48] Toy himself jokes with Howell about attention from women accounting for a missing photograph of the two of them: "Either you or I have made an impression on some heart, most probably female, & our Daguerroetype [photograph] is gone. Can't you come up at the end of the session, if only for a day & Wood will retake us."[49]

The next extant letter from Toy to Howell is dated January 29, 1858, and is written on stationery with the letterhead, "Albemarle Female College," in which Toy inquires about Howell ("are you teaching or practicing Law or both?") and states, "[I] read Greek & teach the youthful female…Eng. Literature and show them Experiments in Chemistry." His next letter to Howell, October 7, 1858, is much more informative. After promising to meet Howell in Hampton, he claims to be "ready to go anywhere in reason. I am prepared to do anything or become anything." He goes on to express a certain satisfaction with his current arrangements: "I am surrounded by all sorts of pleasant circumstances now. My work is moderate and congenial. There are four of us [faculty] who are thrown constantly together, presenting a variety of material and ready at all times to discuss a question of philosophy or philology or…play a game of chess. Two of us are married and two are not." He continues to sing and states that being "able to sing Rossini's 'Stabat Mater' at any time is a luxury."[50] "Reading Hebrew with Mr. Broadus," he relates, "is one of the

---

[45] Una Roberts Lawrence, *Lottie Moon* (Nashville: Sunday School Board, 1927).

[46] For more on the later relationship of Toy and Moon, see the Excursus, "Exploring the Toy/Moon Myth."

[47] Allen, *New Lottie Moon*, 33.

[48] Sarah Ann Strickler [Fife], "Private Diary of Sarah Ann Strickler [Fife]," UVAL; cited by Hurt, "Toy," 37.

[49] Crawford H. Toy to Morton B. Howell, May 16, 1857, ASC, SBTS.

[50] Much of Toy's letters of December 6, 1858, and February 2, 1859, reveal Toy's interest and expertise in classical music and list several upcoming concert opportunities (this despite the fact that Toy, by his own admission, was not allowed to attend theater as a youth). In the latter letter he says, "I wish it were not so unorthodox to go to operas, & that it costs a little less. It's hard to sit still and read of representations in New York of 'William Tell', 'Marriage of Figaro', Robert le Drable', 'The Hugenots', 'Martha', and

pleasant circumstances." He spends a great deal of time discussing goings on at UVA despite his disclaimer that "I have seen very little of the fellows at the University." Then he returns to his situation at the Albemarle Female Institute: "The school here is doing moderately well. I am just engaged for two or three weeks in expounding Chaucer to my Literature class. Pretty tough morsel to some of them."[51]

In his December 6, 1858, letter to Howell, Toy mentions that John Broadus is now associated with the "Theological Seminary" and that it "is the best thing for him now, though the life of the academical training will be a serious one." His thoughts then apparently turn to his "unmarried state," somewhat tongue in cheek: "I went to see Pritchard and his wife a few days ago, and the quietness and...their enjoyment set me to feeling desperate. I told P. it was very unkind of him to do such a thing. Dark thoughts entered my mind. However, a good supper relieved me from this anxious condition, and I am now whole."

After completing his third (and last) year of teaching at the Albemarle Female Institute, Toy, now a ripe old twenty-three, published an editorial in the *Religious Herald*, Virginia's denominational paper, in September 1859. He muses about several items including Alleghany High School for boys, which "is the initiative in Virginia for the denomination, and must be taken hold of, and carried forward." He then turns his attention to the Institute in a segment that is worth quoting nearly in full not only for its content but also because it is one of the first published pieces to come from Toy's hand:

> And in this connection I may refer to a similar institution, which also has a claim on Baptists. I mean the Albemarle Female Institute, located at Charlottesville, with the plan of instruction in which, as well as with the mode of government, and the general results, I have had occasion to become acquainted, my sisters having been pupils there several sessions,[52] and I having been an instructor for three years. I leave teaching for another sphere of duty. I speak, then, as one who has had opportunity to know, when I express my belief that the school does secure the objects of education in respect of both mind and character—that the effect on a

---

twenty others and know that there is no chance of your hearing them. It is some comfort to study the music, however, & I suppose, it is more profitable. It seems singular that the great musicians should have been reserved for those degenerate days. Sacred music reached its highest point in Handel's time, but profane is just now finding its zenith. I have very little confidence in my opinion, but I imagine I see more sublimity in Rossini than in any other secular writer."

[51] Toy to Howell, October 7, 1858.

[52] Three of Toy's sisters, the twins Jennie Santos and Emily Elmore, and their younger sister, Julia Anna, attended AFI; cf. Harris, "My Mother," 349.

young lady can hardly fail to be admirable. I regard this as its characteristic, and commend it to those who are willing to sacrifice something for a solid discipline. The Principal, who has originated and carried out what is good in it, has suffered nothing, not even emolument, to interfere with the establishment of a proper system; and to this system, which is that of the University of Virginia, the good effects are mainly to be ascribed. The principle adopted in the instruction has been, that women are as much profited by a thorough and extensive training as men—that the same means which have been used with advantage in Universities, ought to be used in Female Seminaries—that is, that the thorough study of the Languages (especially the Ancient Languages) and Mathematics, should be made the foundation of education—education being looked on rather as a preparation of the mind for work, than as a process of giving information. So, lectures are delivered, and the examinations are entirely written. And so, some young ladies have read carefully the Latin and Greek authors which are commonly read, as well as the French, Italian, and German; and have studied Mathematics as far as half-through the Differential Calculus, and have shown perfectly good acquaintances with these subjects. They study with similar strictures the questions of History and Psychology. The other departments, scientific, ornamental and historical are not neglected any...not made paramount. The results have been satisfactory.

The fear has been expressed that young ladies were carried too far. But no one need go farther than she chooses and none go into Senior Classes but such as show capacity for it. It would be difficult to make the training too thorough.

It has been supposed that difficulty would arise from the necessity for taking notes of lectures, of writing out long examinations, and of working six days in the week. It is true that hard work is required and performed, and that there needs some trouble to acquire these habits of work. But no good can come without work, and young ladies have shown inclination and capacity for work which equals the application in our Colleges, and with no real detriment to health. Not so much, certainly, as in the case of young men at College; and this may be prevented by care and judicious exercise....

I have thought it just to bear this testimony to the practical working of the system, and to solicit for it the careful examination and kind wishes and assistance of brethren generally.... Yours, C. H. T.[53]

The editorial is remarkable in its progressive view (for the time) of the value

---

[53] *Religious Herald*, September 8, 1859.

of female education, a position on which Toy never faltered for the remainder of his career. He would eventually teach female students at Radcliffe in Cambridge, Massachusetts, and was married to a woman who was educated at a female academy and whose father, Rev. Saunders, served as president of several female institutes in the South.[54]

Toy also writes in this editorial that he is leaving the Institute for "another sphere of duty." It is curious that he does not mention his plans to Howell (at least in the extant letters), although he does say at the close of his June 29, 1859, letter, "There are several things to talk about, but I don't care to write about them."

By that June, Toy's original plans to study languages in Europe had changed. In February 1859, Crawford Toy had responded to a sermon by Broadus and committed himself to the mission field:

> Several times the subject of the ministry was brought specially to my attention, and I gave it thought and prayed in relation to it. After years of reflection I came to the conclusion, and my friends on whose judgment I most relied, concurred with me, that I was not adapted to the work. My temperament, habits of thought and study, and oratory, (or lack of oratory,) seemed to promise rather a life of study and instruction. Accordingly I had determined to go to Europe in the summer of 1859, and spend some years there in preparation for teaching Languages, and especially the Sanscrit, which I wished to have the satisfaction of introducing into my native State. I looked forward to the trip with great delight. The treasures of art, architecture, Painting and Music, would open to me a world of enjoyment. The historical attractions, the scenery, and everything that the Old World offers to youthful imagination, often passed before me. But this was not to be. My plans were completely changed by a missionary Sermon preached by bro. John A. Broadus, in the regular course of his ministry, about February, 1859. The possibility of my being a missionary first presented itself to me. Before I had thought of it, but very vaguely, and very far off. Now it took hold on me. I reflected on it for months, consulted with my friends, and finally offered myself to the Board as missionary to Japan, or wherever else they should think expedient. I did not at first think of preaching. It was missionary work and not properly preaching that I felt called to. But it was necessary to have a better acquaintance with the Bible than I possessed. I must be acquainted with that system of truth which I was to teach to the heathen. I embraced the opportunity afforded by the opening of the So. Bapt. Theolog. Seminary. And it seemed proper that I should go out as an ordained minister of the gospel. So I found myself, what I had not looked

---

[54] See chapter 8 on Nancy Saunders Toy.

to for a long time, a student of Theology, and endeavoring to preach.[55]

We are also aware of Toy's plans from reports in the denominational papers of the day. The *Religious Herald*, for example, reported on June 30, 1859: "License to preach has been recently granted by the Charlottesville Baptist church to Mr. Crawford H. Toy, A.M., graduate of the University of Virginia, and Instructor in Mathematics in the Albemarle Female Institute. The *Jeffersonian Republican* of that place learns that Mr. Toy will attend one session of the Southern Baptist Theological Seminary, Greenville, S.C. and then devote himself to the Foreign Missionary work."[56]

Little is known about the details of Toy's year at the newly formed Southern Seminary in Greenville. He was one of twenty-six members of the first class, ten of whom were from Virginia (no doubt the result of Broadus's ministry and influence in Charlottesville).[57] J. A. Chambliss, a member of that first class, described them:

> The men of '59 were mostly from rural districts of the South. But this does not mean a school of rustics. The most of the refinement and culture for which the South was noted in those days was found in country homes, where the sons and daughters began their education under tutors and governesses, or, in good private schools and then went off to college. The proportion of college men and women in the South before the Civil War was much greater than in the North. The majority of the first students in the Seminary were college men—a number of them distinguished graduates—and nearly all of them were from families of gentle folk.[58]

Charles Ryland, also a member of the inaugural class, specifically mentions Toy (the only member of the entering class from a city—Norfolk): "Of the men from Virginia, two were appointees to the Foreign Mission field. They were Crawford H. Toy and John William Jones. They were to open a mission in Japan."[59] The same J. A. Chambliss cited above attested to Toy's exceptional intellectual talents. Chambliss recounted that Basil Manly, Jr., one of the seminary's four professors, would sometimes consult with Toy on points of Hebrew grammar before meeting the class. Chambliss also referred to Toy

---

[55] Toy, "Sketch of My Religious Life."

[56] *Religious Herald*, June 30, 1859. North Carolina's *Biblical Recorder* runs the same article in its July 7, 1859, issue.

[57] Lyon, "Toy," 4.

[58] Quoted by Charles H. Ryland, "Recollections of the First Year," Address Delivered Before the Seminary at Louisville, Kentucky, Founders Day, January 11, 1911, SBTS.

[59] Ryland, "Recollections of the First Year," 8.

as the best student in Greek.[60] John William Jones, Toy's roommate, corroborated Chambliss's assessment, calling Toy one of the most learned men he ever knew.[61]

Broadus himself concurred with this evaluation. In a letter written in spring 1860 to a Miss Cornelia Taliaferro, Broadus opined, "Brother Toy, who is going to Japan, and Brother Jones (of Louisa), who is going to Canton, are boarding with us now, and we greatly enjoy their society. Toy is among the foremost scholars I have ever known of his years, and an uncommonly conscientious and devoted man."[62] True to these testimonies and according to several witnesses (which may derive from a single source), in one year Toy completed nearly three-fourths of the three-year course of study.[63]

At the end of the spring term, Toy returned from Greenville, South Carolina, to his parents' home in Norfolk, but not before penning "A Sketch of My Religious Life," which he composed on May 24, 1860, in preparation for his missionary commission and/or ordination. The Portsmouth Baptist Association in Virginia resolved in May 1860 to extend patronage to Toy for his mission work in Japan:

> 1. *Resolved*, That this Association adopt Brother Crawford H. Toy, appointed by the Foreign Mission Board of the Southern Baptist Convention a missionary to Japan, as their missionary and agree to raise annually for his support, not less than $1,000.

> 2. *Resolved*, That T. Horne be requested to communicate this to the Board and to Bro. Toy and that he request Bro. Toy to visit the churches of the Association and arrange for such visit.

---

[60] J. A. Chambliss, "Reminiscences of the First Two Sessions," *The Seminary Magazine* 11 (1898): 310; cited by Hurt, "Toy," 29.

[61] John W. Jones, "Recollections of the First Session of the Seminary," *The Seminary Magazine* 5 (1891): 133; cited by Hurt, "Toy," 29.

[62] John A. Broadus to Miss Cornelia Taliaferro, March 28, 1860, quoted in Robertson, *Life and Letters*, 173. This oft-quoted passage continues with a positive, but by comparison less-than-glowing, description of Jones's intellect (see Jones cited above): "Jones you may have seen; he has great zeal, an unusual turn for practical working, and I am sure he will make a very useful man" (173).

[63] Lyon, "Toy," 4; Hurt, "Toy," 28. Drawing on the SBTS *Catalogues* (1859–1860, 37; 1860–1861, 6), Gary Wills concluded that Toy completed requirements for graduation in four of the eight schools: OT interpretation in Hebrew and English; NT interpretation in Greek and English; Systematic Theology; and Ecclesiastical History. Wills further observed, "By later standards Toy would have graduated in seven of the eleven schools, undoubtedly the basis of Broadus's statement that Toy completed two-thirds of the seminary course in one year" (Wills, *Southern Baptist Theological Seminary [1859–2009]* [Oxford: Oxford University Press, 2009], 110).

3. *Resolved,* That we earnestly request every church of the Association to appoint two or more persons for the purpose of collecting some definite daily, weekly, monthly, or annual sums of money for missionary purposes, unless already possessed of some arrangements for securing such moneys, or at least so far as to secure regularly the $1000 salary of our foreign missionary.[64]

In early June, Toy spoke at the Baptist General Association of Virginia in Staunton, Virginia. His remarks were summarized in the June 7, 1860, issue of the *Religious Herald.*

> Brother Toy, one of the three young missionaries for Japan, was introduced, who gave an account of the reasons which induced him to devote himself to the Foreign Mission cause, and why he had chosen Japan as the field of his future labors. All young missionaries, he said, ought to become missionaries to the heathen, unless they could show some good reason for the contrary. He gave quite an extended account of the Japanese nation, and said they would become a great commercial people, and assimilate their manners and habits to those of the Western nations. His remarks were listened to with the undivided and unflagging attention of the audience. Mr. Rohrer, Mr. J. L. Johnson, now a student of this University, and John W. Jones, a graduate of Greenville, are the other young men, who have been accepted by the Southern Board as Missionaries for Japan.[65]

On June 10, 1860, Toy and three others were ordained to the Baptist ministry. The *Religious Herald* (June 30, 1860) reprinted an earlier report from the *Jeffersonian Republican*[66] that an ordination committee (J. B. Taylor, A. M. Poindexter, Charles Quarles, T. G. Jones, John A. Broadus, James Fife, William P. Facist [?], and A. B. Brown) assembled in Charlottesville on June 9 to examine C. H. Toy, J. L. Johnson, J. B. Taylor, Jr., and J. W. Jones. The committee, chaired by J. B. Taylor, Sr., "proceeded to examine the candidates with respect to their conversion, their call to the ministry, and doctrinal views. The result of the examination being highly satisfactory, it was resolved to proceed to the ordination of all the candidates on the next day (Sunday)." Following the regular Sunday morning sermon (delivered by Rev. T. B. Jones),

---

[64] *Virginia Portsmouth Baptist Association, Minutes of the Seventieth Annual Association* (Petersburg, VA: O. Ellyson, 1860), 8; cited by Hurt, "Toy," 32.

[65] This paragraph is quoted nearly verbatim, without attribution, in Charles Ryland's description of Toy's speech to the Association (Ryland, "Recollections of the First Year," 8).

[66] According to Johnson, *Autobiographical Notes,* this account was written by A. B. Brown, pastor of Charlottesville Baptist Church.

the presbytery of clergy laid hands on the ordinands, and Dr. Broadus delivered their charge. "This address was replete with mature wisdom, and pervaded by a tenderness befitting the close relations between the speaker and the young men."[67]

The paper article also noted that three of the four ordinands "have offered for the untried Mission among the Japanese." Those three were Toy, Johnson, and Jones, and all three were close associates. Toy and Johnson had been classmates at the University of Virginia; Johnson had just recently graduated from the university. At the time of the ordination, John Lipscomb Johnson was engaged to Toy's sister, Julia Anna, a student at the AFI. According to Johnson, he "had sought an introduction to his [Toy's] three sisters then at school at Charlottesville" (AFI where Toy had been teaching). When Julia Anna accepted Johnson's marriage proposal, Johnson reports, "I immediately went to her brother, Crawford H. Toy, and told him of the situation. He seemed somewhat surprised, but promptly took my hand and said, 'John, I do not know a living man to whom I'd rather see my sister wedded than to you.'"[68] The engagement occurred in May 1859. By fall 1859, Johnson had responded to a call for foreign missionaries. Johnson recounts, "I went before the Foreign Mission Board (of the Southern Baptist Convention) located in Richmond and was appointed to Japan." Johnson further reports that his appointment "made it necessary to ask the consent of Miss Julia's parents [Thomas Dallam and Amelia Toy] for her to bear me company. I can hardly forget her father's reply, which was about these words: 'If God thinks it well to honor my child by sending her as a messenger of light to the heathen, who am I that I should lift up my voice against Him?'"[69] Originally, two other missionary appointees to Japan, J. Q. A. Rohrer and his wife, were supposed to be the first to sail for the mission, with Toy and Johnson to follow later. After Johnson's marriage to Julia Anna Toy,[70] the FMB decided to send the Johnsons with the Rohrers

---

[67] In a letter to Basil Manly, Sr., on June 16, 1860, Broadus himself commented on the event: "The ordination last Sunday (Toy, Jones, Johnson, Taylor, Jr.) passed off well, and I hope did much good" (Robertson, *Life and Letters*, 174).

[68] Johnson, *Autobiographical Notes*, 118.

[69] Johnson, *Autobiographical Notes*, 121.

[70] In his *Autobiographical Notes*, 123–24, Johnson shares this anecdote: "Over the mantel in my room there had been for many months this legend: 'July 10, 1860.' Most people who came in to see us asked what it meant, and I answered frankly, 'That is the date of my marriage, if it please God.' Because of my very frank answer, nobody believed it." Johnson also recollects the wedding ceremony, telling that he had enclosed a bank-note with the marriage license for the officiating minister, Rev. T. G. Jones, pastor of Freemason Street Baptist Church (the Toys' home church). Jones, according to Johnson, returned the money with a note reading, "Dog don't eat dog!" (124). Crawford Toy also reports on the wedding in a letter to John Broadus on July 27, 1860 (ASC, SBTS).

on the *Edwin Forrest* ship, set to sail for the Orient on August 3, 1860. John Johnson, however, suffered from a combination of measles, typhoid fever, and acute indigestion. He recalls, "The Foreign Mission Board, learning of my condition, advised that I stay in America another year."[71] The Rohrers, therefore, sailed with another couple, Rev. and Mrs. A. L. Bond (assigned to China), but without the Johnsons. The "Edwin Forrest" ship, along with the Rohrers and Bonds, were lost at sea.[72]

John William Jones was also a classmate of Toy's at the University of Virginia and, with Toy, a member of the inaugural class at the Greenville Seminary.[73] Both Toy and Jones had been members of Charlottesville Baptist Church when Broadus was pastor and penned their names to a document protesting the announcement in May 1858 of Broadus's election to the seminary that was to be established in Greenville.[74] Broadus accepted the appointment

---

[71] Johnson, *Autobiographical Notes*, 122.

[72] Edmund F. Merriam, *A History of American Baptist Missions* (Philadelphia: American Baptist Publication Society, 1900), 65; Johnson also reports the loss of his fellow appointee, although he (or the transcriber of Johnson's handwritten manuscript) erroneously identifies him as Rev. John Q. A. Rohun (*Autobiographical Notes*, 122). Catherine Allen writes, "Toy's reason for not being on that boat has never been explained. Perhaps he was looking for a bride to accompany him" (*New Lottie Moon*, 37). Toy's stated intentions, however, were always to sail to Japan at the end of 1860.

[73] For more on Jones, see Christopher Moore, "Apostle of the Confederacy: J. William Jones and the Question of Ecumenism and Denominational Identity in the Development of Lost Cause Mythology" (Ph.D. diss., Baylor University, 2016), forthcoming as a monograph with University of Tennessee Press. Gratitude is expressed to Dr. Moore for sharing pdfs of letters between Jones and Poindexter that reference Toy (see below).

[74] The notice read:

> As to the extent of influence, we doubt whether there shall be really any wider field at Greenville than here; even if it be so, the case stands thus: Another man may be found to supply the place at Greenville, and the denomination and the cause of truth then lose but the difference between the influence for good exercised by such a man, and that which we believe would there be exercised by our pastor. But take away our pastor. There is left a vacancy which we honestly think no other man in the denomination can at all fill. His relations in past time and now to the University, give him an access to the great mass of mind there, sanctified and unsanctified, which no other man in our denomination can have—which no other pastor in Charlottesville has, or can have, so long as the men remain the same. Surely it were great loss to us and Baptists everywhere to lose this advantage. We regard this loss inevitable if our pastor leaves us.

> We think that he is scarcely at all aware of the amount of good he is now doing, how much influence he is now exerting over the young men of our own church, in leading them in the way of Christian duty, and preparing them for future usefulness. (Robertson, *Life and Letters*, 149)

in April 1859, and Jones and Toy also went to Greenville as students. Before departing for Greenville, however, Jones wrote a letter in August 1859 from his home in Louisa, Virginia, to Abram Maer Poindexter (1809–1872), co-secretary of the FMB, volunteering for foreign mission service: "In response to the call made for men by the board, the missionaries, and the cries of perishing millions in heathen lands, I've only to say as did the prophet of old, *'Here am I—send me.'*"[75] Later in that letter, he inquired, "how should I make the application to the Board for an appointment?" He also expressed Japan as his preferred "special field of labor," but assured Poindexter that "I am willing to go anywhere that it may seem I can do the most good."

On December 17, 1859, Jones wrote from Greenville to Poindexter thanking him for "laying my letter before the Board and their action upon it. I will return to Va. first of next June and can appear before the Board either at the June meeting in Staunton or at their next meeting in July."[76] Jones wrote further, "You suggest to me to think of China as my field. I will do so, and wd be glad if you wd furnish me with a statement of your reasons for suggesting that field is preferred to Japan."[77] Jones reiterates his willingness to "go anywhere that it may appear that I can be most useful," but he confesses, "Of course it wd be exceedingly pleasant to me to be in the same field with Bros. Toy & Johnson." By the following July, after the ordination service in June, Jones was "anxious of reaching my field as soon as possible."[78] Having accepted his appointment to China (rather than Japan), he was still hopeful that he might travel with Toy "in the same vessel" because he "had arranged to brush up my Greek with Bro. Toy as we went out together." By September 1860, Jones had heard of Johnson's delay in departing for Japan because of his illness. He wrote tentatively, "It has occurred to me also to suggest in view of the great uncertainty of Bro. Johnson's being able to go to Japan (at least for a year) whether it might not be well to consider the propriety of sending me to Japan with Bro. Toy. I merely throw out the suggestion for you brethren to think about; I hold myself in readiness to go wherever and whenever the Board may

---

[75] John W. Jones to Abram M. Poindexter, August 2, 1860, Missionary File, 1856–1861, SBHLA.

[76] Jones to Poindexter, December 17, 1859. Jones also states: "I am very gratified to hear that bro. [W. L.] Johnson had been accepted, and, from an intimate association with him, I feel confident that he will prove exceedingly useful.... You will also be gratified to learn that three others of the students of the seminary, besides Bro. Toy and myself, have made up their minds to give themselves to the work and that several of the others have the subject under prayerful consideration."

[77] Jones states that he understands that with the appointment of Rohrer and Johnson to Japan, that area was no longer the place of "greater need."

[78] Jones to Poindexter, July 16, 1860.

think best to send me."[79]

Despite his deferential tone in yielding to the wishes of the board, Jones was persistent in pressing the issue of changing his field to Japan, even after it had been publicly announced that he was appointed to Canton, China.[80] The familiar pattern continues in his September 27, 1860, letter to Poindexter:

> Since my last I have learned that Bro. Johnson wd certainly not go out for twelve months at least, and I greatly fear that he will never be well enough to do so—what think you, then, of transferring me to the Japan mission? It wd be exceedingly pleasant for me to be with Bro. Toy and he wd also be very useful to me—but of course all these considerations must yield to the highest one of what is best for the cause and to hold myself ready to go just where the brethren think best that I shd go.

The next extant correspondence is to J. B. Taylor, Sr., SBC FMB secretary, who had made it official that Jones's appointment was to Canton and not Shanghai (or Japan). Jones accepts the appointment, but not without complaining:

> Of course, it will now be impossible for me to go out in the same vessel with bro. Toy—this will be a sad disappointment to me, especially since it has been decided that I am to go out alone, but I must be resigned. You ask if I will be ready to go as early as December. Yes! Or even earlier shd it be deemed best. Indeed but for the hope of going out with Bro. Toy who said he cd not go before Dec. I shd have been ready and anxious to go 1st of Oct.[81]

By the end of June, Toy's plans to launch a mission to Japan had yet to take shape.[82] On the same day (June 28, 1860), he wrote both John Broadus and J. William Jones. He sympathized with Jones's uncertainty about the specific destination of his appointment: "I suppose you feel a little more anxious now to get away as soon as possible." While he waits, Toy advises him to "do the work of an Evangelist. The people need stirring up not only on the subject of missions, but in every department of Christian effort.... Then you can be

---

[79] Jones to Poindexter, September 11, 1860.

[80] In response to that announcement, Jones followed his typical pattern, expressing preference for Shanghai while pledging to "yield to the better judgement of the Board" (Jones to Poindexter, September 27, 1860).

[81] Jones to Poindexter, October 4, 1860. He also indicates that he would travel to Norfolk later in October "to assist bro. Toy in some...meetings in the Portsmouth association."

[82] By September, Toy had commenced his tour of churches by "detached trips." "Regular schedule," he wrote, "not yet made out" (Crawford H. Toy to John W. Jones, September 18, 1860, Papers of the Jones family of Louisa Co., MS 13407, SCUVA).

reading in Missions, & especially on China—this will be of service to you hereafter in writing your Reports & Journal."[83] Toy also offers some pastoral and theological counsel:

> It is hard in your day, to accept such a decision under such circumstances as an indication of Providence. But you know that God uses strange means for indicating His will. The stubborn refusal of a hardheaded Egyptian King indicated to the Jews their duty in leaving Egypt. The malice of some fanatical Jews pointed out to Paul what was clearly providential, the duty of going to Rome. So that the character of the means is no bar to its being a real guidance of God. At the same time it is right to leave no stone unturned to accomplish our lawful desires. Certainly you have done everything that could be done.[84]

Despite his empathy, Toy nowhere expresses the desire to travel or serve with Jones as Jones has done with regard to traveling and/or serving with "bro. Toy."

Toy does confirm to Jones that "I don't think that I will be able to leave before December. I have not yet commenced my visitation of the churches. Forty churches in the Portsmouth Ass. to be seen,[85] several other anniversaries to be visited, a visit to Nashville, perhaps one to N.Y. & a recruiting season." On the same day in a letter to Broadus, Toy makes the same admission: "I have not been able to make any general preparation yet for my tour—shall have to do it as occasion demands"; then he expands, "Have a great deal of visiting to do in town—ah—would be pleasant to a man inclined to visiting, for the people are exceedingly cordial, regard me as a son of the church, & take interest in my plans. I hope they will [be] permanently interested in the work."[86] He also indicates to Broadus that he has "pretty well determined to stay until December, for various reasons." Always the scholar, Toy also muses that "it will be troublesome to take many books out with me, & certainly expensive to get all that I want—so I think I shall bring only critical works, and wait a year or two before ordering others. After providing myself with employment for the voyage, I suppose I need not make provision except for the study of the languages there & Heb & Gr."

All the plans for missionary service came to a complete halt with the

---

[83] Toy to Jones, June 28, 1860.

[84] Ibid.; it is not clear in the letter whether these words are directed specifically toward Jones's frustration in effecting his desires to leave immediately for the mission field or some other incident (which Toy calls "your affair") in which Jones was involved in at the time.

[85] To fulfill the request of the association, which had earlier that month pledged Toy annual support of $1000 (see above).

[86] Crawford H. Toy to John A. Broadus, June 28, 1860, ASC, SBTS.

election of Abraham Lincoln as United States president in November 1860. By the end of the month, rumor had spread that the FMB would suspend any new missionary initiatives. J. William Jones wrote Poindexter on November 24, 1860: "I was truly pained to learn from Bro. [Basil] Manly that the present aspect of political affairs is likely to cause our F. M. Board to retrench its operations, and that our departure to our fields will be indefinitely postponed." Jones goes on to outline the difficult position in which such a decision would put him (and others):

> If the Board shd deem it wise to take this step it will be a sore disap-
> pointment to me. I have fully set my heart on sailing at a very early day—
> have come to look upon Canton as my home, and am eager to enter upon
> my work there at as early a day as possible. Besides if I do not go now I
> shall be placed in a very awkward position for sometime to come. Of
> course, I will not abandon the idea of devoting myself to the foreign mis-
> sion work just as soon as circumstances will admit, and this being the
> case there is no church that wd be willing to employ my services with the
> probability of my leaving there in a short time. So if the Board shd decide
> not to send me now it will become a very serious question with me—
> what am I to do while awaiting the issue of events?[87]

By December, the FMB had, indeed, decided to suspend indefinitely the sending out of new missionaries. According to Jones in a letter to John Broadus in December 1860, Toy was contemplating going out on his own: "The Board have decided not to send out at present any of the missionaries under appointment. Toy talks of going out anyway and taking the chances."[88] By the end of January 1861, however, Toy had abandoned the idea of raising funds to go to Japan on his own. Offered a teaching position at Richmond College, Toy told Broadus:

> I declined at first, not knowing that I might not raise the necessary
> amount of money. But after a few days I became convinced that it was
> impossible to do it. In Portsmouth they really had no money. There was
> even great distress among the Navy-Yard hands, & everybody was more
> or less affected. Elsewhere they thought they had no money. Norfolk did

---

[87] John W. Jones to Abram M. Poindexter, November 24, 1860, Missionary File, 1856–1861, SBHLA.

[88] John W. Jones to John A. Broadus, December 17, 1860, quoted in Robertson, *Life and Letters*, 180. Jones says essentially the same thing in the January 2, 1861, letter to Taylor (cited above): "I very deeply sympathize with Bro. Toy in his purpose to raise (if possible) the means of enabling him to sail at an early day." Jones himself was still exploring possibilities of raising funds and continuing on to China (perhaps inspired by Toy's actions).

not do as well as I had expected.[89]

Richmond College, Toy told Broadus, "presented itself as the most useful position." Richmond College was founded in 1840 as an extension of the Virginia Baptist Seminary. Members of the Virginia Legislature granted a charter for an institution "of learning for the instruction of youth in the various branches of science and literature, the useful arts and the learned and foreign languages."[90] In 1861, when Toy taught there, the college had 161 enrolled students, with 68 alumni. The vacancy had occurred when a Professor Southam grew ill and resigned. Toy described his responsibilities to Broadus:

> My professional duties are not burdensome—three classes every day (except Saturday). I prepare each recitation, but this does not occupy comparatively much time. I find the young men tolerably well prepared. There are one or two that wd do well at G'ville. They have been unfortunate in their instruction. Last session Mr. Adkins taught them very little.... I do not know that any of them contemplate going to the Sem; I shall try to present it to them as strongly as possible. I think you will be inclined to smile a little when I tell you that I have undertaken to form classes in Heb & N.T. Grk.[91]

Toy gives details regarding the proposed Hebrew and Greek classes and also notes that he will offer a study of Romans on Sunday afternoons. "Perhaps," he writes to Broadus, "you will think that I have too many irons in the fire. Well, if it seems to be so, I will take several of them out. But I intended to study Grk & Heb, & these classes only reduce it to form & furnish some incitement."[92]

Toy had clearly adapted quickly to the transition from sudden cessation of his church tour in preparation for missionary service to the academic routine of a college. He reflects:

> It is singular what effect the difference of situation has on me. At home, where I had nothing special to do, & felt a sort of security. I may content to do nothing, to waste hour after hour in smoking, playing chess, reading unimportant things, til I almost lost the capacity to apply myself. Here, having undertaken regular work, I find myself aroused by a desire to do fifty things, & I judge every moment of time that is not spent on

---

[89] Crawford H. Toy to John A. Broadus, January 31, 1861, ASC, SBTS.

[90] "History of Richmond College," University of Richmond, https://rc.richmond.edu/about/history.html.

[91] Toy to Broadus, January 31, 1861.

[92] Ibid.; Toy asks for advice on conducting the classes and asks Broadus to tell Manly "that I have not forgotten so much Hebrew since last May as one wd suppose—partly because there was not much to forget, & partly because I had it well impressed on me."

what I consider profitable employment.

Toy's words indicate a sense of belonging and purpose, and these thoughts cause him to reflect, as he has done frequently in his writings, on the quality of his faith:

> It is very well to be under the power of good habits, but this facility of acting simply fr. regard to duty has sometimes seemed to me dangerous. In religious life it may disguise, I have thought, the absence of Xn emotion by its regular performance of religious duties. It is a difficult question to decide, how far it is just treadmill work & how far the genuine outspeaking of earnest feeling. It has troubled me a good deal. It makes me doubt now sometimes whether my heart has ever been changed. I can only pray God to deepen my Xn feeling & strengthen the internal evidence of my calling.[93]

At the end of the semester, Toy returned home to Norfolk.[94] From May to October 1861, Toy served as pulpit supply for the Cumberland Street Baptist Church in Norfolk.[95] In a letter to Broadus dated October 23, 1861, Toy tells Broadus that Virginia "preachers have not been slow to buckle on fleshly armor" and that he "himself has been divided between desire to take another session at G'ville & inclination to do heroic deeds against our enemies."[96] Toy also tells Broadus that he was "anxious to read Bancroft carefully, in order to trace national character of the two sections, their differences of origin, & their development. I wish to see whether they are distinct nations, & what Slavery

---

[93] Toy to Broadus, January 31, 1861; Toy abruptly turns next in the letter to a discussion of a book on preaching and oratory and another on parables and figurative language.

[94] Within the year, Richmond College shut down its operations because of the Civil War. Most of the faculty and students joined the Confederate army. By war's end, one-fifth of the alumni and many of the students were dead; the campus had been taken over by the Union Army. The college was in complete disarray with no students, no books, and no endowment (https://rc.richmond.edu/about/history.html).

[95] Hurt, "Toy," 34; citing Cathcart, *The Baptist Encyclopedia*, 2:1161.

[96] Crawford H. Toy to John A. Broadus, October 23, 1861, ASC, SBTS. Toy's view here is similar to that expressed by Albert Bledsoe, "Liberty and Slavery," with which Toy was familiar (Crawford H. Toy to Morton B. Howell, February 2, 1859, ASC, SBTS). Toy had mentioned Bledsoe's treatise in the context of asking Howell if he had heard about University of Virginia professor James Holcombe's address, "Is Slavery Consistent with Natural Law?" Toy's only critique of Holcombe's words (which at the time he had not read) was that he doubted Holcombe "has so much philosophy as Bledsoe." Holcombe advocated Virginia's secession at the Richmond Convention in March 1861 and was identified as an early advocate of the Lost Cause movement (see Edward Pollard, *The Lost Cause: A New Southern History of the War of the Confederates* [New York: E. B. Treat, 1867]).

has to do with the difference. I know that you [are] not able to form extreme opinions & that I am." George Bancroft was widely regarded as the preeminent historian of the day, and he was in the midst of writing his multivolume and best-selling *History of the United States*. When the war erupted in April 1861, Bancroft thought that the United States was being guided by Divine Providence and that slavery was "a national sin powerful enough to destroy the American republic and its status as a specially ordained nation."[97] Thus, it is encouraging that Toy was eager to read the respected historian's views and explore the social, political, and economic histories of the two "sections" of the country to decide whether there should be one or two nations. However, Toy did not separate the theological issues that informed and shaped the debate.[98] He makes his own inclinations clear in the next several sentences to Broadus: "A night or two ago, after going to bed, I thought out some analogies behind the relations of Parent & Child & Master & Slave, wh. I afterwards set down. It was suggested to me in a conversation with Dr. Ryland. The carrying out the Analogy seems to me to meet fairly objections against regarding Slavery as a Divine Institution. What do you think of it?"[99] However progressive Toy's views on female education may have been for the mid-nineteenth century, his views on race and slavery thoroughly (and sadly) reflected the views of the dominant white Southern culture. In his extant antebellum letters, Toy rarely refers to African Americans; in fact, only three references have been located, and all of those occur in correspondence with Morton Howell during Toy's college days at the University of Virginia:

"I am very apt to buy cakes or apples or something of the sort from the old darkies that knock at the door every half hour."[100]

"...we have a new Mayor [of Norfolk] who is dreadful to the negroes;

---

[97] William P. Leeman, "George Bancroft's Civil War: Slavery, Abraham Lincoln, and the Course of History," *The New England Quarterly* 81 (2008): 464.

[98] For an analysis of the ways politics, economics, and theology informed the debate about secessionism and slavery, see Mandy E. McMichael, "'We must go out of this Union': The Two Secessions of Basil Manly Sr.," *Baptist History and Heritage* 52/2 (2017): 8–19.

[99] Crawford H. Toy to John A. Broadus, October 23, 1861, ASC, SBTS.

[100] Crawford H. Toy to Morton B. Howell, March 8, 1853, ASC, SBTS. The term "darkie" is clearly offensive to modern ears. Apparently, it was preferred by "genteel" Southern women and men to other slurs (a usage reflected, for example, in Foster's 1852 ballad "My Old Kentucky Home"); cf. Richard Spears, *Forbidden American English* (Lincolnwood, IL: Passport Books, 1990), 49. This was a term imposed condescendingly by those on the outside and in power; black slaves seldom used the term in reference to each other (unlike more offensive terms, such as the "n-" term).

has some whipped every morning & for everything."[101]

"...remember me to the colored folks."[102]

There is nothing explicitly vicious in these references; in fact, there is a hint of passing concern about the welfare of the slaves under the Norfolk mayor and even a hint of (patronizing) endearment in the last. There is no evidence that Toy's family owned slaves. But neither is there evidence that Toy, either in his daily intercourse with the institution and individuals associated with the slave culture or in his studies, showed the kind of intellectual analysis and critique that he demonstrated in most every other arena (including, to some degree, the dominant views of women's role). And he was good friends with some of those, like J. William Jones, who remained unreconstructed "Southerners" and who would become chief architects of the "Lost Cause" movement following the War.[103]

The racism of Southern culture and of its Southern Baptist leaders is often glossed over. David Lyon, for example, says simply, "That Toy should have a part in the war was under all the circumstances inevitable."[104] Furthermore, this racism was in the institutional DNA of the seminary. There was no debate over the injustices of the institution of slavery among the founding faculty, only divided opinion regarding the prudence of Southern secession. Broadus, himself an anti-secessionist, observed, "Brother Boyce is a strong anti-secessionist man, Brother Williams strongly secessionist, Manly mildly so. But neither that, nor anything else, has ever caused the slightest jar among us."[105] Toy himself seemed to indicate a preference for secession as well. In a

[101] Toy to Howell, July 29, 1853.
[102] Toy to Howell, November 9, 1853.
[103] See Moore, "Apostle of the Confederacy."
[104] Lyon, "Toy," 5.
[105] John A. Broadus to Miss Cornelia Taliaferro, quoted in Robertson, *Life and Letters*, 181. Manly's father, Basil Manly, Sr., was a leader in the secessionist movement in Alabama (cf. McMichael, "The Two Secessions of Basil Manly Sr."). Keith Harper, in "What's Wrong with this Picture? James P. Boyce, John A. Broadus, and Reflections on the Lost Cause" (*Journal of Southern Religion* 17 [2015], http://jsreligion.org/issues/vol17/harper.html), has argued that "Southern Seminary is not usually associated with the Lost Cause." The primary reason Harper cites is that, for financial reasons, Boyce and Broadus could not afford to alienate Baptists in the North, since they needed their economic support. He also reports that Boyce and Broadus were anti-secessionists (though Broadus indicated Manly and Williams were, to varying degrees, secessionists, as apparently was Toy). That several of the founding faculty were anti-secessionists hardly makes them abolitionists (Boyce pronounced himself a "pro-slavery" man), and J. William Jones, main architect of the "Lost Cause" movement, worked for a time as a financial agent for the seminary. It is, therefore, more likely that Sampey's "Lost Cause" sympathies (which Harper acknowledges and see below) were not anomalous but rather the more public

letter to Broadus on November 25, 1860, he wrote:

> I suppose you are a secessionist. You have seen the action of the Alabama
> brethren. I hope Doctor Boyce will disentangle himself in New York
> before South Carolina leaves the Union. You all seem inclined to snub
> us in Virginia, hardly willing that we should enter the Southern Confed-
> eracy. In that case we shall have to put ourselves on our dignity, and rely
> on our prestige and our tobacco. *But I hope we shall stand together.*[106]

These racist attitudes continued into the next generation of Southern
faculty, eventually taking the shape of Lost Cause emphases. For example,
SBTS Old Testament professor John Sampey's affection for Robert E. Lee
(whose portrait he kept in his office) was well known.[107]

While it was highly probable that Toy would enter the War on the side

---

manifestation of an ethos, however muted to protect the financial health of the seminary,
that was fertile ground for such sympathies. Recently, Southern Seminary released a report
tracing the involvement of the seminary in slavery, racism, and the perpetuation of Lost
Cause mythology. See *Report on Slavery and Racism in the History of the Southern Baptist
Theological Seminary*, www.sbts.edu/southern-project. For a critique, see Wendell Griffen,
"White Baptists and Racial Reconciliation: There's a Difference between Lament and
Repentance," *Baptist News Global*, January 3, 2019.

[106] Crawford H. Toy to John A. Broadus, Waverly, Sussex County, VA, November
25, 1860, quoted in Robertson, *Life and Letters*, 178; my emphasis.

[107] Dale Moody, longtime professor of theology at Southern, was fond of telling the
anecdote of Sampey asking a student if Robert E. Lee could sin. The student replied, "Of
course," to which Sampey replied, "No. No. No. It was against Lee's nature to sin." For
another version of this story, see "Sampey and Lee," Southern Baptist Theological Seminary, http://archives.sbts.edu/the-history-of-the-sbts/our-lore/sampey-and-lee/. On the
same webpage is a reminiscence of Herschel Hobbs: "One year about the time of Lee's
birthday, Dr. Sampey was asked to conduct chapel at the seminary. He spoke on Jesus. At
one point he said, 'Jesus was a good man. He was a good man. Good as Robert E. Lee.'
Realizing what he had said, he shouted, 'Better, better, BETTER!!'" General Robert E.
Lee's legacy, of course, was at the center of "Lost Cause" mythology, and these "humorous"
anecdotes stand on the surface of a (mostly) unacknowledged racism and white supremacy
rooted in that "Lost Cause" ideology. When I was a student at SBTS, Lee's portrait had
passed to another Old Testament professor in whose office it was proudly displayed. As I
write these words, I am painfully aware that, as much as I would like to think otherwise, in
all likelihood I—like my ancestors from the North Carolina mountains—would have supported the Confederate cause (despite not being slave-owners) and most probably would
have served in the Confederate army (for reasons for this phenomenon, see Nancy Isenberg,
White Trash: The 400-Year Untold History of Class in America [New York: Penguin Books,
2016]). So, as a Southern white male (even a "progressive" one), I acknowledge that the
criticisms leveled here at Toy and (most of) his compatriots are rightly levelled at me as
well.

of the Confederacy,[108] was it "inevitable" (to use David Lyon's word)? Was it inevitable that the racism of Southern slave culture go unchallenged? William and Ann Holcombe were parents of James Philemon Holcombe, Professor of Law at the University of Virginia during Toy's student days. James Holcombe was an avid proponent of slavery who wrote and published a popular treatise, "Is Slavery Consistent with Natural Law?" and later advocated for Virginia's secession from the Union. Earlier in his life during his first year at Yale College, Holcombe's parents, however, freed their slaves. His mother refused a gift of slaves from a childless uncle, and the couple moved to Indiana.[109] Toy's own views on race would evolve somewhat after his move to Cambridge, Massachussetts.[110]

Hurt and his sources all cite October 1861 as the month and year that Toy entered the Confederate army,[111] but the letter cited above is dated October 23, and it shows that Toy has clearly not yet committed to the military. He will write Broadus another letter from Norfolk on November 27, 1861, in which he still has not made a decision: "I have rec'd a proposition for the Cumb. St. Chr., to preach once a week to them, for a small sum. I shall probably accept it, if I do not take a Chaplaincy."[112] According to John Walters,

---

[108] Of course, Toy belonged to a denomination that had already split in 1845 over the theological, political, economic, and social issues focused around slavery. See Robert G. Gardner, *A Decade of Debate and Division: Georgia Baptists and the Formation of the Southern Baptist Convention* (Macon, GA: Mercer University Press, 1995); Walter Shurden, *Not a Silent People: Controversies That Have Shaped Southern Baptists* (Macon, GA: Smyth & Helwys, 1995), 29–38.

[109] Nathaniel Cheairs Hughes, Jr., *Yale's Confederates: A Biographical Dictionary* (Knoxville, TN: University of Tennessee Press), 102.

[110] But not as fully as those of David Lyon, his colleague and former student. The social Darwinism that Toy learned in Germany provided academic and intellectual support for his culturally inherited racist ideology. This is made manifest in his book, *Introduction to the History of Religions* (Boston, MA: Ginn and Company, 1913), published near the end of his career. Marie Griffith has explored Toy's "ascending evolutionary trajectory" from "savage" primitive religions to "higher religions" through the lens of sexuality; see R. Marie Griffith, "Sexing Religion," in *The Cambridge Companion to Religious Studies*, ed. Robert A. Orsi (Cambridge: Cambridge University Press, 2011), 344–46.

[111] Hurt, "Toy," 34; Lyon, "Toy," 5; and Moore, "Toy," 2.

[112] Toy's correspondence, understandably, essentially ceased during his military period. Hurt is reliant here on his sources, Lyon, Moore, and Jones. Since all three were colleagues of Toy at one time or another, they did have firsthand access to Toy's recollections of the war, but it is not clear that they represent independent witnesses at every point. At some points, for example, Moore and Lyon appear dependent on a tribute to Toy upon his retirement from Harvard, published as "Four Professors Retire" in *The Harvard Graduates' Magazine* 17 (1908–1909): 622–26; on Toy, see 622–24. Of course, Crawford Toy may himself have advised on the composition of this tribute. I will note the few points

after his parents closed the drug store and moved to Baltimore in March 1862, Crawford Toy enlisted as a private in the Norfolk Light Artillery Blues and served with that Confederate battery until he became chaplain of the newly formed 53rd Regiment in January 1863.[113] Several stories from Toy's military service serve to portray him as a "scholar solider." In a letter to John Broadus (March 30, 1863) written from Camp Thirteenth Virginia Infantry, Hamilton's Crossing, J. William Jones writes: "I saw Toy ten days ago. He is chaplain in the Fifty-third Georgia Regiment, Seemes' Brigade, McLaw's Division, and is quartered near here. Is Looking very well and seems to be enjoying himself. His Syriac books are in Norfolk and he has, therefore, been compelled to fall back on German for amusement."[114] Another tradition describes Toy in theatric fashion: "In an interval of the suspension at the battle of Cold Harbor, a private soldier lies on the ground poring over an Arabic grammar—it is Crawford H. Toy, who is destined to become the famous professor of Oriental languages at Harvard University."[115] Another source reports Toy's continued devotion to language study: "He [Toy] carried with him through the war his

---

where I can corroborate or challenge (as here in the case of the date of Toy's entrance into the army).

[113] See John Walters, *Norfolk Blues: The Civil War Diary of the Norfolk Light Artillery Blues* (Shippenburg, PA: Burd Street Press, 1997), 300. Walters identifies the unit as the 53rd Virginia Regiment, but all other records refer to it as the 53rd Georgia Regiment. R. Thomas Crew, Jr., and Benjamin H. Trask confirm that Toy enlisted on April 13, 1862, and was later appointed Chaplain (of the 53rd Georgia Infantry) on January 9, 1863 (*Grimes' Battery, Grandy's Battery and Huger's Battery Virginia Artillery*, The Virginia Regimental Histories Series [Lynchburg, VA: H. E. Howard, 1995], 96). In "Seminary Men in the Confederate Army," 134, J. Wm. Jones (mistakenly) states that Toy joined the 51st Georgia Regiment (rather than the 53rd as he states elsewhere and as records indicate), alongside his brother-in-law, W. L. Curry, who served as chaplain in the 50th Georgia Regiment. Curry was a native of South Carolina and, though a Baptist, had received some theological training at Presbyterian Theological Seminary in Columbia, South Carolina, before transferring to the new Baptist Seminary in Greenville in 1859. Jones says Toy and Curry were "true yokefellows" and reports joining them for a revival: "I remember that when Longstreet's Corps came back from East Tennessee and camped near Gordonsville, in the spring of 1864, Toy and Curry wrote for me to come up from my camp, near Orange Court House, and help them in a revival that had begun in their brigade. I responded as promptly as other engagements would permit, and it was a great joy to me to be thus associated with Toy, my old roommate at the Seminary, and Curry, my old classmate there, in these labors in camp…. Brother Curry baptized a number of converts within easy range of the enemies' fire…" (134–35).

[114] John W. Jones to John A. Broadus, March 30, 1863, in Robertson, *Life and Letters*, 197. Hurt, "Toy," 35; Lyon, "Toy," 5; and Moore, "Toy," 2 all cite this passage.

[115] Randolph McKim, "Glimpses of Lee's Army," in *The Soul of Lee by One of His Soldiers* (New York: Longmans, Green and Co, 1918), https://leefamilyarchive.org/reference/books/mckim/09.html.

Hebrew bible and dictionary. This was his diversion. He tramped all the way from the Seven Pines battlefield to Richmond to consult a Hebrew grammar."[116]

Most of the references to Toy's subsequent military career are drawn from a single source, *The Harvard Graduates' Magazine*:

He [Toy] was taken prisoner at Gettysburg on July 4, 1863, and confined, first for a few days in Baltimore and then at Fort McHenry, where the conditions were rigorous in the extreme. But he found it possible to live above the privations of prison life. There was the glee club, the mock dress parade every evening with tin pans for drums, and the class in Italian which Mr. Toy organized and taught. In December, 1863, he was exchanged and rejoined the army, with which he remained until the middle of 1864, when, quite unexpectedly, he was chosen Professor of Natural Philosophy in the University of Alabama, at that time a military training-school for the Confederate army. There he taught applied mathematics until the end of the war, when the university buildings were burned in a cavalry raid.[117]

After the war, Toy accepted a position as "licentiate" and taught Greek at the University of Virginia.[118] At the same time, he returned to teach at the Albemarle Female Institute, where he had previously spent three years. He was viewed there as a demanding teacher. A student at the time, Sarah Ann Strickler [Fife], wrote in her diary, "Mr. Hart says that Mr. Toy compliments my Greek reading very much; I feel honoured to get a word of approbation from that iceberg, especially on Greek."[119] Elsewhere she comments, "I am sick tonight in body and mind—I cannot progress fast enough in knowledge. I wish I had reached the height that Mr. Toy has."[120]

It was this same student who mentioned Toy's plans to continue his studies in Europe:

Mr. Toy spoke to me today about going to Europe in September. Mr.

---

[116] J. S. Dill, *Lest We Forget: Baptist Preachers of Yesterday That I Knew* (Nashville: Broadman Press, 1938), 43.

[117] "Four Professors Retire," 622–23. This paragraph is the basis for the accounts of Lyon and Moore on which Hurt mostly depends. Notes in the *Religious Herald* confirm that Toy was released from prison (October 15, 1863) and went to teach at the University of Alabama (September 23, 1864). Although we know little beyond this brief account of Toy's military service as a chaplain, it is instructive to read analogously his friend J. William Jones's account of his time as a Confederate chaplain; see *Christ in the Camp: Religion in Lee's Army* (Richmond, VA: B. F. Johnson, 1887).

[118] "Four Professors Retire," 623.

[119] Strickler, "Private Diary," 183; cited by Hurt, "Toy," 37–38.

[120] Strickler, "Private Diary," 184; cited by Hurt, "Toy," 38.

and Mrs. Saunders of the South…expect to go to the old country then, and open a school for American girls at Berlin. They will take twenty young ladies, afford them the best masters in music, the languages, etc., and during the year take them traveling over the most beautiful and storied parts of Europe.… Mr. Toy is well acquainted with Mrs. Saunders and expects to go to Berlin very soon.[121]

Strickler also recorded the reaction of her classmates when Toy made his plans public:

> Yesterday morning Mr. Toy announced his intention of leaving on the 10 o'clock train, and never coming back again. We were mute with astonishment; he has known all along that he would leave before the session was out. He expects to start to Germany the 15th of July, and enter the University of Berlin. He will probably stay five years. We all wept when he told us goodbye, and the tears were in his own eyes I think.[122]

European Correspondent

Toy sailed for Europe from New York on the *Denmark*. There is little extant correspondence from Toy during his studies at the University of Berlin; however, Toy did publish a series of articles in the *Religious Herald* about his experiences during his first few weeks abroad. It is unlikely that this journalistic effort was Toy's idea, given his expressed disinterest elsewhere regarding such activities.[123] Nonetheless, he produced ten rather lengthy essays on a variety of subjects from London, Paris, Cologne, and Berlin from July 1866 to

---

[121] Strickler, "Private Diary," 195–96; cited by Hurt, "Toy," 38. In fact, Mrs. Saunders was Toy's cousin, and he would eventually (some twenty-two years later) marry the Saunderses' daughter, Nancy (who was twenty-four years Toy's junior; see chapter 8).

[122] Strickler, "Private Diary," 211; cited by Hurt, "Toy," 40. For Toy's letter to his AFI students, see the beginning of this chapter. Between 1815 and 1914, some nine to ten thousand American students attended German universities (see Konrad H. Jarausch, "American Students in Germany 1815–1914: The Structure of German and U.S. Matriculates at Göttingen University," in *German Influences on Education in the United States to 1917*, ed. Henry Geitz, Jürgen Heideking and Jurgen Herbst [New York: Cambridge University Press, 1995], 195–211). Toy never explains his choice of Berlin as the location for his studies, but by this time it had become the "preferred institution" for American students, outpacing Halle and Gottingen, which earlier students had favored; see Annette G. Aubert, *The German Roots of Nineteenth Century American Theology* (Oxford: Oxford University Press, 2013), 28.

[123] In his letter to J. William Jones, September 13, 1860, he wrote, "I will do what I can in the way of articles for the Herald, though I do not take to such work kindly." Presumably, Jones had suggested that Toy write some articles regarding their missionary plans. It may have been Broadus who recruited Toy as "European Correspondent" (see below).

January 1867. They were published anonymously under the heading "Letter from our European Correspondent" and signed simply, "T." The first letter is dated July 2, and Toy indicates that he had just arrived in London after a twelve-day voyage from New York to Liverpool. He wryly remarks that "As we were unfortunate enough to have no storms, I can give you no thrilling descriptions of howling winds and seas mountain high." Then he reflects theologically on his first experience of an extended voyage on the ocean: "To the Christian who looks at it [the ocean] as God's creation and God's instrument, it is a soothing friend or a terrible messenger, as it lies in calm or rages in tempest—and it has a strange fascination; so that an acquaintance of a few days enabled me to comprehend the almost passionate love that sailors have for their stormy life."[124]

In London, he admires the churches and cathedrals, but with some qualifications: "Undoubtedly, we ought to offer to the Lord houses as noble and beautiful as we can build. But it is an offering that must be prompted by Christian love, and not merely artistic taste; given freely to the Master, not designed to attract the attention of men."[125] The bulk of his column was devoted to an extended description of hearing preach Charles Spurgeon, the pastor of the famous Tabernacle Baptist Church in London. While generally positive, Toy was clearly not overwhelmed by the encounter:

> His face seemed to me an average English one, his head not remarkable, and his expression was sometimes decidedly pleasing. His bearing throughout was exceedingly modest and quiet, and his manner, while it exhibited firmness and decision, had nothing unduly bold or unreverential in it. His voice easily filled the house, but there was, at first, (perhaps only to my unEnglish ear,) some indistinctness of enunciation, which made it difficult for me to understand him. The sermon had in it nothing remarkable in thought, expression or manner…. there was nothing that any man might not have said.[126]

In his next letter, dated July 9, 1866, he returns to the subject of Spurgeon (having first criticized the establishment church). He comments

---

[124] "Letter from our European Correspondent. London. July 2, 1866," *Religious Herald*, August 2, 1866.

[125] Toy also observes that Mr. [John] Smith had established the first Baptist church in London and that there were now about seventy Baptist chapels.

[126] "Letter from our European Correspondent. London. July 2, 1866." Toy also recounted how he was asked to move from his seat for which he had not purchased a ticket. He then conjectured that the seat rentals for the auditorium which held some seven thousand persons might accrue more than twenty thousand dollars annually.

disapprovingly on Spurgeon's practice of open Communion, calling it a "deplorable error." But his next description of Spurgeon's preaching is decidedly more positive:

> Mr. Spurgeon, besides the richness and power of his voice, has the faculty of exciting and sustaining enthusiasm—of making his impress on the hearers—of arousing and carrying on thought. Without being learned or profound he instructs by his spirituality and directness, and the cogency of his appeals to Christian experiences is especially remarkable. Nor is his racy, vigorous English to be overlooked. His language is largely monosyllabic, direct, and with a sometimes Shakespearian fervor and poetry. Such a man cannot be judged as a preacher by a single sermon. Doubtless he is unequal. He has not abandoned those eccentricities that once won the popular applause. But the reality of his power is shown in the profoundly attentive crowds that weekly flock to hear him, and still more in the vigorous life in which he has infused into his church.[127]

Toy's next letter was written from Paris on July 16, 1866. A "good" Baptist, he notes that the people are "given up almost entirely to papistical notions concerning religion, and yet being very pious after their fashion." Still, he admires their piety and devoutness, and especially the churches in a "Roman Catholic country"—"the solemn still which reigns in them—the care bestowed on them—the endless succession of worshippers who come to prostrate themselves before their deities. It is impossible for one unaccustomed to such sights to divest himself of religious awe, especially in the 'dim religious light' and majestic arches of a great cathedral, and to hope there enters into this service somewhat of pure worship which the Infinite Eye will discern and accept."[128]

Toy then turns his attention to church architecture and asserts, "The cathedral of Notre Dame is the gem of Paris." He is struck by these impressive structures and says in an unwittingly foreshadowing remark:

> I hope I may not be thought tainted with foreign heretical notions if I say that, in my opinion, our houses of worship are usually not sufficiently

---

[127] "Letter from our European Correspondent. London. July 9, 1866," *Religious Herald*, August 16, 1866. Toy went on to remark that given Spurgeon's weekly lectures, sermons, correspondence, and work on his journal, *The Sword and the Trowel*, "you have an amount of work not inferior to John Calvin's, and greater than that of ninety men out of a hundred."

[128] "Letter from our European Correspondent. Paris. July 16, 1866," *Religious Herald*, August 30, 1866. He judges, "Leaving out the doctrinal creeds of these people, it is not difficult to say which is more commendable, their devout attentiveness or the irreverential familiarity which marks the worship of many Protestants."

ornate. Or rather, I do not like the word *ornate*; they are not grand enough. We do not spend enough money on them.... I know that a church in Richmond, reputed to be wealthy, abandoned its intention of purchasing an organ, because it seemed inconsistent with the prevailing distress in the churches.... But it is not impossible that the argument, from general poverty is frequently or unjustly or illogically used against the expenditures of money on churches.... Poverty has always existed and will always exist. Yet the Lord exacted from the Jews contributions for the Tabernacle which would now be thought excessive.... And our Saviour blessed the offering of costly ointment which his disciples, some of them conscientiously, thought was wasted, inasmuch as its price might have been given to the poor. He thereby recognized the principle that pure-minded sacrifices to him are as acceptable as deeds of charity.[129]

At the close of the column, thinking of both London and Paris, he applies his missionary zeal, which is still very much with him: "It is necessary to establish a missionary system for great cities no less than for heathen lands, the ignorance being as deplorable in the one as in the other." He returns to this theme in his next letter, dated July 24, 1866, also from Paris: "The contribution of each person is one cent a week, and this system being generally adopted, has worked wonders.... There are, in the South, no less than 200,000 white Baptists, and half a dollar per annum from each would make a very competent income for the Foreign Mission Board."[130]

He also returns in this letter to his critique of Catholic practices as he observed them: "Indulgences are now put to better use than in Tetzel's time.... It looks strange to see votive tablets to the Virgin, offered by men in the nineteenth century, for the cure of disease." Still, he argues, "this is better than utter unbelief. I would rather see men ascribing cures to the Virgin now, than have them explaining the miracles of the Saviour by mesmerism and imagination." Toy was certainly no "anti-supernaturalist" in 1866! Furthermore, the correspondence from Europe reveals that the young man, Toy, is changing and evolving as he confronts new evidence and experience, a foreshadowing of things to come.

By the end of July, he has arrived in Cologne, Germany, curious to see

---

[129] "Letter from our European Correspondent. Paris. July 16, 1866." He does not, however, think one must choose between Foreign missions or "church embellishments": "Many pious men live in handsome, costly houses, and doubtless pray with as much devotion on a carpet as on the bare floor. But the grand church has this advantage over the fine dwelling, that it is an offering to God."

[130] "Letter from our European Correspondent. Paris. July 24, 1866," *Religious Herald*, September 6, 1866.

"the cathedral, the Rhine, and the real Johan Maria Farina."[131] After a short interval, Toy travels on to Berlin, his final destination. In a letter dated August 6, 1866, Toy records his first impressions of Berlin and its people (while claiming at the same time to reserve judgment):

> Berlin is a large and rather ugly place, ugly certainly in comparison with Paris; with which city, however, it is not altogether fair to compare it. For, though six hundred years old, it was, two hundred years ago, still a small place, and has only recently (within a century) a town of political importance.... I will not undertake so soon to form an opinion of the city or of the people, and say nothing now of the commonly expressed opinion of the Germans, that they have learning without uprightness, and wealth without elegance. Certainly they have learning, the results of which the world may thankfully use without too closely criticizing the shortcomings of these worthy Teutons.[132]

As with London and Paris, Toy comments on the religious devotion of the citizens of Berlin: "If the religiousness of a people, as Paul implies in his address to the Athenians, is in proportion to the number of their houses of worship, the Berliners may lay claims to devoutness, according to German standards." He notes that the city has houses of worship belonging to the "National Establishment," French Calvinists, Evangelical Lutherans, Baptists, and Jews. He further notes that the Baptist church is called the "Capella der Baptisten" and thus not even "honored with the name of church [kirche]." About the Jews in Berlin he observed that they had previously enjoyed an able defender in Moses Mendelssohn (1729–1786), grandfather of the composer Felix Mendelssohn, who was a philosopher and a commercial leader in the Berlin textile industry. Mendelssohn

> resisted the repeated efforts of a friend to detach him from the faith of his father, and at last, in self-defence, published an exposition of his

---

[131] "Letter from our Correspondent. Cologne. September 13, 1866," *Religious Herald*, September 27, 1866. Farina was the maker of perfume who had settled in Cologne in the earlier part of the eighteenth century and established a factory—the oldest in the world—there making the scents that took their name from the city and made it famous. Toy had a curiosity about this aspect of the place, joking that "Cologne is not outwardly remarkable. It is not perfumed by the famous preparation to which it has given its name." While in Cologne, the King and his Royal Family attended church, which Toy observed. That experience and others may form the basis for Toy's anecdote reported by David Lyon ("Toy," 6) about the professor who said of the royal family, "Die Allerhöchsten sind in die Kirche gegangen, um den Höchsten anzubeten" ("The Most High have gone to church to worship the Most High").

[132] "Letter from our European Correspondent. Berlin. August 6, 1866," *Religious Herald*, September 20, 1866.

opinions, which is marked by candor, learning and ability. Indeed, the Jews have what more nearly approaches to organization than ever before, and, but for the promises of the Bible, their steadfast and successful opposition to evangelical efforts might lead us to despair of the ultimate conversion.[133]

In his next letter, August 13, 1866, Toy turned his attention to an account of a "favorable specimen of Lutheran preaching," which he found "evangelical and practical."[134] The text was the parable of the Pharisee and the Publican (Luke 18), and Toy summarized what he found new in the exposition: "It was the different views of men taken by the Pharisee and the Publican. The former, in his anxiety to glorify himself, debases his fellow-man." The Publican

stands a far off. So, said the preacher, has it ever been, and is it still.... The humble child of grace represents man as the son of God, created in His image, and endowed by Him with excellent qualities, religious and rational. But the egotistic truster in his own righteousness has originated a philosophy which makes man only a developed ape, and takes away the real divinity of his reason and his conscience.[135]

In this same issue of the *Religious Herald*, John Broadus published a commendation of the still unnamed "European Correspondent":

THE EUROPEAN CORRESPONDENT.—The advertisement of the College will show why one's mind should naturally pass from it to the European letters which the Herald is now publishing, signed T. The writer is one of the foremost young scholars of America, and if he lives twenty years longer, will have few equals in the land in point of real, solid learning. Some persons in our new and extremely practical country, will have little sympathy with his enthusiasm about architecture, music, &c; but the traveller who makes us look at other aspects of life, culture and worship, than those which present themselves around us, and provoke us to inquire whether our opinions and practices are not in some respects defective or erroneous, is the really useful traveler.—He is one of our chiefest benefactors who makes us think. J.A.B. *Greenville, S. C.*[136]

Broadus's unabashed pride in Toy stands out: "The writer is one of the foremost young scholars of America, and if he lives twenty years longer, will

---

[133] "Letter from our European Correspondent. Berlin. August 6, 1866."

[134] "Letter from our European Correspondent. Berlin. August 13, 1866," *Religious Herald*, September 27, 1866.

[135] "Letter from our European Correspondent. Berlin. August 13, 1866."

[136] *Religious Herald*, September 27, 1866.

have few equals in the land in point of real, solid learning." But one wonders if Toy's columns exploring architecture, music, culture, and worship had led to some undercurrents of criticism of the columns, and were the real reason that Toy's mentor, John Broadus, felt compelled to defend.

At any rate, it was not Toy's taste in music or architecture that constituted the basis of published complaints in the next issue of the *Religious Herald*; rather, it was the brief, favorable comments Toy had made about the Lutheran sermon on the parable from Luke 18:9–14. Rev. R. H. Bagby was a Baptist pastor in Virginia who in 1866 was serving as moderator of the Baptist General Association of Virginia.[137] Bagby's letter about Toy is published in the November 8, 1866, issue of the *Religious Herald*. Despite the use of "T." as a byline, the columns of the "European correspondent" were not anonymous to everyone. Bagby begins, "No doubt every reader of the Herald will thank Bro. Toy, and the Editors, for the interesting letters he has written." He then takes a swipe at Toy's suggestion that Baptist churches in America were not "grand" enough: "Whether fortunately or unfortunately, we of the South shall not be able, for some time to come, to build such *splendid* houses of worship, as those he seems to have so much admired. Many a poor church would be very thankful to obtain a house of any kind."[138] Bagby comments also on congregational singing, which had been addressed by Toy in his letters of August 6 and 13 (published in the issues of September 6 and 27). But Bagby writes that "the chief design of this communication is to notice a paragraph in the letter of August 13th. He had heard a sermon in Berlin, on the parable of the Pharisee and the Publican, which was 'evangelical throughout.' Well, we hope it was; but if the passage which Bro. Toy gives us, with seeming commendation, was the best, or even a fair specimen, it 'gives a pause' to our hope." Specifically, Bagby objects to the characterization of the "child of grace" as "a son of God, endowed with excellent qualities, religious and rational," and having "divinity in his reason and conscience" (quoting Toy summarizing the preacher). Bagby goes on: "This language from one of our own preachers, known to be evangelical, would be a little startling; but coming from Germany, the land of 'Olshausen and Stier,' it may well awaken suspicion."

Citing a cacophony of scriptural texts, Bagby argues that this language is a rejection of the "doctrine of human depravity" in favor of rationalism that "has ruined Protestantism in Germany and all over Europe; that is fast infusing itself into the pulpits and churches in the North; and from which we at the South are not entirely free from danger." He writes: "We feel it our duty

---

[137] On Bagby, see George Braxton Taylor, *Virginia Baptist Ministers* (Princeton, NJ: n.p, 1912), 80–93.

[138] *Religious Herald*, November 8, 1866.

to raise a warning voice against these unscriptural and most pernicious senti-ments. It is this rationalism, this high estimate of man's 'excellent religious qualities,' this listening to the supposed 'divinity of human reason,' instead of the teachings of the word and Spirit of God."[139]

Bagby concludes with this biting comment (and another ominous fore-shadowing of things to come for Toy): "It may be well for our young men to visit Germany in search of learning; but it is to be hoped that they will look elsewhere for their theology; and that we of the South shall be spared any communication of the least taint of the heretical doctrines with which that country abounds whether through the columns of the *Herald* or otherwise."[140]

The editors of the *Religious Herald* made no attempt to defend Toy. In a note at the end of Bagby's letter they write:

> We are glad that Bro. Bagby is prompt to notice and correct any latent tendencies to Rationalism, or any other speculative error, that may be found among the articles published in the Herald. We assure him that we are profoundly convinced of the importance of guarding sedulously the foundation principles of our religion, and among these the doctrine of human depravity is not the least important.—Eds. Of HERALD[141]

In addition to quoting Scripture in his critique, Bagby had cited the com-mentary of Hermann Olshausen, professor of Theology in the University of Erlangen, whom Toy had mentioned in passing in his August 13 letter: "It is well Bro. Toy did not consult Olshausen—he might only have been confirmed in the error the German preacher was so insidiously inculcating. He would have learned from that astute and erudite commentator (on Rom vii.11–13,) that 'the germ of the divine image remains, even in fallen man, to which grace knits, in her work of bringing him back to God.'" Toy did not offer any kind of public response to Bagby's criticisms,[142] but he might have taken exception to Bagby's use of Olshausen in his argument. Bagby had focused on Olshau-sen's reference to "fallen man" as indicating Olshausen's embrace of the doc-trine of total depravity. But it is worth noting the larger context of Olshausen's words:

---

[139] Ibid.

[140] Ibid. Bagby's letter, of course, ends with the obligatory expression of regard for the author despite the criticisms: "I need hardly say that no disrespect is here intended to Bro. Toy for whom I entertain the most sincere esteem and affection."

[141] At the time, the editors of the *Religious Herald* were J. B. Jeter and A. E. Dickin-son, who together had purchased the paper in 1865. Both will play a role in Toy's later conflict.

[142] At least not in the *Religious Herald*. It is hard to imagine that Toy did not respond in private correspondence to friends, although such correspondence has not been located or is no longer extant.

Sin is not the nature, the substance of man himself (as evil generally is nothing substantial, but disharmony only, the disturbance of the relations originally ordained by God), rather has *the germ of the divine image remained even in fallen man, on which grace founds her work of bringing man back to God.* (Comp. at Rom. ii. 14, 15) This better germ of life, however, appears in the natural state, when sin has quickened, as suppressed by a foreign power, troubled and obscured in its nature, and hence the operation of grace finds expression in striving to draw it upwards, and to make it prevail.[143]

The issue at hand is not whether Olshausen is reading Paul correctly, but rather whether Bagby is rightly interpreting Olshausen. Toy's anonymous Berlin preacher is describing the "child of Grace," who sounds much like the "fallen man" in Olshausen's exposition who through the "operation of grace" is having the "germ of life"—"troubled and obscured in its nature" by sin—drawn "upwards," presumably to its original state, a state of Grace, freed now from the "foreign power" of sin. Olshausen's language, understandably, is also infused, at least subtly, with the rhetoric of rationalism. At least, his interpretation does not lead directly or explicitly to Bagby's doctrine of "total depravity."[144] So it is easy to imagine that Toy might have retorted that, for the Berlin preacher as for the Erlangen professor, it is precisely God's Grace that differentiates the Publican (the "child of Grace") from the Pharisee (the "egotistical truster in his own righteousness"), so that his "excellent qualities, religious and rational" are themselves the results of divine endowment as Toy's Berlin preacher says.[145]

---

[143] The German edition of *Biblischer Commentar über sämmtliche Schriften des Neuen Testaments zunächst für Prediger und Studirende* was published between 1830–1839. The first American edition of Olshausen's *Biblical Commentary on the New Testament, Adapted Especially for Preachers and Students* was translated by David Fosdick and published by Sheldon & Co. in New York in 1860. It is assumed that Bagby was using this English edition (or one like it).

[144] If Bagby is using an English translation of Olshausen, it is striking to note that the words "depraved" or "depravity" never occur in the translation of his commentary on Romans.

[145] For that reason, it seems somewhat unfair that Paul House can cite this criticism in the *Religious Herald* as evidence that "Toy did not grasp the Rationalistic tendencies of some of the preachers he was hearing" ("Crawford Howell Toy and the Weight of Hermeneutics," *Southern Baptist Journal of Theology* 3 [1999]: 30); further, see chapter 9. That statement seems truer of Bagby than Toy.

Toy published three more letters in the *Religious Herald*, and then the columns ceased.[146] It is not clear why they stopped. Perhaps the editors did not wish to risk more controversy or perhaps Toy was more deeply consumed in his studies. About the details of those studies we know very little. Most of Toy's formal training in Berlin was in ancient languages; in that sense, he was fulfilling plans he had in 1859 to travel to Europe and study languages, plans that had been overturned by his decision to prepare for a career in missions.[147] In Berlin, Toy studied Hebrew with Emil Roediger (1801–1874), who was best known for finishing the *Thesaurus Linguae Hebraicae* by Wilhelm Gesenius (1786–1842). Toy took Sanskrit with Albrecht Weber (1825–1901), a professor of Indian languages and literature, specializing in Sanskrit lexicography, and Arabic with Friedrich Dieterici (1821–1903). Apparently, his only work in theology was with Isaac August Dorner (1809–1884).[148] Dorner was a popular teacher and well-respected scholar whose *History of Protestant Theology* was dubbed "one of the great theological works of the age, peerless in its kind."[149] Steeped in language study and not yet "tainted" by radical German higher criticism,[150] Crawford Howell Toy returned to the United States in late 1868. After a year's stint at Furman, Toy accepted an invitation from Boyce and Broadus to join the faculty of Southern Seminary in 1869.

---

[146] Those letters were published in the January 3, 17, and 24 issues of the *Religious Herald*.

[147] See Toy, "Sketch of My Religious Life."

[148] "Four Professors Retire," 623; Lyon, "Toy," 6; Moore, "Toy," 2–3; Hurt, "Toy," 43–47 (who includes a list of the professors' most important publications). Moore notes that C. A. Briggs was also in Berlin (1866–1869) and that Toy apparently took "no courses in the Old Testament" (3).

[149] "Contemporary Literature," *Presbyterian Quarterly and Princeton Review* 1/1 (1872): 181; cited by Aubert, *The German Roots of Nineteenth Century American Theology*, 33. See also Karl Barth who lavished Dorner with this praise: "Here for the first time we have to deal with a theologian who, while standing amidst the problems of the nineteenth century, points beyond them in his contributions to theological method and poses new questions to us by the new answers that he gives" (*Protestant Theology in the Nineteenth Century: Its Background and History*, trans. Brian Cozens and John Bowden, new edition [Grand Rapids: Eerdmans, 2002], 563).

[150] In "Crawford Howell Toy: Heresy at Louisville," Pope A. Duncan observed: "It is difficult to assess the full impact of the years in Berlin upon Toy's intellectual and religious development. It would appear that they did not greatly alter his religious orientation at the time, but they did serve to sharpen his intellectual tools, to put him in touch with the best theological scholarship, and to whet his appetite for research" (*American Religious Heretics: Formal and Informal Trials*, ed. George H. Shriver [Nashville, TN: Abingdon Press, 1966], 61). We will explore the influence of Toy's educational experience in Germany more fully in chapters 3 and 9.

The early period of Crawford Toy's life was marked by a search for meaning and truth, both religiously and intellectually. Toy was constantly grappling, constantly categorizing, constantly seeking, sometimes desperately it seems, to make sense of his thoughts, experiences, and faith. This quest for truth continues into the next chapter(s) of his life, taking unexpected (and sometimes painful and costly) twists and turns along the way.

Fig. 1

Crawford Howell Toy.
Archives and Special Collections, James P. Boyce Centennial Library,
The Southern Baptist Theological Seminary, Louisville, Kentucky

3

SOUTHERN SEMINARY CAREER AND
CONTROVERSY (1868–1880)

> When Dr. Toy returned to Louisville, and had made his preparations to leave, his colleagues [Boyce and Broadus] who were here went to the railway station. The three happened to stand for a little while alone in a waiting room; and throwing his left arm around Toy's neck, Dr. Boyce lifted the right arm before him, and said, in a passion of grief, "Oh, Toy, I would freely give that arm to be cut off if you could be where you were five years ago, and stay there."[1]

This story was related by John Broadus in his memoir of James P. Boyce as an anecdote to reveal Dr. Boyce's "personal grief" at the forced resignation of C. H. Toy from the faculty of Southern Seminary in May 1879. Broadus himself expressed his disappointment in a letter to his wife: "Alas! The mournful deed is done. Toy's resignation is accepted. He is no longer professor in the Seminary. I learned that the Board were all in tears as they voted, but no one voted against it. ...we have lost our jewel of learning, our beloved and noble brother, the pride of the Seminary. God bless the Seminary, God bless Toy, and God help us, sadly but steadfastly to do our providential duty."[2] The affection between these three men is part of the persistent "Toy myth." Greg Wills described the relationships: "Broadus was his father in the faith and beloved mentor, and Boyce, his admiring benefactor and friend. Both were convinced that his errors were dangerous to the seminary."[3] However much affection shared among the three, according to the Toy myth, doctrinal purity and principle trumped personal friendships.

But that was not how everyone understood the relationships among these three, especially between Toy and Boyce. Their contemporary and colleague,

---

[1] John Albert Broadus, *A Gentleman and a Scholar: Memoir of James P. Boyce* (Birmingham, AL: Solid Ground Christian Books, 2004; repr., New York: A. C. Armstrong and Son, 1893), 263–64.

[2] John Broadus to Mrs. Broadus, May 10, 1879; cited in Robertson, *Life and Letters of John A. Broadus*, 313. On the final vote count, two trustees voted against the motion to accept Toy's resignation.

[3] Wills, *Southern Seminary*, 130.

W. H. Whitsitt, wrote in his private diary: "Toy regarded Boyce with the utmost contempt and this sentiment caused him almost unconsciously to favor the heterodox opinions which he had all the while maintained and conveyed to the students. In fact Toy lost his balance; the sight of Boyce's dunderhead was like a red flag in the eyes of a mad bull."[4] Boyce apparently reciprocated

---

[4] William H. Whitsitt Diary, November 30, 1886, 5:106, VBHS. In 1886, on a snowy wintry evening, Whitsitt reflects back on the events of spring 1879 and remarks on the relationship between Toy and Boyce: "He and Boyce could not well abide each other; he considered Boyce to be supremely ridiculous in the character of a teacher of theology." Likely Whitsitt's own experience with the Boyce family at this time shaped his account of the "Toy controversy," especially with regard to Boyce. After Whitsitt learned in October 1888 that Boyce was very ill (he would die in Paris in December of that year), Whitsitt entered a long entry in his diary regarding another affair that was happening parallel to Toy's:

> The report prevails that Boyce is ill in London. I feel a thrill of regret in view of the early departure of my old enemy. He has been for nearly ten years sternly opposed to me and has done me a deal of damage, but he has many good qualities, and I cannot avoid respecting him. The private occasion of our contention occurred in the spring of the year 1879 at which time I courted his daughter Elizabeth. The trouble about Toy was then in course and it was considered uncertain how the business would result what course I would take. Miss Elizabeth rejected my suit, most likely at the suggestion of her father. The storm passed over. Toy was driven away, but I kept my place. In due time it would have been wise for me to renew my suit. I was too proud to do so, and Miss Elizabeth was left alone in her single misery. On the 4th of October 1881 I married another lady.... Miss Elizabeth had rejected me, but she could never forgive her. The father took up his daughter's grievance and he has nursed it well these seven years: he will carry it with him to the grave. In cultivating his antipathy he has been highly successful. He has deprived me of my just rights in obtaining a full professor's salary and by that process has robbed me of a large amount of money. Poor Miss Elizabeth has had her revenge. I am sorry for her to the bottom of my heart. She has done me a deal of injury: I have done her more. And yet it is better as it is.... Miss Elizabeth has never married and her day is fairly done. One of the saddest sights will be the last that poor Boyce shall behold: his wife and three marriageable daughters without a protector and almost without a friend. Likely none of them will ever marry. What is to befall them none can predict, except that they will be full of bitterness against all mankind. (Whitsitt Diary, October 8, 1888, 9:12–14, VBHS)

There is no mention of Whitsitt's proposal to Elizabeth Boyce in the correspondence with Florence Wallace during this same period of spring 1879, either by Whitsitt or by their daughter, Mary Whitsitt Whitehead, who later edited and curated the letters with commentary and who must have known about the proposal from the diary, which was in her possession (Whitehead, ed., *Mirror*). Whitsitt was right about his salary. On April 1, 1879, Whitsitt received $375 for the quarter compared to Toy, who had only been teaching

this feeling of contempt. Following Toy's resignation, Boyce was reportedly heard to "threaten to publish what will astonish and mortify Dr. Toy's friends, and that he told two distinguished brethren, *en route* to the Miss. Bap. Con. that 'Toy was rotten to the core.'"[5] In the same letter, written to Broadus, the author, Samuel Provence, expressed disbelief with regard to Broadus's apparent charge that Toy had misrepresented his views: "But your letter astonishes me. Surely, Dr. Toy is incapable of acting in bad faith. Do you mean all you say? Does this paper [Toy's letter of resignation] which professes to contain his views of the subject of inspiration really give 'very little idea' of that view? If so, that is dishonest. But can Dr. Toy be dishonest? Has he ever given any other view than this? My trouble increases. I am saddened, amazed, dumbfounded, and unhinged,—and I know not what else."[6] Broadus had often stood between Boyce and Toy,[7] shielding Toy from criticism (whether undue or not), but in the end Toy even "got beyond the boundaries and Broadus, whom Toy led about by the nose during the Greenville period, now went over to the side of Boyce, and the eviction was accomplished."[8] What led to this state of affairs in which Crawford Toy descended from "the jewel of learning" at the seminary to being described as a person "rotten to the core"? What led to the character assassination of Crawford Toy by these two colleagues, James Pettigru Boyce, as chair of the faculty, his superior, and John A. Broadus, his mentor, who baptized Toy, ordained him, preached in the commissioning service for his (failed) appointment as an SBC missionary to Japan, and recommended him for several teaching positions? To answer that question, we begin with his appointment to the faculty of Southern Seminary in 1869.

---

at Southern three years longer than Whitsitt and who had received a quarter's salary of $625 the previous July (Box 2, James Pettigru Boyce Collection, ASC, SBTS). As might be expected for the position of faculty chair, Boyce received a much larger quarterly salary ($875; see salary receipt, April 1, 1879, Box 2, James Pettigru Boyce Collection, ASC, SBTS).

[5] Samuel M. Provence to John A. Broadus, January 7, 1880, Box 8, Broadus Papers, ASC, SBTS. Wills has softened Boyce's criticism by quoting that "Boyce believed that Toy's *beliefs* [and not the man himself] were now 'rotten to the core'" (*Southern Seminary*, 138; emphasis added).

[6] Provence to Broadus, January 7, 1880. For Provence, Boyce's comment paled in comparison to whatever it was that Broadus wrote: "all that didn't trouble me like what I find in your letter this morning."

[7] Broadus, perhaps unconsciously, makes this suggestion in *Memoir*, when he states that "a good many failed to understand Dr. Toy, on the one hand, or Dr. Boyce on the other." Therefore, he argues, "it may be proper to give a plain statement of the facts, which are believed to show nothing in the least discreditable to the character and motives of either party" (261).

[8] Whitsitt Diary, November 30, 1886, 5:106, VBHS.

Southern Seminary (1869–1879)

Upon his return from Europe in July 1868, Toy was recommended by John Broadus for a faculty position at Furman University. In a letter to James Furman on December 18, 1868, Toy accepted the invitation to become chair of Greek Languages and Literature.[9] Plans were already afoot, however, for Toy to move over to the seminary (still, at this time, located in Greenville). In fact, he was tutoring students at Southern during spring 1869.[10] The *Religious Herald* announced his appointment to the seminary faculty at the end of the spring semester:

> The choice for the new Professorship fell on Rev. Crawford H. Toy, of Furman University. Of his fitness for the place, not a doubt can be entertained. He graduated with distinction from the University of Virginia, spent several years of study in a University at Berlin, and is deemed by competent judges, to be one of the best linguists of his age, in this or any other country. Beside his eminent lingual attainments, his sound judgment, amiable manners, and earnest piety will qualify him for the post for which he has been selected. Should his life and health be spared, and circumstances favor the prosecution of his studies, it is confidently expected that he will, at no distant day, rank among the foremost biblical scholars of the world.[11]

Apparently, the abrupt move from Furman to Southern caused no ill will between the leaders of the two institutions. James Furman accepted Boyce's invitation to "perform at the service at the inauguration of Prof. Toy."[12] The faculty decided that the new professor should give an address as part of his inauguration, and he did under the title "The Claims of Biblical Interpretation on Baptists." The printed version of the address was long (over 60 pages) and erudite. Toy argued that "a special obligation in respect to the Scriptures" rested on Baptists, a point he made not out of "denominational arrogance" but

---

[9] "Letter to James C. Furman," in Harvey Toliver Cook, *The Life and Work of James Clement Furman* (Greenville, SC: n.p., 1926), 234–35.

[10] "Minutes of the Faculty of the Southern Baptist Theological Seminary," November 27, 1868, ASC, SBTS; cited by Hurt, "Toy," 51.

[11] *Religious Herald*, May 20, 1869. Broadus commented on Toy's appointment: "The special desire in adding a fifth professor was to relieve Dr. Boyce of teaching Polemics, and Dr. Broadus of Homiletics, as the latter's health was impaired, and Homiletics, in addition to New Testament, was proving too much for him, and as Dr. Boyce was so much hindered by business cares and journeyings" (Broadus, *Memoir*, 211–12).

[12] James Furman to James P. Boyce, August 31, 1869, Box 1, James Pettigru Boyce Collection, ASC, SBTS.

out of the recognition of Baptists' "complete dependence on the Bible."[13] Furthermore, Baptists are not under human authority or any articles of faith "which settle beforehand principles of interpretation" but rather are held "accountable to God alone, and suffer no man's individuality to be swallowed up in the impersonal mass of the body to which he belongs."[14] For these (and other) reasons, Toy argued that it was crucial "to state distinctly the elements of correct exegesis," which for Toy consisted of two elements—an external and an internal.[15] The external dimension deals with "fact, thought and feeling, written by men for men," and requires grammatical and logical investigation. The internal aspect of Scripture is "a revelation by the Spirit of God, given through men filled with a divinely engendered love for God," which, in turn, requires the Spirit's inspiration and guidance.[16] Toy then traced the history of interpretation through an evaluation of these two foci from Jewish exegesis through early Christian interpretation, followed by the medieval and reformation periods, and finally through the gains achieved by the modern "scientific" method. Toy concludes this section: "the word of God has something in common with other books, and something different from all others."[17] Correct exegesis involves determining the meaning of the word, the context of the passage, the character of the writer, and the circumstances of the place and time of writing; in other words, a grammatical-historical investigation.[18] Furthermore Toy's method is grounded on a theory of inspiration that "the Bible, in its assertions being known, is in every iota of its substance absolutely and infallibly true."[19] Such an assertion meant for Toy, at the time, that the apparent conflicts between scientific discovery and the Bible could and would be resolved: "Let Geology first arrive at a satisfactory conclusion, and we may rest in the assured conviction that it will not be in conflict with the inspired record."[20] Thus, Toy combined traditional language regarding the Bible as "infallibly true" with a conviction that scientific discoveries, including evolution should it be demonstrated, "will produce valuable results, and will illustrate rather than denude the Scriptures."[21]

---

[13] Crawford H. Toy, *The Claims of Biblical Interpretation on Baptists* (New York: Lange & Hillman, 1869), 5.

[14] Toy, *Claims of Biblical Interpretation*, 6.

[15] Toy, *Claims of Biblical Interpretation*, 8.

[16] Toy, *Claims of Biblical Interpretation*, 9.

[17] Toy, *Claims of Biblical Interpretation*, 42.

[18] Toy, *Claims of Biblical Interpretation*, 43.

[19] Toy, *Claims of Biblical Interpretation*, 44.

[20] Toy, *Claims of Biblical Interpretation*, 49.

[21] Ibid.

Immediate reaction to the inaugural address was positive.[22] Many used the address to extol theological education for clergy, still a relatively new phenomenon for Baptists. J. C. Hiden warned against an uneducated clergy leading to a "reign of ignorance and superstition in the ministry."[23] A writer to the *Religious Herald* likewise celebrated Toy's erudition: "At last we are on a par with our brethren of other denominations, and our peculiar tenets will no longer be attributed to ignorance and narrow-mindedness."[24]

At this point, Toy was apparently noncommittal regarding Darwin and evolution, advocating that his audience extend "patience in repose even to the Development Theory of Darwin and others. Not that we are called on now to accept it, for it is by no means demonstrated. But we may be sure that the researches which it occasions will produce valuable results, and will illustrate rather than denude the Scriptures."[25] Before the seminary left Greenville to relocate in Louisville in 1877, however, Toy had given a public talk, apparently advocating evolution.[26] For Whitsitt, this event was a harbinger of trouble to come and illustrated his view of Broadus's obsession with Toy, at least at that point in time:

> The manner in which Broadus was subject to Toy in Greenville is one of the wonders of our Seminary history.[27] It would be useless to claim that

[22] Even those who didn't claim to understand it were impressed by the erudition (and length) of the address. John Stout wrote, "Prof Toy delivered the opening address. Subject: 'The Claims of Biblical Interpretation on Baptists' or something to that effect—very profound, but I must say it seemed very long" (John Stout to Fanny Coker, August 31, 1869; September 23, 1869, L–S–C, SCL). More recent evaluations of Toy's inaugural address by conservative scholars have been more critical (especially House and Wills). We will address those critiques in the conclusion when we evaluate Toy's theological method.

[23] J. C. Hiden, *Working Christian*, September 16, 1869; cited by Stephen Hurd, "Confronting an Intellectual Revolution: The Southern Baptists and the Toy Controversy" (M.A. thesis, Vanderbilt University, 1987), 15.

[24] "Professor Toy's Inaugural," *Religious Herald*, March 13, 1870; cited by Hurd, "Confronting an Intellectual Revolution," 16. Hurd comments, "Proud and gratified, the supporters of the seminary believed they had acquired a first-rate scholar who would enhance the quality of theological education in the denomination and provide an intellectual vindication of Baptist beliefs" (16).

[25] Toy, *Claims of Biblical Interpretation*," 49.

[26] Broadus, *Memoir*, 260: "About that time [early 1870s] appeared the most important works of Darwin, Dr. Toy became a pronounced evolutionist and Darwinian, giving once a popular lecture in Greenville to interpret and advocate Darwin's views of the origins of man." George Foote Moore has pointed out a number of issues with Broadus's description of influences on Toy. For example, Darwin's *Origin of Species* was published in 1859, hardly "about that time" that Toy gave his lecture (see Moore, "Toy," 4).

[27] Around this time, Whitsitt also reports to Miss Florence Wallace that his sister, Maggie, had given Toy the nickname, "Great and Mighty." He adds, "She has a talent for

Broadus was not aware of facts that were well known to his colleagues. The Lecture which Toy made on Darwinism before a public audience at the Court House in Greenville could not be concealed. The excitement of Dr. ____ was apparent to all; I heard Broadus concede that the Doctor had spoken to him about the business.[28]

Part of Toy's own evolution in thought occurred when he abandoned attempts to reconcile science with the Bible. For example, he no longer entertained the idea that the word for "day" in Genesis 1 could refer to extended geological periods, and by 1874, he was teaching his students this view as well. It was, Toy argued, manifestly untrue that God infused into the mind of the biblical writer scientific knowledge that did not exist at that time.[29] Tension between Boyce and Toy, which would come to a head in Louisville, was already evident in the classroom in Greenville. One student recalls an anecdote that occurred during the seminary's last year there: "It is recalled that a student went to Doctor Boyce with the statement that 'Doctor Toy taught that the writer of the 16th Psalm had no reference to the resurrection but that Peter said in Acts that it was a direct prophecy of the risen Christ.' 'Well,' said Doctor Boyce, 'as between Doctor Toy and Peter, you and I had better stick to Peter.'"[30] Regardless of the topic, Whitsitt argued, even in Greenville

---

nicknames" (William H. Whitsitt to Florence Wallace, February 9, 1977, in Whitehead, ed., *Mirror*).

[28] Whitsitt Diary, November 30, 1886, 5:110, VBHS. When Toy gave a lecture on Genesis and current ethnological views regarding the unity of race (see Broadus, *Memoir*, 260), he was challenged for "casting discredit on the story related to the confusion of tongues…. Broadus defended Toy with the assurance that it was an inestimable privilege to hear from the foremost scholar in America touching an issue to which he had devoted so much attention" (Whitsitt Diary, November 30, 1886, 5:111, VBHS).

[29] Holt notes on Toy lectures, Class in OT English, September 28, 1874, 148–49, MSS 220.04 H742, ASC, SBTS. David Lyon elaborated further on this point:

In his course on the English Bible many a student heard views expressed which were both novel and disturbing; as when the lecturer told him that the word "day" in the first chapter of Genesis means a day of twenty-four hours, whereas we know the world was not made in six such days but is the result of ages of evolution; or when he said that the author of the book of Daniel was not a contemporary of Nebuchadnezzar but lived in the second century B.C. These commonplaces in the teaching of today were startling to the many minds in the South four decades ago. Dr. Toy never demanded his views on any subject should be accepted without question. ("Toy," 7)

[30] Dill, *Lest We Forget*, 45. Lyon recounts another anecdote that reflects some tension between the two professors, though this one is not about biblical interpretation:

He [Toy] led them likewise into charming and instructive byways, as in a course

61

"whether in public or private Toy was at no pains to conceal his views. But he was not thrown off his balance by any sort of opposition in Greenville; as soon as he reached Louisville he became sensible of opposition; he was not quite regarded in the light of a demigod."[31]

W. H. Whitsitt, who joined the faculty in 1872, recalled this time in Greenville as "the spring time of Toy's fortunes. During that year when he was first 33 years of age he was made a Professor at the Seminary and was the highest toast of Southern Baptists, through the agency of Broadus."[32] It was not just the largesse of Broadus, however, that caused Toy's halo to shine in Greenville. From the beginning, Toy was revered as a teacher. John Stout, a student in Toy's first classes, wrote to his fiancée: "He is so thorough, so true so strong";. "Prof. Toy is a wonderful man—indeed he seems at home on any subject…and I admire his simplicity and plainness so much; he takes such straight-along Common Sense Views."[33] David Lyon enrolled in the seminary in 1876 (and would follow Toy to Louisville). He described Professor Toy's teaching method:

> In the class room he seemed to know everything about the subjects which he taught. He criticized the text-book with freedom, and sought not to fill the mind of the students with facts, though he never minimized the value of fact, but to stir up the mind to the exercise of its own powers. …it was ever his method to set the student at work gathering facts for himself, and thus acquiring at first hand the materials for reaching con-clusions. While his opinions were based on careful study and were firmly held, no man was ever more ready to revise them in the light of additional knowledge. Needless to say, he exercised a profound influence on the thinking of his students.[34]

Other Southern students, whether during Toy's Greenville period

---

of lectures on the fine arts, among which he included dancing. In commenting some days later on the death of John the Baptist, Dr. Broadus remarked to his class, "See what the dance of a silly girl led to." One of the students interrupted the speaker with, "But, Dr. Broadus, Dr. Toy told us the other day that dancing is a fine art." The lecturer replied, "Brother Toy may, but I don't." ("Toy," 11)

[31] Whitsitt Diary, November 30, 1886, 5:111. Whitsitt's comments, especially re-garding Toy's intellectual acumen and promise, must at times be taken *cum grano salis*, since there is no small amount of professional jealousy in his words.

[32] Whitsitt Diary, November 30, 1886, 5:105.

[33] John Stout to Fanny Coker, August 31, 1869, L-S-C, SCL. In the same letter, Stout complained that Professor Toy "requires a great deal of work of us. He asked me the other day if I couldn't manage to put *eight* hours study on each lesson. As it is I do give about six."

[34] Lyon, "Toy," 6, 7.

(1869–1877) or briefer Louisville period (1877–1879), likewise extolled Toy's gifts as a teacher.[35] M. D. Jeffers recalled Toy as "a delightful teacher, a brimful scholar, a sympathetic brother. He taught what he honestly believed."[36]

Toy's commitment to and interest in students went beyond the classroom:

> He was always accessible. In the smallest details of a student's life he was interested. He arranged for the music classes, made provisions for the students' attendance upon lectures or concerts, he visited the sick, he was the inspiration and director of the Missionary Society. His thought and interest, his sympathy and care, touched all of the life of a student from center to circumference.[37]

Toy's piety was also noted by former students: "Dr. Toy's prayers at the opening of his lectures were most earnest cries to God for light upon his study of his word."[38] The cumulative portrait is of an effective teacher committed both to his students and to the subject matter he taught.

In these early years, because of various illnesses and other commitments on the faculty's part, Toy taught a variety of courses besides his own courses in Old Testament and Hebrew, including Greek New Testament, biblical introduction, and Latin Theology.[39] In addition, Toy made substantial changes to existing courses. For example, the course description of Hebrew under Toy's supervision was much more demanding than that offered by his predecessor, Basil Manly.[40] The description of the English Old Testament course

---

[35] Several of these testimonies are recorded also by Hurt, "Toy," 236–37.

[36] M. D. Jeffers, "Reminiscences of My Seminary Life," *The Seminary Magazine,* January 1892, 196–97. Lyon commented, "Dr. Toy's work at the Seminary was not limited to his formal teaching. I have noted that it was his delight to guide his students to independent reading and research" ("Toy," 11).

[37] C. C. Brown, "Letter to the Seminary Magazine," *The Seminary Magazine,* March 1889, 88. Toy also directed the Seminary choir (S. C. Clopton, "Reminiscences of My Life at the Seminary," *The Seminary Magazine,* February 1892, 270). Dill recounts a humorous story from one of the students in the graduating class of 1877 that reveals the way students had imbibed even Toy's phraseology. A certain Ed Dargan "announced to us all that the *terminus ad quem* of his ambition was at least one year of study in Germany. The expression *terminus ad quem* was a favorite with Doctor Toy, and his pupils often used it. At the opening of the next session letters came telling us of the marriage of Ed Dargan. We were forced to the conclusion that he had changed his ambition to a *terminus ad quam*" (Dill, *Lest We Forget,* 52).

[38] Clopton, "Reminiscences," 270.

[39] Moore, "Toy," 3.

[40] Hurt, "Toy," 231–32, citing the *Southern Seminary Catalogue, 1868–69,* 13–14. Among other changes, Toy's iteration includes multiple grammars and lexicons, missing from Manly's description.

was also revised. The original description read, in part, "The Old Testament is studied in chronological order, in the English version with references to the original when necessary. The whole course of the events is considered...as an unfolding of the Great Divine Plan of Providence and Redemption."[41] To this description, Toy adds that "the study of the prophecies is connected with the periods of the history to which they belonged."[42] This commitment to the historical context in interpretation will become a point of contention later.

Like the other professors, Toy spent considerable time, especially in the summers, raising funds for the financially struggling school.[43] He also purchased books in behalf of the seminary and, as Secretary of the Faculty, arranged for advertisements in denominational papers.[44] In 1874, Whitsitt convinced Broadus and Toy to form an extracurricular "Greek Club" to read the "Greek Classics."[45] In addition to all these teaching and administrative responsibilities, Toy tried to establish his publishing career, which at this time included working with Broadus to translate Lange's commentary on First and Second Samuel.[46] It was not all work, however. In addition to encouraging his students to pursue extracurricular activities, Toy also attended concerts and, himself a good musician, occasionally joined in some music-making of his own.[47]

Because of financial difficulties, the seminary moved to Louisville in

---

[41] *Southern Seminary Catalogue, 1868–69,* 13; cited by Hurt, "Toy," 231.

[42] *Southern Seminary Catalogue, 1872–73,* 12; cited by Hurt, "Toy," 233.

[43] Toy sends notes to Boyce detailing funds raised from associations and individuals. See Crawford H. Toy to James P. Boyce, July 4, 1870; August 16, 1870; June 1, 1871; September 15, 1874, Box 1, James Pettigru Boyce Collection, ASC, SBTS.

[44] On book purchases, see Crawford H. Toy to James P. Boyce, July 4, 1870; August 1, 1870, Box 1, James Pettigru Boyce Collection, ASC, SBTS. On advertisements, see Crawford H. Toy to the *Religious Herald*, June 30, 1877, Box 2, James Pettigru Boyce Collection, ASC, SBTS.

[45] W. H. Whitsitt to Florence Wallace, November 10, 1874, and November 24, 1874, in *Mirror*, 52, 54.

[46] Whitsitt to Wallace, February 2, 1875, in *Mirror*, 72. After initially declining to assist Boyce and Toy on the commentary translation, Whitsitt relented the next year, going over the translation (February 2, 1876). Moore admired Toy's superior translation work on an inferior book: "Erdman's commentary is an egregiously bad specimen of a bad kind, and made Toy's task peculiarly difficult. The book is translated with scrupulous fidelity. ...the effort to make a worthless book worth something...must have been a weariness of the flesh and vexation of spirit" ("Toy," 9). Toy did not publish a book of his own during his years at Southern, but he did write numerous articles for denominational and religious publications along with a few technical articles. We will consider Toy's scholarly contributions, particularly in the form of books, in chapter 5.

[47] Whitsitt to Wallace, February 2, 1876, in *Mirror*, 119.

1877.[48] In his letters to Florence Wallace, his fiancée (and later spouse), W. H. Whitsitt provides a unique glimpse into life in Louisville for the seminary community during its first several years there. Both Toy and Whitsitt were "bachelor professors" who, unable to find separate accommodations, became roommates in Louisville, taking up residence in October 1877 in fourth-floor rooms of the Caldwell block, #137 Fourth Avenue (later 415 Fourth Avenue): "Each man had a bedroom and a study, and they shared a common sitting room. The building was in the downtown section with a business establishment on the first floor and apartments above."[49] The relationship between Whitsitt and Toy had its ups and downs. At the beginning, Whitsitt extolled his roommate: "A better man and friend is not often found."[50] In Whitsitt, Toy had also found a kindred spirit who enjoyed opera, though such activities were apparently suspect for Baptist seminary professors in the nineteenth century. Whitsitt reported to Wallace that Toy had wanted to hear famed Austrian opera singer Eugenie Pappenheim, exclaiming, "it's a crime to sit here like brutes and allow all that music to pass unheard away."[51] Whitsitt confessed:

> No, we did not hear Pappenheim.…Speaking of "weak conscience" it is my conscience which is in that condition…. I always went to the opera when I was abroad & I despise myself for neglecting them at home. It is a duty unfulfilled. But on the other hand it is a duty to respect the consciences of other people. In a word there is a hard nut for somebody to work on. I want to be respectful & considerate & gentle & brotherly, "and yet I believe I am not guiltless when I allow a good opera to pass unheard."[52]

---

[48] In despair Broadus wrote to Boyce: "I am more & more wedded to the persuasion that the Seminary must be kept in operation or abandoned. If we can't get these bonds for current support, by summer or early fall at farthest, I should take it as a clear proof that the brethren can't sustain the Sem'y at all. I shd prefer to quit and be done with it than to die a dozen deaths before it is over…. I think, therefore, we had better determine to keep it going or sink it" (March 9, 1976, Box 3, James Pettigru Boyce Collection, ASC, SBTS). Many in South Carolina were unhappy. W. L. Lindsay wrote: "So the Seminary is going to leave us! …I'd rather the Asiatic Cholera should rage from the Sea's bed to Caesar's head! …I am afraid there will be a theological ass tied to the back door of several little high schools down here" (W. L. Lindsay to John Stout, June 5, 1877, L-S-C, SCL).

[49] Whitehead, *Mirror*, 172–73.

[50] William H. Whitsitt to Florence Wallace, December 11, 1877, in *Mirror*, 177.

[51] Whitsitt to Wallace, December 28, 1877, in *Mirror*, 178.

[52] Whitsitt to Wallace, December 28, 1877, in *Mirror*, 179–80. The two professors did go out on New Year's to "pay our duty" to those who had shown them kindnesses. While others were decked out in "swallow-tails and white kids" and rode in carriages, the two bachelors were on foot and "felt that old fellows like ourselves would be excused if we

At the beginning of their second year in Louisville, Whitsitt reports that he and Toy had joined the local Gymnastic Association and "and every evening we may be seen trying our strength on the parallel bars." This activity was much to the amusement of Miss Carrie Davis, a friend of Whitsitt's sister, Maggie, and who was living with the Broadus family in Louisville. She said she expected to find both of them "on the platform dressed in tights the next time a contest occurs at the Exposition."[53] Perhaps the idea was Toy's because Whitsitt was somewhat self-conscious about his participation in the exercise: "I have not dared to report this profane remark to my good colleague for fear he would be scandalized beyond endurance."[54] For a time in Louisville, Toy also took boxing lessons from a "boxing master."[55]

Despite these physical activities, Whitsitt also found himself at times nursing his roommate, whose health did not fare well in the harsher Louisville climate: "I have now become a foot-washing Baptist, and you can hardly believe how proud I am of the distinction. Last night as I was carrying him through his ablutions he [Toy] said, 'Do you know what is the hardest doctrine in the Bible?' 'Predestination, I suppose,' was my answer. 'No,' he replied, 'Oh no, it is "little children love one another,"' and I confess that I almost wept with joy in my lowly service.'"[56] Within a month, Toy had to take his turn as nursemaid. Whitsitt was bedridden with a cold, which he feared would worsen into pneumonia, and "Dr. Toy who meanwhile had improved a good deal stood by me in the kindest way and rendered invaluable assistance."[57]

In February 1879, Toy was instrumental in founding the "Conversation Club" in Louisville, a group of businessmen and professionals who met to

---

neglected to get ourselves up after manner of exquisites" (Whitsitt to Wallace, December 17, 1878, in *Mirror*, 206). James H. Slatton notes that the references to "old fellows" was not entirely hyperbolic (*W. H. Whitsitt: The Man and the Controversy* [Macon, GA: Mercer University Press, 2009], 75). Whitsitt (thirty-seven) and especially Toy (forty-one) were not that far from the expected life span in 1900 of forty-eight years.

[53] According to Slatton, Carrie Davis was a niece by marriage of James Furman and had been a student at the Greenville female college (*W. H. Whitsitt*, 56). She and Maggie and W. H. Whitsitt had shared living quarters for a time in Greenville (ibid.) and had eventually moved to Louisville, where she lived with the Broadus family.

[54] Quotations in this paragraph are from William H. Whitsitt to Florence Wallace, October 3, 1878, in *Mirror*, 199–200.

[55] Whitsitt Diary, November 30, 1886, 5:109.

[56] Whitsitt to Wallace, December 17, 1878, in *Mirror*, 205–206. Whitsitt identified Toy's illness as bronchitis, which kept him from engaging in Christmas parties and festivities that year (*Mirror*, 207).

[57] Whitsitt to Wallace, January 22, 1879, in *Mirror*, 209.

discuss various literary, social, religious, and scientific matters.[58] Toy's role in the Louisville Conversation Club was celebrated in a light-hearted poem composed by Bishop Dudley in 1883:

And Toy, our founder, preacher, scholar, sage,
Who knew all learning, whaso'er its age,
Who dreamed in Arabic, and smoked in Greek,
And read the Zend-Avesta once a week;
As brave as Paladin, as shy as girl,
As bright as diamond, pure as any pearl;
Alas! He too is gone, nor shares our feast,
A Modern Magus, he went to the East.
His learning grew too heavy for his station;
He fell to Boston just by gravitation.[59]

The two bachelor professors, despite the inclement weather and limited opportunities for "high culture" due to their positions as theological teachers, had made a satisfactory transition, along with the other faculty (Broadus, Manly, and Boyce). As noted, stirrings of controversy had already begun in Greenville; now they were about to intensify. From Whitsitt's perspective, the cause of the increasing tension was the reuniting of Boyce and Toy in the same place. Toy's "star was in his ascendant till he came to Louisville…and Boyce got on the track of him." Since 1872, Boyce had spent much of his time in Louisville preparing for the seminary's move. In those five years, Toy had "matured into a self-assured scholar and teacher" and "over the years he had grown bolder" in the application of the "scientific method."[60]

Whitsitt cites one incident in particular as a "fateful" moment in the de-

---

[58] *The Conversation Club* (Louisville: n.p., 1935). Whitsitt remarks on the opening meeting of the club in a letter to Florence Wallace, February 14, 1879; Bishop Dudley was elected President and Toy Vice-president: "There were about twenty persons in the room and we had a satisfactory beginning" (in *Mirror*, 213). Toy would continue to organize these kinds of groups for intellectual discussions at Harvard; see chapter 6 on the Harvard Biblical Club and the History of Religions Club. In the fall following Toy's departure from Louisville, Whitsitt reports that the Conversation Club "appears to be unable to withstand the shock [of the loss of Toy]: there has not been a single meeting this season, and I fear it is doomed to dissolution" (Whitsitt to Wallace, November 5, 1879, in *Mirror*, 244). By December 1880, Whitsitt can report a meeting of the club with "a specially elaborate dinner of seven courses with waiters in white gloves" (Whitsitt to Wallace, December 3, 1880, in *Mirror*, 279).

[59] *Conversation Club*, 60.

[60] Slatton, *W. H. Whitsitt*, 76.

teriorating relationship between Boyce and Toy. The event occurred at a dinner hosted by important seminary benefactors, Dr. and Mrs. Lawrence Smith:

> Dr. Toy was not able to make his usual figure. He was placed at the end of the table and has been unwell of late, but when the Darwinian philosophy came up for discussion he brightened a little and let us know that he believed Mr. Jos. Cook[e] of Boston was a woodenhead. I was sorry for this, for the host had just previously, when Toy's attention was diverted, praised Mr. Cook earnestly. Toy inclines strongly in favor of the philosophy of Mr. Herbert Spencer and his impatience of those who oppose themselves threatens now & then to disturb his really magnificent equipoise.... Dr. Boyce was at a disadvantage at the extreme end of the table.[61]

Reflecting on this event years later, Whitsitt concluded: "One night at a dining that was given to the members of the Faculty by Dr. & Mrs. Lawrence Smith in the autumn of 1878 he [Toy] got in the situation that is vulgarly termed 'regardless' and made a truly ugly display, before the various minsters of other Denominations who had been invited to meet us.... From that evening, I fancy, Boyce began to lay plans to be quit of him, an effort in which he succeeded in the spring of 1879."[62] The embers of conflict were about to burst into full flame.

---

[61] Whitsitt to Wallace, January 25 1878, in *Mirror*, cited by Slatton, *W. H. Whitsitt*, 77–78. Toy also criticized Cooke in a letter to T. T. Eaton, claiming "Cooke's 'Biology' has some good points, only he doesn't know the difference between religion and science" (December 17, 1877, SBHLA; see also Crawford H. Toy to T. T. Eaton, January 28, 1878, SBHLA). Exchanges such as this probably contributed to Eaton's animosity toward Toy.

[62] Whitsitt Diary, November 30, 1886, 5:105–106. There is a discrepancy in Whitsitt's memory of the date of the dinner (here autumn 1878) in the diary and the date of the letter (January 25, 1878) in which he recounted the event to Florence Wallace. But there is no doubt he is referring to the same event. Boyce was also irked by the relationship between Toy and Abraham Jaeger, a Jewish convert who had studied at the seminary and for whom Toy lobbied in 1876 to replace temporarily an ailing William Williams. Boyce objected that Jaeger's views were contrary to the seminary's abstract of principles (James P. Boyce to John A. Broadus, February 11, 1876, Box 6, Broadus Papers, ASC, SBTS). Jaeger was not hired and eventually became an Episcopalian and took a position at the University of the South. Boyce was "much disturbed in his temper" when Jaeger returned for a visit to the Seminary in 1878, and Broadus was apparently not happy that Toy "left his duties" to attend Jaeger's wedding in Sewanee, TN. Whitsitt observed, "There was not another man in existence to whom he would have showed such a favor" (Whitsitt Diary, November 30, 1886, 5:111). Elsewhere Whitsitt commented, "Nobody comprehends him [Jaeger] or appreciates or loves him like Toy" (William H. Whitsitt to Florence Wallace, March 17, 1878, in *Mirror*, 189). The friendship with Jaeger (whose view on inspiration Boyce did not trust) did nothing to help the tension between Toy and Boyce (see Wills, *Southern Seminary*, 124–25; Slatton, *W. H. Whitsitt*, 77–79).

The Controversy (1879)

There is some confusion as to the nature of the controversy regarding Toy's teaching. Greg Wills asserted that "Toy's dismissal precipitated a denominational controversy concerning the doctrine of inspiration."[63] And there is much to support this view that the controversy focused on the inspiration of Scripture. After all, Crawford Toy's resignation letter acknowledges this in the opening sentence: "It having lately become apparent to me that my views of Inspiration differ considerably from those of the body of brethren, I ask leave to say my opinions on that subject before you and submit them to your judgment."[64] Indeed, it was the question of inspiration.that prompted Broadus through Boyce to encourage Toy to prepare this statement and offer his resignation to the Board of Trustees meeting in Atlanta in May 1879. Rumors of Toy's views on inspiration began to spread as early as 1876. On June 20, 1876, Boyce informed Broadus that "in a postscript to a letter to Toy I broke into a gentle remonstrance and earnest entreaty on inspiration."[65] The spread of Toy's views was due, in part, to the efforts of South Carolina pastor William Lindsay, who wrote under the pseudonym "Senex" and promoted Toy's ideas (without naming him) in *Working Christians*, the South Carolina Baptist newspaper.[66] Though the connection between Senex and Toy was not widely recognized, Boyce saw that the writings of "Senex" were "some of the fruits of

---

[63] Wills, *Southern Seminary*, 136.

[64] Crawford H. Toy, Letter of Resignation, ASC, SBTS.

[65] Cited in Robertson, *Life and Letters of John A. Broadus*, 301.

[66] See Wills, *Southern Seminary*, 124. Lindsay told his friend, John Stout:

I have some new game "a foot". Look out in the next two issues of W. P. for two letters to My Friend by *Senex*. By all means keep me incog. "Saxon" had by various means become known, & I had to "double" again. These letters were struck off rather hastily; but this, understand, effected only their "get up" & not their matter.... I do not think you will yet endorse them in full, but they will at least furnish you a "cud", & that is more than "our" paper generally does.... I am determined to stir up this stagnant pool of religious thought which has settled like a Dead Sea over the minds & hearts of our ministry. We are standing like a pillar of salt, while the mighty tide of thought, bearing the world's intellect upon its bosom, is surging about us, sapping our ancient & rotten foundations, & tossing the truth about us as a thing of ridicule & scorn. There is almightiness in the Bible or it would go to pieces & go down under such treatment.... I struck boldly & hard—may God himself guide the blow. (William L. Lindsay to John Stout, May 20, 1877, L-S-C, SCL)

Toy's teaching."[67] Boyce wrote to Broadus:

> I have a letter from Bro. Toy setting forth his theory, in itself well
> enough. In so doing, I do not know that he goes beyond the statements
> of others. The trouble is when he enters, as he did in Virginia, into the
> details and begins to knock away one part and another. I think however
> that the ice being broken we shall be able to keep all right. His letter to
> me was very kind, if anything too flatteringly so. I do hope we can keep
> all right for I prize Toy more than all. I love him very much. He is a
> noble fellow and adds greatly to the glory of our institution.[68]

Broadus reports that by the end of the first session in Louisville in 1877,
"it became known to his colleagues that Professor Toy had been teaching some
views in conflict with the full inspiration and accuracy of the Old Testament
writings."[69] Whatever love Boyce had for Toy continued to sour, and among
the faculty he openly opposed Toy's views, thinking they would do harm to
the seminary, its students, and the sponsoring churches. Boyce communicated
these concerns to Toy through Broadus in spring 1878. Toy, however, "was
convinced that the views he had adopted were correct, and would, by removing many intellectual difficulties, greatly promote faith in the Scriptures."[70]
Still, Toy promised that he would refrain from posing such "theoretical questions," a promise he was unable to keep because students pressed him with
questions in class and he "found it impossible to leave out those inquiries, or
abstain from teaching the opinions he held."[71]

In summer 1878, Rev. W. B. Carson wrote Boyce to say he had heard
from another minister who thought the "doctrinal parts of the Bible are inspired," but the rest is as "liable to error as any other book," and, further, that
this was also the view of Toy (and Whitsitt).[72] The conflict over Toy's view
on inspiration came to a head in December 1878 when an editorial appeared

---

[67] James P. Boyce to John A. Broadus, June 15, 1877, Broadus Papers, ASC, SBTS.
For more on the "Senex" episode, see Thomas J. Nettles, *James Petigru Boyce: A Southern
Baptist Statesman* (Phillipsburg, NJ: P & R Publishing, 2009), 324–31.

[68] Boyce to Broadus, June 22, 1877.

[69] Broadus, *Memoir*, 262.

[70] Ibid.

[71] Ibid. Whitsitt claimed that Broadus was aware of Toy's behavior in the classroom
because he regularly attended Toy's Old Testament History class (Whitsitt Diary, November 30, 1886, 5:114).

[72] W. B. Carson to James P. Boyce, June 11, 1878, Box 2, Boyce Papers, ASC, SBTS.
Carson went on to query: "If we go thus far, I do not see how we can stop short of the
rejection of the whole. Is there better evidence of the inspiration of the doctrinal than of
other portions? If ¾ of an army are routed, how can the others hold their ground if they
have no stronger position than the routed?"

in the *Religious Herald* complaining about professors in Baptist theological schools being of unsound doctrine:

> One does not believe in the inspiration of Moses, nor, indeed, of various other parts of Scripture. I do not know by what rule he declares on the inspiration and non-inspiration of various parts of the Bible, but surely he must regard himself as either infallible or inspired, that he may be able to decide what part to receive and what to reject. In fact, he must regard himself as better authority than Christ, on the subject of inspiration; for he does not consider David inspired—unless in spots—and Christ did, for Christ declared that David "spoke by the Holy Ghost."[73]

Should not such professors be replaced, the author asks, "by men who will teach what the denomination wishes taught and pays to have taught?" At the end of the editorial, the author, who signs as E. T. R., muses, "Suppose the Professor who has no faith in Moses teaches Hebrew—he will lack that reverence which all should be trained to as he reads Genesis."[74]

The author did not name Crawford Toy, but there was little question as to his identity and, as it turns out, the identity of the author as well. On the same day the article appeared, Broadus wrote Boyce: "I do not know whether you are informed that E. T. R. of the *Rel. Herald*, who has of late been Dickinson's pet sensation, & who this week attacks Toy, is Miss Josephine Eaton." Although Broadus judged her comments "unfair, impudent and foolish," he was concerned that "Toy will be obliged to go before the Board in May & state what he holds & what he teaches. The point is not covered by our Articles of Belief, but his views differ widely from what is common among us." He then suggested that Toy might need to "tell the Boards & tender his resignation. If he cannot satisfy them he ought not to retain the position. If they are satisfied, we need not care for E. T. R. & Co." He encouraged Boyce to inform the chair of the trustees, Dr. Jeremiah Jeter, and to "talk it frankly over with Toy at once." With these words, Broadus outlined the terms of what, in fact, would unfold a few months later. Apparently, Boyce did talk with Toy (as eventually did Broadus as well?) and convinced Toy to set his views in writing. Following Broadus's lead, Toy claimed to teach in accordance with, and not contrary to, the seminary's article on Scripture but admitted that his views on inspiration did not reflect the common position among the churches, and he tendered his resignation.[75]

But Toy's view of inspiration may not have been the only reason for the

---

[73] *Religious Herald*, December 12, 1878.

[74] Ibid.

[75] John A. Broadus to James P. Boyce, December 12, 1878, Box 3, Boyce Collection, ASC, SBTS.

controversy, and certainly not as the discussion developed in the convention. Billy Hurt, Toy's first biographer, was apparently unaware that the *Religious Herald* article by E. T. R. implicated (but did not explicitly name) C. H. Toy as holding an unsound doctrine of inspiration, because he wrote, "In the years prior to 1879…there was no criticism of Toy made openly in the popular Baptist papers of the South."[76] Hurt then suggested that the precipitating factor was Toy's treatment of the suffering servant passages in Isaiah, which he published in the *Sunday School Times*, a publication widely used by pastors and Sunday School teachers. In the April 12 and 19, 1879, issues, Toy suggested that the servant should be primarily identified with Israel and not Jesus: "Some students of this passage suppose that in some passages the prophet means by the 'Servant of Jehovah' the Messiah directly; but this view is hard to reconcile with the frequency and clearness with which the servant is called 'Israel.' It seems better, therefore, to suppose a primary reference to the nation, with a final fulfilment in Christ."[77] In the April 19 issue, Toy dealt with Isaiah 53 and again concluded that Israel was the primary referent of the "servant" language with a "higher fulfillment" in Christ.[78]

Reactions to Toy's articles first appeared in non-Baptist publications.[79] *The Christian Intelligencer*, a Reformed publication, published "A Deplorable Oversight" in which the *Sunday School Times* was excoriated: "The Christian public may properly demand from them [*Sunday School Times*] a full apology for such a publication or unite in condemning the paper from all the pulpits and from the desk of every evangelical Sabbath-School." But the publication saved its most damning (and damnable) words for Toy: "The exposition is a base surrender of the chapter to unbelieving, Christ-hating Jews, and infidel neologists."[80] A Baptist paper, *The Journal and Messenger* (with offices in Cincinnati, Indianapolis, and Parkersburg, WV) extended the criticism of *The*

---

[76] Hurt, "Toy," 128. Nor does Hurt cite Broadus's letter to Boyce on December 12, 1878, in which the idea of Toy offering his letter of resignation was first broached. Hurt repeats this claim on page 148.

[77] Crawford H. Toy, "Critical Notes," *Sunday School Times*, April 12, 1879, 231. He continues: "This is not a 'double sense' in prophecy, but simply a necessary result of the fact that Christ was by divine appointment the consummation of all of God's revelations of truth in ancient Israel, a fact that seems more wonderful, more divine, the more we study it" (231).

[78] Crawford H. Toy, "Critical Notes," *Sunday School Times*, April 19, 1879, 246–48.

[79] For most of what follows regarding Toy's *Sunday School Times* articles, see Hurt, "Toy," 128–43.

[80] *The Christian Intelligencer*, April 24, 1879, 8. George Foote Moore observed that Toy's "by no means novel exegesis provoked a violent denunciation from the *Christian Intelligencer*, in the role of *inquisitor haereticae pravitatis* which the editors of denominational newspapers in those days often assumed" ("Toy," 4).

Christian Intelligencer and took aim directly at Toy: "We are sorry to find this evidence of a rationalistic tendency in one who has heretofore enjoyed the confidence of his brethren as a teacher of young men in the Baptist Theological Seminary, for we regard it as indicative of a state of mind boding danger to those who may come under his instruction."[81]

North Carolina's *Biblical Recorder* was the first Southern Baptist paper to criticize Toy's *Sunday School Times* articles, largely reproducing the criticisms of *The Journal and Messenger* and calling for Toy's resignation:

> If Dr. Toy holds and teaches these views, we believe it to be our duty to ask the Board of Trustees of the Southern Baptist Theological Seminary at its next meeting, either to dispense with the Chair of Professor Toy or request his prompt resignation of the position he fills in that institution. Whatever may be Dr. Toy's learning and capacity, it seems that he is teaching error, and error, too, strikes at the very foundation of the Christian religion. We built the Seminary for other purposes. We sustain it only as it teaches and defends the truths of the revealed word of God.[82]

The *Biblical Recorder* article appeared on May 7, 1879, the same day that Crawford Toy submitted his resignation to the trustees meeting in Atlanta. For that reason, scholars have often diminished or ignored the importance of Toy's *Sunday School Times* articles on Isaiah's suffering servant.[83] Stephen Hurd contends that the "Trustees in Atlanta…could not have read that paper [the *Biblical Recorder*], which came out the first day of the Convention."[84] There is evidence, however, that some of the trustees had read or heard of the criticisms leveled against Toy, and at least one trustee even questioned him about them in a second session. Trustee Matthew Hillsman from Tennessee stated that a few (but not many) of the trustees were aware of the *Sunday School*

---

[81] *The Journal and the Messenger*, April 30, 1879.

[82] *Biblical Recorder*, May 7, 1879.

[83] Wills mentions Toy's "Critical Notes" on Isaiah 42 and 53 as part of his "theological pilgrimage," but he does not give those notes any particular significance in the controversy that erupted in the 1879 (*Southern Seminary*, 121). Wills also mentions Toy's "Critical Notes" of January 12, 1879, in which Toy proposed a late date of the composition of the Pentateuch, but Wills noted that the article drew little attention in the Baptist papers, save for those who defended Toy (e.g., J. C. Hiden, "Our Field Glass," *Baptist Courier*, February 7, 1878, 2; Wills, *Southern Seminary*, 125–26).

[84] Hurd, "Confronting an Intellectual Revolution," 24–25. Hurd acknowledged that Toy may have reacted partially to criticism leveled at his *Sunday School Times* notes on Isaiah 42 and 53 (p. 28).

Times criticism.[85] Further, Trustee Thomas H. Pritchard reported that

> when I asked him his views as to the 53rd chapter of Isaiah, I was assured that while he regarded the chapter as fulfilled in the history of Israel, it was more fully and gloriously fulfilled in the character of Christ, and his friends complained that the *Journal and Messenger* had done him injustice in its review of his paper in the *Sunday School Times*. After reading the articles in the *Times* I incline to the same opinion, though it must be confessed that the statement of his views in that article, while clear enough as far as they go, are not so full as to be desirable.[86]

The role of the *Sunday School Times* articles in the board's decision is unclear, but the assertion that they played a role was widely held by many people at the time, most likely including Toy himself, given the fact that he was questioned about them at the trustees meeting.[87] Certainly it was the view of William Whitsitt, Toy's colleague and roommate, that Toy's interpretation of Isaiah's servant was a significant point of discussion at the 1879 trustees

---

[85] Matthew Hillsman, "Elder Provence and the Seminary," *The Baptist Reflector*, February 19, 1880, 2; this article was reprinted with editorial comment as "Dr. Toy's Resignation and the Seminary," in the March 3, 1880, issue of the *Biblical Recorder*. Hillsman was responding to the sharp criticism of the trustees' action by Samuel Provence, who had taken his concerns public in the *Baptist Reflector*.

[86] T. H. Pritchard, "Dr. C. H. Toy," *Biblical Recorder*, May 21, 1879. The article is dated May 8, 1879, and Pritchard seems to imply that his questioning of Toy occurred during the trustees meeting. Elsewhere, Pritchard commends Toy who "acted very honourably in this whole matter, and evinced a spirit of candor which made it all the more painful to part with him as a professor" (ibid.). This statement suggests Pritchard may have been a(n unnamed) member of the smaller committee that met with Toy.

[87] This would account for the prominent role that Toy's interpretation of Isaiah's servant plays in the accounts of David Lyon and George Foote Moore, both colleagues of Toy who may have gotten much of their story from his account (see Lyon, "Toy," 9; Moore, "Toy," 4). Lyon comments: "It seems not unlikely that the episode of the *Sunday School Times* had something to do with Dr. Toy's resignation. Though not mentioned by Dr. Broadus, this episode must have made him and Dr. Boyce anxious lest the Seminary should become involved in suspicion of heterodoxy, a suspicion which, for a variety of reasons, they would be loth to have it bear" ("Toy," 9, footnote 4). Below we will see that Broadus had several reasons to focus the Toy controversy on his view of inspiration and uncouple the emerging controversy from his views of Isaiah's suffering servant.

meeting.[88] But Whitsitt added a new wrinkle to the story.[89] John Broadus had also published a lesson on Isaiah 53 about the same time, holding to a view very similar to Toy's that Israel was the primary referent of the servant:

> Broadus was almost on the side of Toy in his theological opinions. In the early spring of 1879 they were both writing comments on the Sunday School Lessons; Toy for the *Sunday School Times*, and Broadus either for the *Baptist Teacher* or for the *Kind Words*. When they came to the 53rd chapter of Isaiah the explanation which Broadus gave lacked but little of being as suspicious as that given by Toy. Both of them, if I remember correctly, were assailed in the newspapers for this bit of work. That was the sorest point in the world to Broadus for many months. It was amusing at Atlanta, where Toy was deposed, to observe the degree of vehemence with which Broadus would protest that Toy's exposition of the 53rd of Isaiah had nothing to do with the business. If that had been made one of the counts in Toy's indictment it would have laid almost as truly against Broadus.[90]

---

[88] Whitsitt recalls the events of 1879 in a diary entry on November 30, 1886. He was prompted to recall those events because he was reading the "trashy" Baptist history by Toy's uncle and namesake, R. B. C. Howell. Interestingly, Whitsitt is silent in his May 10, 1879, letter to Florence Wallace, though he certainly knew of the events as they unfolded. Rather, he celebrates a speech he had made to the convention "on the resolution to publish a catechism": "I never had so clear a triumph in my life. Gov. Jos. E. Brown told me that I had a better reason to feel satisfied with myself than any other person in the body." He then informs Wallace that he has been chosen to deliver the convention sermon for the following year, anxiously recording, "There I shall lose all my laurels; for you know I can't preach worth a farthing" (William H. Whitsitt to Florence Wallace, May 10, 1879, in *Mirror*, 218)! It is possible that the news of Toy's resignation had not yet broken publicly or that Whitsitt was simply self-absorbed in his own accomplishments (and anticipated failures). At any rate, writing from Nashville on May 14, 1879, he does refer to Toy's demise: "One of the greatest sorrows of my life has now befallen me in the resignation of my beloved and admired colleague, Dr. Toy, and we are going forward to break up our chambers and separate, I fear forever" (in *Mirror*, 218).

[89] Whitsitt's perspective on the Toy controversy is also explored in Slatton, *W. H. Whitsitt*, 73–86.

[90] Whitsitt Diary, November 30, 1886, 5:106–107. Years later, after a contentious faculty meeting with Broadus, Whitsitt returned to the topic: "Broadus was almost captured by the influence of Toy. His exegesis of the 53rd of Isaiah in the Sunday School Lessons, as published in 'Kind Words' in the spring of 1879, was very like that made by Toy the same spring in the *Sunday School Times* at Philadelphia. I was astonished that he should go so far, and it was a sore point with him to meet the questions of brethren when the cataclysm appeared on the first of May in Atlanta. Now he has forgotten all that and is quite as solicitous about his orthodoxy as Jerome was after the conflict with Rufinus" (Whitsitt Diary, January 24, 1893, 15:84, VBHS). By now, Whitsitt has misremembered

Whitsitt was right on several counts. Broadus had indeed published a short note on Isaiah 53 in *The Baptist Teacher* on May 1, 1879.[91] He argued that "the primary reference is to Israel, as God's despised and suffering servant; who has, nevertheless, a mission to bless the world. But there is a typical relationship between Israel and Messiah…and the prophet, whether consciously or unconsciously, is here led to use many expressions which but dimly describe Israel's suffering and mission, and very distinctly and strikingly describe those of Messiah."[92] The line of argument is essentially the same as Toy's; the only difference is Broadus's caveat: "For more intelligent classes, all this should be carefully explained, having first been carefully studied. For most classes, better say at once that it means the Saviour."[93]

Whitsitt was also correct that Broadus was in the crosshairs along with Toy for his interpretation of Isaiah 53. A letter in *The Journal and the Messenger* by a Baptist layperson from Cincinnati complained to the editor about both Toy and Broadus. After reading the editorial on Toy from the week before, the author turned to the *Baptist Teacher* for help in preparation for the week's Sunday School lesson. There the contributor, "F. B. B," read Broadus's interpretation (cited above) and determined it was basically the same as Toy's as described in *The Journal and the Messenger*:

> Mr. Editor, do you think God inspired Isaiah to write the fifty-third chapter to teach one lesson and have it "consciously or unconsciously" teach another? …If this lesson refers primarily to Israel, why not teach it as such? If the lesson refers to Christ, why imply that it means Israel?
>
> Now, Mr. Editor, though I am young, I have a large amount of respect for "old fogey" ideas when they are right, and if the lesson refers to Christ, and that favors "the old fogey expositor," give me the old fogey's exposition every time. But if Isaiah wrote about Israel, and meant Israel, and the "old fogey" would have us believe otherwise, then away with "old fogyism." …
>
> Can't you help me out of the dilemma into which Dr. Broadus and Professor Toy have placed me?[94]

It is not clear whether Broadus was aware of this particular critique in

---

that Broadus's article appeared in *The Baptist Teacher* and not *Kind Words*, but he is spot on in his recollection of the similarity between the two interpretations.

[91] John Broadus, "How to Teach the Lesson," *The Baptist Teacher* 10/5 (May 1, 1879): 70.

[92] Ibid.

[93] Ibid.

[94] *The Journal and Messenger*, May 7, 1879, 4.

The Journal and Messenger during the Atlanta Convention, since it appeared on May 7 during the meeting. But Broadus, as Whitsitt suggests, may have been anxious to keep Toy's interpretation of the suffering servant out of the discussion of the trustees, since eventually he could also be implicated with a similar kind of criticism.[95]

A week later, on May 14, 1879, after the SBC meeting but before Toy's resignation had been reported in the papers, Landmark Baptist A. S. Worrell—then professor at Mount Pleasant College (Huntsville, MO)—published an article in *Baptist Battle Flag* that again criticized the interpretations of Toy and Broadus.[96] Most of the criticism was reserved for Toy's interpretation, but Broadus was also denounced for interpreting Israel as the primary referent of Isaiah 53. But Worrell extended the critique to include Broadus's advice regarding how to teach the lesson: "If it is certain that 'most' preachers, as well as 'most classes,' need to be taught 'at once,' 'that it means the Saviour, as shown by the New Testament.' And yet, if the text refers to Christ only in a typical sense, or indirectly, why not teach just what *it* teaches, and teach the same thing to *all* classes?"[97] The double edge of Worrell's critique not only chastised the interpretation of the text but also recognized that Broadus's advice to teachers bordered on duplicity. These criticisms of Broadus apparently never made it to the more widely read denominational papers of Baptists in the South.[98] This point is significant because many of the initial reactions to the announcement of Toy's resignation were "judged almost exclusively on the basis of his expositions of the Sunday school lessons in the *Sunday School Times* on Isaiah 40:1–10 and Isaiah 53:1–10."[99] This is in part because Toy's letter of resignation had not yet been made public and in part because the Board of Trustees were initially reluctant to release details of their decision.[100]

---

[95] While it is unlikely that Broadus knew of *The Journal and Messenger* essay in Atlanta, it is not entirely impossible since the meeting continued through May 12, 1879.

[96] For more on Worrell, see C. Douglas Weaver, *Baptists and the Holy Spirit: Interactions with the Holiness Pentecostal-Charismatic Traditions* (Waco, TX: Baylor University Press, forthcoming).

[97] A. S. Worrell, "Drs. Toy and Broadus on Isaiah 53," *Baptist Battle Flag*, May 14, 1879, 156; cited by Hurt, "Toy," 193.

[98] Hurt, "Toy," 193, points out that *The Biblical Recorder*, in the context of another issue regarding a resolution at the SBC meeting, objected to Broadus's interpretation of the resolution, arguing that it, "like some other of his interpretations, is fanciful and unreliable." This article appeared in the May 28, 1879, issue and might have been read as a muted criticism of Broadus's interpretation of Isaiah (see *The Biblical Recorder*, May 28, 1879).

[99] Hurt, "Toy," 142.

[100] A letter published by one of the trustees (probably Chambliss or Hiden or both together) in the May 22, 1879, issue of the *Baptist Courier* stated: "Though a member of

Boyce read Toy's letter of resignation on May 7, 1879, to the whole board, who were meeting at the First Baptist Church, Atlanta, and the meeting was adjourned until the next day.[101] In the letter, Toy affirmed that he had always taught "and do now teach in accordance with and not contrary to" the first article of the "Fundamental Principles" of the seminary, which reads, "The Scriptures of the Old and New Testament were given by inspiration of God and are the only sufficient, certain and authoritative rule of all saving knowledge, faith and obedience."[102] In the letter, Toy makes much the same argument as he did in his inaugural address, with several expansions. He continues to speak of the twofold nature of Scripture (its "outer" and "inner" dimensions), which he now describes in Christological terminology: "I believe that the Bible is wholly divine and wholly human."[103] Beyond that understanding, he eschews any kind of a priori theory of inspiration, relying instead on Scripture itself, which testifies to "the *fact* of divine inspiration" while saying nothing of the "*manner* of its action."[104] He has also abandoned the language of "infallibility" as well as efforts to harmonize Scripture with the findings of science (geography, astronomy, and other physical sciences). Toy anticipated the trustees' concern about whether his views were consistent with biblical teaching and whether they violated the Abstract of Principles. His letter was designed to answer yes to the first and no to the second. The committee was reluctant to address either issue.[105]

---

the Board, we do not feel it is our duty to act apart from our colleagues; but we suppose that the Board will, in due time, officially inform the public of the reasons for such action as was taken by them" (*Baptist Courier*, May 22, 1879). Two of the trustees (Jeter and Winkler) were editors of denominational papers (*Religious Herald* and *Alabama Baptist*, respectively), which initially refused to publish articles on the trustee decision for fear of fanning the flames of controversy and dissent. The Kentucky *Western Recorder*, Georgia *Christian Index*, and North Carolina *Biblical Recorder* announced the resignation but did not foster public discussion of the issue, at least at the beginning. The South Carolina *Baptist Courier* (earlier called *Working Christian*) was the exception and was decidedly pro-Toy in its publications (many of which were written by W. C. Lindsay and J. A. Chambliss, one of the dissenting trustee votes). After the *Courier* published Toy's letter later in fall 1879, the *Religious Herald* reluctantly entered the fray (see Hurd, "Confronting an Intellectual Revolution," 40–44). Toy himself published several articles in the *Religious Herald* in 1880. On reactions to Toy's resignation, see chapter 4, "Ripple Effects."

[101] Hurt, "Toy," 141, citing the Minutes of the Annual Meeting of the Board of Trustees of The Southern Baptist Theological Seminary, May 1879, ASC, SBTS, 14.

[102] Toy, Letter of Resignation. For the full text, see Appendix 2.

[103] Toy, Letter of Resignation, 2. In recent times, Toy would be accused of Nestorianism in his views of the two natures of Scripture (Wills, *Southern Seminary*, 114). See chapter 9.

[104] Toy, Letter of Resignation, 1.

[105] See Wills, *Southern Seminary*, 124.

J. C. Hiden presented materials that Toy wished to add to his original letter in an attempt to clarify that "in the majority of cases I hold that the New Testament quotations correctly represent the sense of the Old Testament, and that there is always a true spiritual feeling controlling them."[106] A committee was then appointed to discuss the statement and make a report to the full board.[107] At some point the committee apparently met with Toy, and on Saturday, May 10, the committee made the following report:

> The Committee to whom was referred the communication of Dr. Toy beg leave to report—
>
> …They sought conference with Professor Toy, and in addition to the carefully expressed paper presented to the Board along with his resignation, they had a very free and candid expression of his opinions on some of the points less fully expressed in his written communication.
>
> While deeply impressed with the beautiful Christian Spirit of our beloved brother, they cannot but recognize what he himself asserts; that there is a divergence in his views of inspiration from those held by our brethren in general. In view of this divergence, your Committee feel constrained to recommend to the Board the acceptance of Professor Toy's resignation. In this recommendation they concur unanimously.
>
> In behalf of the Committee,
> James C. Furman, Chairman[108]

After discussion, the trustees approved the report and accepted the resignation, and a copy was sent to Dr. Toy. The only reason given by the board was the one stated by Toy himself that his view diverged from commonly held beliefs. Later, Dr. Jeremiah Jeter attempted to provide additional information

---

[106] Toy inserted page 6 of his "Letter of Resignation." Interestingly, he cites the example of Acts 2 to say that Peter's sermon "gives the true spiritual sense of the passage in Joel." Remember that this passage was one of the classroom disputes between Boyce and Toy.

[107] Minutes of the Annual Meeting of the Board of Trustees of The Southern Baptist Theological Seminary, May 1879, ASC, SBTS, 14. Trustees in attendance: Furman, Hillsman, Tichenor, T. P. Smith, Shuck, J. C. Smith, Wharton, Chambliss, Hiden, Thayer, Jeter, Henderson, Jones, and Pritchard. Sources state that committee, based on Hillsman's report (cf. footnote 40), was comprised of five members: J. C. Hiden, James C. Furman, W. D. Thomas, T. G. Jones, and Basil Manly (Wills, *Southern Seminary*, 130, who mentions a committee of five without listing names; Hurd, "Confronting an Intellectual Revolution," 28–29). This committee met with Toy. But Pritchard's note suggests he was also involved in the smaller group interview with Toy (and Hillsman does say [in Paul-like fashion] "if there was another his name has escaped me" (*Biblical Recorder*, March 3, 1880).

[108] This report is appended to the end of Toy's resignation letter; see Appendix 2.

in a report published in the *Religious Herald*: "the Trustees deemed it inexpedient to subject it to the disadvantages which would inevitably arise from a protracted controversy on an important theological subject, especially while efforts are being made to obtain an endowment."[109]

On Monday, May 12, two board members, D. W. Gwin and J. A. Chambliss, opposed the trustees' action, protesting that the board should have evaluated Toy's presentation of his view of inspiration before accepting the resignation.[110] Instead, the trustees appeared to yield to majority rule among Baptists rather than challenging Toy's assertion that he taught in accordance with the Abstract of Principles. In a sense, the decision did little to establish a process to decide when and how a professor had violated doctrinal limits of the Baptist denomination.[111] The final vote count was 16-2 to accept the resignation.

---

[109] *Religious Herald*, May 22, 1879.

[110] Minutes of the Annual Meeting of the Board of Trustees, May 12, 1879, cited by Hurt, "Toy," 212. Later, Hillsman ("Elder Provence and the Seminary," 2) would point out that one of these two (Gwin) was married to Toy's cousin and entertained Toy while he was in Atlanta, and the other was Toy's classmate at Southern (who had also married Toy's love interest from the 1860s). But, as Jeter pointed out, several other trustees had long-standing friendships with Toy (e.g., Pritchard) and yet still voted to accept the resignation.

[111] See Duncan, "Heresy at Louisville," 77–78. For this reason, subsequent interpreters have tried to reverse design the decision, beginning with some of the trustees. Wills acknowledged that the trustees' dismissal of Toy did not include a charge of heresy, and to many Southern Baptists (especially among the seminary's alumni) the dismissal "appeared to be an unmanly capitulation to public feeling" (*Southern Seminary*, 134). Nonetheless, Wills concluded that "Trustees judged that Toy's views, whether contrary to the Abstract [of Principles] or not were contrary to the Bible" (134). He also asserted, "Most trustees…seem to have been convinced that Toy's view of inspiration was erroneous, inconsistent with scripture, and damaging to the faith" (135). Wills's assertion is largely based on Trustee J. B. Jeter's defense published in the *Religious Herald* (November 13, 1879) several months after the trustees' decision in response to the outcry of those opposing the view. The point remains that in the official trustee report, the only rationale given was that Toy's views on inspiration diverged "from those held by our brethren in general." As early critics of the decision pointed out, majority opinion seems a shaky foundation on which to judge theological orthodoxy and a poor warrant and precedent for future such decisions (see J. A. Chambliss, "The Trustees of the Seminary and Dr. Toy's Resignation," *Baptist Courier*, June 12, 1879, 2; cited by Wills, *Southern Seminary*, 136). Partially at stake was the question as to whether the Abstract of Principles was the "maximum standard of orthodoxy for faculty" (so Chambliss) or whether it was "the minimum standard of orthodoxy," a view imputed by Wills on the 1879 trustees and not a view expressed in their official response (*Southern Seminary*, 134). The reverse engineering of the trustees' decision began weeks after the decision in May 1879 and continues to this day. The subsequent attempts to clarify their rationale for the decision to accept the resignation suggest, at the least, that the

Toy expected to be vindicated by the board; he certainly did not expect his letter of resignation to be accepted.[112] Whitsitt provided this account of the matter in his diary:

> He did not anticipate the action of the Board of Trustees deposing him from his position in May 1879. When he wrote his letter he must have believed that it would…reassure the Board. He expected that Broadus at least would stand by him and represent to the Board that his sentiments were harmless and correct enough. I half suspect that Broadus had permitted himself to make some sort of representations to that effect which Toy leaned on too heavily. It was pitiful to a man who could see Broadus on the other side to perceive how truly Toy depended upon his good offices and support.[113]

Whitsitt was at the convention and got wind apparently of what the investigative committee intended to recommend to the board:[114]

> When I told him [Toy] I understood that the Board had already been advised by the Committee whom they had charged with the duty of investigating the business and that it was believed they would unseat him at the meeting which they should hold that morning he appeared for the first time to become aware of his peril. He was almost frantic with solicitude; it was nearly inconceivable that they should lay violent hands upon him. He wanted to find Broadus; he wanted me to go and speak to various members before the hour should arrive; but I was fully aware that the scheme of Boyce and Broadus was now coming to a successful issue. The Letter to the Board of Trustees, so far from bringing repose to their minds had been used by Boyce and Broadus the more effectually to stir up their minds. It was a cruel fate. If he could have seen the end from the beginning he would have hesitated long before placing himself by this process in the hands of Boyce and Broadus; he would have stood upon his might and replied to the suggestions of Broadus to the effect that he did not believe the minds of the Board were any way discontented with him; they had sent him no notice of their discontent; he would wait to receive charges and specifications before he accepted the conclusions

---

original declaration may have been too hastily made, an expedient path taken to ensure that a financially insecure institution not suffer collapse from a prolonged controversy. For more on the ensuing "inspiration controversy," see chapter 4 and Wills, *Southern Seminary*, 136–49.

[112] Wills, *Southern Seminary*, 127.

[113] Whitsitt Diary, November 30, 1886, 5:113.

[114] Whitehead, *Mirror*, 219, wrote that Whitsitt "seemed always to know what went on in the meetings of the Board of Trustees."

which Broadus advanced.[115]

Whitsitt was convinced that Boyce and Broadus had Toy's dismissal as their goal from the outset: "Broadus and Boyce are believed to have anticipated this turn of affairs; I should not wonder if the former had his charges and specifications all made out; ...Boyce and Broadus could well afford to look through their finger, and smile at the ease with which they captured the poor silly bird."[116]

---

[115] Whitsitt Diary, November 30, 1886, 5:113–14. At the end of this remarkable diary entry, Whitsitt unpacks the cautionary aspects of the Toy episode (5:114–15):

> I conceived that Broadus had given me an object lesson which it would be well enough to bear in mind as long as I lived. And I have acted upon it much to my profit and peace of mind. In the month of June 1880 when I was at the 5th Avenue Hotel in New York I had a very tender epistle from Broadus desiring that before I sailed for England I should give him a full statement of my views touching the inspiration of the Holy Scriptures...and speaking pleasant words about the complete unreserved of our friendship. The net is spread in vain in the sight of any bird. I was mindful of the feat which Boyce and Broadus had accomplished in the overthrow of my colleague the year before and I "denied the allegation and defied the alligator."

> There has never been the slightest trace of unreserved between Broadus and myself since I observed his conduct about...the deposition of Toy in 1879. I keep to my side of the house and allow Boyce and Broadus to keep to their side of the house. Our official relations, the Lord be thanked, are peaceful enough; I desire to cultivate no other relationship with them. Toy cultivated exceptionally kind relations with Broadus and I have shown above what came of it. Is there any good reason why I should imitate his example? Boyce is not a person whom it would be profitable to associate with on intimate terms; he is a very uninteresting person, and except in the way of business without any kind of importance. After what I have observed of him I cannot avoid to feel that Broadus upon occasion may be insincere. I prefer to bestow my confidence & to ask for advice elsewhere, when I chance to need advice.

(The pun on "allegations and alligator" apparently comes from Richard Sheridan's 1775 play *The Rivals*.)

[116] Whitsitt Diary, November 30, 1886, 5:114. This conclusion is the opposite of that drawn nearly a century later by Billy Hurt ("Toy," 193–94): "The evidence seems to support the view that Broadus was not actively engaged in securing Toy's resignation from the Seminary. His efforts were certainly not such as to cause a breach in the relationships which existed between the two men. Also the very fact that Broadus had himself come in for criticism on the question of the interpretation of Isaiah 53 would have weakened the effectiveness of any intercession which he may have attempted on Toy's behalf." Hurt, however, did not have access to Whitsitt's diary or, apparently, the letter from Broadus to Boyce in which the idea of Toy's resignation was first broached. The evidence, therefore,

Even more remarkable is Whitsitt's view that the encouragement of Toy to write a letter of resignation by Broadus and Boyce was a trap laid to ensnare him:

> Toy was silly enough to allow Broadus to entrap him into the nonsense of writing a letter to the Board of Trustees in which he made a clean breast of the business and with which he expected the Board to be content. If he had waited for charges to be proffered he would have been a far uglier customer; there can be little question that he would have destroyed the Seminary root and branch. It was almost on its last legs at the moment.... When his communication to the Board of Trustees was read at Atlanta in May 1879, Dr. Jeter the President of the Board, broke silence first of all with the remarks: "Well, I see nothing wrong about that." Boyce was horrified to hear this word.[117]

Why did Toy offer his resignation, especially if, as has been widely reported, Toy did not think he had violated the Abstract of Principles? Broadus himself acknowledged that "it was hard for Dr. Toy to realize that such teaching was quite out of the question in this institution. He was satisfied that his views would promote truth and piety."[118] Broadus's summary of the events in 1893 seemingly remove Boyce (and Broadus) altogether from the decision-making process: "While not perceiving that the opinions he was teaching formed a just ground for his leaving the seminary, Dr. Toy concluded to send to the Board of Trustees at its approaching session in Atlanta, May 1879, a statement of the views that he had adopted, and of his persuasion that by teaching them he could do much good; and, in order to relieve the Board from restraints of delicacy, he tendered his resignation."[119]

Given the correspondence between Broadus and Boyce in December

---

appears to favor Whitsitt's interpretation that Broadus and Boyce were actively involved in the removal of Toy from the faculty.

[117] Whitsitt Diary, November 30, 1886, 5:106–107. Whitsitt was not the only one who suspected an inside conspiracy to rid the seminary of Toy. Trustee Matthew Hillsman quoted Samuel Provence as claiming that "it is known to a few to be a fact, that the pressure to remove Dr. Toy from the Seminary was not from without but *from within*." Hillsman replied that he was not prepared to say that Provence's charge was not true but that he "to the contrary believe[s] if it is not a fact, it ought to be." Finally, Hillsman concluded, "If Drs. Boyce, Broadus, and Whitsett [sic], who had the best opportunity for judging, believed Dr. Toy's views so radically unsound as to desire his leaving the Seminary, that is sufficient to settle the question" (*Biblical Recorder*, March 3, 1880). That may have been the view of Broadus and Boyce, but certainly, judging from his private diary, it was not the position of Whitsitt!

[118] Broadus, *Memoir*, 262. It is clear from this assessment that Broadus stood on the side of Boyce in the matter.

[119] Broadus, *Memoir*, 263.

1878, however, it is obvious that Toy did not come to the decision to offer his resignation on his own but was encouraged to do so by Boyce and Broadus, whom he trusted. The precipitating event was apparently a single pseudonymous letter criticizing unnamed professors. Questions linger. Why such a precipitous preemptive strike? Was it the proverbial straw that broke the camel's back for Boyce and Broadus? And why were no efforts made to identify the other professor who embraced "universalism" in order to root out that heresy as well?[120] Whatever degree of responsibility historians might assign to Broadus and Boyce for Toy's resignation, Toy himself, judging from his extant subsequent correspondence, seems to have harbored no ill will against either man.[121] It seems unlikely that Toy was completely unaware of the role of Broadus and Boyce, since they (Boyce in behalf of Broadus) were the ones who approached him about setting his views down in the context of a resignation. Whitsitt claimed that "the gift of reticence is one of Toy's undeniable virtues. He made no utterance prejudicial to the honor of his quondam friend."[122] Less than a month after his resignation. Toy wrote Alvah Hovey, who was editing the American Commentary on the New Testament Series, to which both Toy and Broadus were scheduled to contribute:

> May I be permitted to say a word about Dr. Broadus' comm'y on "Matthew"? I know that he is giving his best strength to it, and is in position to make a noteworthy book. But he is much hampered and harassed by the limits within which he is confined, so that his health has suffered. If

---

[120] It would seem that Whitsitt would be the most likely candidate for the professor among the Southern faculty, and while he would come under fire a few years later for his views on Baptist origins, I am unaware of any charges of universalism against him.

[121] In a sense, it was also business as usual for Broadus as well. Broadus sought Toy's opinion regarding possible candidates to succeed him in teaching Hebrew at the seminary. Boyce would have none of that, however: "Yours just received enclosing letter of Bro. [C. H.] Toy.... As to Toy's list of men, so far as I know none would do at all except [E. C.] Dargan or [W. R. L.] Smith. I am in favor of getting some older man from some place, and leaving Manly there unless we are sure of the right young man. If we go through this year and get what we hope in endowment, I think we four can work for some years to come however without further help. Why could not Whitsitt turn his attention to Hebrew and be transferred to that chair? He could then get some other man for Ecc[lesiastical] History or get Manly to teach that, or change in some other way. Manly would do well at Church History." (James P. Boyce to John A. Broadus, August 23, 1880, Broadus Papers, ASC, SBTS)

[122] Whitsitt Diary, November 30, 1886, 5:115. David Lyon concurred: "Dr. Toy accepted the decision without reproaches or bitterness, supported by the consciousness of rectitude, and by that catholic, philosophic spirit which never failed him in any crisis" ("Toy," 9–10). Toy's fondness extended to the whole seminary: "Louisville and especially the Seminary will always be a home to me" (Crawford H. Toy to John A. Broadus, December 14, 1881, Broadus Papers, ASC, SBTS).

the Soc'y could allow him a larger space it would relieve him, and by no means injure the sale of the book.[123]

One cannot dismiss the fact that there were serious philosophical and theological differences between Boyce and Toy. Hurd has pointed out that Boyce's education at Brown University and Princeton was grounded in Scottish Common Sense philosophy, which rejected German speculative theology and *a priori* reasoning, relying instead on empirical realism and a conviction of the stability of truth. And at Princeton, Boyce studied with Charles Hodge and also imbibed a Princeton theology that included an embrace of the infallibility of Scripture and a plenary view of inspiration that ensured the factuality of the Bible.[124]

Toy, of course, had been educated in Germany, whose speculative philosophy and theology Boyce despised. Toy had not fully embraced German

---

[123] Crawford H. Toy to Alvah Hovey, June 9, 1879, Alvah Hovey Collection, ANTS. Toy had been asked to write the commentary on 1 and 2 Thessalonians and later also the Pastoral Epistles for the commentary series (see Toy to Hovey, December 21, 1876; January 27, 1877). In this same letter, Toy informed Hovey that as a result of his research he had concluded Paul was the author of 2 Thessalonians but, "after repeated readings and comparisons, I have found it impossible to attribute the Pastoral Eps. to him." First Timothy was patterned after a Pauline letter and 2 Timothy and Titus were formed out of "general Pauline material" by "an author quite different from Paul." Toy wrote to say he was aware his conclusions "may not meet with the approbation of the Publication Soc'y" and wished to know if he should continue with the work. "If critical freedom is allowed, it will be a pleasure to me to do the work," he concluded. By August, Toy had received his answer from Hovey that the publication committee wished Toy to withdraw from the series, which he did: "I accept your decision, though I greatly regret the position of affairs which seems to you to require such a decision. I heartily wish success to the enterprise" (Toy to Hovey, August 15, 1879). Meanwhile Broadus received a letter from Hovey in which Broadus gratefully acknowledged that Hovey had recommended to the committee that he be granted "more space" to write, apparently unaware of Toy's efforts in his behalf to secure a larger page count. In contrast, Broadus says only this to Hovey about Toy: "I am sorry, and not surprised, that my dear friend Toy has reached such conclusions about the Pastoral Epistles…. Of course you can do nothing else than leave him" (John A. Broadus to Alvah Hovey, August 8, 1879, Alvah Hovey Collection, ANTS). I am grateful to Diane Yount, Archives and Special Collections, Andover Newton Theological Seminary, for providing pdfs of these letters, especially during a time when the manuscript materials were being readied for transit as the school was moving to affiliate with Yale Divinity School.

[124] Hurd, "Confronting an Intellectual Revolution," 21; see also Sydney E. Ahlstrom, "The Scottish Philosophy and American Theology," *Church History* 24 (1955): 257–72.

philosophical idealism; in fact, his strength was his ability to amass information in a variety of disciplines, but, as Hurd recognized, "He revealed little inclination to engage in systematic theology and little aptitude for philosophical speculation."[125] Personality issues aside, Boyce and Toy were simply not going to see eye to eye on issues of biblical interpretation.

But it is important to recall the historical context of the controversy:

> The year was 1869, not 1925. The division among Southern Baptists was not between liberal and conservative methods of interpreting the Bible, but between the supporters of theological education and those indifferent or hostile to it. Advocates of theological education shared Toy's confidence that the intellectual and the spiritual could be reconciled.[126]

This point was recognized by at least one of the participants in the debate. W. L. Lindsay, a prominent South Carolina pastor who published several articles in the *Baptist Courier* from the progressive's point of view, commented that "not Toy but higher education is the cause of these liberal 'views.'"[127]

Diminishing controversy over the efficacy of formal theological education was crucial at this time because the seminary, which had moved to Louisville because of financial straits, still faced fiscal difficulties. A controversy which held that ministerial education ruined the minister could have a direct impact on the school's ability to draw students and financial support from Baptist congregations. Even Whitsitt, Toy's supporter, recognized the dangers of a full-blown controversy: "If he [Toy] had waited for charges to be proffered he would have been a far uglier customer; there can be little question that he would have destroyed the Seminary root and branch. It was almost on its last legs at the moment."[128] The situation was dire enough as it was. Whitsitt reported that in the next academic year, the numbers of students had decreased "and Boyce suggested to me in private…that Manly [Toy's replacement] was in fault."[129] The financial stress of the seminary was relieved in February 1880 when J. E. Brown, former Governor of Georgia, made a gift of $50,000 to the school.[130] Whether such a gift would have been forthcoming

---

[125] Hurd, "Confronting an Intellectual Revolution," 14. Whitsitt actually criticized this aspect of Toy's scholarly personality (Whitsitt Diary, November 30, 1886, 5:109): "His crying weakness is the passion to be considered a *Polyhistor*. There can be no question of his powers to acquire and retain, but he wants to acquire and retain too much…. He has dabbled in everything."

[126] Hurd, "Confronting an Intellectual Revolution," 15.

[127] W. L. Lindsay to John Stout, September 19, 1881, L-S-C, SCL.

[128] Whitsitt Diary, November 30, 1886, 5:107.

[129] Whitsitt Diary, November 30, 1886, 5:110.

[130] See Wills, *Southern Seminary*, 158–61.

if Toy had remained on the faculty is a matter of speculation. In any case, after Brown's initial gift spurred additional giving in the amount of $150,000, Boyce was able to exclaim, "The seminary is now safe—humanly speaking."[131]

---

[131] James P. Boyce to M. T. Yates, July 13, 1881, Letterpress Copy Book 7, June–November 1881, 434; cited by Wills, *Southern Seminary*, 160.

4

RIPPLE EFFECTS (1879–1881)

For weeks in the summer of 1879, a young theological student, David Gordon Lyon, who had studied with Crawford Toy both in Greenville and Louisville, struggled with where and how to continue his studies in light of his professor's forced resignation. Should he remain in Louisville and complete the requirements for his degree? Or should he follow in his mentor's steps and continue advanced studies in Germany? On June 28, 1879, Lyon had reached a momentous decision and made the following entry in his diary:

> And now with the fear of God before my eyes, with no desire if I know my own heart except to fit myself for usefulness & leaving it to the future to decide whether I act wisely or not, after a prayerful review of the arguments pro and con, I believe it to be my duty to go to Europe. If I wrongly interpret God's will concerning me, I shall pray him to show me my mistake before the time for my departure arrives.[1]

God did not reveal a judgment in error on Lyon's part, and so he left for Germany later that summer (only to return later to play a significant role in the next chapters of Toy's life).[2] The aftermath of the Toy controversy extended in several different directions. The lives of individuals, like David Lyon, and the missional trajectories of institutions, both inside (SBTS) and outside Baptist life (Harvard University), were changed as a result of the departure of Crawford Howell Toy from Southern Seminary.

The Controversy's Aftermath in Denominational Papers

There was neither an announcement at the Atlanta convention regarding Toy's resignation nor was it included in the SBC Minutes. The only report concerning the seminary described the appeals for financial assistance by Boyce and Broadus.[3] Given this relative swiftness of the board's action (the

---

[1] David Gordon Lyon Diary, June 28, 1879, HUG 1541, Box 6, Volume 3, HUA.
[2] See chapter 7.
[3] Hurt cites the SBC Proceedings 1879, ASC, SBTS ("Toy," 143). Hurt has an excellent summary of the subsequent debate regarding the Toy controversy in denominational papers; see Hurt, "Toy," 142–73.

matter was heard and resolved practically over a weekend) and the silence immediately surrounding the reasons for the action, there was a delayed response to Toy's resignation, and the reasons for it, in the denominational papers. But once the reactions began, they did not stop for over a year.

The resignation is first reported in *The Journal and the Messenger*, the journal that first carried criticism of Toy's *Sunday School Times* articles on Isaiah. The journal actually reported it twice. The first occurrence is a report on events of the second day of the Southern Baptist Convention. The tone is measured but sympathetic to Toy. After describing the financial appeal of Boyce (see above), the report states:

> In connection with this matter [appeal for funds], it may be as well to refer to the resignation of Rev. Dr. Toy, as one of the Faculty. Dr. Toy, in tendering his resignation to the Board of Trustees, gave a succinct statement of his views in reference to the inspiration of Scriptures, and some other points about which he has been supposed to differ with his brethren. It is just to him to say that he holds to the fundamental articles of evangelical Christianity, and says he can still conscientiously sign the Confessions of Faith, in accordance with which the professors are required to teach in the Seminary. The resignation was accepted with great reluctance, and Dr. Toy is universally loved and esteemed as a scholar and sincere Christian gentleman, by his brethren throughout the South. Yet he deems it his duty to avoid even the semblance of seeming to stand in the way of the beloved Seminary by remaining in the Faculty while suspicions, however unjust, may be entertained against his Baptist orthodoxy. Rev. B. Manly, D.D., President of Georgetown College, has been elected to Dr. Toy's vacated chair, and he has accepted the position. Dr. M. formerly occupied this chair in the institution.[4]

The other notice was apparently by the editors and reflected the critical tone of the previous evaluation of Toy's writing:

> As will be seen by readers of our report…it has seemed good to the Board…that Prof C. H. Toy, D.D., LL.D., should be separated from its corps of instructors. It is said that Dr. Toy declared that he could subscribe to all the "Articles of Faith" as held to by Baptists, and that therefore there was no good and sufficient reason why his brethren should not sustain him in his chair. But the difficulty with Prof. Toy is of too subtle a character to admit of a precise statement in the short compass of an "article of faith," and it is far from ingenuous for a man to teach after such a manner as Dr. Toy has done in his exposition of Isaiah, and yet claim that he can subscribe to the first article in the "New Hampshire

---

[4] *The Journal and the Messenger*, May 21, 1879.

Confession." We are glad to believe that there is a certain unwritten creed in vogue among Baptists that is even more definite than is that article in the Confession, and that no man can maintain good standing in a Baptist Theological Seminary who does not find more of Christ in the prophecies of Isaiah than Prof. Toy does. Baptists greatly prefer the doctrines of Philip and Paul, and Jesus, to those of Prof. Toy.[5]

Two points need to be noted. The editor ignores the detail in the convention report that it was Toy's views on inspiration that were at variance with the majority of Baptists, focusing instead on his interpretations of Isaiah, which had come under fire in the earlier article in the journal. The editor also applauds the notion that an "unwritten creed" had been applied to Toy's views and they had been found lacking, an arguably "unbaptistic" criterion to put into play.

On the following day, May 22, 1879, notice of Toy's resignation appeared in several Southern denominational papers.[6] Most of them expressed regret at the news and praised Toy's Christian character. The comments in Kentucky's *Western Recorder* were typical. After reporting the resignation, the article continues, "We are assured that the resignation has been accepted with undiminished kind feeling on the part of all concerned. Dr. Toy is a man of signal ability, extraordinary learning and very noble character."[7] This positive assessment was a constant note sounded by most participants in the debate,

---

[5] Ibid. While the seminary's Abstract of Principles on Scripture resembles the New Hampshire Confession, they are not identical. The New Hampshire Confession states:

> We believe that the Holy Bible was written by men divinely inspired, and is a perfect treasure of heavenly instruction; that it has God for its author, salvation for its end, and truth without any mixture of error for its matter, that it reveals the principles by which God will judge us; and therefore is, and shall remain to the end of the world, the true center of Christian union, and the supreme standard by which all human conduct, creeds, and opinions should be tried.

The SBTS Abstract of Principles reads, "The Scriptures of the Old and New Testaments were given by the inspiration of God, and are the only sufficient, certain, and authoritative rule of all saving knowledge and obedience."

[6] See, for example, *The Christian Index*, May 22, 1879; *Religious Herald*, May 22, 1879; *The Texas Baptist Herald*, May 22, 1879.

[7] *Western Recorder*, May 22, 1879. The *Western Recorder* was actually quoting from an article in the Louisville *Courier-Journal*, which it reprinted. It is generally thought that Broadus was the author of the original article. If so, and given the fact that the resignation was originally Broadus's idea, it is ironic that the article asserted that Toy, "himself seeing in these views no sufficient reason for his ceasing to teach in the Seminary, …has thought proper to state them to the Trustees and tender his resignation."

leading one scholar to quip that "never was a heretic more beloved by his accusers!"[8]

South Carolina's *Baptist Courier* announced the resignation, and the editors, responding to another essay in the same issue calling for the Board of Trustees to give a public explanation of its actions, wrote, "Though a member of the Board, we do not feel it our duty to set apart from our colleagues; but we suppose that the Board will, in due time, officially inform the public of the reasons for such action as was taken by them."[9] In fact, it would be several months, and after numerous criticisms, before anyone from the board would give a specific version of the actions.

The same issue of the *Baptist Courier* contained two responses to the Toy resignation, both of them vigorous defenses of Toy. The first, by "A Layman," is critical of the *Biblical Recorder* for reprinting the April 30 article in the *Journal and Messenger* that criticized Toy's interpretation of Isaiah. In particular, "A Layman" objects to the fact that the article accuses Toy of being guilty of "rationalism" but does not engage any of the specifics of Toy's arguments. "Why is it that Dr. Toy's objectionable exposition is not first carefully and critically examined? And why should not he be allowed to vindicate himself, that we might have a fair opportunity to learn where and on which side of the question the weight of testimony is to be found?" The writer goes on to argue that "the world is progressing and that what we in our ignorance may fancy to be true may be shown by Dr. Toy to be either untrue, or sadly mixed with error." Because of this, he urges, "let us exercise that freedom of thought that is our natural heritage."[10]

Early attention in the major Baptist papers focused on Toy's interpretation of the Isaianic servant passages (but, interestingly, not on Broadus's).[11] Some of these comments defended Toy. For example, "A Layman" wrote in the June 5, 1879, issue of *The Baptist Courier*, "if his Toy's interpretation of Isaiah 53 is a fair specimen of his rationalism, I sincerely hope the good Lord will send us speedily a whole host of just such rationalists—the sooner the better for our denomination."[12]

---

[8] John Powell Clayton, "Crawford Howell Toy of Virginia," *The Baptist Quarterly* 24 (1971): 50.

[9] *Baptist Courier*, May 22, 1879.

[10] Ibid.

[11] Hurt speaks of "four distinct phases" in the reactions of Baptist newspapers in the South to Toy's resignation, but this seems too schematized ("Toy," 142). While the focus did shift as more and different kinds of information became available, the responses were more ad hoc and organic than moving in any particular direction that could be characterized as "distinct phases."

[12] *Baptist Courier*, June 5, 1879.

This article is immediately followed by an editorial, delighting in the fact that a "layman" wrote the preceding opinion: "when the private members of the Church begin to read; to think; to investigate—we have a fancy that the pulpit will become healthily uncomfortable to the consecrated dullness and the traditional stupidity which too often characterize it." The editor then goes on to claim that "Brother Bailey [editor of the *Biblical Recorder* who accused Toy of rationalism] is the Rationalist—not Prof. Toy. Prof T. studies Isaiah; finds out exactly what the Prophet meant, and then like an honest man, devoutly tells us just what it is that 'is spoken of Jehovah by the Prophet.'"[13]

The May 22, 1879, issue of Virginia's *Religious Herald* published a statement by J. B. Jeter, SBTS Board of Trustees chair. In it, Jeter reiterated the position taken by the board at its May meeting in Atlanta:

> This was in no sense a trial of Dr. Toy. He was held in the highest estimation for his scholarship and piety by all the Trustees. There was, however, a conceded divergence in his views from those generally held by the supporters of the Seminary; and the Trustees deemed it inexpedient to subject it to the disadvantages which would inevitably arise from a protracted controversy on an important theological subject, especially while efforts were being made to obtain an endowment.[14]

Once again, the "charge" was the one to which Toy had admitted, holding views not held by the majority of Southern Baptists, and the action of the trustees in accepting the resignation were shaped by a desire to avoid damaging the seminary, especially its financial outlook. Jeter also indicated that there had been published reports in circulation that Toy's views on inspiration were "at variance with those generally held by the denomination."[15]

Jeter's statement prompted a sharp retort from the *Baptist Courier*: "The public, and especially the Baptist public, have the right to know more than has yet been published about the discontinuation of Prof. Toy's services in the Southern Baptist Theological Seminary. There has been an air of mystery, or

---

[13] *Baptist Courier*, May 22, 1879. Though unsigned, the editorial is presumably by J. C. Hiden, since the author states he was a graduate of Virginia Military Institute (VMI). Both Hiden (editor) and J. A. Chambliss (associate editor) were SBTS trustees, but only Hiden attended VMI. Interestingly, Hiden comes to Toy's defense even though he voted to accept his resignation. A Boston publication, *The Watchman* (May 22, 1879), likewise defended Toy: "It is not to be understood that his views are necessarily heterodox, for he entertains opinions shared in common by some of the ablest, purest, and most evangelical of scholars" (cited by Hurt, "Toy," 145).

[14] *Religious Herald*, May 22, 1879.

[15] Ibid. Apparently, Jeter was referring to the anonymous letter of December 1878 to which Boyce had brought his attention.

at least a degree of reticence."[16] The editor then posed three questions with responses: "Why was the resignation tendered? Why was it accepted? Why did two of the Trustees protest against the acceptance?"

Contrary to other reports, the *Courier* contended that Toy did not submit his resignation because he felt bound to vacate his chair; rather, Toy, realizing that his views diverged from the "body of his brethren," took the initiative to bring the matter before the board but "was astonished at the action of the Trustees in accepting." He believed that after "carefully considering his views the Trustees would be satisfied that he was not a dangerous heretic."[17]

With regard to why two trustees dissented from the majority, the *Courier* repeated the objections of the trustees themselves: "Having a strong conviction that the resignation of Dr. Toy should not have been accepted until after a decision reached by the Trustees that the views expressed by him on the subject of inspiration are inimical to the true program of Christianity, we respectfully ask to be placed on record as protesting against the policy and the action of the Board in this matter." The essayist further asserts that "the subject of inspiration is one with respect to which Baptists have no distinctive principles. …the subject of inspiration is one with respect to which neither Baptists nor any other denominations have any canon beyond the very broad one that 'the Scriptures of the Old and New Testaments are given by inspiration of God,' which truth Prof. Toy expressly stated he had constantly held and taught." To release the professor for "divergent views" also violated conditions of employment set forth by the constitution of the seminary. It is unreasonable to expect that a seminary professor "must not go outside or beyond the circles within which the mass of the people who sustain the Seminary find their opinions, however nebulous those opinions may be, or however shifting the limits that encircle them."[18]

The debate took a turn when W. C. Lindsay announced that he had obtained a copy of Toy's letter and distributed it to a number of persons for review across six states who claimed to hold views on inspiration similar to Toy's. Lindsay also challenged Jeter's claim that criticism of Toy had been in circulation. He correctly speculated that the essay Jeter had in mind was the one that had so vexed Broadus months before. But Lindsay contended, "an anonymous writer in the *Religious Herald* did charge some Theological Pro-

---

[16] *Baptist Courier*, June 19, 1879.

[17] Ibid.

[18] Quotations from the preceding paragraph are taken from *Baptist Courier*, June 19, 1879.

fessor with unsoundness: but Dr. Eaton, who it seems ought to know, emphatically denies that this anonymous writer referred to Dr. Toy."[19]

Responses to Lindsay's claim were widespread. A certain A. Broaddus (apparently no relation to John Broadus) wrote in the *Religious Herald* that "justice to the Seminary—to the Trustees—to Dr. Toy—demands that his paper be published, and that the whole matter, from alpha to omega, be fully ventilated."[20] Trustee J. O. B. Dargan did respond to the "feverish excitement in reference to the resignation" in the December 4, 1879, issue of the *Religious Herald*. In addition to reminding readers that the trustees were elected from several states to oversee interests of the seminary, he further reports that if a professor cannot subscribe to the articles of faith, "his election is void." According to Dargan, the board had no alternative but to accept Toy's resignation.[21] Dargan failed to mention that Toy had asserted that he was, in fact, teaching in accordance with the Abstract of Principles, a point made by John Stout (who would later be denied missionary appointment because of his own views).[22] The week after Dargan's response, the *Religious Herald* published Toy's letter of resignation.[23]

Once Toy's resignation letter was available, debate turned squarely to the issue of inspiration and continued from the end of 1879 throughout much of 1880. The *Baptist Courier* published a variety of articles in late 1879 through early 1880, most of them favorable to what was understood of Toy's views on inspiration.[24] Attention to this point was still focused on the (in)appropriateness of the trustees' actions.[25] The *Religious Herald* countered with articles critical of Toy's views.[26] One of the most critical, however, was by E. T. Winkler and reprinted in the *Baptist Courier*. Winkler took aim at Toy's notion of the dual divine-human nature of Scripture, especially his description of the "Human Element." He queried, "Who can tell us what part of the Bible is

---

[19] *Baptist Courier*, October 30, 1879. This assertion, of course, is contrary to that provided to Broadus in December 1878.

[20] A. Broaddus, "Dr. Toy and the Seminary," *Religious Herald*, November 20, 1879. Broaddus further commented: "I humbly suggest that they [the managers of denominational enterprises] are sometimes too distrustful of their constituents—too reluctantly frankly and fully to make known facts, especially when those facts are unfavorable to the work they have in hand. I believe the rank and file among the Baptists may be trusted."

[21] J. O. B. Dargan, "Dr. Toy and our Seminary—How It Appears to a Trustee," *Religious Herald*, December 4, 1879.

[22] John Stout, "The Relation of Dr. Toy's Position to a Fundamental Baptist Principle," *Baptist Courier*, December 25, 1879.

[23] *Religious Herald*, December 11, 1879.

[24] See *Baptist Courier*, November 13, 20, December 4, 1879; February 26, 1880.

[25] See Hurt, "Toy," 163.

[26] *Religious Herald*, December 11, 18, 25, 1879.

human and what part is divine?"[27]

John Stout took Winkler to task, claiming he "either failed to understand the position taken by Dr. Toy…on the Inspiration of Scriptures, or failed to state it fairly." Toy, Stout claimed, argued not that "'a divine revelation is *somewhere* in the Bible,' but that the Bible *is* a divine revelation…. *As a whole they [the Scriptures] are the revelation of God to man.*" Thus, Stout asserted, "'The Human Element' in the revelation is apparent to all. The real question upon which division has occurred is, Is any error to be found in this Human Element? Dr. Winkler takes the negative—Dr. Toy the affirmative." He continued, "Let it be remembered…that the errors of physical science—chronology, or what not—which have been found, or may be found, do not vitiate, or in any way detract from, the value of the spiritual truth with which they are incidentally connected."[28]

In January 1880, Crawford Toy himself joined the debate, and attention turned more squarely to discussions of the inspiration of Scripture.[29] Toy published a series of essays in which he attempted to clarify his views, especially

---

[27] E. T. Winkler, "Dr. Toy on Inspiration," *Baptist Courier*, February 26, 1880, reprinted in the *Alabama Baptist*. Winkler continued, "The only safe position that we as Baptists can hold, is that the Bible is free from error." E. T. W. is identified by John Stout as E. T. Winkler, a prominent pastor who served congregations in South Carolina and Alabama. In a private letter, W. L. Lindsay took exception to Winkler's characterization of Toy's argument:

> I did so much want somebody to take Winkler's assertion, "Toy's views will destroy the Bible," & ask the readers of the *Courier* to take it and go through Toy's paper with it paragraph by paragraph and at the close of each paragraph ask themselves if *that* would "destroy the Bible." It would be a good thing if it were done in *writing* and *published*. (W. L. Lindsay to John Stout, March 10, 1880, L-S-C, SCL)

[28] John Stout, "The *Alabama Baptist*, Entitled Dr. Toy on Inspiration," *Baptist Courier*, March 11, 1880. Despite the title, Stout is responding to the reprint of Winkler's article in the *Courier*, noting "this article…must furnish satisfaction to the brethren who have been complaining of the one-sidedness of the discussion had in *THE COURIER*." Stout included a back-handed compliment to Winkler: "To say 'that there is no error in the Bible' is a remarkable thing for a scholar to say—and Dr. Winkler is a scholar. Will he state what he understands by 'the Bible' in that proposition? No matter what—English version—or the best available edition of the Scriptures in their original languages, the necessity of confessing error will stare him in the face…. Suppose a chronological mistake *is* discovered? Suppose a plain case of inexact physical science is pointed out. What is to be done? …Shutting one's eyes does not remove them—nor do they vanish before the most vehement declarations that they are not." Stout and Lindsay were writing private letters of encouragement to each other during this period. See W. L. Lindsay to John Stout, March 10, 1880, L-S-C, SCL.

[29] Crawford H. Toy, "Letter," *Religious Herald*, January 8, 1880.

with regard to his conviction that theories of inspiration had to be secondary to what the Scriptures themselves claimed.[30] The most compelling of the essays was the one titled "A Bit of Personal Experience," in which Toy traced his own journey in coming to terms with the relationship between the creation account of Genesis 1 and the findings of modern science. Once again, he appealed to the dual nature of Scripture: "this chapter [Gen.1] is a revelation of divine truth in human speech and modes of thought…so here I distinguish between form and spirit." Although essays continued to appear sporadically throughout 1880, the debate was essentially exhausted by the last of Toy's essays.[31] Despite the exchanges, little progress was made in finding common ground between those who adhered to a view of plenary verbal inspiration and those who did not.

Stout-Bell Inspiration Controversy

The inspiration controversy reignited a year later in 1881 when two appointees of the SBC Foreign Mission Board were subsequently denied appointments because of their theological views.[32] John Stout, an established pastor in South Carolina and a former student and active defender of Toy during the exchanges in denominational papers, and T. P. Bell, a recent graduate of SBTS, had been appointed in 1881 to serve as missionaries in China.[33] Neither candidate had been questioned regarding their views on inspiration during their initial interviews with the FMB. Apparently, it was Stout who

---

[30] Crawford H. Toy, "The Outward Form of Divine Revelation," *Religious Herald*, January 22, 1880; "Inspiration and Criticism," *Religious Herald*, February 5, 1880); "The Historical Books of the Bible," *Religious Herald*, March 11, 1880; "A Bit of Personal Experience," *Religious Herald*, April 1, 1880; "Destruction for Reconstruction," *Religious Herald*, April 22, 1880; and "Genesis and Geology," *Religious Herald*, May 6, 1880.

[31] Hurt, "Toy," 171. Basil Manly wrote to his mother, "the Inspiration discussion drags itself along in the *Courier* and *Herald*. Toy and Lindsay are having it now pretty much to themselves" ("Letter to Sarah Manly," quoted by Hurt, "Toy," 171). Lindsay told Stout in February 1880: "I have a great deal to say, but too lazy to say it. One more art. on canon will finish up that so far as I'm concerned, unless some carnivorous animal bites into one…. My next general subject (according to my plan) will be the 'Composition' of the Bible (about two articles), followed by its 'Preservation & Transmission' (about half doz articles!)—heigh-ho! It makes me groan to think of it; but the people know nothing (nor the minister either (?) on this subject—so I *must* write & (?) *you*?" (W. L. Lindsay to John Stout, February 20, 1880, L-S-C, SCL). By the next month, Lindsay confessed, "For myself, I have, for the present, laid down the pen, unless I am forced to take it up" (Lindsay to Stout, March 10, 1880).

[32] See Wills, *Southern Seminary*, 144–45.

[33] For the impact of their failed appointments on Baptist missions in China, see the Excursus, "Exploring the Toy-Moon Myth."

originally pressed the issue.[34] In a letter to Stout following the SBC annual meeting in May 1881, Foreign Mission Board Corresponding Secretary H. A. Tupper, wrote:

> At the Convention you proposed to send to me your views on Inspiration. As I stated to you, at the time of your coming before the Board the matter did not occur to me, and no question on the subject was raised by the Board. Since my return from the Convention some communications, written and with regard to the action of the Board have come to me.... I start by reminding you of the offer to send me your views to be used at my discretion. Does bro. Bell think with you? Do confer with him.[35]

Stout followed Tupper's advice and wrote to Bell, who then consulted W. L. Lindsay, another South Carolina pastor who had been heavily involved in the denominational papers' exchange on the side of Toy. Lindsay wrote to Stout:

> Bell sent me Tupper's letter to you, along with his paper on his views of inspiration, which he means to present to Tupper. It is a strong paper, substantially the same as that of Toy. Really there seems to be a possibility of complications ahead of us. But Tupper's letter (which you will carefully preserve of course) leaves but one course open to you two, viz. to make a clear full statement of your opinions to the Board and leave the rest to God. Bell will send me a copy of his paper, and you must do the same.[36]

Lindsay then speculated that the objections to which Tupper referred were coming from Marion, South Carolina, and Louisville, Kentucky: "They see what the real significance of sending you two is, in that the denomination is veering around from the position it occupied when it silenced Toy—the body which silenced him for entertaining certain opinions is now sending

---

[34] William R. Estep remarked, "If Stout had not raised the issue of inspiration of the Scriptures, neither Tupper nor the board would have done so" (cf. *Whole Gospel—Whole World: The Foreign Mission Board of the Southern Baptist Convention 1845–1995* [Nashville: Broadman and Holman, 1994], 139; see also Wills, *Southern Seminary*, 144).

[35] H. A. Tupper to John Stout, May 21, 1881, L-S-C, SCL. One of those who objected to the appointments of Stout and Bell was James P. Boyce, who had reported to H. A. Tupper (Boyce's brother-in-law) that Stout and Bell were not "sound in the faith" (see Estep, *Whole Gospel—Whole World*, 137–39; citing 1881 correspondence of Tupper and Boyce in JMLA). For the story on how Boyce became aware of the position of Bell (and Stout), see Wills, *Southern Seminary*, 144.

[36] W. L. Lindsay to John Stout, May 27, 1881, L-S-C, SCL.

forth as its accredited teachers two men who hold substantially the same opinions."[37]

Both Bell and Stout sent Lindsay copies of their statements concerning inspiration, which they had prepared and sent to the FMB. Lindsay had refused to comment on either paper until submitted. "This was necessary, because a hint of collusion would hurt the truth…. Both papers, now that they are written & in, let me say, are strong and clear as far as they go; & I don't see how the Board can stultify itself by withdrawing the appointments because of anything contained in either."[38]

The Foreign Mission Board drew different conclusions than Lindsay. Tupper informed Stout of the withdrawal of his appointment:

> I enclose the result of the prayerful, painful, and protracted consideration of the paper presented by you to our Board. If it is not the highest wisdom, the Board saw nothing wiser to do. The noble and Christian spirit manifested in your communication gives assurance that you will appreciate our struggles, and credit us with doing what was thought best for the cause of missions and the glory of God. Our hearts are all with you personally. We love you. We honor you for your manliness and your spiritual fervor. But you charged us not to be influenced by personal considerations. We have done what seems the will of God. Will you not unite with us in the constant prayer that all may result to the praise of his name?[39]

Friends and foes alike were puzzled by the decision. Luther Broaddus wrote to Stout, "Differing as I do from you, widely and I think radically, on the subject of inspiration, I still could not see nor can I now, that this difference of opinion furnished any good reason why you could not represent me in preaching the gospel to the heathen."[40] Unlike Toy, both Stout and Bell remained within the [Southern Baptist] Convention; "both would-be missionaries continued to serve the denomination that refused to send them as missionaries."[41] Toy himself got involved, writing Stout to encourage him to write

---

[37] Ibid.

[38] Lindsay to Stout, June 7, 1881.

[39] H. A. Tupper to John Stout, June 18, 1881, and W. L. Lindsay to John Stout, May 27, 1881, L-S-C, SCL.

[40] Luther Broaddus to John Stout, July 19, 1881, L-S-C, SCL. On a lighthearted note, ally Pastor C. C. Brown wrote Stout: "You may be unfit to preach to the heathen in China; but I think we heathen in Sumter [SC] may not be led hopelessly astray by your ministrations…. Can't you come over and preach for us?" (C. C. Brown to John Stout, September 4, 1881, L-S-C, SCL).

[41] Estep, *Whole Gospel—Whole World*, 138–39. Bell would later serve a stint as Corresponding Secretary of the Sunday School Board. Stout continued as a pastor and was a

and print his experience with the board to be distributed to prominent SBC leaders. Toy asserted that it was "desirable that the facts be known & they will not be known from Bapt. Newspapers."[42] Toy offered to cover one-fourth of the expenses of printing around a thousand copies.

The Teaching of the Old Testament at Southern Seminary

Before the trustees disbanded at the Atlanta convention in May 1879, they had not only accepted C. H. Toy's resignation but had also hired his replacement, Basil Manly, Jr.[43] Manly had been an original member of the Southern Seminary faculty and was a safe choice to replace Toy. When Toy was added to the faculty in 1869, Manly shifted his teaching assignment away from Old Testament and Hebrew. His accommodation to the addition of Toy was viewed differently. John Broadus commented, "Dr. Manly, who was highly versatile, and quite varied in his attainments, consented to take Polemics and Homiletics in connection with Biblical Introduction, which he retained."[44] William Whitsitt, on the other hand, argued that Manly "had been crowded out of his position as Prof of Hebrew by means of Broadus' passion for Toy."[45] According to Whitsitt, Manly, who left SBTS in 1871 to accept the presidency at Georgetown College, "had his revenge against Toy in 1879…when at the deposition of Toy, the seminary was compelled to take him back again. There was no other man that pretended to know any Hebrew whose orthodoxy could be trusted in that bitter time."[46]

With the return of Manly to the faculty, the teaching of the Old Testament took a decidedly traditional turn. Manly took over the Old Testament in English class that Toy had been scheduled to teach in the 1879–1880 academic year. A brief comparison of student notes on Genesis compiled that year with notes taken on the same course taught by Toy in 1874–1875 is instructive.[47] In the notes on Genesis, Toy rejected various attempts to harmonize the creation account with geological reconstructions of earth's history.

---

great advocate of the Baptist women's missionary societies in the South. Friends and relatives contributed funds for building a hospital in China, which was named after Stout. See *Life History of Reverend John Stout* (Stout Memorial Hospital, 1894).

[42] Crawford H. Toy to John Stout, August 5, 1881, L-S-C, SCL.

[43] *The Journal and the Messenger*, May 21, 1879.

[44] Broadus, *Memoir of James P. Boyce*, 211–12.

[45] Whitsitt Diary, November 30, 1886, 5:109.

[46] Whitsitt Diary, November 30, 1886, 5:109–10.

[47] The notes for Manly's course, "Notes on Basil Manly by H. C. Smith at SBTS, 1879–80," ASC, SBTS, run to about 35 pages. "Notes on C. H. Toy by Holt at SBTS, 1874–75," ASC, SBTS, contain about 105 pages. Of course, one must bear in mind these

He concluded that the word for "day" "cannot mean a long geological period of time. If it were true, we must suppose that God had infused into the mind of the writer a knowledge of science that was entirely before the times. God did not infuse a knowledge of science into the mind of Moses."[48] At the same time, Toy stated it was possible for a Christian to affirm the theory of evolution, that "God made the earth and heaven, stars, etc. through long processes of development."[49] Although he referred to Moses as the "author" of Genesis, Toy clearly presented the document as being the result of a long compositional history. Over several class periods, Toy said that differences are to be explained as the result of the perspectives of the "Jehovist" editor or the Elohist.[50] He rarely referred to the New Testament in these early lectures, and when he did it was to claim that the New Testament "does not tell us anything" about the authorship of the Pentateuch.[51] Toy did not address the question of inspiration in any systematic way in these lectures on Genesis.

The first point made by Manly in the semester's first class, on the other hand, was that "the OT is divinely inspired. Whatever sanctity God can give to a book is given to this book."[52] Manly avoided addressing the relationship of the account of creation in Genesis to science and, after a brief survey of compositional theories, offered an extended defense of the Mosaic authorship of the Pentateuch, citing the very New Testament evidence that Toy had rejected in support of his view.[53] In fact, many of the student notes included New Testament references peppered among references to the Old Testament. Furthermore, lectures often closed with what appeared to be sermonic notes

---

are student notes, so detailed comparisons are not warranted. Still, the differences in the substance and style, even filtered through the medium of student class notes, are striking.

[48] Holt, "September 28, 1874 Notes," ASC, SBTS.

[49] Holt, "September 30, 1874 Notes," ASC, SBTS. Elsewhere, Toy asserted that evolution "is entirely consistent with the Christian religion or rather one can be a Christian and still be an Evolutionist" (Holt, "October 9 Notes, 1874," ASC, SBTS).

[50] Holt, "October 7, 9, 1874 Notes," ASC, SBTS.

[51] Holt, "October 9, 1874 Notes," ASC, SBTS. We will return to an analysis of Toy's SBTS lectures when we compare them to his Harvard lectures in chapter 5.

[52] H. C. Smith, "First Lecture, September 3, 1879 Notes," ASC, SBTS. Smith did not consistently give dates for classroom lectures, opting at times to number them. Subsequent references to the lectures, therefore, will give the date or, in the absence of that, the lecture number. Manly would later publish a book expressing a traditional view of inspiration; see Basil Manly, Jr., *The Bible Doctrine of Inspiration Explained and Vindicated* (New York: A. C. Armstrong, 1888).

[53] H. C. Smith, "Fifth Lecture; Tenth Lecture," ASC, SBTS. Manly's view on the authorship question is especially striking when compared to his 1868–1869 lectures in which he seems to hold open the possibility of multiple authors for Genesis; see "Notes on Basil Manly by D. T. Smith at SBTS, 1868–69," ASC, SBTS.

on such topics as "The Philosophy of the Plan of Salvation" or "The Beginning of the Church."[54] Manly also pointed out various passages that served as "primal battlegrounds"; for example, on infant baptism, he was recorded to say, "When you converse with a pedobaptist, he goes to the OT. ...If we would understand the NT, we must understand the Old."[55]

Basil Manly, Jr., was certainly aware of being in a "fish bowl." He wrote Lulie Manly on May 13, 1879: "If I agree with him [Toy], I shall be censured for unsoundness, if I differ, I shall be thought to be actuated by prejudice or narrow views, clinging to orthodoxy rather than Truth."[56] In his lectures, Manly clearly chose the side of orthodoxy; whether he did so to the neglect of Truth is a matter of debate.

David Lyon's Changing Plans

In the initial days following Toy's resignation, one of the most intriguing stories associated with Toy's story began developing. The decisions of one seminary student regarding his future path hardly seems on a par with the upheaval caused by the controversy in the Southern Baptist Convention. Yet those decisions would later have an impact on the development of the study of Semitic and other ancient languages in North America, if not around the world.

David Gordon Lyon was born May 24, 1852, to Sara Caroline and Isaac Lyon, his father being a physician in Benton, Alabama. David attended William Jewell College in Liberty, Missouri (1869–1872) and transferred to Howard College, now Samford University, in Birmingham, Alabama, where he graduated in 1875. He began theological studies at The Southern Baptist Theological Seminary in 1876, which was then located in Greenville, South Carolina. The seminary relocated to Louisville, Kentucky, in 1877, and Lyon was part of the group of faculty and students who moved. While at Southern, Lyon came under the tutelage of Professor Toy and became an enthusiastic linguist, studying Greek (Koine and classical) with Professor Broadus, and Hebrew and Syriac with Professor Toy.

On May 13, 1879, David Lyon heard that his professor, C. H. Toy, had been pressured to tender his resignation to the Board of Trustees. On May 14, Lyon had tea with Dr. John Broadus to learn "the particulars of Dr. Toy's resignation."[57] On the next day, May 15, Toy and Professor Whitsitt arrived

---

[54] Smith, "First Lecture," ASC, SBTS; "October 2, 1879," ASC, SBTS.

[55] Smith, "First Lecture." ASC, SBTS.

[56] Cited in Joseph P. Cox, "A Study of the Life and Word of Basil Manly, Jr." (PhD diss., Southern Baptist Theological Seminary, 1954), 283.

[57] David Gordon Lyon Diary, May 14, 1879, HUG 1541, Box 6, Volume 3, HUA.

back in Louisville.[58] The following day, David Lyon and two other students assisted Professor Toy in packing his books for a train trip back east. Toy gave several books to Lyon as a gift of gratitude: Athanasius in Latin, Conant's *Proverbs*, and Howell's *History of Early Baptists*.[59] The next day he was back at Toy's residence packing more books. He wrote that he saw Toy's works on the Life of R. B. C. Howell, a commentary on 1 Samuel, and a commentary on 1 and 2 Thessalonians and 1 Timothy.[60]

After Toy's resignation, Lyon found himself torn between feelings of loyalty to Southern Seminary and a deep desire to continue his studies in Europe. At first, his two favorite professors, Broadus and Toy, advised him to remain in Louisville. In the Saturday, May 19, entry of his diary, Lyon reports that Dr. Broadus "has changed his mind as to the desirability of study in Germany and advises me to return to [the] Sem. next session." Lyon goes on to note that Broadus "says that I will certainly have to teach in some one of our denominational institutions," and he ends with a foreshadowing note: "he [Broadus] has in mind some plans which he cannot yet speak because their execution is dependent on other persons."[61] Broadus's rationale is that "the popular prejudice vs. going to Germany, while unreasonable, is sufficient to make a man ask whether he may not do to himself more harm than good by going." Broadus concludes that Lyon, at this point, should finish his degree and then "enter the pastorate."[62]

At first, Toy also counseled Lyon to remain in Louisville and finish his studies.[63] Despite the fact that both professors advised Lyon to remain in Lou-

---

[58] Lyon Diary, May 15, 1879.

[59] Lyon Diary, May 16, 1879. Conant's *Proverbs* is a philological and exegetical commentary on the Hebrew text of Proverbs by Thomas Jefferson Conant (New York: Sheldon & Co., 1872). In the same journal entry describing the Toy episode, Whitsitt comments that he had been reading *History of Early Baptists of Virginia* by Toy's uncle, R. B. C. Howell (which Toy gave to Lyon) and reckoned it "a poor trashy book, stitched together mainly of Semple." He asked, "What was the use of writing such a book? ...Toy who wrote the preface was too much ashamed of his uncle and the book to subscribe any name to it" (Whitsitt Diary, November 30, 1886, 5:104).

[60] Lyon Diary, May 17, 1879. Howell was a prominent pastor and Toy's uncle (after whom he was named). Toy never finished the biography of his uncle or the last work mentioned, the commentary on 1, 2 Thessalonians and the Pastorals, which was being written by Toy for the American Commentary Series, a series edited by Alvah Hovey and published by the American Baptist Publication Society. Because of his views on the authorship of the Pastorals, Toy's commentary was never published.

[61] Lyon Diary, May 19, 1879. Several times over the next several years, Broadus will allude to this "plan," which eventually he will fully disclose.

[62] Lyon Diary, May 19, 1879.

[63] Lyon Diary, May 15, 1879.

isville, he confesses in his diary that he feels "strongly inclined to go to Germany this summer. My only question now is which is best."[64] On June 7, David Lyon wrote Dr. Broadus a ten-page letter "on the subject of going to Germany."[65] Two days later he wrote Toy, presumably about the same matter.[66] In the letter to Broadus, Lyon rehearses the arguments pro and con. Against going now, he says, are "1) my love for the Seminary, 2) a desire to finish the course, 3) the injury which I may do myself by going." He then spends the next several pages unpacking the arguments against study abroad. Under love for the seminary, Lyon asserts, "My love for Dr. Toy was not less than that of any other student, but my love to the institution exceeds that which I feel toward any one of its instructors. But it does not seem to me that leaving the institution now for a greater good shows any lack of devotion."

Lyon then indicates that he lacks only two courses to fulfill graduation requirements, a course in Church History and another in Latin Theology, admitting he prizes "the latter more for the Latin than for the Theology" and that he does not expect to devote "any special & extended labor on the former." He offers that he could return to the seminary in two or three years and complete his course of study since the "possession of a diploma from such an institution is an honor & is desirable," but he concludes, "real scholarship in special branches seems to me a nobler ambition."

In regard to injury to himself from contact with German Rationalism, Lyon says he recognizes the danger, but he counters, "I believe that he who stands on the gospel & who keeps his heart by habits of devotion, in sympathy with the gospel, will stand unmoved by the storm. On the other side, the application of reason to the interpretation of Scripture is one of the most valuable lessons which I have learned from your instructions." He then acknowledges that injury to his reputation could occur not because there was prejudice against German study per se as "against all such study" and "which in my particular case will weigh in proportion as a man shows by his intercourse with the people that much study has not made him mad."

On the other side of the ledger are two reasons in favor of going to Germany: a desire for scholarship and providential indications. Regarding his desire for scholarship, Lyon writes passionately:

It has been an ambition of my life to make the most of what God has

---

[64] Ibid.

[65] Lyon Diary, July 7, 1879. Lyon mistakenly skipped June in his diary, and the entry regarding the Broadus letter is mismarked for July 7. But this letter is held in ASC, SBTS, and is marked June 7, 1879.

[66] Lyon Diary, June 9, 1879. The erroneous calendar dating has now been corrected by Lyon.

given me. I have been taught by all our professors to regard a mastery of the German language as indispensable to scholarship, because the German language contains the richest treasures of modern thought & because the German spirit of inquiry is most conducive to progress. I care nothing for the name of going to Germany, even if the mere fact of going gave one an enviable position, but I do desire to be able to handle the excellent instrument which I am sure the German language must be. In Germany I can acquire such facility as I should perhaps never gain in this country.

Whether his calling is to teach or whether his "life is to be given to the glorious work of preaching," Lyon says, "I have the same need to be scholarly, for I regard nothing so important to the Christian ministry as to know what is God's word & what is the meaning of that word." With regard to providential indications, Lyon simply says that a year ago he did not have the financial means to undertake study abroad, but now "the ability has been placed within my reach." He queries Broadus, "I rejoice to believe that in my college course & in my Seminary course, God has led me along, always opening the way which at times was dark & closed. In believing that he has now prepared the way to go to Germany & that his dealings point that way, am I mistaken?" Finally Lyon admits, "One trouble opposes me. I have learned to regard you & Dr. Toy as two of my best & wisest friends, & you both three weeks ago advised me to remain here. I do not know but this is a providential indication more weighty than the one above referred to." Lyon ends by asking Dr. Broadus for a "short reply."[67]

As Lyon reported to Broadus, Professor Toy had originally advised Lyon to stay in Louisville. But all that changed on June 18, when David Lyon recorded in his diary that he had received a "letter from Dr. Toy telling me to go to Germany now." Lyon then says that "after dinner I wrote a long letter to Dr. Broadus telling him that I must go to Europe this summer." He also writes that he gave an answer to the objections raised by Broadus in a letter from June 14. His next statement is remarkable both for its prescience and for the insight and intuition shown by one who is barely twenty-seven years old: "This day will be memorable in my history as the one on which I decided the momentous qu[estion] of quitting the Sem[inary] for Germany. I am influenced in the decision by nothing but a desire to enlarge my capabilities for usefulness." He ends his June 18, 1879, diary entry with this prayer: "May God grant that it shall be so."[68] He copies his letter to Dr. Broadus on the following day

---

[67] Quotations in the preceding paragraphs are taken from David Gordon Lyon to John Broadus, June 7, 1879, Broadus correspondence, Box 8, Folder 46.
[68] David Gordon Lyon Diary, June 18, 1879, HUG 1541, Box 6, Volume 3, HUA.

and on the day after that writes Toy informing him of his decision to go to Germany.

We do not have Lyon's letter to Toy, but his eight-page letter to Broadus on June 18 does survive. Lyon tells Broadus he read his letter over and over "with that respectful attention which I always pay to your opinion." Broadus had raised again objections to Lyon's study abroad, focusing, according to Lyon's response, on "(1) injury to the Seminary, (2) Prejudice against myself, (3) importance of completing the course." Lyon again addresses the objections point by point and with many of the same arguments made in his previous letter. In addition to these objections, Broadus again alludes to some future plan for Lyon. Lyon writes:

> I think that I discern what you have in mind when you speak of plans & hopes which you entertain in respect to my future. Profoundly grateful do I feel, my beloved Teacher, but my sense of gratitude does not exceed my sense of unworthiness for the position. I have always been looking to the Christian ministry & I do not feel that I should be blamed if I now cast a glance in another direction toward a station which is admitted to be contingent & to perform the duties of which I am most sincerely conscious of my inability. And however much I might desire the position if it could be purchased only by denying myself the means of becoming an interpreter of God's Word, I am ready to lift my hands & say, Go, forever.

Lyon goes on:

> I have tried to pray over this matter. I have tried to persuade myself that I ought to remain. But the conviction deepens that I should go now. What am I to do? How shall I act contrary to positive conviction of duty? In devotion to the Seminary I am determined to be surpassed by no other student. I would not willingly give the trustees just ground of offence.... I am very anxious in such an important movement to have the sanction of yourself or at least your benediction (which benediction & sanction I should prize beyond computation); but all these considerations cannot silence what seems to me the voice of God bidding me to go.

Lyon then made his impassioned resolve to go to Germany (cited at the beginning of the chapter). He ended the letter to Broadus with these words: "For your patience & kindness in reading my long letter & in writing to me, I feel very deeply grateful. My only regret is that I have to act contrary to your advice, but with the reasons for my action in your hands, as contained in this & a former letter, I shall hope not to forfeit that friendship which in the past

I have found so valuable."[69]

In this emotionally filled and rhetorically charged letter, David Lyon has left out very little in presenting his case to Dr. Broadus for his decision to study in Germany. In fact, he seems to omit nothing from his decision-making process save one point. Nowhere in the letter does he inform Dr. Broadus that he has heard from Dr. Toy and that Toy has now advised Lyon to go to Germany that very summer. On Saturday June 28, Lyon records that he received a letter from Dr. Broadus "saying that he loved me none the less for my decision to go against his advice."[70]

Toy's Transitions (1879–1880)

Whatever ripple effects others experienced from the Toy controversy, no one was more affected than Crawford Toy himself. According to most versions of the Toy myth, when Crawford Howell Toy stepped off the platform onto the train in Louisville, he was unknowingly headed to Hell in a Unitarian handbasket via Harvard! Or at least into "secular" oblivion. W. O. Carver observed that Toy

> might have become the leader of a new era of insight and interpretation of the Old Testament and of a better understanding of the Hebrew religion and of the principles of religion in general. He might have given to this Seminary an outstanding position in Old Testament scholarship such as it achieved in the New Testament field [with A. T. Robertson], and such as it has waited for until just now. However this may be, the openings which came to Dr. Toy for the pursuit of scholarship in his field led him into an environment wholly conducive to the secularistic interpretation of the history of religions in what was already an essentially humanistic environment.[71]

Reflecting in 1886 on the aftermath of the Toy controversy, his friend and former roommate, W. H. Whitsitt commented:

> He is one of the most disappointing men in the world; he always subsides just as he is in the act of doing something great. If he had simply kept his tongue he would have been a great figure in the Baptist history of

---

[69] David Gordon Lyon to John Broadus, June 18, 1879, Broadus Correspondence, Box 8, Folder 46, SBTS.

[70] Lyon Diary, June 28, 1879.

[71] W. O. Carver, "Recollections and Information from Other Sources concerning the Southern Baptist Theological Seminary" (Louisville, KY: n.p., 1954), 28, MSS 922.6173 C256r, ASC, SBTS.

America. If he had died in 1879 or 1880 his name would have been immortal; his power would have been felt for a whole generation. But he's now a dead cock in the pit.[72]

But Toy didn't go to Hell or Harvard, at least not immediately, nor did he fade into oblivion or die a martyr's death. Instead, he returned home to Norfolk, Virginia. On May 16, Toy had received a telegram from Norfolk that his father, Thomas D. Toy, was "in a very precarious condition" and requesting his immediate return home.[73] Toy wrote Broadus on May 23 to tell him of his father's ailing health.[74] Thomas Dallam Toy died on May 28, 1879, at the age of 65.[75]

Toy's mother, Amelia Rogers Toy, had died in 1873. Toy's brother-in-law described the effect her death had on the elder Toy: "Since the death of his wife in 1873, he [Thomas D. Toy] had been as though another man. He had lost all interest in the thriving drug business, wholesale and retail, which he had conducted for many years in Norfolk, and finally closed it out. If one may speak of such things with certainty, he died of a broken heart."[76] Whitsitt, however, attributed Thomas Toy's death to the events surrounding the forced resignation of Crawford Toy: "Dr. Toy's father was not able in the feeble state of his health to sustain the shock which was occasioned by the events in Atlanta, and so passed away last week at Norfolk. It is one of the saddest things

---

[72] Whitsitt Diary, November 30, 1886, 5:108. Whitsitt is certainly sharp-tongued in his portrayal of the three principal players, Boyce, Broadus, and Toy, but neither does he mince any words when it comes to his own shortcomings in comparison (see 5:116): "It is no consolation to me in criticizing the life of other good men to find that I have not succeeded in ordering my own life as wisely as they have ordered their lives. Broadus is likely a better man than I am though I am not able to trust him far. Toy has enjoyed higher success than I have though I consider him but an ordinary mind. Boyce has obtained a far superior station, though I can hardly see any but ridiculous features about him."

[73] William H. Whitsitt to Florence Wallace, May 16, 1879, in *Mirror*, 240.

[74] Crawford H. Toy to John A. Broadus, May 23, 1879, ASC, SBTS.

[75] The *Religious Herald*, June 26, 1879, carried a touching obituary for "Deacon Thomas D. Toy."

[76] Johnson, *Autobiographical Notes*, 222. Johnson went on to quote a poem he wrote about his father-in-law:

Five years have slowly rolled away;
Five of longing day by day;
Five years of grief so meekly borne;
Five years of pilgrimage alone!
'Tis over now; thy sorrows done,
Thy cross laid down, thy crown is won
And all is well. The Savior's breast
Thy pillow now; take then thy rest.

connected with the whole sad affair. 'No man liveth to himself.' The consequences of our acts are often apparent in quarters where beforehand we little dreamed of observing them."[77]

Southern Seminary was not the only institution facing crisis at the 1879 May meeting of the Southern Baptist Convention in Atlanta. Furman College had for several years been in financial straits. At this May meeting, the trustees were contemplating closing the school or reducing the number of faculty. Professor Charles H. Judson, who was also the treasurer at the university, offered his resignation to the Furman Trustees, who were meeting in Atlanta in conjunction with the SBC.[78] In the course of the meeting, President Furman also tendered his resignation. Both were accepted; later the rest of the faculty also resigned.[79]

On June 17, 1879, the Board of Trustees at Furman College in Greenville, South Carolina, (re)elected Dr. Judson as professor of mathematics, Dr. Furman as professor of English, and Dr. E. G. Winkler as president and professor of languages, effectively reducing the number of faculty to three. Winkler refused the offer by telegram ("Thanks for the offer but can't accept."), and Furman and Judson requested time to consider the proposal.[80] The board then elected Crawford Toy as president and professor of languages.[81] Toy re-

---

[77] William H. Whitsitt to Florence Wallace, June 6, 1879, in *Mirror*, 223.

[78] Robert Norman Daniel, *Furman University: A History* (Greenville, SC: Furman University, 1951), 90.

[79] W. J. McGlothlin, *Baptist Beginnings in Education: A History of Furman University* (Nashville: Sunday School Board, 1926), 140. Furman later published a letter to the "Baptists of South Carolina" in the *Baptist Courier* in which he explained his resignation at the trustees' meeting:

> In the course of some remarks he [Judson] alluded to existing dissatisfaction with the internal working of the University, but without specifying any particular ground of complaint. This was followed by a remark from a member of the Board [Dr. Hiden] which seemed to me necessarily to imply a failure of duty on my part. Under the circumstances, self-respect in my judgment demanded the vacation of my office. Though subsequent events have shown that I felt too keenly what was said, yet the effect was my resignation. I could bear to suffer for the University, but I could not bear that the University should be even supposed to suffer through me. (Quoted in Harvey Toliver Cook, *The Life and Work of James Clement Furman* [Greenville, SC: n.p., 1926], 275)

[80] McGlothlin, *Baptist Beginnings*, 141. Daniel, *Furman University*, 91, narrates essentially the same story, but he puts the date of the meeting at July 1, 1879.

[81] Cook, *James Clement Furman*, 274.

plied by telegram: "It is with extreme regret and grateful affection that I decline your generous offer."[82] Judson, who by now had accepted his reinstatement, was asked to go to Virginia to "persuade Dr. Toy to accept the presidency."[83] Judson reported to the board meeting in Columbia in July that Toy had again refused the offer of the Furman presidency.[84] Although no reason was stated, it is reasonable to think that Furman's dire financial situation weighed heavily in Toy's decision, not to mention the fact that the position would have presumably kept him under the close eye of Baptists who only weeks before had forced him out of Southern, or at least stood by and allowed it to transpire.

On the other hand, why would the board at Furman elect someone who only weeks earlier had been forced to resign from the seminary that had once been a neighbor? McGlothlin conjectures, "South Carolina Baptists were very fond of Dr. Toy who had left the Seminary faculty in May, and many resented his virtual dismissal by the Seminary Board which had made no public statement of the reasons for their action. This fact explains the earnest efforts made to secure him [Toy] as President."[85]

For whatever reason, Toy turned down the presidency of Furman and remained that summer in Norfolk where he served as pulpit supply[86] at his home church, Freemason Street Baptist Church, for Rev. William D. Thomas, D.D., who had left the Baptist church in Greenville to accept the pulpit in Norfolk in 1971.[87] Still, Toy had no further offers for fulltime employment. In July 1879, Toy was elected president of the American Philological Society, which as W. H. Whitsitt observed was "an office of distinguished honor, but of no benefit."[88] By then, Toy had decided to relocate to New York City in October 1879 in hopes of finding employment.[89] By the first of November, Toy had moved to New York and "settled on 24th St. but has not

---

[82] Cited in Daniel, *Furman University*, 91.

[83] Daniel, *Furman University*, 91.

[84] Ibid.

[85] McGlothlin, *Baptist Beginnings*, 140–41.

[86] William H. Whitsitt to Florence Wallace, September 29, 1879, *Mirror*, 240.

[87] George Braxton Taylor, "William Dandridge Thomas," *Virginia Baptist Ministers* (Lynchburg, VA: J. P. Bell, 1913), 391–92.

[88] Whitsitt to Wallace, August 5, 1879, in *Mirror*, 230. Whitsitt goes on: "I greatly rejoice with my friend in this acknowledgement of his talents and acquirements, but I am sorry that no sphere of labor has been opened to him…. His election to the position just indicated will be of advantage, giving him an introduction & character throughout the country, and by that means it may be possible for him to get on."

[89] Whitsitt reported, "For the present he will settle in New York, where he will do any work that may come to hand" (Whitsitt to Wallace, August 5, 1879, in *Mirror*, 230). Cf. Whitsitt to Wallace, September 15, 1879, in *Mirror*, 230, in which Whitsitt specifies

formed any plans for the future."[90]

Soon, however, Toy "found very modest employment in the office of the *Independent*,"[91] a magazine that had been especially critical of the seminary in its handling of the controversy. As Toy himself described his situation, "At present I am living very quietly, writing an occasional article for a newspaper, and doing a little work for the *Independent* of this city."[92] Toy continued his research during this interval, working in the Semitic materials in the Astor Library.[93] He wrote to David Lyon, "At a recent meeting of the Oriental Society in Boston, I read a short paper on Noun-inflection in Sabean (Himyaritic), and I shall probably read something at the meeting of the American Philological Society at Philadelphia next July."[94] In a letter to Broadus, Toy expressed concern about the state of university language studies, noting that at Johns Hopkins eighteen of sixty-four students were "pursuing languages...of which twelve are in Greek. That does not look well for the humanities. But I have faith in men's sense of the useful in the long run; I do not doubt that, allowing for temporary movements in one direction and another, the world will give us as much attention to Greek and Latin as they deserve."[95]

---

that Toy "expects to settl in New York on the first of next month, and engag in teaching Hebrew, privately. He has no position except that of President of the American Philological Society, which is a station of great honor but of no profit at al." It is worth noting, in passing, that in this correspondence, Whitsitt used a hybrid of phonetic spelling, no doubt under the influence of Toy, who had been advocating phonetic spelling in his work and associations with the APA.

[90] Whitsitt to Wallace, November 5, 1879, in *Mirror*, 245.

[91] George F. Moore, "An Appreciation of Professor Toy," *American Journal of Semitic Languages and Literatures* 36 (1919): 5.

[92] Crawford H. Toy to David Lyon, New York, February 23, 1880; cited in Lyon, "Toy," 12–13. Toy's niece presented a dim, if not dire, view of Toy's responsibilities with the *Independent*: "His work, according to his wife, included writing the funnies (whatever the funnies of 1879 were), and we can picture the biblical scholar sitting at his desk, grinding out laughs. In none of his writings that I have seen is there evidence that a sense of humor was among his gifts, but he did the job and got away with it" (Jane Toy Coolidge, "Crawford Howell Toy, 1836–1919," [n.p.], 7). Toy does, in fact, demonstrate a keen sense of humor from his earliest letters through the height of his Harvard career. For example, in his diary of 1900 he related the following anecdote: "the man who takes care of his house at Bar Harbor; being asked of what Mr. Thayer was professor, he replied, 'oh, he's professor of the whole damn thing'" (Toy Diary, March 8, 1900, Chest of 1900, HUA 900.11, Box 4, HUA). Furthermore, Toy himself describes his work as "not unpleasant and not without utility" (Crawford H. Toy to John A. Broadus, November 10, 1880, ASC, SBTS).

[93] Toy to Broadus, March 10, 1880.

[94] Crawford H. Toy to David Lyon, New York, May 29, 1880; cited in Lyon, "Toy," 13.

[95] Crawford H. Toy to John A. Broadus, October 31, 1879; cited by Hurt, "Toy," 69.

In May 1880, Whitsitt stopped off to see Toy in transit from New York to England, where he spent the summer continuing his research on Baptist origins. He wrote to his fiancée: "I arrived yesterday. Toy took dinner with me at 5 p.m. and staid for the evening. I have taken to smoking with Toy. It is too bad, is it not? He staid until 10 o'clock last night: we sat together on Madison Square which lies just in front of the hotel and had much talk and communion."[96]

In the course of his work for the *Independent*, Toy apparently solicited some essays from Whitsitt on his developing views of Baptist beginnings. Whitsitt had shared a letter he had written to a Mennonite scholar, J. G. de Hoop Scheffer of Amsterdam, concerning his findings regarding the origins of the English Baptists: "Dr. Toy wrote me last week that my letter to Dr. Scheffer was to him a revelation in regard to Baptist history, and begged me to allow him to retain it until he should have time to lay it before some friends in New York. I really felt complimented to have him express himself so plainly, and show such an evident interest in the subject."[97] Four articles by Whitsitt appeared in the *Independent* on June 24, September 2 and 9, and October 3 while Toy was still working there.[98] Whitsitt argued that baptism by immersion was not practiced among English Baptists until 1641, thereby challenging the "trail of blood" mythology held by Landmark Baptists that traced the practice of immersion through various dissident groups back to John the Baptist. Whitsitt also suggested that Roger Williams was not immersed at all.[99] The articles were published anonymously, and the views, met with "much disapproval and sneers from many quarters,"[100] were not immediately connected with Whitsitt.[101]

---

[96] William H. Whitsitt to Florence Wallace, May 26, 1880, in *Mirror*, 255. In June, while still in New York, awaiting departure for England, Whitsitt later recalled: "In the month of June 1880 when I was at the 5th Avenue Hotel in New York I had a very tender epistle from Broadus desiring that before I sailed for England I should give him a full statement of my views touching the inspiration of the Holy Scriptures seeing that these had been brung in question in certain quarters; and speaking pleasant words about the complete unreserved of our friendship. The net is spread in vain in the sight of any bird. I was mindful of the feat which Boyce and Broadus had accomplished in the overthrow of my colleague the year before and I 'denied the allegation and defied the alligator.'" The allusion here is apparently to Richard Sheridan's 1775 play *The Rivals*, in which a character "resents the allegation and alligator." See Whitsitt Diary, November 30, 1886, 5:115.

[97] Whitsitt to Wallace, November 5, 1879, in *Mirror*, 244.

[98] Duncan, "Heresy at Louisville," 73–74; Slatton, *W. H. Whitsitt*, 98.

[99] Slatton, *W. H. Whitsitt*, 98.

[100] Ibid.

[101] Duncan, "Heresy at Louisville," 74.

In May 1880, at the time of Whitsitt's visit, Toy had no immediate prospects: "I suppose I shall be in this city for several months to come. I am still writing for the *Independent* newspaper, and have other matters at hand."[102] Little did Toy know at that moment how his circumstances were about to change—and change dramatically—as a result of the efforts and vision of Charles W. Eliot, then president of Harvard University.

Eliot had been elected president of Harvard in 1869 and set about to move the university from a regional school, whose claim to fame to that point had been as a training ground for Unitarian ministers, to an educational institution of national prominence. By 1879, Eliot had turned his attentions to reforming the Harvard Divinity School (which had become a distinct entity within the college about sixty years earlier). He laid out his vision for the divinity school in a fundraising letter written in September 1879 and distributed it to prominent ministers presumably for the purpose of soliciting contributions from wealthy congregants.[103] His vision began with funding five professorships that were "inadequately endowed." Eliot made the case that all the positions (Hebrew, New Testament Criticism and Literature, Ecclesiastical History, Homiletics, and Theology and Ethics) were or could be taught in an unsectarian way. Some of these subjects, according to Eliot, were more obviously appropriate to the mission of a university. The professorship in Hebrew was one of these: "Nobody questions that this is a proper University professorship—in every respect fit & indispensable."[104] Eliot concluded his appeal

---

[102] Crawford H. Toy to David Lyon, New York, May 29, 1880, cited in Lyon, "Toy," 13.

[103] The rough draft copy in the Eliot papers contains two similarly worded letters to Rev. E. B. Wilbon and Rev. H. N. Brown. Ellipses indicate that portions of the letter were reproduced verbatim in the two versions, but also tailored for the individual addressees; cf. Charles W. Eliot to E. B. Wilbon and H. N. Brown (rough draft), September 16, 1879, HUA 5.150, Box 9, Records of the President of Harvard University, Charles William Eliot, HUA. Eliot's aim was to raise $130,000 for the five positions (the equivalent of more than three million dollars in 2018; cf. https://www.officialdata.org/).

[104] Eliot to Wilbon and Brown (rough draft), September 16, 1879. New Testament Criticism and Literature was likewise a subject that "is thoroughly unsectarian—a purely scholarly and scientific subject," which as Eliot pointed out was "taught now by a layman, who is confessedly the best New Testament scholar in the country" (Ezra Abbot). Likewise for ecclesiastical history, which was "as suitable for liberal training as any other branch of history." But Eliot also made a case for homiletics: "No one can doubt the necessity and fitness of this professorship in a University except those who...think the clerical profession has no longer any function and therefore that a University should not train ministers at all." Theology at Harvard was "treated in our school historically,—as it should be—without the least attempt to impose any set of opinions upon the student. The professor has his own opinions of course and doubtless exhibits them." Eliot then compared theology with American history, a subject everyone recognized as an indispensable part of the curriculum

by providing three reasons for his "interest in this matter":

> As President of the University I desire that five important professorships
> should be adequately endowed: 2. Believing firmly in the permanent use-
> fulness and influence of the clerical profession—through all changes, so-
> cial or other—I wish to see the University training ministers: 3. As a
> Unitarian I am proud to see them doing what seemed to me a very wor-
> thy thing.[105]

Eliot soon set about to fulfill his vision by seeking to fill the professorship
of Hebrew and other Oriental languages. Eliot had heard that across the Atlantic in Aberdeen, Scotland, a "heresy" trial had been raging for quite some
time. In 1870, William Robertson Smith had been elected to the chair in He-
brew/Oriental Languages and Exegesis of Old Testament at the Free Church
College in Aberdeen. In 1875, Smith incited an ecclesiastical conflict with an
article on "Bible," which he published in the ninth edition of the *Encyclopaedia
Britannica*. While he would eventually be charged with eight counts of libel
by the Free Church General Assembly, the most controversial view was
Smith's denial of Mosaic authorship of Deuteronomy. The controversy lasted
five years, complete with "heated debates and temporary suspensions";
although his views were never formally declared heretical, he was dismissed
from his chair in 1881.[106] In January 1880, during the midst of this turmoil,
while Smith was in Jeddah, Saudia Arabia (during a forced suspension from
teaching), he received a proposal from Charles Eliot, president of Harvard
College, to accept the chair of Hebrew and other Oriental Languages at Harvard.[107] In a follow-up letter in February, Eliot sought to reassure Smith of
his academic freedom should he accept the position:

> As regards opinions, modes of teaching, and means of influence, a pro-
> fessor is absolutely free. He is responsible to no person and to no body
> of men as to what he believes or does not believe, teaches or does not
> teach. None of our professors subscribe any creed or are in any way in-
> quired as to their beliefs. He may adopt a pure lecture method or may

---

"though it is impossible to get a teacher who will not incline either to the Federalists or the
Democrats."

[105] Eliot to Wilbon and Brown (rough draft), September 16, 1879.

[106] William Johnstone, "Introduction," *William Robertson Smith: Essays in Reassessment*, ed. William Johnstone, JSOTSup 189 (Sheffield: Sheffield Academic, 1995), 19–20.

[107] John Sutherland Black and George Chrystal, *The Life of William Robertson Smith*
(London: Adam and Charles Black, 1912), 340. A handwritten, rough draft of this letter
is preserved in the Harvard University Archives (UAI 5.150, Box 9, Records of the President of Harvard University, Charles William Eliot).

require his students to translate and recite or answer questions. A professor is expected not to go far out of his own department but within his sphere he is master. He may be strict or lax as to discipline in his lecture-room; he may cultivate social relations with his pupils.[108]

In response to a question posed by Smith regarding the nature of the position, Eliot confessed that there was "a serious difficulty in answering your inquiry, because what ought to be, and what might be, is so very different from what is. This year, the present incumbent is instructing four students from the college, and about twenty from the Divinity School."[109] With regard to the student body, Eliot commented: "I have no means of knowing to what churches the Divinity students belong, or propose to belong.... The majority of the Divinity students doubtless have Unitarian predilections—the term Unitarian designates with us a great variety of non-evangelical opinions—but members of evangelical denominations are usually found among them."[110]

Eliot states his goal for the position plainly: "What we want is a fresh start—a revolution in the department—a new enthusiasm for Oriental studies. We are absolutely unprovided with a teacher of Arabic and the study of Hebrew has been for years pursued in a perfunctory manner." Eliot then makes his pitch to Smith, declaring that "Harvard University is the oldest, richest, most independent and most vigorous institution of learning in the United States, no matter what test of wealth, independence and vigor you may apply. By taking this chair, you would take the best position in America in your department of scholarship, so far as salary, accessible libraries, comfort in living, and width of influence are concerned." Eliot states that he is aware (through the endorsement of Francis Peabody) that Robertson Smith is "the best possible man for the vacant professorship." He concludes with this open-ended invitation: "We should be glad to have your services for any term of years not

---

[108] Charles W. Eliot to W. Robertson Smith (rough draft), February 23, 1880, HUA 5.150, Box 9, HUA.

[109] Ibid. Eliot goes on to comment, "You will at once perceive that this state of things, considering that there are this year 1356 students in the University, is exceedingly unsatisfactory." Clearly, Eliot is unhappy with these numbers: "In fact, if Hebrew and the cognate languages had been taught for ten years past with success, we should not now be looking for a competent professor." These remarks reflect Eliot's dissatisfaction with the current holder of the Hancock Chair of Hebrew, Edward James Young. Gary Dorrien commented, "Edward James Young, Hancock Professor of Hebrew and Old Testament...flopped as a scholar and teacher and was forced to resign in 1880, ostensibly to make room for a non-Unitarian" (*Social Ethics in the Making: Interpreting an American Tradition* [Malden, MA: Wiley-Blackwell, 2011], 8).

[110] Eliot to Smith (rough draft), February 23, 1880.

less than five, if such an arrangement would be more agreeable to you."[111]

Finally, with rhetorical flourish Eliot lays out his vision for the divinity school—one might claim for the university as a whole—and invites Smith to join the enterprise:

> The work which is here proposed to you is undoubtedly pioneer work; but I hope that it will attract you on that very account. Interest in oriental literature and in Biblical research is to be aroused anew; an important department in the University is to be recreated; and theology is to be freely cultivated and developed side by side with history, philosophy, philology, and natural science in a well established institution of learning, independent alike of church & of State, and governed by lay boards.[112]

How could anyone refuse the opportunity to join such a grandiose position? William Robertson Smith found a way. Smith replied on March 10, 1880: "I may say at once that a post in your University such as you describe is just what I should like to hold if I had no one but myself to consult in the matter." The opportunities to teach Old Testament and Hebrew alongside other "Semitic dialects" and with "absolute freedom of opinion" were "exactly what I most desire and what I do not think can be secured anywhere better than at Harvard." Still, as much as Smith desired the kind of "religious freedom" Eliot described, Smith worried that "it would hurt the whole liberal party in the Free Church of Scotland very much if it were possible to get up a cry that I had gone over to a Unitarian Divinity School." Smith reassured Eliot that he himself had "no personal objections whatever to be associated with earnest and independent thinkers of any denomination," but "there are plenty of people in Scotland as elsewhere who don't know what toleration means." In any case, Smith conveyed that his fight against heresy charges was as yet unfinished (he suggested that "the fight will probably be decided in May").[113]

The offer remained open until June. Smith was "at first disposed to regard this as perhaps a providential call by which he, his friends, and the Church might be relieved from a situation that had become in so many ways

---

[111] All quotations in this paragraph are from Charles W. Eliot to W. Robertson Smith (rough draft), February 23, 1880. Eliot also informs Robertson Smith that two more appointments in ecclesiastical history and ethics and homiletics would be filled within eighteen months by "the most learned and influential men to be had without regard to their theological opinions."

[112] Eliot to Smith (rough draft), February 23, 1880.

[113] Quotations in this paragraph are from W. Robertson Smith to Charles W. Eliot, March 10, 1880, HUA 5.150, Box 9, HUA. Smith's other concern was that he did not wish to be a candidate for a position that he might not actually be offered, that is, he did not want to be a failed candidate, for whatever reason.

embarrassing."[114] Eliot replied to Smith's concerns, apparently alleviating them. Smith confirmed that Eliot had "made it quite clear to me that candidature for a chair in your University could not be interpreted as a desertion of the doctrinal position which I have hitherto maintained."[115] He then reasserted that no decision could be made before his denomination's General Assembly in late May.

On May 27, 1880, a motion was made at the Free Church Assembly to admonish Smith for "unguarded and incomplete statements" but to leave him in his chair; the motion passed by a vote of 299-292.[116] So Smith sent a telegraph to Eliot stating that he would not be able to consider the invitation to join the faculty at Harvard. He followed with a letter on June 4, 1880, in which he wrote:

> The telegram which I sent you on the decision of the Assembly has already let you understand that I can no longer think of leaving Aberdeen. ...Yet I ought not to close our correspondence on the subject without saying how much I have felt attracted towards Harvard by all I have heard from you and others, and how deeply I am touched by the kindness with which many friends on the other side of the Ocean held out their hands to me when I seemed almost deserted at home. I shall always feel towards Harvard as towards a place where I have personal friends.

Smith goes on to recommend Harnack for the position in ecclesiastical history and Wellhausen for the chair in Hebrew, asserting that he is "by far the ablest coming man in O.T. studies....if you had him in Harvard your university would have the man who for the next ten or 15 years is likely to influence O.T. study more than any living person, Kuenen not excepted."[117] Eliot

---

[114] John Sutherland Black and George Chrystal, *The Life of William Robertson Smith* (London: Adam and Charles Black, 1912), 340. Smith's colleagues, however, were divided on the issue.

[115] W. Robertson Smith to Charles W. Eliot, n.d., HUA 5.150, Box 9, HUA. The letter was probably written in late April or early May.

[116] Quoted in Black and Chrystal, *Life of William Robertson Smith*, 358.

[117] W. Robertson Smith to Charles W. Eliot, June 4, 1880, HUA 5.150, Box 9, HUA. On the relationship between Smith and Wellhausen, see Rudolf Smend, "William Robertson Smith and Julius Wellhausen," in *William Robertson Smith: Essays in Reassessment*, ed. William Johnstone, JSOT 189 (Sheffield: Sheffield Academic, 1995), 226–42. Ezra Abbot, based on a "testimonial" from C. R. Gregory of Leipzig, also recommended Harnack for the position in ecclesiastical history (Ezra Abbot to Charles W. Eliot, April 8, 1881, HUA 5.150, Box 9, HUA). See also James Hardy Ropes, "Theological Education at Harvard," *Harvard Alumni Bulletin* 17/15 (January 13, 1915): 251. Harnack chose to go to Berlin, and Ephraim Emerton was appointed to the Winn professorship in church history. As it turned out, Smith was eventually removed from his position at Aberdeen in 1881. According to Black and Chrystal, *Life of William Robertson Smith*, 406, when Eliot

replied, "I have not seen any intelligible account of the proceedings of the General Assembly. The vote seemed too close to be decisive, but you evidently count it a battle won once for all. The Free Church is much to be congratulated on the result."[118] Eliot went on to inform Smith that Harvard's governing body "had appointed an American heretic whose views on Isaiah had offended the Baptist communion to which he had belonged."[119]

That "American heretic" was Crawford Howell Toy. Eliot's interest in Toy had begun at about the same time that he contacted Smith.[120] Harvard's Ezra Abbott, Bussey Professor of New Testament Criticism and Interpretation, presumably at the request of Eliot, wrote John Broadus on February 12, 1880:

> Professor Young has resigned his office as professor of Hebrew and other Oriental Languages at Harvard University. As you have been associated with Professor C. H. Toy, I venture to ask you to give me frankly and somewhat fully your opinion of him as a man, a scholar and a teacher. We want the very best man who can be obtained to fill this vacant place without regard to his denominational connections. Any information you can give me concerning Prof. Toy, or concerning any other scholar whom you regard as eminently qualified for such a position will be thankfully received.
>
> I am, dear Sir,
> Very respectfully yours,
> Ezra Abbot[121]

Broadus responded that Toy's resignation was due to his holding views

---

heard of Smith's dismissal, he offered him a chair of ecclesiastical history. Smith ended up at Christ's College, Cambridge University.

[118] Quoted in Black and Chrystal, *Life of William Robertson Smith*, 375.

[119] Ibid. Reference to Toy's interpretation of Isaiah is another indication that this was Toy's understanding of the cause of his forced resignation. Eliot's description of Toy as an "American heretic" was cited (without attribution to Black and Chrystal) in an article by George Hodges, "Censured Saints," *Atlantic Monthly* (April 1913): 511. Toy wrote Hodges after the article appeared to say, "I did not know before of President Eliot's letter to Robertson Smith" (Crawford H. Toy to George Hodges, May 29, 1913, Harvard Houghton Library, Autograph File, T, 1580–1975, HUA). Toy also remarked, "We have all enjoyed it, and my wife and her mother (Mrs. Saunders) are particularly pleased at the way you bring me in."

[120] Moore's and Hurt's accounts seem to suggest that Eliot did not turn his attention to Toy until after Smith's withdrawal from consideration, but this correspondence from Abbott proves otherwise.

[121] Ezra Abbot to John A. Broadus, February 12, 1880, ASC, SBTS.

similar to those of the German scholars, Kuenen and Wellhausen.[122] G. F. Moore comments, "After getting what information he could from others, he [Eliot] sought out Toy in his narrow journalistic quarters in New York, and by an interview with him promptly satisfied himself that both in learning and in spirit he found the kind of man he wanted."[123]

Eliot had wasted little time in moving forward after Smith's withdrawal. Years after the fact, Eliot recounted the original meeting with Crawford Toy in his own words:

> In 1880 there was a vacancy in the Hancock Professorship of Hebrew and other Oriental Languages and it was important that the Vacancy should be filled with the best possible scholar. Having heard that Professor Crawford Howell Toy had been dismissed from the Southern Baptist Theological Seminary at Louisville, Kentucky because his views on Inspiration were not satisfactory to the Trustees at that institution and that he was at the moment employed in the office of *THE INDEPENDENT* in New York City, I met Dr. Toy by appointment in the bare cell in which he was working daily for the journal. We had never seen each other before, so that I had to ask questions about his education, previous labors and desires, and he had many questions to ask me about what I wanted of him, and what sort of a place he could have at Harvard University and how free he would be there.[124]

Though the specifics of the exchange between Eliot and Toy in Toy's "bare cell" at *The Independent* are unknown, it is doubtful Eliot spent as much time wooing Toy as he had done with Robertson Smith. Still, the results were positive for both sides: "As a result of that conversation, I made up my mind that Harvard University wanted Dr. Toy and Dr. Toy made up his mind that he would like to take the offered professorship in Harvard. Both decisions

---

[122] Broadus, *Memoir of James P. Boyce*, 264. Abbot thanked Broadus for his "full and satisfactory" responses to his queries (Abbot to Broadus, February 23, 1880; cited by Hurt, "Toy," 70, footnote 176).

[123] Moore, "Toy," 5.

[124] Charles W. Eliot to Mr. Hulburt, November 23, 1920, UAI 5.150, Box 231, HUA. Eliot had been asked to prepare brief statements for the Cambridge Book Club on Toy and W. G. Farlow, famed Harvard botanist, both of whom had died in 1919. Eliot decided to treat the scholars together "partly as contrasts, but chiefly as men of the same spirit and similar careers." Of the differences, Eliot wrote, "one was of Southern birth and a soldier in the Confederate Army and always in very narrow circumstances, the other was the son of a rich Massachusetts merchant, whose father gave him every possible educational advantage and furthered his early scientific career." Eliot concluded, "In many external ways, they were different men, but at heart they were strikingly alike. In all fields of scholarship and research, the modern scholar is moved by the same intense love of truth and wins from the ardent pursuit of it the same satisfying reward."

held."[125]

In a letter to Broadus dated June 8, 1880, Toy summarized the whirlwind of events:

> Many thanks for the letter you mentioned having written to Ezra Abbot in reply to his inquiries; I am sure that your opinion had great weight with him & with the authorities of the University. I supposed at the time that it was improbable their choice would fall on me. I knew that they had a European scholar in mind and in fact they did elect Robertson Smith but his restoration to the Assembly occurred about that time, & he naturally preferred to stay in Scotland. After that the Corporation of the University presented my name to the Board of Overseers, and the election will take place the 30th of this month. I went to Boston last week & saw Presd't Eliot & Ezra Abbot, and also James Freeman Clarke, who is one of the committee to whom the nomination was referred. The two first named seemed to regard the election as a matter of course; but it will be just as well to wait and see.[126]

The Harvard Board of Overseers did meet on June 30, 1880, at 9:00 a.m. The minutes record that the "Hon. Mr. Endicott for the Committee on the election of Crawford Howell Toy, D.D., reported in favor of concurrence & the Board voted to concur in the election of Crawford Howell Toy, D.D. as

---

[125] Eliot to Hulburt, November 23, 1920. Neither Eliot nor Toy indicated any controversy regarding Toy's appointment. Whitsitt, however, suggested that there was some resistance of which he became aware in March 1881: "Have you seen the remark about Dr. Toy that is now going the rounds of the papers? President Eliot of Harvard it seems was called upon for an explanation of the fact that a Baptist had found a chair in the Theological Faculty of the Institution. His reply was that no questions were asked as to his religious connections: they took him 'merely because he was the most eminent Semitic scholar that could be obtained'" (William H. Whitsitt to Florence Wallace, March 9, 1881, in *Mirror*, 284). In his next correspondence, he indicated that Toy's position "is entirely secure. ...the men at Harvard seeming to make a merit out of the circumstances that they are free enough to employ a theological teacher of another communion merely on the score of superior scholarship" (Whitsitt to Wallace, March 14, 1881, in *Mirror*, 285).
[126] Crawford H. Toy to John A. Broadus, June 8, 1880, John A. Broadus Papers, Box 9, ASC, SBTS. Apparently, Broadus had informed Toy of his recommendation. He communicated the same point to Lyon in a letter written from New Jersey and dated August 3, 1880: "I hope to see Toy before the week closes. You know he has been appointed Professor of Hebrew and other Shemitic Languages at Harvard. I had the great satisfaction of laying myself out on a letter to the appointers. I am persuaded he will do great things there for Shemitic Philology" (cited by Lyon, "Toy," 14).

Hancock Professor of Hebrew and Other Oriental Languages & Dexter Lecturer of Biblical Literature."[127] Toy held the Hancock chair until his retirement in 1909.[128]

How did Toy's appointment fit with President Eliot's vision for the Harvard Divinity School? In an address reflecting on his forty-year presidency (1869–1909), Eliot remarked about the need for "the development of the Harvard Divinity School from a local School, undenominational in principle but in fact supported and used by Unitarians, into a broad School of Scientific Theology and independent research."[129] Eliot was committed to creating a "model research university at Harvard" and saw the divinity school as having a crucial part in fulfilling those aspirations. At the time of Eliot's appointment, the divinity school had four professors—Convers Francis, George Rapall Noyes (who held the Hancock/Dexter professorship), Frederick Henry Hedge, and George E. Ellis. Eliot wasted little time in appointing Charles Carroll Everett (1869 and dean in 1878) and Ezra Abbot as a lecturer in New Testament (1871) and later as the Bussey Professor of New Testament Criticism and Interpretation (1874).

Toy's appointment was part of a second wave of professors recruited by Eliot and appointed to the faculty by the Board of Overseers. In 1881, Francis

---

[127] "Minutes from June 30th Meeting," *Overseer's Records*, Volume XI, 1871–1882, UAII.5.2, HUA.

[128] *Harvard University: Quinquennial Catalogue of the Officers and Graduates (1636–1930)* (Cambridge, MA: Harvard University Press, 1930), 23. The Hancock Chair was established in 1764 by the will of Thomas Hancock. The chair was first held by Stephen Sewell (1764–1785). Subsequent chair holders were Elophalet Pearson (1786–1806), Sidney Willard (1807–1831), George Rapall Noyes (1840–1868), and Edward James Young (1868–1880). In 1840, the Dexter Lectureship on Biblical Literature was united with the Hancock Chair. The Dexter Lectureship on Biblical Criticism was established in 1811 with the will of Samuel Dexter. The title was changed to the Dexter Professorship of Sacred Literature in 1819 and then to the Dexter Lectureship on Biblical Literature in 1840. According to the *Overseer's Minutes*, Toy was elected to both posts. He would relinquish the Dexter Lectureship in 1903–1904, when it was joined with the Bussey Professorship of New Testament Criticism and Interpretation and assigned to James Hardy Ropes. Before the Dexter Lectureship was united with the Hancock Chair, its holders were Joseph Stevens Buckminster (1811–1812), William Ellery Channing (1812–1813), Andrews Norton (1813–1830), and John Gorham Palfrey (1830–1839).

[129] Charles W. Eliot, Addresses, 1916, 43; cited by George H. Williams, ed. *The Harvard Divinity School: Its Place in Harvard University and in American Culture* (Boston: Beacon, 1954), 168.

G. Peabody filled the Parkman Chair.[130] In 1882, Ephraim Emerton was appointed to a newly formed Chair of Winn Professor of Ecclesiastical History,[131] and Toy's former student at Southern, David Gordon Lyon, was appointed to the Hollis Professorship of Divinity.[132] James Henry Thayer was appointed in 1883 and succeeded Abbot as Bussey Professor of New Testament Criticism and Interpretation in 1884.[133] These six professors—Everett, Toy, Peabody, Emerton, Lyon, and Thayer—would form the nucleus of the Harvard Divinity faculty until the end of the century.[134]

George Williams has summarized what Eliot was trying to accomplish with three adjectives: "unsectarian," "scientific," and "broad."[135] In 1879, even before his election to the faculty, Francis G. Peabody had argued before the Board of Overseers that the divinity school should be an "Unsectarian School," like those known in Germany (where Peabody himself had studied): the "fundamental objects of instruction" were properly "sound methods, broad knowledge, and quickened interest."[136] In this regard, Peabody's words echoed those by Eliot in his fundraising appeal also in 1879.[137] By "scientific," Eliot and the Harvard faculty meant a method that "called for objectivity in viewing the material to be treated. Nothing was to be considered so 'sacred' that it

---

[130] Peabody had been appointed as lecturer in ethics and homiletics in 1880 before being named to the Parkman Professorship Chair in 1881; cf. Williams, *The Harvard Divinity School*, 166. On Peabody's role in the development of social ethics on the landscape of nineteenth century American theological education, see Dorrien, *Social Ethics in the Making*, 15–20.

[131] According to Williams, *The "Augustan Age,"* 125, footnote 9. Eliot first tried to hire Adolf von Harnack for the Winn Professorship, but von Harnack chose to go to Berlin; see also Ropes, "Theological Education at Harvard," 251.

[132] On Lyon, see chapter 7.

[133] See Williams, *The Harvard Divinity School*, 147, 167.

[134] Williams, *The Harvard Divinity School*, 167. Williams notes that all the professors except Thayer had studied in Germany (167, footnote 6).

[135] Williams, *The Harvard Divinity School*, 168.

[136] *Reports of the Committees of the Board of Overseers*, 1878–1879, 20–27; cited by Williams, *The Harvard Divinity School*, 168. As one example of Peabody's commitments to "unsectarian" education, Williams cites Peabody's successful efforts, as Plummer Professor of Christian Morals, to move Harvard to become one of the first colleges to "adopt a system of voluntary religious exercises in place of compulsory chapel" (*The Harvard Divinity School*, 169).

[137] Gary Dorrien has noted, "Years later Peabody took pride by setting the Divinity School free from monolithic Unitarian influence. Formally at least, Harvard opted for university theology which he called 'the highest Unitarianism'" (*Social Ethics in the Making*, 16). Dorrien notes that the appointment of Toy (among others) was part of this new stance for "objective theological scholarship" (ibid.).

could not be required to undergo impartial scrutiny."[138] The "broad" aspect of Eliot's vision took shape in terms of the elective system, in which students could choose their courses from a variety of options rather than following a rigid, prescribed course of study. The elective system took root in the divinity school in the 1880s, and Toy, with help from his colleagues over the next decade, expanded the language offerings in the divinity school and at the university.[139]

It was in the context of Eliot's effort to fulfill this vision of an unsectarian, scientific, and broad divinity school with strategic faculty appointments and curriculum revision that Crawford Howell Toy accepted the invitation to join the faculty of Harvard University as the Hancock Professor of Oriental and Other Semitic Languages and Dexter Lecturer of Biblical Languages.[140] Toy arrived in Cambridge, Massachusetts, in September 1880. He wrote to his protégé, David Lyon, on September 30: "I begin work tomorrow under fairly favorable circumstances."[141] On October 1, 1880, Crawford Howell Toy entered a strange, new world.

---

[138] Williams, *The Harvard Divinity School*, 169. Williams cites Francis G. Peabody, "Voluntary Worship, 1886–1929," *The Development of Harvard University Since the Inauguration of President Eliot: 1869–1929*, ed. Samuel Eliot Morison (Cambridge: Harvard University Press, 1930), li–lviii.

[139] Williams, *The Harvard Divinity School*, 172–76.

[140] George H. Williams has produced the magisterial history of the Harvard Divinity School in three volumes. For the period of Eliot and Toy discussed above, see *Divinings: Religion at Harvard from Its Origins in New England Ecclesiastical History to the 175th Anniversary of the Harvard Divinity School, 1636–1992*, vol. 2 of *The "Augustan Age": Religion in the University, the Foundations of a Learned Ministry and the Development of the Divinity School*, ed. Rodney L. Peterson (Göttingen: Vandenhoeck & Ruprecht; Newton, MA: The Boston Theological Institute, 2014).

[141] Letter from Crawford H. Toy to David G. Lyon, September 30, 1880; cited in Lyon, "Toy," 13–14.

PART 2: HARVARD UNIVERSITY:
THE NEGLECTED DECADES (1880–1919)

Fig. 2

Crawford Howell Toy.

Andover-Harvard Theological Library, Harvard Divinity School, Harvard University

5

Teaching and Scholarship

At the opening ceremony of the Semitic Museum, Harvard President Charles Eliot lauded the efforts of Professors Crawford Toy and David Lyon:

> It is only ten years since Professor Toy began to develop here the study of the classical Aramaic and of Arabic, in addition to the Hebrew, and of the political, social and religious history of Israel.... Within a few years of the coming of these two scholars to the University, the range of instruction was greatly increased, and the number of students as well.... The growth of the department has, therefore, been extraordinary.[1]

TEACHING

Crawford Toy was involved in a number of teaching endeavors at Harvard. In this section, we consider his impact on the Harvard curriculum in Semitic studies, his participation in Harvard's Summer School of Theology, and the style and specific content of his teaching, and his published scholarship.

The Harvard Curriculum in Semitic Studies

Eliot described the growth of Semitic studies at Harvard during Toy's tenure as "extraordinary," and this seems an apt, even understated, portrayal. In the academic year before Crawford Toy joined the Harvard faculty (1879–1880), course offerings in Semitic languages by Hancock Professor Edwin Young were limited to courses in Hebrew language and history at the divinity school: introductory Hebrew (three times a week); Hebrew literature (selected passages from Poets and Prophets) (once a week); Lectures on Old Testament, Antiquities, Chronology, Calendar, and Customs of the Jews (once a

---

[1] "Opening of the Harvard Semitic Museum: Addresses by Pres. Eliot, Prof. Toy, Curator Lyon and Mr. Jacob H. Schiff," *The American Hebrew* (May 13, 1892): 67–70; here 67, Records of the President of Harvard University, Charles William Eliot UIA 5.150, Box 217, HUA. Williams, *The "Augustan Age,"* 139–40, noted that "Eliot's two Southern Baptist appointees to the Divinity Faculty, Crawford H. Toy and David Gordon Lyon, were most directly responsible for the development of ancient and particularly Near Eastern comparative studies in Scripture and religion."

week); and Hebrew readings (twice a week).[2] According to Eliot, there were a combined total of twenty-four students in those courses (four undergraduates and twenty from the divinity school), a number that, given a student body of 1,356, Eliot found "exceedingly unsatisfactory."[3]

In his first year (1880–1881), Toy was forced to teach the curriculum he had inherited from Young, which consisted mostly of Hebrew courses. He added Aramaic the first year and added a course of "evening readings" on Arabic Poets. Indeed, he hit the ground running. After his first full year, Toy reported to Broadus:

> I gave no lectures on Arabic poetry, but only readings, translation of half a dozen poems. They were as well received as expected, & next year I hope to do better. I have to create a public. I have had one pupil in Arabic. In Hebrew I have succeeded in arousing a new interest in the linguistic part of the course. I have not had a fair chance in the other departments, historical and critical. You can imagine that, with six lessons a week for the whole, I have been cramped. For the present I must take things as they are, but my efforts at extension are cordially received and seconded by my colleagues and the President.[4]

The following year he offered a readings course on the book of Job.[5] By the 1885–1886 academic year, with the addition of David Lyon (in 1882), the course offerings had expanded in breathtaking proportions. In that year, Toy and Lyon offered the following classes:

Introductory Hebrew. 3 times a week. (Lyon)

Hebrew (second course)—syntax. Prophets, Poetical Books, Textual criticism. Twice a week. (Toy)

Classical Aramaic (Syriac). Peshitto version of NT. ½ year. (Lyon)

Jewish Aramaic. Targums, Daniel, Ezra. Second half year. (Lyon)

Assyrian. Grammar. (Lyon)

Assyrian. Second course. (Lyon)

---

[2] *Harvard University Courses of Instruction for 1879–80, Divinity School,* 27, HUC 8500.16, Courses of Instruction, Box 1, HUA. The introductory course was also open to undergraduates as "Biblia Hebraica" (*Harvard University, 1879–80, Courses of Instruction in Harvard College,* 3).

[3] Charles W. Eliot to W. Robertson Smith (rough draft), February 23, 1880, HUA 5.150, Box 9, HUA.

[4] Crawford H. Toy to John A. Broadus, June 4, 1881, Broadus Papers, ASC, SBTS.

[5] Lyon, "Toy," 14.

Sumero-Akkadian. Cuneiform Inscriptions of Western Asia. ½ course. (Lyon)

Arabic. Thousand and One Nights. (Toy)

Arabic. Second course. (Toy)

General Semitic Grammar. ½ course. (Toy)[6]

In addition to these courses, a non-credit class known as the "Semitic Seminary" met twice a month. In subsequent years, the name was changed to the "Semitic Conference," and a purpose statement was provided in the course catalogue:

> This conference, which is composed of instructors and students in the Division of Semitic studies, meets twice a month throughout the academic year. Its object is a more detailed discussion of special topics than is ordinarily possible in the class-room. At each meeting a paper is read, which is expected to give the results of independent investigation in the subject presented.[7]

By 1885, not only had the profile and interests of students populating the Semitic Department shifted, but the numbers were also improving. Toy observed in a letter to Broadus in fall 1885:

> The classes are in general larger than they have ever been before, and what is noteworthy, the majority of the Semitic students are not members of theological schools, but college students. In Arabic, I depend almost exclusively on college men, and I have some now studying who are studying the poetry simply for literary ends. With these men I pay comparatively little attention to the details of grammar, but read as much as I can. So Lyon's Assyrian men have most of them undertaken the study

---

[6] *Harvard University 1885–86, Courses of Instruction in Harvard College*, 2nd edition, (Harvard University Press, June 1885), HUC 8500.16, Courses of Instruction, Box 1, HUA.

[7] *Harvard University, Courses of Instruction in Harvard College* (1897–98), 9, HUC 8500.16, Courses of Instruction, Box 1, HUA. Toy was primarily responsible for the Semitic Conference (see Lyon, "Toy," 17–18), and for a few years, the year's topic was published (and often coordinated with Toy's or Lyon's current research interests): The Names of Semitic Deities (1897–1898); Recent Explorations and Discoveries in Semitic Lands (1898–1899); The Early Narratives in Genesis (1899–1900); Survivals in the Old Testament of Early Ideas (ancestor-worship, totemism, etc.) (1900–1901); First Book of Kings (1901–1902); Relations between Egypt and Canaan (1902–1903). No topics for the Semitic Conference are listed after the 1902–1903 academic year.

for scientific purposes.[8]

In the next year, 1886–1887, Babylonian-Assyrian History (1/2 course; Lyon) and Ethiopic (Toy) were rotated into the course offerings (omitting third-year Assyrian and General Semitic Grammar).[9] By the time Eliot gave his remarks in 1892, he could quantify the success of the program: "I find that last year [1890–1891] there were 69 choices of the eleven courses given in the Semitic Department, and that these students came from the Divinity School, the Graduate School and from all classes in the Colleges, except the Freshman. For the current year [1891–1892] there are 65 students divided among twelve courses, and again they come from the Divinity School, and the Graduate School, and from all classes of the College."[10]

By 1899, David Lyon could assert:

Although a certain amount of instruction in Semitic subjects has been offered in Harvard College from the foundation of the institution, the development of a Semitic Department in the University began in 1880. Since that time new courses have been gradually added until *to-day a student may pursue here nearly all the subjects taught in the best European universities.* Six languages are represented, and there are historical courses related to the Hebrews, the Arabians, and the Assyrians. The

---

[8] Crawford H. Toy to John A. Broadus, October 10, 1885, Broadus Papers, ASC, SBTS. Toy also commented on his classes at the divinity school: "In the Divinity School my work has also begun under favorable auspice. My class in the history of Israel (English) is much larger than it has ever been before, and the men seem to be all of good type. The material of my class in the religion of Israel is also particularly good, and the work there is interesting as any that I have."

[9] *Harvard University 1886–87. Courses of Instruction in Harvard College*, 2nd edition (Harvard University Press, June 1886), HUC 8500.16, Courses of Instruction, Box 1, HUA. In 1896–1897, Toy introduced a course on the Talmud.

[10] "Opening of the Harvard Semitic Museum: Addresses by Pres. Eliot, Prof. Toy, Curator Lyon, and Mr. Jacob H. Schiff," 67, UAI 5.250, Box 217, Folder 47.2, Records of the President of Harvard University, Charles William Eliot. Despite lavishing praise on the numerical success of the Semitic Department, Eliot did, at least twice, raise questions about the number of courses offered, first out of concern for Lyon's teaching load in particular. Even President Eliot took note of Lyon's ambitious teaching schedule. After reviewing the proposed curriculum for the Semitic Department for 1885–1886, Eliot wrote Lyon, "Have you not proposed too much work for yourself next year? Eleven hours divided into seven courses makes a hard year's work. Might not one or more of these courses be bracketed for next year?" (Charles W. Eliot to David Lyon, April 28, 1885, HUG 1541, Papers of David Gordon Lyon, Box 12, HUA). The other instance regarding the number of offered classes had to do with the financial situation of the university.

Hebrew historical courses treat the political and social history, the literature, and the religion.[11]

Eventually, other lecturers, part-time and full-time, would be added to enrich and enhance the curriculum in Semitic languages and history. Most notably, the eminent scholar, George Foot Moore, left Andover Theological Seminary and joined the Harvard Faculty in 1903. According to George H. Williams, Moore "was roughly the counterpart, for Hellenistic Jewish studies, of David Gordon Lyon—with the latter's second tenure, as seventh Hancock Professor—in primordial Semitic languages and biblical Hebrew with the pan-Semitic vision of an Assyriologist, while Moore was a pioneer Christian scholar of the Judaism of the first two centuries of the Christian era."[12] Moore added several new courses to the curriculum in his first years such as History of Jewish Literature from the earliest Times to 200 A.D; Old Testament: Principles and Practice of Criticism; Phoenician and Aramaic Inscriptions.[13]

Toy himself over the years would offer a range of courses that were taken by college, divinity, and doctoral students. These included Arabic, Ethiopic, the Talmud, general Semitic grammar, the history of Israel, the religion of Israel, Old Testament quotations in the New Testament, Old Testament introduction, Pentateuchal criticism, Chronicles, the formation of Genesis, the Spanish califate, and the Bagdad califate.[14] By the time Crawford Toy retired in 1909, the Semitic Division at Harvard University had established itself as one of the world's leading seats of study of Ancient Near Eastern languages and cultures.[15]

---

[11] "A Semitic Building for Harvard University" flyer, D. G. Lyon, Curator of the Semitic Museum (Cambridge, MA, June 15, 1899), Records of the President of Harvard University, Charles William Eliot, UAI 5.150, Box 52, HUA (emphasis added).

[12] Williams, The "Augustan Age," 177.

[13] Harvard University. Courses of Instruction in Harvard College (1905–1906; 1906–1907), HUC 8500.16, Courses of Instruction, Box 2, HUA.

[14] Lyon, "Toy," 15.

[15] Today, Harvard's Department of Near Eastern Languages and Civilizations consists of fourteen professors, four associate professors, six lecturers, and nine preceptors. In the brief history on its website, the department traces its roots back to Crawford Toy:

> The Department of Near Eastern Languages and Civilizations (NELC) has a rich and long history at Harvard. The Division of Semitic Languages, created in 1880, was precursor to NELC. Professor Crawford H. Toy taught courses that greatly expanded the curriculum and increased enrollment. He taught Arabic as well as Hebrew and Aramaic. The division was later renamed the Department of Semitic Languages and History. In 1961, reorganization resulted in the Department of Near Eastern Languages and Civilizations. For over a century,

Summer School of Theology

From 1899–1910, the Harvard Divinity School sponsored a Summer School of Theology that was open to clergy and laity, male and female alike. The faculty was composed of both HDS professors as well as other professors from the Greater Boston area. Crawford Toy participated in most of the sessions. Beginning in 1905, the Summer School of Theology was held in the new Semitic Museum, containing a lecture room that was advertised as "one of the quietest, coolest, pleasantest in the University, thoroughly ventilated, and well shaded."[16] The purpose of the school, according to the prospectus, was "to provide a place where clergymen and divinity students may gather for the study of subjects which have intrinsic and current theological interest, and where they may feel the inspiration which comes from direct contact with the best and most recent results of modern scholarship." Teachers of the Bible, history, and philosophy, as well as teachers in "more advanced classes in Sunday School," were encouraged to attend.[17]

The first session featured lectures on the Old Testament, theology, and church history. The Old Testament lecturers were Toy and Lyon from Harvard, Hinckley Mitchell from Boston University, and George F. Moore from Andover Theological Seminary. Toy was the featured Old Testament speaker for the first week on the topic "The History of Early Israelitish Institutions," delivering individual lectures on "Offerings and Feasts," "The Priesthood," "Sabbath and Circumcision," and "Relation of these Institutions to the Moral Life of the People."

In 1904, Toy spoke on "The Development of Monotheism." His first lecture (indicative of the then current evolutionary method of history of reli-

---

through name change and reorganization, the department has resided at the Semitic Museum. (https://nelc.fas.harvard.edu/academics)

Today the NELC

encompasses the study of ancient and modern peoples, languages, literatures, cultures, and societies of the Near and Middle East. Languages include Akkadian, Arabic, Aramaic, Armenian, Babylonian, Egyptian, Hebrew, Persian, Sumerian, Turkish and Yiddish. NELC has three general fields of study for graduate students (A.M. and Ph.D.) and has four tracks for undergraduate concentrators. Currently, the department enrolls 60 graduate students and 17 undergraduate concentrators. (https://nelc.fas.harvard.edu/academics)

[16] *Divinity School of Harvard University. Summer School of Theology. Seventh Session: The Bible. July 5–21, 1905* (Cambridge: Harvard University Press, February 10, 1905), 12.

[17] *Divinity School of Harvard University. Summer School of Theology. First Session. July 5–21, 1899* (Cambridge: Harvard University Press, 1899), 3.

gions) was titled "Theory of a primitive revelation. Supposed traces of mono-theistic belief among savages." In subsequent lectures he traced the "general lines of movement toward monotheism" in Egypt, China, and Japan (lecture 2); Brahmanism, Buddhism, Bábism (3); Greece (4); Rome (5); Persia (6); Babylonia, Arabia, the Hebrews (7); Christianity and Islam (8); and finally ended with "Religious value of the monotheistic idea. Modern doubts" (9).[18] The following year's prospectus reprinted testimonials from students who had attended the previous year's summer school. One minister wrote that Toy's lectures on monotheism "made us realize that in other religions, even the most polytheistic, there were some who reached out toward a Supreme Being, and that the 'unitary conception' was widespread, though the Hebrews alone made it a part of the life of the world."[19] In 1905, the general theme was "The Bible," and Toy offered a week of lectures on "The Old Testament Prophetic Thought."[20] The next summer school saw as its theme "Christian Theology in its Origin and Development," and Toy lectured on the "Scriptural Basis of Christian Beliefs." The abstract of Toy's lectures offered this description: "After describing briefly the development, in Old Testament and Apocrypha, of Old-Hebrew and Jewish theistic, soteriological, ecclesiastical, and eschatological ideas, the course will consider the religious situation in the world in which Christianity arose, the point of view of Jesus of Nazareth, and the subsequent New Testament conceptions of God, of the Christ, of salvation, and of the future."[21]

The 1908 Summer School of Theology was on a topic, "The Relation of Christianity to Other Religions," that had proven to be of great interest to Crawford Toy in his later years at Harvard. Toy's lecture topic was "The Origin and Development of Religion" with individual lectures on "The Historical Beginnings," "The Higher Social Organization," "The Scientific

---

[18] *Divinity School of Harvard University. Summer School of Theology. Sixth Session. July 5–21, 1904* (Cambridge: Harvard University Press, March 30, 1904).

[19] "Letter from Rev. Edwin H. Byington in the *Congregationalist and Christian World*. Boston, August 6, 1904," in *Summer School of Theology. Sixth Session*, 6.

[20] *Divinity School of Harvard University. Summer School of Theology. Seventh Session. 1905* (Cambridge: Harvard University Press, February 10, 1905). With the publication of this prospectus, the format changed, and individual lecture topics were no longer listed. In addition, beginning in 1901, general themes were chosen (the first two years had advertised lectures on disciplines)—1901: The Relation of Minsters to Social Questions; 1902: Current Problems in Theology; 1903: Principles of Education in the Work of the Church; 1904: Contributions to Historical Theology.

[21] *Divinity School of Harvard University. Summer School of Theology. Eighth Session. July 5–21, 1906. Subject: Christian Theology in its Origin and Development* (Cambridge: Harvard University Press, February 21, 1906).

Movement," "The Ethical Movement," and "Spirituality and Unity."[22] In 1909, the eleventh of the divinity school's summer sessions focused on "Present Religious Conditions and Prospects." Toy gave two lectures on "General Causes of Variation in Religious Interest,"[23] but the highlight of the summer school was the final address of the session given by President Eliot, who had retired the previous May, having served as Harvard president for forty years. His speech titled "The Religion of the Future" that was to be reprinted several times and translated into French, was considered "in many ways the magisterial summary of the evolving concept of a religion of the humanely educated of the North Atlantic community, just five years before the outbreak of World War I and just eight years before the Russian Revolution."[24] Eliot begins by tracing what the "religion of the future" would *not* be and then presents what he calls the "positive elements" of the "new religion." This remarkable essay reflects the peak of nineteenth-century progressive, liberal Protestantism. Eliot ends with these words of "prophecy":

> This twentieth-century religion is not only to be in harmony with the great secular movements of modern society—democracy, individualism, social idealism, the zeal for education, the spirit of research, the modern tendency to welcome the new, the fresh powers of preventive medicine, and the recent advances in business and industrial ethics—but also in essential agreement with the direct, personal teachings of Jesus, as they are reported in the Gospels. The revelation he gave to mankind thus becomes more wonderful than ever.[25]

This iteration of the summer school ended in 1910 with a theme on "The

---

[22] *Announcement of the Summer School of Theology. Tenth Session. July 1–18, 1908. Subject: The Relation of Christianity to Other Religions* (Cambridge: Harvard University Press, 1908), 10.

[23] *Announcement of the Summer School of Theology. Eleventh Session. July 7–22, 1909. Subject: Present Religious Conditions and Prospects* (Cambridge: Harvard University, 1909), 9.

[24] Williams, *The "Augustan Age,"* 188–89. The essay was first published as "The Religion of the Future," *Harvard Theological Review* 2 (October 1909): 389–407.

[25] Eliot, "The Religion of the Future," 407. Eliot's prediction, *inter alia*, that the "new religion" will be anti-authoritarian rings hollow to modern ears, since Eliot could not imagine the resilience and pervasiveness of fundamentalism—Christian, Islamic, and otherwise—in the late twentieth and early twenty-first century (one may say that his hope in secularism rings hollow as well with the moral failure of modern "secular" societies in the twentieth century: e.g., USSR, Germany, Italy, Poland, USA, etc.). See *The Fundamentalist Project,* a multivolume series edited by Martin Marty and Scott Appleby (Chicago: University of Chicago Press, 1994–2004).

Parish Minister."[26] Judging strictly by its overall numbers, the Harvard Summer School of Theology would seem to have been deemed a success. Below are the statistics for attendance for 1899–1910:

Year	Total Registered Attendance	Registered Females
1899	105	9
1900	54	2
1901	89	5
1902	78	4
1903	58	4
1904	47	1
1905	61	7
1906	68	9
1907	103	11
1908	66	5
1909	64	5
1910	36	2
Total	829	64

In terms of denominational distribution over the twelve-year period, it is interesting to note that the largest group of clergy came from orthodox Congregationalists (197), followed by Episcopalians (154), unitarian Congregationalists (93), universalists (72), Methodists (70), and Baptists (48). Twelve other denominations were represented by thirty or fewer clergy, some having a single attendee.[27] Over the years, attendees came from at least thirty-five

---

[26] No reason for its cancellation was made public. *The Divinity School of Harvard Catalogue of 1911–1912* simply reported, "No Summer School will be held this year. This does not necessarily mean that the School has been permanently discontinued but only that, in the circumstances, it has been deemed unadvisable to hold a session in the summer of 1911" (Cambridge, MA: Harvard University Press, 1912, 31). The reason for the school's termination may lie in a combination of the last year's significant drop in attendance and the change to a new administration under President Lowell that was generally less supportive of the divinity school. The Harvard Summer School of Theology would be revived in 1920 with the support of the Unitarian Laymen's League, which paid the full tuition and one-half travel and living expenses for Unitarian minsters in attendance.

[27] *Divinity School Catalogue 1911–12*, 30. The statistics represent attendees for each year and do not account for repeat attendees, of which presumably there would have been a significant number. Also, the published numbers suggest that 729 of 829 attendees were clergy, meaning that 100 were laypersons. Since 64 women attended (and were presumably not ordained), that would mean some 36 laymen were in attendance (again, the numbers do not account for repeat attendees).

states, the District of Columbia, British West Indies, Japan, Nova Scotia, Ontario, and Quebec.[28]

It may appear from this survey of Toy's participation in the Harvard curriculum, whether of the college or divinity school, that his interests were narrow and focused. It is true, of course, that he was a specialist in philology, languages, and ancient cultures. But Toy also had a clear sense of the overall mission and purpose of higher education. In a remarkable lecture, "Ethical Influences in University Life," delivered at President Eliot's invitation to the Harvard Graduate School of Arts and Sciences on October 5, 1905, Toy laid out his understanding of the intellectual and moral dimensions of the university as well as the ethical significance of the inter-relatedness of disciplines.[29]

> Knowledge of the work of our fellows has a definite ethical value. The intention of the university…is to cover the whole field of human knowledge—nothing that pertains to intellectual life is alien to it—and he who imbibes its spirit will not turn his back on any field of thought. The intimate relation existing between all branches of knowledge and the constant association among the various specialists tend naturally to enlarge the view, to broaden sympathy and to quicken insight. In the march of learning the philosopher moves shoulder to shoulder with the biologist, the historian and the economist with the mathematician, the student of art with the student of language—every one with every other.[30]

Teaching Style

There are fewer testimonials about Crawford Toy's teaching style at Harvard than at Southern. That is partially due to the fact that "from the nature of his material his class room attracted thoughtful and earnest students, but never considerable numbers."[31] What is available confirms his previous reputation as a reflective and effective teacher. His colleague, George Foot Moore, wrote that Toy

---

[28] Combining the statistics in the *Divinity School Catalogue 1911–12*, 31, with the *Summer School of Theology. Seventh Session. 1905,* Table 3.

[29] The address was published as Crawford H. Toy, "Ethical Influences in University Life," *International Journal of Ethics* 16 (1906): 145–57.

[30] Toy, "Ethical Influences in University Life," 156.

[31] Lyon, "Toy," 15. His colleague, G. F. Moore, also commented on the quality of Toy's students at Harvard: "though, from the nature of the subjects taught, most of his courses had but a slender attendance, he attracted some of the best students in the college, among them men whose special interests lay in other fields" (Moore, "Toy," 6).

was an admirable teacher, exact in his own knowledge of the matter, orderly in its disposition, lucid in exposition, patient with stupidity and even with opinionatedness, taking a warm personal interest in his pupils and an encouraging estimate of their abilities and possibilities, and setting them a high example of love and learning and single-minded pursuit of truth, whithersoever the quest might lead. His character and the spirit and method of his instruction were themselves an education in the true aims and temper of scholarship.[32]

His colleague and former student David Lyon also elaborated further about Toy's teaching style:

His instruction was characterized by fulness and accuracy of learning, orderly arrangement, comprehensiveness and lucidity of statement. His aim was always, however, less to impart knowledge than to quicken the mind of his pupils, to indicate sources and methods, to guide into the ways of research and productivity.

As lecturer Dr. Toy's utterance was measured and easy, always compact with thought, always choice in expression. He inclined to the conversational style, and encouraged the asking of questions. His manner towards students was deferential and considerate, almost paternal. He never put one of them to shame by irony or rebuke, however strong the temptation may have been. The urbanity of the well-bred gentleman never forsook him. Such considerateness he manifested indeed towards all men, especially to such as were in need. What endless hours he gave to those who submitted their manuscripts to him for criticism![33]

These accolades praising Toy's classroom teaching style are hardly surprising. After all, this is the same person who as a sixteen-year-old first-year student at the University of Virginia complained about time wasted in class:

I am entirely opposed to this mode of teaching by lectures, the copying off occupies more time than would be sufficient to learn double the quantity of matter. It took me today about an hour and a half to write one of Courtenay's Syllabi; which I could have learnt in fifteen minutes. Why not teach by text-books, and if there is any remark omitted in the text-books, let the professor make it and the students take it down. If you take up four or five hours every day in merely copying down lectures which you are to study afterwards, where is the time to study?[34]

---

[32] Moore, "Toy," 6.
[33] Lyon, "Toy," 15.
[34] Crawford H. Toy to Morton Howell, October 11, 1852, ASC, SBTS.

Teaching Substance

While we have little direct evidence of Toy's pedagogical style, there do exist student notebooks that preserve the content from Toy's classroom lectures. Toy's lectures on the history of the religion of Israel and lectures on the Old Testament (1888–1890) as taken by Earl Morse Wilbur and on the History of Hebrew Literature by Raymond Calkins (1895–1896) provide a glimpse into Toy's approach to various topics associated with the Old Testament.[35] Occasional comparison with SBTS student notes will further highlight the distinctives of Toy's Harvard classes.

Earl Morse Wilbur became a well-known Unitarian educator and historian. He would serve as dean and president of the Pacific Unitarian School for Ministry in Berkeley and author a two-volume history of Unitarianism.[36] In 1888–1889 and again in 1889–1890, Wilber was a student in Toy's Old Testament Introduction. One of the first points of interest is that while he did not ignore questions of the relationship between Genesis and science, Toy spent much more time exploring the compositional issues surrounding Genesis and the rest of the Pentateuch. For example, in his lecture on Genesis 2–3, Toy disaggregates among various strands of tradition, identifying J (Yahwist), E (Elohist), JE (an editor who combined J + E), D (Deuteronomistic editor), P (Priestly writer), and R (the final redactor).[37] With regard to the overall redaction of the Hexateuch, Toy posited two layers, one priestly and one prophetic. Wilbur recorded, "The *priestly* has elaborations of ritual, a quiet settled monotheism and uses the name Elohim.... It includes such passages as Gen 1, 5, 17, Exodus 12, 20:1–17, chs 25–31, 36–40, through most of Leviticus and most of Numbers." The prophetic, on the other hand, "has different strata, one using Elohim, the other Jahweh....[and has a] freshness and

---

[35] Earle Morse Wilbur's "Lectures on Old Testament Introduction, by Crawford Howell Toy, 1888–89," Wilbur, Earl Morse, Notebooks, AHTL HDS, bMS 466, Box 1. The notebook contains approximately 275 pages of notes on the first and second years of Toy's Old Testament Introduction. Raymond Calkin's "Lectures on the History of Hebrew Literature by Professor Toy," AHTL HDS, notebook contains roughly 200 pages of extensive coverage of Hebrew literature, especially the Pentateuch. Toy appears to have adopted a hybrid canonical and chronological approach to his lectures, with questions of composition appearing prominent. We will, at points, compare these Harvard lectures with Holt's lectures from SBTS (see chapter 3).

[36] Alan Seaburg, "Earl Morse Wilbur," in *Dictionary of Unitarian and Universalist Biography*, http://uudb.org/articles/earlmorsewilbur.html; cf. Earl Morse Wilbur, *A History of Unitarianism*, 2 vols. (Boston: Beacon Press, 1945).

[37] Wilbur, "Toy Lecture Notes, 1888–89," 13–14.

flexibility of anthropomorphic closeness of ritual."[38] This concern for compositional sources extended beyond Toy's analysis of Genesis. For example, he concluded that the plagues in Exodus represented a late tradition. Toy argued that the final editor combined plague and sign traditions from JE and P, noting tensions and discontinuities that remain in the text.[39]

Toy also placed stories within an imagined cultural and historical context. For example, regarding the story of Cain in Genesis 4, Wilbur recorded Toy as saying: "Ch. 4 is a Jehovistic story coming from Jahwistic circle. The fact that Cain was let go and not killed indicates that the story was likely written at the time when the law of blood revenge—that the murderer should be killed by the nearest relatives of the murdered—was giving way…. Exactly *when* this was written, we cannot say."[40] Similarly, regarding the detail that Canaan is cursed for Ham's sin (Gen 9:18–24), Toy noted that the "origin of it is to be probably referred to time when Israel was struggling in Canaan or had just conquered them."[41]

Toy was also sure to "remove" Christianized interpretations from the students' purview. For example, regarding Genesis 11:7 ("let us go down and confuse their language"), Toy asserted that the plural ("let us") was not "to indicate the Trinity nor is it 'plural of majesty,' but probably refers to the angels or a polytheistic conception."[42]

Toy also suggested that the Hebrews possessed "mythical materials" when they entered Canaan that included many of the stories found in Genesis 1–10 (and beyond) and that were similar to ones found in Assyrian and Babylonian literature (seraphim and cherubim, Gen 3:19, 24; intermarriage of the "sons of God," Gen 6:2; Jahweh riding a storm-chariot, Ps 18:10; Rahab-Leviathan serpents, Isa 29:1, 30:4; Job 3:8, 9:13; anti-godly star-spirits, Isa 24:21–23). This mythic material, however, did not include mythical poems, such as the Iliad (or if it did, they are now lost).[43]

In 1895–1896, Raymond Calkins, later minister of the First Congrega-

---

[38] Wilbur, "Toy Lecture Notes, 1889–90," 36.

[39] Wilbur, "Toy Lecture Notes, 1888–89," 58–59. In all, Wilbur took four pages of notes on the compositional history of the Exodus plagues.

[40] Wilbur, "Toy Lecture Notes, 1888–89," 15.

[41] Wilbur, 19.

[42] Wilbur, 23.

[43] Wilbur, "Toy Lecture Notes, 1889–90," 20.

tional Church in Cambridge, took a course with Toy on the "History of Hebrew Literature."[44] Perhaps, given the nature of the course, Toy spent much more time summarizing pertinent secondary literature on the topic; most of the first class period was spent on a bibliographic overview.[45] Again, Toy mentioned the tension between science and the Genesis account, but he was much more interested in the tradition history of the materials. He also expanded on his interpretation of the "let us" reference in Genesis 11:7:[46]

> What does *Let us* infer? a) This is the plural of majesty. The royal we. But this is a usage elsewhere unknown in the OT. b) The plural is merely grammatical conformity since *Elohim* is a plural word. But before had God *said*, the verb is singular. c) The only [workable] explanation: It supposes a council on the [?] the divine Being. cf. Genesis 11:7. Is this council of *the angels*? This would not do, for angels are messengers, not counsellors. This expression is the survival of the old [idea] when Jahweh was surrounded with other deities with whom he would take counsel. See Job 1 where the sons of the Elohim appear before Jahweh and Satan based on agreement with Jahweh who prevails him to do as he pleases.... This is *a very old* conception. Jeremiah could not have said that, nor Ezra.[47]

Toy then discussed the "image of God" and argued that the phrase referred to the bodily form of God: "This was the universal belief of antiquity that God was in man's form."[48] Throughout this section of lecture notes, Toy drew repeatedly on parallels between the Genesis accounts and other (mostly) Babylonian stories.

Toy's interpretation of Isaiah, especially the servant songs, was one of the points of contention in the debates of 1879. Toy continued to find that Isaianic passages traditionally interpreted by Christians as messianic usually referred to people or groups in the preexilic or exilic periods. In the notes to his 1874–1875 class at SBTS, Toy had affirmed that while the servant songs had as their primary referent an individual or group, the passage "typically" also referred to Christ. The passage is "fulfilled in one case by Israel but more

---

[44] Calkins would deliver the Lyman Beecher Lecture at Yale in 1926. His sister, Mary Calkins, studied with William James at Harvard but was denied the doctorate degree because she was a woman. She taught at Wellesley College and was the first female to serve as president of the American Psychological Association.

[45] Calkins, "History of Hebrew Literature," September 30, 1895, 1–2.

[46] Or perhaps Calkins just took better notes! Here Toy seems to confirm his opinion regarding the "majestic plural" interpretation.

[47] Calkins, "History of Hebrew Literature," 10–11.

[48] Calkins, 11.

so in Christ."[49] In his lectures at Harvard, Toy presented the case for the suffering servant to be either corporate Israel or an individual "ideal Israelite" without taking a stance.[50] He explored the notion of the servant as a vicarious sufferer, but he no longer dealt with a possible christological reading, rather pointing out that the term "messiah" is not used in the context.[51]

In general, Toy gave much more attention to critical issues of compositional history and parallels with comparative, contemporary literature in his Harvard lectures than he did in his lectures at Southern, in which he attended more to theological issues (often in a corrective vein) that would be of interest to Christian readers. In part, this shift reflected Toy's change in institutional settings. A number of his students were college undergraduates and not divinity students, and those who were divinity students represented an ever-widening span of theological traditions. Equally, if not more, important was the shift in Toy's own interests. His participation in the Harvard History of Religions Club (which he founded in 1891) encouraged and expanded his interest in placing his expertise in the history of Hebrew religion within the emerging comparative study of the religions of antiquity. These shifting interests would also eventually present themselves in his published, scholarly works.

SCHOLARSHIP[52]

Apart from working with John Broadus to produce a translation of, and critical notes for, C. F. D. Erdman's Lange commentary on Samuel,[53] most of Crawford Toy's publications during his career at Southern Seminary comprised essays and articles. His published work divided between devotional materials for religious magazines and publications and highly technical articles on various linguistic topics in scholarly journals.[54] The move to Harvard

---

[49] Holt, "SBTS Lectures," 242 [244].

[50] Wilbur, "Toy Lecture Notes, 1888–89," 107.

[51] Wilbur, 107–108.

[52] This section of the chapter was co-written with Nathan Hays, a doctoral student in Old Testament/Hebrew Bible at Baylor University.

[53] Christian Friedrich David Erdmann, *The Books of Samuel*, ed. John Peter Lange, trans. and enlarged by Crawford H. Toy and John A. Broadus (New York: Charles Scribner's Sons, 1877). George Foot Moore was critical of the commentary itself, while praising Toy's work on the project: "Erdman's commentary is an egregiously bad specimen of a bad kind, and made Toy's task peculiarly difficult. …the effort to make a worthless book worth something by a kind of supercommentary must have been a weariness of the flesh and vexation of spirit" (Moore, "Toy," 9).

[54] For a summary and analysis of Toy's publications, both devotional and technical, during the Southern period, see Hurt, "Toy," 238–48. Toy's religious publications often

proved a boon to Toy's productivity as a scholar. What follows is a summary of the contents of Toy's published books, along with a brief survey of the work's scholarly reception and, where applicable, its continuing influence in contemporary scholarly discussions.[55]

The History of the Religion of Israel (1882)[56]

Summary. Toy designed this book for Sunday school teachers of pupils twelve years old and upwards and provides a section of reference books for these teachers to consult and for church libraries to acquire.[57] In about 150 pages and 30 chapters, the book described the growth and development of the religion of Israel, structured chronologically and complete with a brief bibliography and questions at the end of each chapter. Toy narrated the history of the religion of Israel as a progressive development from fetishism through polytheism to monotheism. The Israelite/Jewish religion moved from the formative period (earliest times to about the end of the ninth century BC) to the prophetic (to the exile), to the priestly (from the return to about the first century BC), to the scribal (from then until the eighteenth century AD), to the modern (since then). All religions develop according to some of the same rules, although not all reach the advanced monotheistic stage. At the same time as this development toward monotheism, Israel's religion progressively recognized the holiness of God and sought through laws to produce holy living in Israel. These laws over time became "burdensome and injurious."[58] Jesus showed that "holiness was reached, not by rules, but by the inward disposition

---

included observations based on higher criticism. These kinds of comments, of course, formed part of the basis for resistance to Toy's views (see chapter 3). In addition to technical articles on the Hebrew language (cf. "On Hebrew Verb-Etymology," *Transactions of the American Philological Association* 7 [1877]: 50–72; "On the Nominal Basis of the Hebrew Verb," *Proceedings of the American Philological Association* 8 [1877]: 29–30), Toy also published a learned article on "The Yoruban Language," *Transactions of the American Philological Association* 9 (1878): 19–38. Hurt conjectured that this article "may have some connection with his previous missionary commitment and with his continued interest in the area of missions, an interest he retained as long as he was a part of the Seminary Faculty" ("Toy," 244).

[55] For the sake of space, I do not deal in depth with Toy's published articles. Points of contact between the content and/or method of those articles with the published monograph will be noted. For a summary and analysis of selected articles published during Toy's Harvard career, see Hurt, "Toy," 277–88.

[56] Crawford H. Toy, *The History of the Religion of Israel: An Old Testament Primer* (Boston: Unitarian Sunday School Society, 1882).

[57] Toy, *History of the Religion of Israel*, iii.

[58] Toy, *History of the Religion of Israel*, 149.

of love to God."[59] After Jesus, Judaism has only the semblance of life. Therefore, "Christianity may be called the development of the pure spiritual elements of the faith of Israel."[60]

Reception. Probably owing to the book's popular character, *The History of the Religion of Israel* received little attention in other scholarly works. The two reviews that did appear were negative. Nevertheless, the book ran into at least sixteen editions (in 1910).[61] The anonymous review in *The Hebrew Student* noted that the book is "from the standpoint of the most advanced school of German criticism" and perhaps too advanced for children of twelve years old.[62] The reviewer quoted some passages where Toy casts significant doubt on the historical reliability of the biblical materials. The review then concluded that the adoption of Toy's view would lead people no longer to believe in the inspiration of the Old Testament and away from knowing how to interpret the New Testament.

The review in the *Independent* made similar claims. It found that the work does not show even the traces of Christianity but rather tends toward Jewish Deism and pure rationalism.[63] Toy's outline of the history is quite speculative but given in a dogmatic style. According to this reviewer, the manual ultimately seeks to replace belief in a personal God among children with naturalistic conceptions.[64] In his 1919 tribute to Toy, George F. Moore claims that the work "is a brief and popular presentation of the views of Kuenen and of his popularizers."[65]

Robert Moore-Jumonville, echoing the review of *The Hebrew Student*, pointed to this work as "another example of…unmitigated use of critical methods in the Sunday School class."[66] Moore-Jumonville noted that Toy saw the Sunday school teacher as a specialist, providing a lengthy reading list that included many volumes in German! In an interesting side note to the reception history of this work, Charlotte Perkins Gilman, an important feminist

[59] Ibid.

[60] Toy, *History of the Religion of Israel*, 150.

[61] Apparently, none of the subsequent editions was changed from the first, although the title page does use the term "edition." Toy does not update the preface.

[62] Review of *The History of the Religion of Israel: An Old Testament Primer*, *The Hebrew Student* 2 (1883): 328–29; here 328.

[63] For Baptist reactions to this work, mostly negative even among those generally supportive of Toy, see Wills, *Southern Seminary*, 148.

[64] Review of *The History of the Religion of Israel: An Old Testament Primer*, *The Independent* (January 4, 1883): 35.

[65] Moore, "Toy," 12.

[66] Robert Moore-Jumonville, *The Hermeneutics of Historical Distance: Mapping the Terrain of American Biblical Criticism, 1880–1914* (Lanham, MD: University Press of America, 2002), 152.

thinker best known for her short story "The Yellow Wallpaper," purchased this volume on October 19, 1882. In her diary, she wrote, "Buy Prof. Toy's Manual, 'Hist of Religion of Israel' (.50) and enjoy the Bible class." Gilman was from a Unitarian family but later moved beyond traditional religion, which she perceived as too masculine.[67]

Quotations in the New Testament (1884)[68]

Summary. Toy wrote this book in order to fill the need for a book detailing "a general view of the texts, and a precise comparison of the [New Testament] quotation with its original."[69] Many of the existing treatments of this topic are based "on defective biblical texts and unsound exegesis."[70] Toy notes that people may disagree with him but says that he aims at exactitude, not irreverence.[71] He writes, "I believe that the ethical-religious power of the Bible will be increased by perfectly free, fair-minded dealing, and by a precise knowledge of what it does or does not say." Toy avers that the prevalent belief of "the mechanical infallibility of the Bible" is attenuating the Bible's influence.[72]

After an introduction that summarized the different versions and gave a general overview of types of quotations and formulas of quotation, the rest of the book was arranged in canonical order of the New Testament, covering each quotation in turn. Toy translated the Hebrew, the relevant versions, and the New Testament text. He then discussed the quotation, comparing the Old Testament and New Testament contexts and also discussing any text-critical issues. He found that the New Testament writers generally quote from the Septuagint but at times depart from the Greek and follow an oral Aramaic translation. They never show direct contact with the Hebrew.

Reception. Toy's book appears frequently in New Testament scholarship from the time of its publication through the first half of the twentieth century, indicating that it was considered a standard reference work for Old Testament quotations. Indeed, in a review in *The Critic* of Toy's later *Judaism and Christianity*, the author of the review states that *Quotations in the New Testament* "is the standard work on this subject in probably a majority of the theological

---

[67] See her diary and Gary Scharnhorst and Denise D. Knight, "Charlotte Perkins Gilman's Library: A Reconstruction," *Resources for American Literary Study* 23 (1997): 215.
[68] Crawford H. Toy, *Quotations in the New Testament* (New York: Charles Scribner's Sons, 1884).
[69] Ibid., vi.
[70] Ibid.
[71] Toy, *Quotations*, vii–viii.
[72] Both citations from Toy, *Quotations*, viii.

seminaries in this country."[73] In addition to the book's use as a reference, perhaps the most enduring idea of Toy's book is that of the oral Aramaic translation of Scripture that stands behind some of the Old Testament quotations not aligning with the Hebrew or Septuagint.[74] Contemporary scholars of the Targum no longer adhere to this view, and it never seems to have gained much of a following, but it stands as a landmark idea in the history of research.

Several scholars situated Toy's work within the history of investigations into the Old Testament in the New.[75] Christopher D. Stanley places the book within the upswell of interest in the nineteenth century in Old Testament quotations in the New.[76] The reviewer of the *New York Evangelist* confirms Toy's contention that there was a need for the investigation. Other books were apologetic or, in the case of Böhl, concerned with investigating a particular theory.[77] There was not a book—especially in English—giving a broad overview of such quotations. The author of the review in *Unity* (with the initials G. L. C.) concurred.[78] Andrew Dickson White's 1955 book on the conflict between science and theology finds that the question of "mistaken quotations" in the New Testament "was apparently the most difficult of all matters divid-

---

[73] Review of *Judaism and Christianity, The Critic: A Weekly Review of Literature and the Arts* (February 14, 1891): 80.

[74] See Toy, *Quotations*, 9; E. Earle Ellis, "Quotations in the New Testament," *ISBE* 4:19; Benjamin B. Warfield, "Recent American Literature on the New Testament," in *The Expositor* 3/2, ed. W. Robertson Nicoll (London: Hodder and Stoughton, 1885), 145; Moore, "Toy," 11; George M. Soares Prabhu, *The Formula Quotations in the Infancy Narrative of Matthew: An Enquiry Into the Tradition History of Mt 1–2*, AnBib 63 (Rome: Pontifical Biblical Institute, 1976), 64; Christopher D. Stanley, *Paul and the Language of Scripture: Citation Technique in the Pauline Epistles and Contemporary Literature*, SNTSMS 69 (Cambridge: Cambridge University Press, 1992), 13, 23. See also Emerson B. Powery, *Jesus Reads Scripture: The Function of Jesus' Use of Scripture in the Synoptic Gospels*, BibInt 63 (Leiden: Brill, 2003), 14 n. 54, on Toy's assessment that no New Testament writers knew Hebrew.

[75] In addition to the scholars in this paragraph, Garrick V. Allen briefly mentions Toy's book as departing from the "history of religions school" approach to biblical allusions in Revelation ("Scriptural Allusions in the Book of Revelation and the Contours of Textual Research 1900–2014: Retrospect and Prospects," *CurBR* 14 [2016]: 321).

[76] Christopher D. Stanley, "Paul and Scripture: Charting the Course," in *As It Is Written: Studying Paul's Use of Scripture*, ed. Stanley E. Porter and Christopher D. Stanley, SBLSymS 50 (Leiden: Brill, 2008), 3–4.

[77] See also George Foot Moore's review, 113.

[78] G.L.C., "Quotations in the New Testament," *Unity: Freedom, Fellowship and Character in Religion* 11 (1884): 74.

ing the two forces [i.e., conservatives and those employing literary criticism]."[79] In the late nineteenth and early twentieth centuries, Christians were becoming more comfortable with critical inquiry into these quotations. In his 1919 tribute to Toy, George F. Moore claimed that Toy did not primarily intend the book to be a reference work but rather "a methodical investigation of the way in which the Old Testament is interpreted and applied by the writers of the New, the outcome of which is that the latter used the Old Testament after the manner of the Jewish exegesis of their time, and that the peculiarities of their interpretation are chiefly due to their peculiar messianic beliefs."[80] In this way, Toy emphasized that one must interpret the Old Testament in its original context rather than allowing Jesus and the apostles to have the final say.

Responses to Toy's book come in several forms. Several question Toy's methodology entirely. For instance, Benjamin B. Warfield—who resists the "modernist" approaches to biblical interpretation that Toy embraced—criticizes Toy for applying "personal theories" to the subject.[81] According to Warfield, Toy's New Testament exegesis is "sometimes mechanical, external and inadequate," and his Old Testament interpretation is hampered by his problematic understanding of Israel's history.[82] Toy also unjustly dismisses typological and allegorical approaches to the Old Testament (see p. xxvi in Toy's work). The review in *Christian Union* raises the same point.[83] Along similar lines, the reviewer in the *New York Evangelist*, although generally positive toward Toy's work, suggests that Toy "does not sufficiently estimate the divinity of our Lord, and the divine force of inspiration in the words of His Disciples."[84]

There are also scholars who respond to particular points of Toy's work. In a relatively lengthy review, George F. Moore questions Toy's idea that Hebrew was entirely dead and that there was an oral Aramaic translation of

---

[79] Andrew Dickson White, *A History of the Warfare of Science with Theology in Christendom* (New York: Braziller, 1955), 391. White cited Toy's book as an example of critical investigation into Old Testament quotations in the New.

[80] Moore, "Toy," 11.

[81] Warfield, "Recent American Literature on the New Testament," 144.

[82] Warfield, 145. On a similar methodological note, the review in *Zion's Herald* disagreed with Toy's "frank and unqualified acceptance of the modern 'higher' or destructive criticism upon the Pentateuch and portions of the prophetic Scriptures" (review of *Quotations in the New Testament*, *Zion's Herald*, March 5, 1884, 74).

[83] Review of *Quotations in the New Testament*, *Christian Union*, May 28, 1885, 21.

[84] Review of *Quotations in the New Testament*, *New York Evangelist*, March 20, 1884, 1.

Scripture.[85] Twenty-five years later, Moore also observes that Toy's reliance on Vaticanus for the text of the LXX would be judged by subsequent scholarship as too simplistic.[86] Perhaps the most sustained negative response to Toy is the 1896 study of Old Testament quotations by Franklin Johnson, professor at the University of Chicago.[87] Edward Hincks, in a review of Johnson's book, calls the work "a polemic treatise aimed at proving that certain scholars…have not done Paul and the author of 'Hebrews' justice in respect to their use of Old Testament literature."[88] Toy and Kuenen are chief among those scholars Johnson attacks, and indeed references to Toy appear throughout the work.

Toy's work received mention from time to time in works of the late twentieth century to the present day, especially in dissertations that by their nature have deeper bibliographies.[89] Usually, however, Toy is simply mentioned in lists of citations rather than utilized in any decisive way. Michael Knowles, for instance, briefly mentions and dismisses the view of Toy on Matthew 27:9–

---

[85] On this point, see also Warfield, "Recent American Literature on the New Testament," 145. The review in *Christian Union* also speaks of the lack of evidence of an "Aramaic Version" (21).

[86] Moore, "Toy," 11.

[87] Franklin Johnson, *The Quotations of the New Testament from the Old: Considered in the Light of General Literature* (Philadelphia: American Baptist Publication Society, 1896). Johnson had been Toy's pastor at Old Cambridge Baptist Church in the early 1880s. For more on Johnson's critique of Toy, see chapter 6.

[88] Edward Y. Hincks, review of Johnson's *The Quotations of the New Testament from the Old in The New World: a Quarterly Review of Religion, Ethics, and Theology* (March 1897): 171. It is interesting to note that Toy was one of the editors of the periodical in which this review appeared; see chapter 6.

[89] E.g., Charles Kimball, *Jesus' Exposition of the Old Testament in Luke's Gospel*, JSNTSup 94 (Sheffield: JSOT Press, 1994), 13, 47; Guy Prentiss Waters, *The End of Deuteronomy in the Epistles of Paul*, WUNT 2/221 (Tübingen: Mohr Siebeck, 2006), 18; Paul Jankowski, *Shades of Indignation: Political Scandals in France, Past and Present* (New York: Berghahn, 2007), 5–6 (surprisingly); Benjamin Gladd, *Revealing the Mysterion: The Use of Mystery in Daniel and Second Temple Judaism with Its Bearing on First Corinthians*, BZNW 160 (Berlin: de Gruyter, 2008), 146 n. 127; James A. Meek, *The Gentile Mission in Old Testament Citations in Acts: Text, Hermeneutic, and Purpose*, LNTS 385 (London: T&T Clark, 2008), 17, 63; Christopher A. Beetham, *Echoes of Scripture in the Letter of Paul to the Colossians*, BibInt 96 (Leiden: Brill, 2008), 2, 3, 4; Reimar Vetne, "The Influence and Use of Daniel in the Synoptic Gospels" (PhD diss., Andrews University, 2011), 53, 136, 178, 210; Seth M. Ehorn, "The Citation of Psalm 68(67).19 in Ephesians 4.8 within the Context of Early Christian Uses of the Psalms" (PhD diss., University of Edinburgh, 2014), 108; Donald Lee Schmidt Jr., "An Examination of Selected Uses of the Psalms of David in John and Acts in Light of Traditional Typology" (PhD diss., Southwestern Baptist Theological Seminary, 2014), 100, 183, 227.

10.[90] In the more than thousand-page evangelical commentary on the New Testament use of the Old Testament from 2007, Toy receives mention once.[91] Richard Hays does not mention Toy in his books on scriptural echoes in the Gospels or in Paul.[92]

Judaism and Christianity (1890)[93]

Summary. Toy wrote that the volume began as a continuation of *Quotations in the New Testament* in that it would show how religious thought developed from the Old Testament to the New Testament.[94] Yet, as he worked on the project, he decided to give "a general historical survey of the period reaching from the distinct legal organization of the Jewish people to the close of the New Testament Canon."[95] The book has 435 pages of content.

Chapter 1 surveys the literature, and chapters 2–8 cover particular topics: the doctrine of God, subordinate supernatural beings, man (the longest chapter), ethics, the kingdom of God, eschatology, and the relation of Jesus to Christianity. Toy begins his study of Judaism with Ezra's time, since it was then that the Israelite religion developed into the first stage of modern Judaism.[96] In the fifty-one-page introduction, Toy lays out some of the fundamental ideas for the entire work. He states that Christianity developed out of Judaism "in conformity with a well-defined law of human progress."[97] One can recognize these laws when religion is treated as it ought to be—namely "as a product of human thought."[98] There are various laws that affect social entities (such as empires), and these same laws, mutatis mutandis, affect religion as well.[99] Religions naturally develop from national to universal forms; only three

---

[90] Michael Knowles, *Jeremiah in Matthew's Gospel: The Rejected Prophet Motif in Matthean Redaction*, JSNTSup 62 (Sheffield: Sheffield Academic, 1993), 62.

[91] Peter Balla, "2 Corinthians," in *Commentary on the New Testament Use of the Old Testament*, ed. G. K Beale and D. A Carson (Grand Rapids: Baker Academic, 2009), 767, on the similarity between the LXX and MT of Isa 49:8 in the discussion of the quote of Isa 49:8 in 2 Cor 6:2.

[92] Richard B. Hays, *Echoes of Scripture in the Letters of Paul* (Yale University Press, 1993); *Echoes of Scripture in the Gospels* (Waco, TX: Baylor University Press, 2016).

[93] Crawford H. Toy, *Judaism and Christianity: A Sketch of the Progress of Thought from Old Testament to New Testament* (Boston: Little, Brown, and Co., 1890).

[94] Ibid., v.

[95] Ibid.

[96] Toy, *Judaism and Christianity*, 47.

[97] Toy, *Judaism and Christianity*, 1.

[98] Ibid.

[99] Toy, *Judaism and Christianity*, 5.

cases exist for universal religions today: "Brahmanism into Buddhism, Judaism into Christianity, and the old Arabian faith into Islam."[100] In time, these universal religions will control the entire population, as they already control the majority of people.[101] Yet Christianity will ultimately triumph. Toy writes, "Religion follows in the wake of social progress, and it is this last that determines the relations among nations. Christianity (to say nothing of its moral and spiritual superiority) is the religion of the great civilized and civilizing nations of the world, in whose hands are science and philosophy, literature and art, political and social progress."[102] Europeans and Americans naturally plant Christianity throughout the world as they "encroach" on the rest of the world.[103] Much of the existing non-Christian civilizations and religions will disappear. Yet Christianity will also change through this encounter because it will be "standing always in close contact with the world's highest thought."[104] It will thus attain closer and closer to the "purest ethical-religious conception of life."[105] Relatedly, science has already been helping in this process. In an earlier section on science and religion, Toy observes, "Science has been the handmaid and friend of religion, relieving it of the burden of superstitions, of false relations between phenomena, and pushing it to the conception of the spiritual relation between man and God."[106]

Chapter 8 begins with a summary of the book thus far.[107] Jesus of Nazareth transformed Judaism, "the religion of a nation," into Christianity, "a religion for the world."[108] Whereas the prophets, psalmists, and apocalyptists were thinking of an ultimate earthly blessedness, "Jesus made the essence of the new law to be the purity of the individual soul."[109] At the same time, pre-Christian Jewish literature still "reached very high conceptions of the principles of moral conduct and of the nature of religion (Proverbs, Psalms, Wisdom of Solomon, Wisdom of the Son of Sirach, Hillel)."[110] The best minds yearned for something greater than they had and rejected "the extreme Pharisaic party" that insisted on "external details up to the point of forgetting sincerity and spirituality."[111] Jesus's principles tended to "abolish outward distinctions, and

---

[100] Toy, *Judaism and Christianity*, 39.
[101] Toy, *Judaism and Christianity*, 44.
[102] Toy, *Judaism and Christianity*, 45.
[103] Ibid.
[104] Toy, *Judaism and Christianity*, 46.
[105] Ibid.
[106] Toy, *Judaism and Christianity*, 15.
[107] See Toy, *Judaism and Christianity*, 415–16.
[108] Toy, *Judaism and Christianity*, 415.
[109] Ibid.
[110] Toy, *Judaism and Christianity*, 417.
[111] Ibid.

to lead to the conclusion that all men stood in the same relation to God."[112] Paul then did away with the ceremonial that Jesus had "depressed" and allowed for the full acceptance of Gentiles.[113] Under the influence of Greek philosophy, Jesus came to be understood as the eternal Word. Jesus probably did not see himself as a sacrifice for sin or as divine.[114]

Reception. Writing in 1919, G. F. Moore stated: "It does not speak well for the discrimination of American readers that this volume, the fruit of thorough and first-hand studies, made little impression when it appeared and has received little attention since. It is seldom quoted, even by writers whose footnotes resemble—in more ways than one—the bibliography of a doctor's dissertation, and bristle with the titles of books of warmed-over learning."[115] Indeed, the book appears only rarely in contemporary bibliographies.[116] An influential *JBL* article on Pauline theology in 2004, however, does cite Toy as representative of the view that universal religions are superior to ethnoracially linked ones.[117]

Nevertheless, Charles Dudley Warner included the book in his *Library of the World's Best Literature*, writing in 1896, "The tone of the book is undogmatic; and its fine scholarship, clearness of statement, and delightful narrative style, make it agreeable and instructive reading for the laic."[118] The review in the *Unitarian Review* naturally praises Toy's belief that Jesus is "truly a man" and states that "Few discussions of the Bible are better fitted to make converts to a liberal theology than this substantial work."[119]

Toy's book garnered praise from several writers for shedding greater light on the lesser-known period between the two Testaments.[120] Toy shows that

---

[112] Toy, *Judaism and Christianity*, 416.

[113] Toy, *Judaism and Christianity*, 415–16.

[114] Toy, *Judaism and Christianity*, 419, 422–23. These statements will sound harshly inaccurate to those with the "New Respective" ears.

[115] Moore, "Toy," 14.

[116] See, for example, Y. Michael Barilan, "The Vision of Vegetarianism and Peace: Rabbi Kook on the Ethical Treatment of Animals," *History of the Human Sciences* 17/4 (2004): 79; Chaim N. Saiman, "Talmud Study, Ethics and Social Policy: A Case Study in the Laws of Wage-Payment as an Argument for Leo-Lamdanut," *Villanova University School of Law Public Law and Legal Theory Working Paper* No. 2016-1024 (2014): 226. Saiman presents this book as part of the nineteenth century critique of rabbinic legalism. On this point, see also Solomon Schechter, "The Law and Recent Criticism," *JQR* 3 (1891): 754–766.

[117] Denise Kimber Buell and Caroline Johnson Hodge, "The Politics of Interpretation: The Rhetoric of Race and Ethnicity in Paul," *JBL* 123 (2004): 240.

[118] Charles Dudley Warner, *A Library of the World's Best Literature XLV: Synopses of Famous Books & General Index* (New York: Cosimo, 2009), 455.

[119] Review of *Judaism and Christianity*, *The Unitarian Review* 35 (April 1891): 325.

[120] See review, *Unitarian Review*, 325; David G. Lyon, "Judaism and Christianity," *The Old and New Testament Student* 12/6 (1891): 367–73; George Foot Moore, "Judaism

it was not a period of stagnation but one of significant development. G. F. Moore wished that Toy expanded his scope, bringing the story down to the time of the redaction of the Mishnah.[121]

More substantially, G. F. Moore questioned some of Toy's points about the origins of religion, the dating of prophetic materials, and the relationship between the Gospel of John and Paul.[122] Moore later also critiqued the book for not investigating the teaching of the Palestinian schools and synagogues.[123] Instead, Toy focused on the apocalypses, which, in fact, are less important for understanding the Gospels than these Palestinian sources. Moore admitted that Toy authored *Judaism and Christianity* at a time when the critical study of rabbinic literature was still in its infancy,[124] and Moore decried its continued neglect in 1919.[125] Moore also noted that scholars became less confident in the decades after Toy in the existence of or ability to determine "laws of historical development" and began to understand history in a less scientific way.[126]

In a lengthy review of this book, S. Schechter praised Toy for recognizing the positive value of the law in the history of religion, which proves that "Toy is not only up to his date, but beyond it."[127] Nevertheless, Toy still had to find problems in the law: "The general idea seems to be that, as the doctrine of the resurrection of Christ must be loosely interpreted in a spiritual sense, it must logically have been preceded by a universal spiritual death, and the germs of the disease which brought this death are to be sought for in the law."[128] Schechter then responded at length to Toy's claims that Judaism was overly interested in the minutiae of ceremonies. Schechter also asserted that the legal

---

and Christianity by Crawford Howell Toy," *Magazine of Christian Literature* (May 1891): 116–17; review of *Judaism and Christianity, Christian Union*, March 12, 1891, 350.

[121] Moore, "Judaism and Christianity," 116. This same critique appears in Moore, "Toy," 12–13.

[122] Moore, "Judaism and Christianity," 117.

[123] Moore, "Toy," 13.

[124] For a brief assessment of G. F. Moore's importance for understanding ancient Judaism, see E. P. Sanders, *Paul and Palestinian Judaism: A Comparison of Patterns of Religion* (Philadelphia: Fortress, 1977), 33–59. Sanders claims that Moore's 1921 article ("Christian Writers on Judaism," *HTR* 14 [1921]: 197–254) "should be required reading for any Christian scholar who writes about Judaism" (33).

[125] Moore, "Toy," 13–14.

[126] Moore, "Toy," 14. This criticism could be applied broadly to those in biblical studies who attempted to apply the "laws of evolution" of "social Darwinism" to the development of religions.

[127] Schechter, "The Law and Recent Criticism," 754–66, here 755.

[128] Schechter, "The Law and Recent Criticism," 755.

tendency in Judaism led to a flourishing literature, as one can see in the wisdom literature, the book of Job, and Psalms.[129] Indeed, the law brings many Jews joy.[130] Nevertheless, Schechter concluded by noting how Toy was influenced by so many works that denounce legalism and few if any that give a positive image, so he "has done the best he could with existing materials, and produced a meritorious work deserving of wide recognition and approval."[131]

At the time of its publication, the most controversial aspect of Toy's book was the fact that he treats religious history like all other history. For instance, the review in *American Catholic Quarterly Review* strongly condemned Toy as a rationalist, Spencerian, eliminating "every vestige of inspiration."[132] According to the reviewer, Toy's work was speculative and contradictory, and Toy acted as if he knew the thoughts of Christ regardless of Christ's words. Henry Preserved Smith acknowledged that Crawford Toy was the "coryphaeus of the higher criticism in this country" and wrote that he did not necessarily agree with Toy's purely "naturalistic" point of view.[133] The reviewer in *The Monist* echoed this remark.[134] At the same time, Toy's colleague, D. G. Lyon, argued: "Prof. Toy does not deny divine guidance in the history. He would allow a fashioning hand, a leading thought, behind all the phenomena. Only it is the same hand and thought which show themselves in all human development. They lie beyond our comprehension."[135] Despite these disagreements, several writers stated that the book provides helpful information even to those who do not accept Toy's approach.[136] As to the relationship of this book to Toy's later work, G. F. Moore declared that this book "contains...a prophecy of Professor Toy's latest and ripest contribution to a subject in which he had long been deeply interested, his *Introduction to the History of Religions*."[137]

---

[129] Schechter, "The Law and Recent Criticism," 761–62.

[130] Schechter, "The Law and Recent Criticism," 762–65.

[131] Schechter, "The Law and Recent Criticism," 766. See also Moore's critique above.

[132] Review of *Judaism and Christianity*, *The American Catholic Quarterly Review* (January 1891): 220.

[133] "Henry Preserved Smith, "Toy's Judaism and Christianity," *The Andover Review* 16 (1891): 311, 313–14.

[134] Review of *Judaism and Christianity*, *The Monist* 2 (October 1891): 123–24, here 123.

[135] Lyon, "Judaism and Christianity," 372–73.

[136] See the Lyon, "Judaism and Christianity," 373; review of *Judaism and Christianity*, *The Critic* 19 (1891): 80.

[137] Moore, "Toy," 15.

The Book of the Prophet Ezekiel (1899)[138]

Summary. This work, part of the Sacred Books of the Old and New Testaments series, consists of two volumes, one a critical edition of the Hebrew text with about 75 pages of notes (mostly text-critical), and the other a new English translation with about 115 pages of notes in English designed for the average reader. The latter is based on the Toy's critical Hebrew text and includes about 120 charts and illustrations. The illustrations in the series are usually in color (giving rise to the "Rainbow Bible" or "Polychrome Edition" as a popular name for the series), but this particular volume is not in color. Many of the illustrations in this book indicate parallels in Ancient Near Eastern artwork and architecture. Toy viewed the book of Ezekiel largely as a compositional unity. He was perhaps drawn to the book because of its connections to Ancient Near Eastern literature, as well as to parts of the Pentateuch. Indeed, Toy had already explored Babylonian connections in a *JBL* article in 1881.[139] His lectures in 1895–1896 also explored the connections between Ezekiel 28 and Genesis 3, as well as the influence of Babylonian elements on Ezekiel (and Genesis 1–3).[140] Toy may also have been drawn to the book because of its many interesting text-critical issues—a subject he had already explored an 1896 article.[141] Toy later wrote the Ezekiel entries for *Encyclopaedia Biblica* (1901) and *Encyclopaedia Britannica* (1910).

Reception. Even though the book appeared in a series that has not had much of a lasting impact, it continues to be cited to the present day. Toy's book has had the most influence in the areas of text-criticism and translation.[142] The brief review by J. G. Tasker was positive.[143] In 1919, Moore claimed that Toy worked with "judicious conservatism," not suggesting too many alterations to the Hebrew text and recognizing the limitations of our

---

[138] Crawford H. Toy, *The Book of the Prophet Ezekiel: A New English Translation, with Explanatory Notes*, ed. Paul Haupt, Sacred Books of the Old and New Testaments (New York: Dodd, Mead, and Co., 1899).

[139] Crawford H. Toy, "The Babylonian Element in Ezekiel," *JBL* 1 (1881): 59–66.

[140] Calkin, "Lectures on the History of Hebrew Literature," 63.

[141] Crawford H. Toy, "Text-Critical Notes on Ezekiel," *JBL* 15 (1896): 54–58.

[142] See, for example, Leslie C. Allen, *Ezekiel 20–48*, WBC 29 (Dallas: Word, 1990), 157, 200, 244, 273, 276; Leslie C. Allen, "The Structure and Intention of Ezekiel I," *VT* 43 (1993): 151 (quoting Toy on the intention of Ezekiel 1); Ka Leung Wong, "A Note On Ezekiel VIII 6," *VT* 51 (2001): 399 n. 5; Michael A. Lyons, "'A Barley Cake' (Ezek 4:12a): Syntax and Redaction," *JNSL* 40 (2014): 81.

[143] J. G. Tasker, review of *The Book of the Prophet Ezekiel*, *London Quarterly Review* (April 1900): 358–59; see also Tasker, "The Sacred Books of the Old Testament, Ezekiel," *Expository Times* 11 (1900): 225.

understanding.[144] Friedrich Giesebrecht, however, did not find this conservativism to be a virtue.[145] Giesebrecht argued that Toy's work does not move Ezekiel research much beyond Cornill's work. Giesebrecht also responded to some particular technical text-critical issues in Toy's book.[146]

In her 2005 commentary on Ezekiel, Margaret S. Odell cited Toy (wrongly as "Charles Toy") as an example of a scholar who correctly observes the relevance to Ezekiel of Assyrian architecture and iconography.[147] After all, Toy included many line drawings of Assyrian parallels in his book. Many subsequent scholars, however, did not pay much attention to such parallels because of Ezekiel's *Babylonian* context, but Odell suggested that the time is ripe to return to such comparisons. Interestingly, Toy's 1881 article[148] on Babylonian influence in Ezekiel also continues to be cited in the scholarly literature.[149] Daniel Bodi claims that Toy "was among the first to identify the Babylonian ideas and motifs found in the Book of Ezekiel."[150]

A Critical and Exegetical Commentary on the Book of Proverbs (1899)[151]

Summary. In the same year that the critical edition and translation of Ezekiel was published, Toy's most enduring contribution to scholarship, the ICC commentary on Proverbs, also appeared. At about 580 pages of content, this commentary on Proverbs takes the standard form of the ICC series of an introduction followed with passage-by-passage translation and commentary.

---

[144] Moore, "Toy," 10. J. G. Tasker agreed, declaring that Toy is "more conservative than…such critics as Cornill and Winckler" (review of *The Book of the Prophet Ezekiel*, 359).

[145] Friedrich Giesebrecht, "The Sacred Books of the Old Testament," *Orientalistische Litteratur-Zeitung* 12 (1900): 455–56.

[146] Ibid.

[147] Margaret S. Odell, *Ezekiel*, Smyth & Helwys Bible Commentary 16 (Macon, GA: Smyth & Helwys, 2005), 25. Odell cites Austen Henry Layard as a forerunner of this idea.

[148] Crawford H. Toy, "The Babylonian Element in Ezekiel," *Journal of the Society of Biblical Literature and Exegesis, Including the Papers Read and Abstract of Proceedings for June 1–December* (1881): 59–66.

[149] See, for instance, Jose M. Bertoluci, "The Son of the Morning and the Guardian Cherub in the Context of the Controversy Between Good and Evil" (ThD diss., Andrews University, 1985), 110 n. 2; Brian Neil Peterson, *Ezekiel in Context: Ezekiel's Message Understood in Its Historical Setting of Covenant Curses and Ancient Near Eastern Mythological Motifs*, PTMS 182 (Eugene, OR: Pickwick, 2012), 21, 118–19.

[150] Daniel Bodi, *The Book of Ezekiel and the Poem of Erra*, OBO 104 (Göttingen: Vandenhoeck & Ruprecht, 1991), 45.

[151] Crawford H. Toy, *A Critical and Exegetical Commentary on the Book of Proverbs*, ICC (New York: Charles Scribner's Sons, 1899).

Toy places much of the book of Proverbs in the late Persian period, with continued textual growth until 200 BC (xix–xxxi). George Foot Moore claimed that Jewish wisdom had always had an attraction for Toy.[152] Toy later wrote the Proverbs entries for *Encyclopaedia Biblica* (1902) and *Encyclopaedia Britannica* (1910). Toy discussed the book at length in the Calkins notes (1895–1896), and in *Judaism and Christianity* he expressed appreciation for the "very high conceptions of the principles of moral conduct and of the nature of religion (Proverbs, Psalms, Wisdom of Solomon, Wisdom of the Son of Sirach, Hillel)."[153]

Reception. Toy was part of a time prior to the publication of the Instruction of Amenemope, and Egyptian wisdom text, in 1924 in which scholars frequently placed much of Proverbs relatively late in the Persian period.[154] Toy also generally saw wisdom theology as compatible with the rest of the Old Testament[155]—a view that would not remain unchallenged as scholars increasingly noted the relative dearth of references to the *Heilsgeschichte* in wisdom literature.

Due to the importance of the ICC series as one of the main biblical commentary series, this book has proven to be Toy's most influential work.[156] The ICC series tends to be strongest with regard to philology and text-criticism, as indeed most of the citations of Toy's Proverbs commentary have to do with text-critical or translational issues.[157] Nonetheless, Toy's literary reconstructions and structural observations also continue to find a voice. As late as 1993,

---

[152] Moore, "Toy," 9.

[153] Toy, *Judaism and Christianity*, 417. Toy expressed similar praise of Proverbs in the commentary (*Proverbs*, ix).

[154] See R. N. Whybray, *The Book of Proverbs: A Survey of Modern Study*, History of Biblical Interpretation 1 (Leiden: Brill, 1995), 1–2, 151. Johnny E. Miles writes of this commentary that, along with the work of Franz Delitzsch, it "helped to pave the way for historical-critical interests in sources, genre, social background and redactional stages" (*Wise King—Royal Fool: Semiotics, Satire and Proverbs 1–9*, JSOTSup 399 [London: T&T Clark, 2004], 4). See also Bruce K. Waltke, *The Book of Proverbs Chapters 1–15*, NICOT (Grand Rapids: Eerdmans, 2004), 28–29 (who still affirms the value of Toy's commentary).

[155] Whybray, *The Book of Proverbs*, 134, 151.

[156] GoogleScholar—which often significantly underestimates total number of citations—shows 133 citations.

[157] E.g., Riad Aziz Kassis, *The Book of Proverbs and Arabic Proverbial Works*, VTSup 74 (Leiden: Brill, 1999); Miles, *Wise King*, 65; Karin Finsterbusch, *Weisung für Israel: Studien zu religiösem Lehren und Lernen im Deuteronomium und in seinem Umfeld*, FAT 1/44 (Tübingen: Mohr Siebeck, 2005), 91, 102, 110; Sun Myung Lyu, *Righteousness in the Book of Proverbs*, FAT 2/55 (Tübingen: Mohr Siebeck, 2012), 73, 86; Knut Martin Heim, *Poetic Imagination in Proverbs: Variant Repetitions and the Nature of Poetry*, BBRSup 4 (Winona Lake, IN: Eisenbrauns, 2013), 16, 100–101, 102, 321, 448; Ernest Lucas, *Proverbs*, Two

Daniel C. Snell could declare that this volume is still "the most useful commentary currently available."[158] Pieter Venter, in a review of James Loader's HCOT on Proverbs 1–9, compared the commentary to Toy, the paradigm of the technical Proverbs commentary.[159]

The reviewers of the time praised this book.[160] Still, there were minor criticisms. The reviewer in *The Methodist Review* expresses astonishment at Toy's relatively sparse English bibliography,[161] and *The Bookman* states that the bibliography is "too brief."[162] Similarly, J. F. McCurdy complains that the introduction is "too brief."[163] John P. Peters's review of the book expresses doubt as to Toy's arguments for the late dating of the work.[164] After all, Peters observes, Toy "has nothing to say regarding the lack of references in the book of Proverbs to the legal and scribal conceptions of law and religion, which dominated the Jewish life of the period to which he would refer the book of Proverbs."[165] Peters brings up some other interpretive issues as well, but he generally praises the book.[166] To sum: Toy's commentary on Proverbs repre-

---

Horizons Old Testament Commentary (Grand Rapids: Eerdmans, 2015), 66, 67, 121, 146, 164, 346.

[158] Daniel C. Snell, *Twice-Told Proverbs and the Composition of the Book of Proverbs* (Winona Lake, IN: Eisenbrauns, 1993), 85.

[159] Pieter Venter, review of *Proverbs 1–9*, by James Alfred Loader, *HTS Teologiese Studies/Theological Studies* 72/4 (2018): 1–8, here 8.

[160] See, for instance, Review of *A Critical and Exegetical Commentary on the Book of Proverbs*, *The Methodist Review* 49 (1900): 462–63; "The Bookman's Table," *The Bookman* (January, 1900): 124; J. F. McCurdy, Review of *A Critical and Exegetical Commentary on the Book of Proverbs*, *The Biblical World* 16/5 (1900): 379–81; Georg Beer, Review of *A Critical and Exegetical Commentary on the Book of Proverbs*, *Theologische Literaturzeitung* 11 (1901): 284–87, here 287.

[161] *The Methodist's Review*, 463.

[162] "The Bookman's Table," 124.

[163] McCurdy, review of *Book of Proverbs*, 379.

[164] John P. Peters, review of *A Critical and Exegetical Commentary on the Book of Proverbs*, *The American Journal of Theology* 4/4 (1900): 825–28, here 826.

[165] Peters, Review of *Book of Proverbs*, 826. The review of *A Critical and Exegetical Commentary on the Book of Proverbs* in *The Athenaeum*, May 12, 1900, 589, also questioned Toy's dating. This subject would become more important within the history of research into wisdom literature.

[166] Peters, review of *Book of Proverbs*, 827–28. Numerous modern studies continue to cite Toy's commentary on Proverbs; see, *inter alia*, Michael V. Fox, "The Pedagogy of Proverbs 2," *JBL* 113/2 (1994): 233–43; Michael V. Fox, "Who Can Learn? A Dispute in Ancient Pedagogy?" in *Wisdom, You Are My Sister: Studies in Honor of Roland E. Murphy on the Occasion of His Eightieth Birthday*, ed. Michael L. Barré (Washington: Catholic Biblical Association of America, 1997), 62–77; 233–43; Andrew E. Steinmann, "Three Things...Four Things...Seven Things: The Coherence of Proverbs 30:11–33 and the

sents his most significant contribution to Old Testament studies; in fact, Rudolf Smend claimed Toy's ICC commentary took the "crown" for the Proverbs commentary with the "reputation for having most furthered understanding" in the nineteenth century.[167]

Introduction to the History of Religions (1913)[168]

Summary. The *Introduction to the History of Religions* represents both a departure from Toy's previously published books and a culmination of his life's work, especially over the last two decades of his career.[169] The 583 pages of content are divided into 11 chapters (consisting of 1,173 sections). After an introductory chapter ("Nature of Religion"), Toy takes up the following topics: The Soul (chapter 2); Early Religious Ceremonies (chapter 3); Early Cults (chapter 4); Totemism and Taboo (chapter 5); Gods (chapter 6); Myths (chapter 7); Magic and Divination (chapter 8); The Higher Theistic Development (chapter 9); Social Development of Religion (chapter 10); and Scientific and Ethical Elements in Religious Systems (chapter 11). The book draws heavily on the work of anthropologist Sir James George Frazer (whose most famous work, *Golden Bough*, appeared in its third edition in 1911).[170]

In the first sentence of the preface, Toy succinctly states the purpose of the book: "The object of this volume is to describe the principal customs and ideas that underlie all public religion."[171] Consistent with the methodology of

---

Unity of Proverbs 30," *Hebrew Studies* 42 (2001): 59–66; Glenn D. Pemberton, "The Rhetoric of the Father in Proverbs 1–9," *JSOT* 30/1 (2005): 63–82; Alan Lenzi, "Proverbs 8:22–31: Three Perspectives on Its Composition," *JBL* 125/4 (2006): 687–714; Timothy J. Sandoval, "Revisiting the Prologue of Proverbs," *JBL* 126/3 (2007): 455–73; Barbara Böck, "Proverbs 30:18–19 in the Light of Ancient Mesopotamian Cuneiform Texts," *Sefarad* 69/2 (2009): 263–79; Ronald L. Giese, Jr., "'Iron Sharpens Iron' as a Negative Image: Challenging the Common Interpretation of Proverbs 27:17," *JBL* 135/1 (2016): 61–76; Arthur Keefer, "A Shift in Perspective: The Intended Audience and a Coherent Reading of Proverbs 1:1–7," *JBL* 136/1 (2017): 103–16.

[167] Rudolf Smend, "The Interpretation of Wisdom in Nineteenth-Century Scholarship," in *Wisdom in Ancient Israel: Essays in Honor of J. A. Emerton*, ed. John Day, R. P. Gordon, H. G. M. Williamson (Cambridge: Cambridge University Press, 1998), 257–68.

[168] Crawford H. Toy, *Introduction to the History of Religions*, Handbooks on the History of Religions Series 4, ed. Morris Jastrow, Jr. (Boston: The Athenaeum Press, 1913).

[169] See Toy's previous essays and articles published in this area: "Taboo and Morality," *JAOS* 20 (1899): 151–56; "Creator Gods," *JAOS* 23 (1902): 20–37; "Recent Discussions of Totemism," *JOAS* 25 (1904): 146–61; "An Early Form of Animal Sacrifice," *JAOS* 26 (1905): 137–44; "Mexican Human Sacrifice," *Journal of American Folk-Lore* 18 (1905): 173–81.

[170] There are more than 100 references to Frazer's work in Toy's *History of Religions*.

[171] Toy, *History of Religions*, vii.

the times, Toy traces what he sees as the evolutionary development of religion from primitive animism to higher forms of monotheism.[172] Toy surveys practices and beliefs in a wide-ranging number of religious traditions in a variety of locales: Hindu, Egyptian, Greek, Roman, Hebrew, Christian, and many others, seeking to describe both common and distinct elements in each of the major topics.

Reception. The volume was widely acclaimed from the beginning and was still being reprinted as late as 1948. One reviewer, Joachim Wach, noted that "it speaks well for a text when a reprint after thirty-five years can still serve a useful purpose."[173] The reviewer in *Bibliotheca Sacra* claimed that the volume (along with one by Toy's colleague, George Foot Moore) "can be depended on as authoritative and fair representations of the facts relating to the subjects treated."[174] Hutton Webster claimed that Toy's volume enjoyed "the distinction of being the first in any language to attempt this task [of comparing different faiths by analyzing what they shared in common] from a purely objective standpoint and in a comprehensive manner. The difficulties attending such a pioneer study are immense; to have overcome them so successfully is an achievement for which the author will receive congratulations of every serious student."[175] Toy's objectivity, celebrated by various reviewers, is a departure from the kind of apologetics that often colored investigations of religious traditions at this time, but, of course, Toy, despite his attempted objectivity, still had a Western bias.[176] G. F. Moore attributed the success of this volume

---

[172] Toy was building on the work of anthropologist Edward Tylor, whose two-volume work, *Primitive Culture* (London: John Murray, 1871), popularized the evolutionary view of the development of religion. In "Sexing Religion," R. Marie Griffith (*The Cambridge Companion to Religious Studies*, ed. Robert A. Orsi [Cambridge: Cambridge University Press, 2012], 338–59, esp. 344–46), has traced the evolutionary underpinnings of Toy's work through his portrayal of the development of sexual practices in the "phallus worship" of primitive religious groups to its presence among religions of the "highest civilization" which "discarded here and there its more bestial forms" until "finally it vanished from religious usage" (Griffith, 346, quoting Toy, *History of Religions*, 520).

[173] Joachim Wach, review of *Introduction to the History of Religions, Journal of Religion* 32 (1952): 74–75, here 74. Wach was a significant early figure in the phenomenological approach to religious traditions. See also P. W. Schimdt, review of *Introduction to the History of Religions, Anthropos* 20 (1925): 356–58.

[174] Review of *History of Religions*, by George Foot Moore, and *Introduction to the History of Religions*, by Crawford Howell Toy, *Bibliotheca Sacra* 71 (1914): 168–69, here 169.

[175] Hutton Webster, review of *Introduction to the History of Religions*, HTR 7 (1914): 441–46, here 442. Hutton went on to predict, "This book is likely to remain for many years *the* text on comparative religion in American universities" (446).

[176] Toy distinguished between the "Impersonal Whole" and "Personal Power," indicating a familiarity with Eastern religious traditions. But he also occasionally lapsed into

(and others) to the fact that Toy "had a native scientific bent which gave him a reverence for facts and held him to patient and painstaking endeavor to ascertain and verify them and to state them exactly as they are. His judgment was formed deliberately on an unprejudiced consideration of all the evidence."[177]

Moore also called this work "the latest and ripest contribution to a subject in which [Toy] had long been deeply interested."[178] Moore connected the *Introduction to the History of Religions* to Toy's previous work, *Judaism and Christianity*, claiming that it contained "we may say, a prophecy" of this 1913 book.[179] At any rate, this work does seem to be the fruit of Toy's scholarship not only on the Bible but also on a variety of other cultures.

The book did not escape criticism among early reviewers, however. Ethnologist Pliny Gottard noted that for "the ordinary scholarly reader and student with the current views concerning the less advanced peoples and their psychology this book ought to prove thoroughly satisfactory"; however, "the few ethnologists who have had field experience and intimate contact with the people chiefly concerned in the subject matter of the book will of course have many doubts as they turn the pages."[180] Gottard spelled out the concerns of ethnologists as follows:

> They will doubt the value of many of the documents cited as the sources of the information given. It is not an easy thing to know the religious ideas of an alien people, usually a people speaking an unknown language. They know, too, that many of the terms used, such as totemism, animism, gods, and demons, do not stand for blocks of stone of uniform substance and size, capable of being combined into artistic and stable structures. To them they are parts of the bedrock of life which split off with uneven cleavage into blocks of all sizes and shapes.[181]

---

judgments reflecting a certain "Western" bias. For example, Toy's definition of religion as an attempt to understand powers that act on humanity "intentionally" (*History of Religions*, 1) would seem foreign to advocates of Eastern religions (especially Buddhists), for whom the sacred presence does not have personal agency. My thanks to my colleague, Blake Burleson, for sharing with me these (and other) observations on Toy's work in comparative religions.

[177] Moore, "Toy," 16.

[178] Moore, "Toy," 15.

[179] Ibid.

[180] Pliny E. Goddard, review of *Introduction to the History of Religions*, *American Anthropologist* 18 (1916): 277–78, here 277.

[181] Goddard, review of *Introduction to the History of Religions*, 277. Goddard labels Toy's attempt to present a general and comprehensive overview as a "stupendous task" for

Goddard's solution was for field ethnologists to complicate the "writing of such books as this by piling a greater mass of conflicting data from the peoples with whom they are thrown."[182]

Toy's book has continued to be cited from time to time by various specialists. George A. Barton, for instance, refers to Toy with regard to the religiousness of all people, the beliefs about the dwelling places of the dead, Egyptian religion, and totemism.[183] John Murphy cites Toy on the definition of a fetish.[184] H. L. Mencken is evidence of some popular reception of the book. He cites Toy on Central Australia as evidence that primitive people conducted ceremonies without emotion except for desire of gain.[185] Mencken dismissed the emotive element of religion, citing Toy that the love of God is unknown to primitive peoples, and among civilized peoples it is more a fancy to be cultivated than reality to be experienced.[186] In a bibliographic note, Mencken writes, "Perhaps the best of them [i.e., handbooks of religion] is Crawford H. Toy's 'Introduction to the History of Religions' (Cambridge, Harvard University Press, 1924). It is impartially written, and contains a great deal of curious and interesting matter."[187]

Crawford Toy's interest in comparative work in religious traditions joined with others who labored with Toy at Harvard at that time (*inter alia*,

---

those who understand "how difficult it is to learn much about any one particular religious system" (277).

[182] Goddard, review of *Introduction to the History of Religions*, 278. L. L. Bernard, in "The Sociological Interpretation of Religion" (*Journal of Religion* 18 [1938]: 1–18), explored the critical disagreements between science and theology, using Toy's first chapter in *Introduction to the History of Religions* as an example of the "liberal theologian's" approach to the relationship between science and religion (in contrast to the "scientist" and the "orthodox theologian"). Given his past "employment history" at Southern Seminary, Toy's remarks about the relationship between science and religion are fascinating: science and religion "clash when an old nonreligious belief, adopted by religion, is confronted by an antagonistic scientific discovery; the first result is a protest, but the mind demands harmony, and religion always ends by accepting a well-attested scientific conclusion, and bringing it into harmony with its fundamental belief," he wrote (*History of Religions*, 574). In a footnote, Toy specified the Copernican and Newtonian theories, the "magnitude of the stellar universe," biblical criticism, and the theories of evolution and conservation of energy as examples of "well-attested scientific conclusions" (ibid., n. 1).

[183] George A. Barton, *The Religions of the World*, 2nd ed., University of Chicago Publications in Religious Education (Chicago: University of Chicago Press, 1919), 3, 6, 37, 361.

[184] John Murphy, *The Origins and History of Religions* (Manchester: Manchester University Press, 1952), 70.

[185] H. L. Mencken, *Treatise on the Gods*, 2nd ed. (New York: Knopf, 1946), 51.

[186] Mencken, *Treatise on the Gods*, 272.

[187] Mencken, *Treatise on the Gods*, 297.

G. F. Moore, William James, C. R. Lanman, F. W. Putnam) and/or who participated in the Harvard History of Religions Club, which Toy founded in 1891.[188] Later, such interests were developed and extended by William Ernest Hocking (Harvard Philosophy) and Arthur Darby Nock (HDS), which eventually led to the establishment of the Center for the Study of World Religions (CSWR) at Harvard. While there is no direct line from Toy to the CSWR, Toy's role in expanding teaching and research into the newly established academic study of religions should be acknowledged.[189]

From 1880 until 1909 (and beyond in the case of his publications), Crawford Toy was an effective classroom teacher and a productive scholar. His accomplishments were recognized with honorary doctorate degrees from Wake Forest College, Howard College, the University of North Carolina, and finally, and perhaps most meaningfully for Toy, from Harvard University in 1904. But Crawford Toy's contributions to the intellectual life at Harvard University were not limited to the lectern or the monograph. He was also active in a variety of intellectual, social, and religious activities beyond the normal course of his duties as a professor. He was a great organizer of people and ideas and apparently took delight in bringing order to chaos, whether in a scholarly discussion or in the pages of a curated journal. We explore the "citizenship" of Crawford Toy in the following chapter.

---

[188] See chapter 6.

[189] On the history of the CSWR, including the dispute over the legitimacy of the label "history of religions" for the project, see John B. Carman and Kathryn Dodgson, eds., *Community and Colloquy* (Cambridge: Center for the Study of World Religions, 2006). To place Toy's efforts and interests in the history of religions on the larger canvas of the emergence of the academic study of religion in late nineteenth century-early twentieth century America, see D. G. Hart, *The University Gets Religion: Religious Studies in American Higher Education* (Baltimore: Johns Hopkins University Press, 1999). Interesting also (but beyond our scope here) is the relation of Toy's comparative approach to the commonalities in belief and practices of various religious groups with what has come to be known as the phenomenological approach to religion; cf., e.g., James L. Cox, *An Introduction to the Phenomenology of Religion* (London: Continuum, 2010).

Fig. 3

Old Cambridge Baptist Church.
Old Cambridge Baptist Church Archives

6

University, Community, and Church Citizenship

After three semesters at Harvard, Crawford Toy reflected on his experiences:

> I am more at home here now & find the people very kind—no stranger could have been more pleasantly received. Of all the life here—the readings by professors…of my efforts to have attendance on morning-prayer made voluntary, of the lectures by foreign & other celebrities…of my pleasant table-companions, of the Div'y professors & the School, it would take a small volume to tell.[1]

For those outside the rhythm of most academic communities, it may come as something of a surprise to learn how little Toy remarks on classroom teaching and scholarship, the subjects of the previous chapter. The amount of a professor's time spent engaged in activities cannot easily be categorized, strictly speaking, as teaching or scholarship. Such is certainly true of Crawford Toy's career at Harvard.

Scholarly Organizations and Clubs

Like many professors, then and now, Crawford Toy was a member of several professional societies. He had served (as previously noted) as president of the American Philological Association and also the American Oriental Society, and he was a founding member of the Society of Biblical Literature and Exegesis, which formed in 1880.[2] In addition to these national learned societies, Crawford Toy was also responsible for founding and sustaining several others in the larger Boston area in conjunction with Harvard University.

Harvard Biblical Club (HBC). At the beginning of Toy's second semester at Harvard, he organized the Harvard Semitic Club.[3] Toy sent invitations for

---

[1] Crawford H. Toy to John A. Broadus, December 14, 1881, Broadus Papers, ASC, SBTS. It is interesting to compare these musings with those of the fifteen-year-old Toy, newly arrived at the University of Virginia (see chapter 2)!

[2] See Ernest W. Saunders, *Searching the Scriptures: A History of the Society of Biblical Literature, 1880–1980* (Chico, CA: Society of Biblical Literature, 1982), 22.

[3] Harvard Biblical Club, vol. 1, January 1881–May 1897, HUD 3211, Box 2, Records of the Harvard Biblical Club, HUA. Unless otherwise noted, all information on the Biblical Club are taken from the minutes in these archival materials. This activity was typical

a first meeting in the Wadsworth House on January 22, 1881. A severe snow-storm on the previous day prevented many from attending, so the first official meeting was held on February 5.[4] Seven of nine professors from the Boston area who had been invited were in attendance. Several actions were taken: C. H. Toy was elected president and G. H. Whittemore secretary/treasurer, po-sitions,[5] by annual election, the two would hold for years to come; the name "Harvard Semitic Club" was officially adopted; and the group agreed to meet at 11:00 a.m. on the first and third Saturdays of each month from October to June. In that first official meeting, Toy lead the group in a reading of Ezekiel 1–3. The first few meetings were held in the homes of participants until a more permanent location in Boston's New Church Seminary could be secured.

At the last meeting of the spring on May 21, 1881, the group decided to open its membership to Biblical Greek scholars and authorized its officers to offer membership to qualified individuals with the restriction that the total membership should not exceed twenty. In the following December, the group officially changed its name to the Harvard Biblical Club. The founding group signed the record book in January 1882: Ezra Abbot, Ezra Gould, Alvah Hovey, C. M. Mead, Selah Merrill, F. O. Paine, John Orne, Jr., O. L. Stearns, P. H. Steenstra, C. H. Toy, G. H. Whittemore.[6]

In the first three years, papers were presented on a variety of subjects: the identification of the "Red Sea" with the Serbonian Lake (Paine), the construc-tion of Romans 9:5 (Abbot), Exodus 33:7–11 (Mead), the intersection of "biblical geography" with biblical exegesis (Merrill), Paul and the law (Gould), and reading Matthew 6:13 as the "Evil One" (Thayer). In addition to a read-ing of Ezekiel, Toy presented papers on the various explanations of Matthew 2:23 ("he shall be called a Nazarene") and the date of Deuteronomy (February 1884). Some of the presentations were in defense of "traditional" positions in light of the critique of higher criticism. For example, Alvah Hovey argued for

---

for Toy; he was instrumental in founding the Conversation Club in Louisville (see chapter 3).

[4] David Lyon, "Minutes on Crawford Howell Toy, presented to the Harvard Biblical Club at its meeting in Boston, Saturday, December 13, 1919," Papers of David Gordon Lyon, Diary Ephemera, 1919, HUG 1541, Box 3, Folder 3, HUA.

[5] Whittemore was a Harvard graduate and a seventh-generation descendant of Har-vard's first president, Henry Dunster. He was a Baptist minister who taught for eight years at Rochester Theological Seminary. He published several books, including one on Horatio Hackett (a professor of biblical literature at Newton Theological Institution, 1839–1868). After he returned to Boston, he served as pulpit supply in various churches and was a dea-con at Old Cambridge Baptist Church (see Church Covenant Meeting, February 1, 1889; OCBCA). Whittemore would pass away at the age of 81 less than two years after the dissolution of the HBC; see *Cambridge Tribune* (May 14, 1921).

[6] A number of others, including David Lyon, joined in the coming months.

the view that the Apostle John was author of the Fourth Gospel.[7] At the March 1883 session, Ezra Abbot argued that there was no conflict regarding the timing of the Last Supper in the accounts of the Synoptics and the Fourth Gospel.

Over the next several years, a number of other topics were explored by Biblical Club members: the bearing of Babylonian-Assyrian religion on Old Testament doctrine and ritual (Lyon), the (dis)connection between the destruction of Judea and Christ's prediction of his Parousia in the Synoptic tradition (Hicks), and Paul's view of Christ, namely that he did not view him as equal to the Deity (Hall). In December 1888, Professor Gould presented a paper defending the historicity of Jesus' miracles. He concluded, "Nothing but the arbitrary rejection of the miraculous can prove an unfavorable test of the miracles of Jesus, the historical Christ."[8] At the very next meeting, Professor Mead continued the theme with a paper titled "The Agnostic View of the Evidential Value of Miracles." According to the abstract, Mead argued that "to believe in a Christ who did not perform miracles is to believe in a Christ we know nothing of—either Christianity is a delusion, or the supernatural is inseparable from it."[9]

A year later, Professor Ryder presented a paper titled "The Practical Gains of the Higher Criticism," which met with the general approval of the group. His abstract, copied into the HBC minutes, claimed the paper aimed

> to show that the traditional view that the Scripture is an infallible rule of faith and practice, limits its usefulness, makes faith in its inspiration difficult, and fixes attention upon its formal and temporary features rather than upon those which are spiritual and eternal; and that the freer ideas of the nature and origin of the Bible, now held by many scholars, tend both to an increase of true faith in the Scriptures and also a recovery of a more just idea of the constant presence of God's spirit with pious souls and with the church.[10]

Despite their apparent differences in biblical interpretation, the group developed strong interpersonal relationships. David Lyon commented that the HBC "has ever been the abode of harmony and goodwill, to which every

---

[7] At the January 6, 1883, and the January 5, 1884, meetings of the club. This was the same Hovey who was editor of the American Commentary Series and who withdrew the invitation to Toy to write the series commentary on the Pastoral Epistles in light of Toy's conclusion regarding the pseudonymous authorship of the Epistles.

[8] December 1, 1888, Minutes of the Harvard Biblical Club, HUA.

[9] January 5, 1889 minutes.

[10] January 4, 1890 minutes. The language here is reminiscent of the arguments laid out during the Toy controversy a decade earlier.

member could bring the results of his study with the assurance of sympathetic hearing and frank discussion."[11] All the members were saddened at news of the death of one of the club's founding members, Professor Ezra Abbot, in spring 1884. A special session was called to hear a "special item" from J. B. Thayer to be entered into the association's minutes and presented to Abbot's family. The special session was held on May 10, 1884,[12] and Professor Thayer presented the following eloquent tribute in memory of Ezra Abbot:

> By the death of Professor Abbot, D.D. L.L. D, the Harvard Biblical Club has been deprived of one of its original, most useful, most valued members.
>
> His constancy in attendance in spite of accumulating bodily infirmities, his keen and broad interest in everything pertaining to the Sacred Scriptures, the thoroughness of his research, the extent and accuracy of his knowledge, the clearness and candor of his discussions, his modest estimate of himself, and his generous appreciation of the efforts of others, render his name for us the synonym of scholarly and Christian worth:--an associate to be beloved, a scholarly example to be imitated, a loss to be deplored, a memory to be reverently cherished.[13]

Following the reading of the minutes, several professors shared recollections of their associations with Abbot. Secretary Whittemore summarized Toy's remarks about his friend and colleague (who had sought from Broadus in 1880 a "frank and somewhat full account" of Toy's personal and scholarly qualities): "The President, Dr. Toy, spoke of the esteem and love which had grown up in him for his late colleague, in the close relations of the last four years, not only official, though his example of scholarly fidelity to truth would have an abiding influence, but in the delightful intercourse of the home to which he had been so often and kindly welcomed."[14] In addition to the shared scholarly knowledge that the Biblical Club (and other professional societies) provided Toy and his colleagues, the personal affection that grew out of these regular associations was surely a benefit highly prized by Crawford Toy.

Over the years, Crawford Toy made several presentations to the HBC (besides the two already mentioned). Those included:

---

[11] Lyon, "Minutes on Crawford Toy," December 13, 1919, Harvard Biblical Club, HUA.

[12] Three more members were elected to the club representing the Episcopal Theological School, Andover Seminary, and First Parish Church, Cambridge. Not everyone who was elected to membership accepted, however, often because of "other pressing duties."

[13] May 10, 1884 minutes.

[14] Ibid.

"Recent Theories on the Pentateuch" (December 5, 1885)

"Biblical Demonology" (December 7, 1889)

"The Final Redaction of the Book of Proverbs" (October 11, 1891)

Daniel 5:25 (April 9, 1892)

"The Alleged Conflict between Literary and Archaeological Old Testament Criticism" (March 14, 1896)

"The introduction of the Jahweh cult into Israel" (October 10, 1903)

Many of Toy's papers, as well as others' presentations, would eventually be published;[15] a number of them appeared in the *Journal of Biblical Literature*. Toy's paper on "Biblical Demonology" deserves special comment. The recording secretary, George Whittemore, typically recorded the name of the presenter, the title of the paper and, when available, a brief abstract provided by the presenter. On rare occasions, Whittemore would comment on the quality of the discussion prompted by the presentation. In the case of Toy's "Biblical Demonology," Whittemore was effusive in his praise:

> Professor Toy read a paper on Biblical Demonology, presenting the view that the revised refined & purified Hebrew Scriptures, chronologically considered, exhibit no distinct, malevolent spirit until the Satan of Job, a composite, slowly developed not altogether consistent conception, due largely it may be, to Persian ideas. He is found in the New Test to represent the combined evil agencies of the Old, and to be at the head of the demonical realm, a conception also largely foreign and gnostic in origin & development. This is a most imperfect hint at the contents of an essay of admirable order and lucidity, the discussion indeed embracing the expression of some doubt as to whether the actual history could have presented so clear an evolution.[16]

Beyond being an active presenter, Toy was also a steady and official presence at the meetings. In his role as president, he chaired each session and guided the discussion. He also ran the meetings, which observed established and formal procedures and protocols. For example, when one member asked about the impact of absences from meetings, Toy, as chair, replied that there "was no limit to the absences of a member of the Club, provided they did not

---

[15] E.g., C. H. Toy, "The Present Position of Pentateuch Criticism," *Unitarian Review* 24 (1886): 47–68.

[16] December 7, 1889 minutes. Whittemore nowhere else commented with this detail about any other of Toy's presentations (striking down the possibility that Whittemore was simply seeking to curry the favor of the club's president). A version of the paper was published as "Evil Spirits in the Bible," *JBL* 9 (1890): 17–30.

interfere with filling his appointment on the Calendar; and that the standing of those unable to attend through change of residence or other good cause was that of honorary members."[17] Crawford Toy as president and George Whittemore were the only officers the HBC ever had, and each January, the members went through the ritual of reelecting the officers to another annual term.

Only once in the minutes does it appear that the HBC departed from its mission to encourage presentation and discussion of scholarly papers on biblical topics. In January 1893, the HBC members voted that "the Secretary be empowered to write to the President Elect of the United States, at such time as may seem fitting, requesting in the interest of the Biblical and archaeological studies to which this Club is devoted, the retention of the Rev. Dr. Selah Merrill in the consulship at Jerusalem." Selah Merrill had been a founding member of the HBC when he taught at Andover Theological Seminary. He was appointed to the consulship in Jerusalem during Benjamin Harrison's presidential administration. With the election of Grover Cleveland, a Republican, Merrill's appointment was in jeopardy. Over the next year, the HBC lobbied for their colleague Merrill to keep his post, but it was to no avail. On January 13, 1894, the minutes report that Merrill's position had been terminated.[18]

In later years, because of his failing eyesight and other physical ailments, Toy was unable to attend many of the meetings of the HBC. After he missed several meetings at the beginning of 1918, Nancy Toy (Crawford's wife) sent a note to the club that was read by the secretary "explaining our President's physical disability, but continued interest." In its heyday from about 1897–1906, the HBC averaged anywhere from fourteen to eighteen in attendance.[19] Attendance during those last years began to decline. In 1911, the average attendance was eleven or twelve. In February 1919, the club's secretary reported that the average attendance for 1918 had dwindled to eight.[20] The attendance in 1919 (Toy died in May 1919) was as follows: January—four; February—eight; March—five; April—six; November—nine; December—nine. At the

---

[17] As reported by the secretary in the May 12, 1900, Minutes of the Harvard Biblical Club, vol. 2, October, 1897–December 1919, HUD 3211, Box 2, Records of the Harvard Biblical Club, HUA.

[18] Later, with yet another change in the administration, Merrill returned to the American consulate in Jerusalem.

[19] See the January annual reports in the minutes of the Harvard Biblical Club from each year, which included an average attendance (as well as the high and low attendance for the previous year).

[20] The report that year had been delayed until February because only four members attended the January meeting.

November meeting—the first meeting since Toy had died—Secretary Whittemore made the formal announcement of Toy's death. A printed tribute to Toy was inserted into the minutes following the November 1919 minutes.

The December 1919 meeting turned out to be the last of the HBC. In addition to the nine members present at the meeting were two guests, one of whom was Henry J. Cadbury, a Harvard PhD who had just returned to Cambridge to join the Harvard faculty and who, after a brief stint at Bryn Mawr, would return to Harvard in 1934 and have a distinguished career as writer well beyond his retirement in 1954. Poor attendance was compounded by the fact that the secretary had been unable to set a calendar of presentations for the 1920 spring meetings. David Lyon read a tribute prepared for the HBC. He concluded:

> Dr. Toy's long connection with this Club has left a memory of the most pleasing nature. We all admired his ample and accurate scholarship, his ability to seize and express the essential thought, his fairness in stating the views of others and his modesty and considerateness in urging his own, his respect for the opinions of others and his genial manner in expressing dissent, the soundness of his views, always based on careful study and reflection. He was the personification of urbanity and gentlemanliness, the charming companion, the lover of learning, the reverent student of the Bible. He rejoiced in good work, not only his own but that of others. He was guileless as a child, unselfish, and free from self-seeking. He sought to achieve for himself and to impart to others the highest ideals of conduct and of scholarship. He thus served his generation well, always abreast and often in advance of his times…. Among the satisfactions of life he probably found none more real and enduring than that connected with the worthy task worthily performed.[21]

Following the tribute, discussion about the future of the club ensued, and the nine members present decided to dissolve the club as a way to honor Toy's memory. They passed the following motion:

> After utterances by several speakers (the Secretary having earlier reported a failing Calendar for papers), recognizing the difference in the situation of questions of Biblical Criticism now and a generation ago, when the Club flourished; with an expression of sentiment that Dr. Toy had been the life as well as the founder of the Club,—and that perhaps his memory could hardly be more honored on our part by action as follows it was voted (*nem.con.*) [without dissent] that the Club be dissolved at the close

---

[21] Lyon, "Minute on Toy," vol. 3, January 11, 1919–December 13, 1919, HUD 3211, Box 2, Records of the Harvard Biblical Club, HUA.

of the present meeting.[22]

Following the resolution, George Foote Moore presented a paper on "The Word *Messiah*," and the HBC closed its doors forever.[23]

History of Religions Club (HRC). In November 1891, Crawford Toy hosted another meeting of scholars, this time for those interested in the study of religions. Thus, the Harvard Religions Club (later the History of Religions Club) was born. On December 5, 1891, the group again was hosted by Toy in his home, and he gave a sketch of the history of the study of religions. The purpose of the club, he proposed, was to explore "the comparative study of religions." Present at the December meeting were Toy, C. C. Everett, James B. Greenenough, John Wriglit, Charles Lanman, George Kittredge, Morris Morgan, William Newell, and David Lyon.[24] The participation of Everett,

---

[22] December 13, 1919, Minutes of the Harvard Biblical Club, HBC, HUA. The language of the motion echoed the sentiments of Lyon in his tribute in which he spoke of C. H. Toy as "not only the Founder but he was ever the life and mainspring of the Club. For all that he was to us as an organization and as individuals we are profoundly grateful." Following the vote to dissolve, David Lyon moved for a vote of thanks to George Whittemore, who was "the only survivor of the original group, for faithful, efficient and devoted service."

[23] December 13, 1919 minutes. Whittemore ended the last recorded minutes with these words:

> Dr. Moore presented a paper on The Word Messiah, after consideration of which came
> Finis,
> George Henry Whittemore
> Secretary and Treasurer of the Harvard Biblical Club, Feb. 5, 1881–Dec. 13, 1919

[24] History of Religions Club Minutes, Papers of C. R. Lanman, HUD 3454.500, HUA. The minutes were apparently supplemented with information from the diary of David Lyon. Later, famed Harvard anthropologist F. W. Putnam would join the group, and by 1905 he had become an integral part of the group (see correspondence from Crawford H. Toy to F. W. Putnam in February and December 1905, History of Religions Club Minutes). Toy had taken to sending postcards to members announcing the date and topic for the month. G. F. Moore claimed the HRC "counted among its members some of the most distinguished scholars in the University—philologists, archaeologists, and anthropologists" (Moore, "Toy," 7). George Foot Moore himself added to the luster of the group. Moore was professor and then president at Andover Theological Seminary until he joined the Harvard faculty in 1902. In Moore, according to George Williams, "the historian of religion had emerged as a new socio-academic type, distinct from both the college chaplain and the university professor of Christian theology" (Williams, *The "Augustan Age*," 177–78; see also Morton Smith, "George Foot Moore," *Harvard Library Bulletin* 15 [1967]: 169–79).

then dean of Harvard Divinity School (1879–1900), was especially significant. Everett "for the first time anywhere made the study of world religions a necessary part of systematic theology."[25]

The group was more loosely organized than the Harvard Biblical Club. There was no George Whittemore to keep meticulous minutes, and the club had no elected officers. According to Lyon, however, "Dr. Toy kept the record as long as he was able, and by unanimous consent he was always looked up to as president."[26] It was also smaller than HBC, with a membership that hovered around twelve; during the years 1892–1919, the group averaged seven members in attendance, ranging mostly from five to eight.[27] While perhaps less well organized than the HBC, the History of Religions Club represented the area of most interest to Toy toward the end of his career. "Dr. Toy's chief interest during the later years of his life was the broad field of religion, and he was rarely happier than in the monthly meetings of this group of congenial friends."[28]

As noted above, the records for the HRC were not as thorough as for the HBC. Still, we are able to get a sense of the wide variety of topics presented to the group, which included in the first few years papers on such subjects as "Medieval Monasticism" (Emerton, February 1892); "Stoic Ideas in Christianity" (Greenenough, March 1892); "Religious Heresy in Ancient Athens" (Tarbell, May 1892); "Christian Saint Worship" (Newell, February 1893); "Human Sacrifice," (Wriglit, May 1893); "The Horse in Religion and Especially in Greek Religion" (Morgan, December 1894); "Druidism" (Sheldon, January 1895); "The Art of the American Indians" (Putnam, March 1895).[29] Toy gave papers on "Evil Spirits in Heaven" (November 1896); "Semitic Chthonic Deities" (May 1898); "Belief in the Death of the Soul" (October 1903); "He thought it not robbery to be equal with God" (May 1906); "Some Differences between Semitic and Indo-European Gods" (October 1910).

---

[25] Williams, The "Augustan Age," 141.

[26] Lyon, "Toy," 18.

[27] History of Religions Club Minutes, HUA.

[28] Lyon, "Toy," 18. Toy's interest would culminate in the publication of *Introduction to the History of Religions* (Boston, MA: Ginn and Company, 1913), but he had published other articles that indicated his shifting interests in this direction: see, e.g., "Myths and Legends as Vehicles of Religious Teaching," *Christian Register* 72 (1893): 404–405; "Taboo and Morality," *Journal of the American Oriental Society* 20 (1899): 151–56; "The Relation between Magic and Religion," *Journal of the American Oriental Society* 20 (1899): 327–31; "An Early Form of Animal Sacrifice," *Journal of the American Oriental Society* 26 (1905): 137–44.

[29] History of Religion Club Minutes, HUA. One of the more interesting topics was the paper on "Vampires" presented by Kittredge at the March 1897 meeting.

CRAWFORD HOWELL TOY

In May 1905, the HRC held a dinner at the Parker House in Boston to honor Toy's twenty-five years at Harvard. Professor Kittredge presided, and David Lyon presented Toy with a commemorative silver cigarette box. A dozen members attended.[30] David Lyon and George F. Moore also edited a Festschrift in honor of Crawford Toy's seventy-fifth birthday (March 23, 1911). The volume appeared in 1912 and consisted of essays related to the study of the history of religions. A number of the contributors had been participants in the HRC, and the club's influence on the topics is evident.[31] The HRC also presented Toy with a gift on his eightieth birthday in 1916, although by now, Toy's health was making his attendance at this and other meetings more difficult.[32]

Unlike the Harvard Biblical Club, which ceased to exist with Toy's death, the History of Religions Club continued for several more decades. The relationship of the HRC to the emergence of the history of religions as a mode of inquiry at Harvard would be an interesting topic to pursue at another time. Apparently, President Eliot consulted with David Lyon about creating a professorship in the study of history of religions.

> I have delivered your message to Dr. Toy, and he will write to you. After leaving you this morning I wondered at myself for not suggesting Dr. Toy himself for the history of religions. This has for years been a special interest of his, and he founded about a dozen years ago the Harvard Club for the Study of Religions....
>
> Dr. Toy and I have often spoken of the desirableness of a University department for the study of religions. If such a department is to be created, I believe that all the members of the Club which I have mentioned would think of Dr. Toy as the man for the place. If he should be thus appointed, might not G. F. Moore be chosen to do the linguistic work now done by Dr. Toy? G. F. Moore would also be admirable for the history of religions, but he has not, I think, given to the subject so much attention as Dr. Toy. I will only add that Dr. Toy is now engaged to write a book of introduction to the study of religion.[33]

In 1904, Eliot named George F. Moore (and not Toy) as the first holder of the Frothingham Professorship of the History of Religion at Harvard.

---

[30] History of Religions Club Minutes, HUA; see also David Gordon Lyon Diary, May 6, 1905, HUG 1541, Box 6, Volume 3, HUA.

[31] David Lyon and George Foot Moore, *Studies in the History of Religions* (New York: The Macmillan Company, 1912). See Appendix 4 for the Table of Contents. Jacob Schiff helped pay for the printing of the volume (on Schiff, see chapter 6).

[32] History of Religions Club Minutes, HUA.

[33] David G. Lyon to Charles W. Eliot, May 24, 1901, Papers of President Charles W. Eliot, UAI 5.150, Box 52, HUA.

Although not active members of the HRC, Harvard philosophers Josiah Royce, George Herbert Palmer, William James, and later William Hocking also advanced the academic study of comparative religions at Harvard.[34] The phrase "history of religions" is a contested one, its appropriateness being disputed from nearly the time of its introduction at Harvard.[35] Toy's own comparative approach (typical of many practitioners in late nineteenth century), which was heavily influenced by an evolutionary model that traced the development of religions from "primitive" to "advanced," also came under fire.[36]

Editorial Work: New World. Charles Everett (1829–1900), dean of Harvard Divinity School, was one of the founding editors of *New World: A Quarterly Review of Religion, Ethics and Theology* in 1892. The journal was in print until 1900. During this eight-year period, Crawford Toy was part of the editorial board, along with Everett, Orello Cone, and N. P. Gilman (who was named managing editor). The journal's stated purpose was to be open to able and constructive thinkers without regard to sectarian lines. For the editors, this *New World* was one that develops under the influence of modern science, philosophy, criticism, and philanthropy—all of which, rightly viewed, are the friends and helpers of enduring religious faith. The journal planned to publish 200 pages in each issue and included book reviews in additions to articles. The lead articles of the first issue were essays titled "The Evolution of Christianity" by Lyman Abbott and "The Historic and the Ideal Christ" by editor Charles Carroll Everett.[37] Everett makes the interesting claim that "everyone who believes that God is a spirit is thereby a Trinitarian." Everett's Trinity, however, "has nothing in common with that of the creeds" but rather is based on the view of Dorner (Toy's former teacher) that the "Trinity is made up of the elements that enter into the various aspects of all complete spiritual consciousness." Thus, the Father is the "I" of divine self-consciousness, the Son is the "me," and the Holy Spirit "stands for the unity of the two."[38]

Over its thirty-six issues, Toy contributed six articles and seventy-four book reviews.[39] Most of Toy's contributions to the journal came through his editorial efforts. We get a glimpse of Toy's work in the March 1900 diary Toy

---

[34] Williams, *The "Augustan Age,"* 180–81.

[35] See John B. Carman and Kathryn Dodgson, eds., *Community and Colloquy* (Cambridge: Center for the Study of World Religions, 2006), 15.

[36] Again, almost from the beginning. G. F. Moore, in his tribute to Toy, criticized him for utilizing this evolutionary model in his understanding of first-century Judaism ("Toy," 13–14).

[37] Lyman Abbott, "The Evolution of Christianity," *New World* 1 (1892): 1–13; Charles Carroll Everett, "The Historic and Ideal Christ," *New World* 1 (1892): 14–29.

[38] Everett, "Historic and Ideal Christ," 15.

[39] Lyon, "Toy," 21.

contributed to the Harvard time capsule. On March 2, Toy recorded that he "went to Dr. Everett's (found him suffering with cold) and talked over *New World* matters. Managing Editor Gilman is to make a trip to Europe, and the labor of bringing out the June & Sept. nos. of *New World* falls on Dr. Everett & me."[40] Three days later, Toy returned to Everett's home and found him still ill, so Toy "arranged some *New World* matters" which included rejecting a submission on "The Hamadyad." The next day (March 6), he wrote to Gilman, the managing editor of *New World*, for assistance in recruiting an article on popular religions of India. On March 9, Toy visited Riverside Press (Houghton, Mifflin & Co.), publishers of *New World*, "to arrange for sending to them of copy for the *New World*, & receiving proofs." The following day, Toy looked over books for review in *New World*. On Sunday, March 11, Toy visited Everett again and "got articles and books for *New World*" and spent part of the mornings of March 12, 13, and 14 reading articles for the journal. After a week occupied with other responsibilities, Toy was back to reading articles for *New World* on March 21. On that same afternoon, Toy visited Everett "to talk over articles and book indices for *New World*." He returned to work on *New World* on March 23 (Toy's birthday). On March 25, after church, the Toys dined with Dr. Everett and his daughter, Mildred. After lunch, Everett and Toy "settled some *New World* matters." Toy read *New World* articles again on the morning of March 28 and in the afternoon picked up books for review. On March 29, Toy went to the College Library to check a reference to Antoninus Pius's *Scriptores Augustae historiae* for an article in the June issue of *New World*. On March 30, Toy again worked on *New World* articles, and on the afternoon of March 31, he visited Everett again (who was still not well). All told, Toy reports spending parts of sixteen days working on *New World* matters: rejecting or recruiting essays, proofing articles, collecting books for reviews, checking the accuracy of references in an article, arranging for the printing of the journal, and consulting with Everett.[41]

In the final issue of *New World*, published after the death of Everett, the last pages are devoted to a tribute to C. C. Everett by Toy. He describes Everett's philosophical assumptions and gives a rather detailed account of two of Everett's lecture courses on theology and Asiatic religions. About Everett's work with *New World*, he writes:

---

[40] Diary of Crawford H. Toy, March 2, 1900, Chest of 1900, 900.11, Box 4, HUA. Other references in this paragraph are also from the diary.

[41] Perhaps Toy's activities during March are atypical, given that Gilman was indisposed and Everett was sick. Still, Toy clearly invested significant time into the management of the journal.

It is with deep sorrow that we record the death of Charles Carroll Everett, the Senior Editor of the *NEW WORLD*. He was one of its founders, and was a member of its editorial board from the beginning. He gave it much of his time, contributing to it a number of articles, and being always ready with helpful suggestions in its conduct. He was largely instrumental in determining its tone and spirit, and in giving it whatever power for good it may have possessed.[42]

Editorial Work: Jewish Encyclopedia. Replacing George Foot Moore very early in the planning stages, Crawford Toy served as the only non-Jewish editor of the *Jewish Encyclopedia* with particular responsibilities for the departments of Hebrew philology and Hellenistic literature.[43] According to the preface of the encyclopedia, Hebrew philology

> possesses peculiar interest. The history of the Hebrew alphabet, in its origin and changes, shows the relation of the Jews in the most ancient times to their Semitic neighbors, while its development follows certain lines of cleavage which indicate actual divisions among the Jewish people. Certain peculiarities of grammar and vocabulary, when traced historically to their source, determine whether the Jews developed their language solely on their own national lines or whether they borrowed from other nations, of their own or of different stock.[44]

The description of Hellenistic Literature included in the encyclopedia is also instructive:

> The *Jewish Encyclopedia* aims to acquaint the student with the results of modern research in many fields that are altogether new and bristling with interesting discoveries…. The nineteenth century witnessed a great advance in the investigation of Hellenistic literature. The forms and syntactical constructions of the Hellenistic dialect have been set forth in dictionaries and grammars, so as greatly to facilitate the study of the

---

[42] Crawford H. Toy, "Charles Carroll Everett," *New World* 9 (1900): 714. Toy ended his tribute by noting that Everett's "life was an illustration of the principles inculcated in his teaching; he lived truly in that pure atmosphere of religion which he regarded as the end and outcome of the world" (725). Harvard philosopher, Josiah Royce, also provided an analysis of Everett's philosophy in "Professor Everett as a Metaphysician," *New World* 9 (1900): 726–41.

[43] Lyon, "Toy," 21. He was also a contributor to all twelve volumes. On the history of the encyclopedia and the issues surrounding its controversial founding editor, Isidore Singer, see Shuly Rubin Schwartz, *The Emergence of Jewish Scholarship in America: The Publication of the Jewish Encyclopedia*, Monographs of the Hebrew Union College 13 (Cincinnati: Hebrew Union College Press, 1991).

[44] "Preface," *Jewish Encyclopedia*, http://www.jewishencyclopedia.com/preface.

documents. ...The result has been to determine with some definiteness the relation of the Hellenistic literature to the Jewish and Greek thought of the period, and its position in the general intellectual development of the age which produced Christianity. In these investigations Jewish scholars have taken a distinguished part. It has been the aim of the *Jewish Encyclopedia* to present in the most thorough manner the results achieved by critical investigation in the domain of Hellenistic literature. Of all Hellenistic productions of Jewish interest critical accounts and critical discussions are given; and the necessity of apprehending the ideas contained in them as products of their times, and of tracing their origin and development and their influence on contemporary and on later life, has constantly been kept in view.[45]

George Foot Moore remarked regarding Toy's service to the *Jewish Encyclopedia* that while he "wrote little for it himself, he put a great deal of time and labor into the revision of the many articles to which his editorial initial is affixed as a kind of imprimatur."[46] Since Toy had only recently begun his work for the *Jewish Encyclopedia*, his March 1900 diary is less revealing of his editorial work there than for *New World*. Nonetheless, there is reference to Toy's work as a contributor for articles on "Abraham" (March 1–3), "Anakim" (March 5–6), and "Ariel" (March 6–7) for the encyclopedia. On March 10, Toy responded to a query from the publishers of the *Jewish Encyclopedia*, Funk & Wagnalls, as to whether B.C./A.D. or B.C.E./C.E. should be used for dates. Toy advised the "use of the former [B.C./A.D.] on the ground that they were the common conventional symbols & did not carry belief in Xty."[47] Toy did not return to his work for the *Jewish Encyclopedia* until the end of the month (March 30).

Participation in the Academic Life at Harvard

University Committees. Crawford Toy served on several committees during his long tenure at Harvard. He was on the Harvard Library Council and the Graduate School administrative board.[48] Even as he closed in on retirement, Toy continued to serve on various committees. In 1907, as chair of the

---

[45] Ibid.

[46] Moore, "Toy," 8.

[47] Toy's advice does not seem to have completely won the day. In the list of abbreviations for the *Jewish Encyclopedia*, one finds "B.C." for "before the Christian Era" (and not B.C.E.) and "C.E." for the "common era" (but no A.D.). A perusal of the online version of the 1906 edition, however, shows both A.D. and C.E. used in individual articles, although "B.C." seems to be used consistently throughout; see http://www.jewishencyclopedia.com/abbreviations_listings#0.

[48] Lyon, "Toy," 16.

divinity committee on the chapel organ (!), he had to write President Eliot to ask if he were authorized to order repairs to the organ that might be in excess of $40.[49] He was also an active, if at times bemused, participant in Harvard faculty meetings. In his first year at Harvard, Toy was impressed with the quality of the discussion meetings. He wrote to Broadus about "the faculty-meetings with discussions of all sorts of educational questions."[50] In 1883, Toy wrote Broadus again and mentioned attending "the largest Faculty-meeting I have seen (48 men present) and the best debate. The discussion [about conferring the A.B. degree without requiring Greek] will probably go on throughout the college-year."[51]

Within a decade, Toy's view of the efficacy of faculty meetings was slightly less enthusiastic. In those days, Harvard faculty meetings were regularly held in the evening, and on one particular occasion, Toy reported that J. H. Thayer had brought up a "well-worn question" about degree requirements that "the majority of the Fac'y don't care to discuss." But, he added, "the Pres't, who had been taking short naps, waked up and had a dialogic argument with Thayer for half an hour, the rest smiling & yawning for it was approaching 11 o'clock, & we knew that the thing was endless."[52] No doubt this was the kind of meeting Toy's old friend and Harvard colleague, William James, had in mind when he wrote from his European research leave to Toy: "Don't I just *not* envy you all the soul- and body-destroying committees, which you must be having to attend! They are what are losing Harvard University. Da durch wird sie zu grunde gerichtet."[53]

Informal Influence. Toy was also involved in the informal channels of information and chains of command, which have apparently long been part of the fabric of academic life. Toy was particularly interested in faculty appointments. At one point early in his career at Harvard, and perhaps emboldened by his presumed participation in the appointment of David Lyon to the faculty,[54] Toy wrote John Broadus with a proposal that Broadus fill a vacancy in the divinity school:

---

[49] Crawford H. Toy to Charles Eliot, November 20, 1907, Records of the President of Harvard University, Charles W. Eliot, UAI 5.150, Box 68, HUA. Eliot's assistant, Mr. Warren, gave approval for the repairs (Warren to Crawford H. Toy, November 25, 1907).

[50] Crawford H. Toy to John A. Broadus, December 14, 1881, Broadus Papers, ASC, SBTS.

[51] Toy to Broadus, December 5, 1883.

[52] Diary of Crawford H. Toy, March 26, 1900, Chest of 1900, 900.11, Box 4, HUA.

[53] William James to Crawford H. Toy, May 3, 1893, William James Papers, 1842–1910, bMS Am 1092.92.9 (3818), Harvard Houghton Library, HUA. The German translates: "As a result, she is judged."

[54] For details of Lyon's appointment, see chapter 7.

The authorities here are anxious to have a trinitarian Prof of Syst. Th[eolog]y in the Div'y School, and, failing the money now for a chair, have established a lectureship, filled last year by a Congregat.l clergyman of Cambridge. Negotiating with two men (Thayer, late of Andover, & Newman Smyth) have deferred the matter till I felt it would be useless to write you for this year; but I should like to know whether you would be willing to come, if we could arrange for next year or the year after (that is, the Spring of '84 or '85). A course in ten or twelve lectures on any theological subject, as, an exposition of Romans, or one of the Gospels, or a sketch of N.T. Christology, or a systematic exposition of some doctrine; wide choice of subjects is possible. The sum offered is inconsiderable (about $300); but I hope that you would find a visit here pleasant, as I know it would be greatly enjoyed by us all.[55]

We do not possess Broadus's response, but he did not take up Toy's offer. Toy's next extant letter to Broadus is from April 1884, and Toy acknowledged Broadus's expression of condolences in light of the death of Ezra Abbot. Once again, Toy was involved in the faculty recruitment process:

Nothing has been done towards filling the vacant chair. It is a question whether we shall try to get a text-critical man, or one more devoted to exegesis and historical criticism. Do you know C. R. Gregory of Leipzig? & have you any opinion as to his general scholarship & ability? ...Or if you know any accessible able man, could you give me his name? It is possible that J H Thayer may be our choice; but while we like him a good deal, we wish to see whether there is anybody we might like better. This, of course, *inter nos*.[56]

Unable to attract Broadus to a vacant faculty position at Harvard in 1884, in summer 1886 Toy tried to induce him to speak in Appleton Chapel (despite the fact that the honorarium was "only $50"):

I hope you will be able to come, and you will come to my house, of course, prepared to stay not less than a week. We are all very much interested in this new experiment of religious service in Harvard. The problem is to get and to hold the attention of fourteen hundred men of all varieties of disposition and belief. I incline to think that there is no little basis here of sound, honest, religious sentiment—much kicking, of course, against the community received orthodoxy, or rather a great indifference to it, yet at the same time a deep interest in fundamental religious truth in its bearing on life. I think you may hope to effect a good

---

[55] Crawford H. Toy to John A. Broadus, December 8, 1882, Broadus Papers, ASC, SBTS.

[56] Toy to Broadus, April 7, 1884. Thayer was ultimately appointed to the vacancy.

deal by coming.[57]

Broadus did, indeed, receive an invitation to speak in chapel at Harvard and sought Boyce's counsel. Boyce responded:

> I see no objection to your doing as you please about preaching at Harvard, but were I you I should not plan to do so. There is great danger in any encouragement we give to Dr. Toy and Lyon. We do not know what harm we may do by making people think that their differences from us are not of importance. Besides, I do not like to see the Unitarians helped by favors from others, and especially by sermons from which the "gospel" must be left out so as not to say what would be unacceptable to Unitarians.[58]

Broadus heeded Boyce's advice and declined the invitation. Toy wrote Broadus to say: "I am very sorry that you cannot come. We had promised ourselves great pleasure in having you with us for a few days and in having your name associated with the celebration of the college. But I understand how great a pressure there is now to you and what an interruption it would be to come. What you say of your health gives me great concern."[59]

The correspondence between Toy and President Eliot also illuminates Toy's informal but influential role in university matters. The president often consulted Toy with regard to curricular matters in the university and divinity school. Toy gave permission for a female student to attend his Hebrew Religion course (Semitic 13) as a guest.[60] Just a month later, with the university facing financial difficulties, Eliot apparently suggested canceling some Semitic courses as a cost-saving measure. Toy responded:

> I do not think that any pecuniary gain of the College would result from the suspension or omission of any of the courses. The two professors are teaching 11 and 12 ½ hours, a fair amount but we cannot omit anything. If I have not answered your question satisfactorily, I should like to speak

---

[57] Toy to Broadus, July 22, 1886.

[58] James P. Boyce to John A. Broadus, August 14, 1886, Broadus Papers, ASC, SBTS. Boyce's letter seems to presume that Toy (and Lyon?) were on the side of the Unitarians, but at this point, both Toy and Lyon were still active members of OCBC. Boyce also presumes that there was no room for "trinitarian" sermons in the Harvard chapel, which also seems not to be the case.

[59] Toy to Broadus, October 29, 1886. Apparently, Broadus used being busy and unwell as his excuse to decline the invitation.

[60] Crawford H. Toy to Charles Eliot, December 16, 1893, Records of the President of Harvard University, Charles W. Eliot, UAI 5.150, Box 68, HUA.

with you about the matter. We recognize the serious position of the College, and would gladly do what we could to give relief.[61]

Toy was also apparently responsible for finding teachers to cover his classes during his sabbatical. In April 1894, Toy wrote Eliot five times to sort through proposed replacements. Toy was responsible as well for negotiating with the replacements regarding course times and payment.[62]

Toy also lobbied the president regarding potential purchases for the university, mostly in relation to Semitic studies and the Semitic Museum. Eliot, however, did not always follow Toy's expert advice. Regarding the Landberg collection, Toy wrote:

> The editing of these MSS would illustrate one of the great civilizations of the world; the obligation of Europe (and America) to Moslem culture has not yet been fully set forth. And further, this Moslem literature, historical, biographical, poetical & theological is valuable in itself as literature; the poetry is of a distinct and charming sort, and the narrative prose is unexcelled in the world for freshness and dramatic power.[63]

Toy then informed Eliot that the manuscripts were selling for $20,000, which Toy assured was "relatively not large." He thought Jacob Schiff, benefactor for Harvard Semitic studies, would contribute $15,000 if Harvard would commit $5,000.[64] Eliot was not impressed, especially given the fact that the manuscripts were copies and not originals. He denied the request. In a follow-up letter, Toy accepted the president's decision but tried to defend the proposed expenditure, explaining that copies of Hebrew and Arabic manuscripts rarely "differ among themselves by scarcely a letter." Thus the cost of the Landberg collection was justified, even though it consisted primarily of copies. Toy explained: "The precautions taken by Count Landberg justify us in regarding his copies as absolutely faithful. Originals have of course a superior sentimental value. And it is also true that though one may be convinced of the fidelity of a copy one feels just a little more absolutely certain of the originals. Yet practically the difference does not amount to anything."[65]

---

[61] Toy to Eliot, January 18, 1894.

[62] Toy to Eliot, April 14, 21, 24, 27, 29, 1894. One of the replacements, George Foot Moore, would eventually join the Harvard faculty, with Toy's support (see below).

[63] Crawford H. Toy to Charles Eliot, May 12, 1900, Records of the President of Harvard University, Charles W. Eliot, UAI 5.150, Box 126, HUA.

[64] Ibid.

[65] Toy to Eliot, May 17, 1900. Morris Ketchum Jesup, New York banker and philanthropist, purchased the Landberg collection, consisting of 835 manuscripts, in 1900 for the price of $20,000 and presented the collection to Yale University, where it is still housed in the Beinecke Rare Book and Manuscript Library.

Professor Toy's most active involvement in Harvard affairs was in the area of personnel. Toy was constantly making recommendations to President Eliot regarding faculty appointments, visiting lecturers, and even candidates for honorary degrees. Perhaps the most significant appointment that Toy was directly involved in was the selection of George Foot Moore to join the faculty. Moore had been serving as professor, and then president, of Andover Theological Seminary. He was well known to Toy through various professional associations, including the Harvard Biblical Club and History of Religions Club. In his March 1900 diary, Toy recorded that Moore and his brother, E. C. Moore, had come to the Toys' home for dinner and discussed "theological absurdities," and then attended the History of Religions Club. G. F. Moore spent the night and attended church with the Toys. After Sunday dinner, "Moore spoke of his plan for reorganizing Andover Sem'y so as to get it out of the clutches of the creed—this done, the Sem'y might be brought to Cambridge."[66] Toy wrote to Eliot, who was considering making an offer of a faculty appointment to Moore: "In regard to Professor G. F. Moore I have to say I think he would be a great addition to our force, and I should be very glad to see him in the Harvard Faculty. His specialty is Semitic history and literature, and his learning in this field is wide and exact; but his reading embraces much besides this. I know nothing about his ability as a teacher beyond the fact that he appears to have given satisfaction the year that he taught here. I regard him as one of the ablest men in this country."[67] Moore was appointed to the Harvard faculty in 1902.

Toy, however, was not always so successful in his recommendations. In 1907, Toy informed Eliot that Professor Max Margolis of Hebrew Union College in Cincinnati had left his post "on account of dogmatic differences with the President." Margolis would "be glad to come to Harvard. He is a scholar of recognized ability and has undertaken a great work—a revision of the concordance of the Septuagint." Toy wondered if Harvard could offer a "sufficient salary."[68] Eliot's assistant, Jerome Greene, replied to say that the president "did not think it would be practicable to offer Professor Max Margolis a place here without assuming a greater obligation than the University is in a position to assume at present."[69]

---

[66] Diary of Crawford H. Toy, March 18, 1900, Chest of 1900, 900.11, Box 4, HUA.

[67] Crawford H. Toy to Charles Eliot, May 1, 1901, Records of the President of Harvard University, Charles W. Eliot, UAI 5.150, Box 68, HUA. Moore's younger brother, E. C. Moore, would also join the faculty as Parkman Professor of Theology. Toy was also instrumental in the appointments of David Lyon and George Reisner (see chapter 7).

[68] Toy to Eliot, March 12, 1907.

[69] Jerome Greene to Crawford H. Toy, March 18, 1907, Records of the President of Harvard University, Charles W. Eliot, UAI 5.150, Box 68, HUA.

Occasionally Toy would weigh in with the president regarding the qualifications of certain individuals for honorary degrees. Toy suggested B. D. Eerdmans of Leiden University for an honorary degree because he would be in town during commencement, was a recognized scholar, and it would be "an appropriate compliment to the eminent University of which he is a member."[70] Eerdmans did not receive the recognition. On the other hand, when asked to say something in support of an honorary L.L.D. degree for Morris Jastrow, Jr., of the University of Pennsylvania, Toy acknowledged that Jastrow was an "excellent Semitic scholar," but then concluded that he could "not say that he stands decidedly above all other Semitic scholars in this country."[71]

The last couple of years of Toy's career at Harvard were marked by several misunderstandings. First, a clerical error on the part of Jerome Greene, the president's assistant and secretary to the Harvard Corporation, had resulted in Toy being promised a salary of $6,000 for 1908, which was $500 over the maximum allowed for a full professor in the College of Arts and Sciences.[72] In response to Toy's query of "how the matter stands?" Jerome replied that Toy would receive one-fourth of his compensation at the rate of $6,000 and three-fourths at the rate of $5,500.[73] Compensation was becoming a concern to Toy, whose retirement pension was about to cut his income nearly in half.

There was also confusion regarding the timing of Toy's retirement from the university. Part of the confusion was due to Toy's indecision about when to retire. Apparently, he had engaged in a conversation with the president about retiring at the end of the 1907–1908 academic year but was persuaded not to do so by Eliot. In spring 1907, Toy wrote to Eliot, "On reconsideration (as you suggested) I have decided not to offer my resignation—I think I see my way to getting time for my book, and I recognize a certain obligation to the University."[74] Confusion emerged again in 1908, when it appeared Toy

[70] Crawford H. Toy to Charles Eliot, April 25, 1902, Records of the President of Harvard University, Charles W. Eliot, UAI 5.150, Box 126, HUA.

[71] Toy to Eliot, March 4, 1907, Records of the President of Harvard University, Charles W. Eliot, UAI 5.150, Box 68, HUA. Jastrow and others had been involved in a dispute with his Penn colleague, Hermann Hilprecht, to which Toy also alluded in his letter, expressing hope that Jastrow would "come out victorious in his struggle with Hilprecht."

[72] Jerome Greene to Crawford H. Toy, February 21, 1908 (2 letters), Records of the President of Harvard University, Charles W. Eliot, UAI 5.150, Box 68, HUA.

[73] Crawford H. Toy to Jerome Greene, February 22, 1908, Records of the President of Harvard University, Charles W. Eliot, UAI 5.150, Box 68, HUA. The reply is written in a different hand at the bottom of Toy's letter and was presumably communicated to Toy.

[74] Crawford H. Toy to Charles W. Eliot, March 4, 1907, Records of the President of Harvard University, Charles W. Eliot, UAI 5.150, Box 68, HUA.

intended to resign at the end of the 1908 calendar year: "My expression 'next year' was, I see, ambiguous. ...My purpose is to send in my resignation soon to take effect at the end of the present College year."[75] On December 26, 1908, Toy offered his resignation as Hancock Professor of Hebrew and Oriental Languages "to take effect September 1st, 1909."[76]

In writing in behalf of the president to acknowledge Toy's plans for retirement, Jerome Greene had also explained that according to the calculations of the Carnegie Foundation's formula, Toy would be entitled to an annual compensation of $2,658.33. If Toy's ten years of service at Southern Seminary were included in the calculations, those benefits would raise to $3,236.00.[77] Toy countered by providing a list of all of his previous teaching posts, no doubt in hopes that his compensation could be enhanced.[78] Toy's final compensation is unknown, but clearly it was not enough to allay Toy's fears that he would not be able to maintain his residence on Lowell Street into retirement.[79]

Extracurricular Teaching. In his early days at Harvard and in addition to his regular teaching duties, Toy offered other lectures outside the established curriculum in the hopes of stirring up interest in biblical studies generally and Semitic studies more specifically. Toy described his efforts to Broadus:

> I have introduced two novelties, which may be considered doubtful experiments. I offer a lecture on Israelitish history and messianic thought (about such as you heard from me) once a week to the whole Div'y School

---

[75] Toy to Eliot, November 6, 1908. Jerome Greene wrote to Toy within the week to confirm that the president had communicated to the Corporation Toy's "intention to send in your resignation to take effect at the end of the present college year" (Greene to Toy, November 11, 1908, Records of the President of Harvard University, Charles W. Eliot, UAI 5.150, Box 126, HUA).

[76] Crawford H. Toy to President and Fellows of Harvard College, December 26, 1908, Records of the President of Harvard University, Charles W. Eliot, UAI 5.150, Box 68, HUA.

[77] Jerome Greene to Crawford H. Toy, November 11, 1908, Records of the President of Harvard University, Charles W. Eliot, UAI 5.150, Box 126, HUA.

[78] Crawford H. Toy to President and Fellows of Harvard College, December 26, 1908, Records of the President of Harvard University, Charles W. Eliot, UAI 5.150, Box 68, HUA. He listed Women's College, Charlottesville, VA 1856–59 (3 years); Richmond College, January–April 1861 (3 months); University of Alabama, 1864–65 (6 months); University of Va. (as Licentiate), 1865–66 (1 year); Furman University, Greenville, S.C. 1869 (6 months); Southern Baptist Theological Seminary, 1869–79 (10 years); Harvard University, 1880–1909 (29 years). This would have given Toy an additional five years and three months of service. In a subsequent communication to Greene, Toy provided his rank and title at the various institutions (Crawford H. Toy to Jerome Greene, July 24, 1909, Records of the President of Harvard University, Charles W. Eliot, UAI 5.150, Box 126, HUA).

[79] Jane Toy Coolidge, "Toy," 16; see also chapter 7.

(but you will understand that the whole Un'y doesn't rush to it); it is tolerably well attended so far, & it seems to have awakened some interest in O.T. study. Then – what is of questionable wisdom – I offer a Sunday afternoon lecture on Paul – meant especially for students, tho I have graciously (or ungraciously) granted admission to ladies. It is a somewhat rash undertaking. Students are so belectured here that it would seem a pity to force knowledge on their Sundays also. But I wish to contribute my mite to religious work among them, & thought that a few might be glad to hear familiar talks on "Paul of Tarsus & the beginnings of X'ty" – at any rate they have the privilege of staying away. …attendance has been rather better than I expected. There is no little earnest religious feeling in the College, but it is not attracted by the ordinary church services & I hope that talking freely as an historical student, I shall be able to impress religious truth.[80]

Crawford Toy's participation in and leadership of various learned societies and organizations reveal an academic fully engaged in the life of the mind, whose interests were wide-ranging and whose knowledge ran both deep and wide. After reviewing his professional activities, David Lyon's assessment seems quite on the mark: "On coming to Harvard, Dr. Toy's great learning was promptly recognized by his colleagues. Perhaps it is no exaggeration to say that they regarded him as the most widely informed member of the Faculty."[81]

Faith Communities

One of the most contested of Toy's "extracurricular" activities was his participation in faith communities. According to the Toy myth, after leaving Louisville, Crawford Toy was either denied admission to the Old Cambridge Baptist Church or was excommunicated from that congregation several years later. Neither is true.

Toy was a member of Broadway Baptist Church while in Louisville. He returned to his parents' home in Norfolk in May 1879. On September 17, 1879, Broadway Baptist granted upon request Toy's "letter of dismission."[82] According to W. H. Whitsitt,[83] Toy had spent the summer preaching at Freemason Baptist Church, since its pastor, Rev. William Thomas, had accepted

---

[80] Crawford H. Toy to John A. Broadus, December 14, 1881, Broadus Papers, ASC, SBTS. It is unclear how long Toy continued to offer these kinds of extracurricular lectures for the Harvard community.

[81] Lyon, "Toy," 16.

[82] OCBCA. The letter was not immediately transferred to a sister church, and on March 29, 1882, the letter was renewed "by order of the church" for sixth months.

[83] W. H. Whitsitt to Florence Wallace, September 29, 1979, in *Mirror*, 240.

a pastorate elsewhere.[84] We have no record of Toy's church involvement while working for the *Independent* in New York. At some point after accepting the position at Harvard, Toy began attending the Old Cambridge Baptist Church.

Baptist beginnings in Massachusetts were less than auspicious. In 1635–1636, erstwhile Baptist Roger Williams was banished from the Massachusetts Bay Colony for heretical "diverse, new, and dangerous opinions."[85] The centennial history of Old Cambridge summarizes the attitude of the Massachusetts religious establishment toward non-conforming Baptists: "Baptists have not always been highly esteemed in Massachusetts. In fact, the Puritan authorities of three centuries ago regarded Baptists as pestiferous trouble-makers, dangerous to the established order, sometimes guilty of subversive practices and therefore rightly subject to censure, to chastisement, and even to banishment."[86]

The first Baptist Church in Cambridge was founded in 1817, and despite the fact that prejudice against the non-conformists prevented the original congregation from purchasing land in Harvard Square, the church grew to the point that it established other churches in the area, beginning with Second Baptist Church (now defunct) in East Cambridge in 1827. In 1844, First Baptist organized a church in the village of Old Cambridge to alleviate the overflow of attendees at services. Old Cambridge Baptist Church began meeting in August 1844 at a member's home. They voted to hold services at Lyceum Hall (where Harvard's Coop store now stands) near Harvard Square until a house of worship could be erected. The first minister, Rev. Ezekiel G. Robinson of Norfolk, Virginia, accepted a pastoral call in July 1845 and the new church building was dedicated that September. Robinson remained only for a year, leaving to become a professor of Hebrew at the Theological Institute in Covington Kentucky. Later, he would serve as professor (1852–1868) and then president of Rochester Theological Seminary (1868–1872) and Brown University (1872–1889). A new church building (erected in its current location on Massachusetts Avenue) was dedicated in 1868. It was this impressive structure that Crawford Toy encountered upon his arrival in Cambridge.

In 1881, Toy wrote to Broadus, "I go frequently to hear a sermon from Dr. Johnson, the Bapt. Pastor, with whom my relations are cordial, tho his people are not quite satisfied as to my orthodoxy."[87] Based on a letter by A.

---

[84] See chapter 3.

[85] Glenn W. LaFantasie, ed., *The Correspondence of Roger Williams* (Hanover, NH: University Press of New England, 1988), 1:12–23.

[86] Cecil Thayer Derry, *A Brief History of the Old Cambridge Baptist Church 1844–1944* (Cambridge, MA: The Cosmos Press, 1944), 3.

[87] Toy to Broadus, December 14, 1881, Broadus Papers.

M. Kendall to John Broadus, historian Greg Wills concluded that Toy withdrew his application for membership at Old Cambridge Baptist Church "when some church members objected to admitting him because of his new doctrines."[88] Thus, according to Wills, Toy was never allowed to join the Baptist church. Contrary to Wills's assertion, the records of Old Cambridge Baptist Church show that the congregation voted to receive Crawford Toy into its membership on May 26, 1882.[89] Admission to church membership at OCBC was not taken lightly:

> The student of our records is impressed by the numerous cases of church discipline in our first fifty years. So seriously did that earlier generation take the Baptist belief in a regenerate church membership, that entrance into the church was carefully guarded against unqualified persons. ...It was no easy matter to gain admittance to the church; for a long period not only must the applicant satisfy the Standing Committee, and the church that he was a child of God, but he must also submit to be visited and questioned by a committee of the more solid members of the church, who sought to make certain that he was a regenerate soul. ...It was a solemn and significant experience to be admitted to the church.[90]

Whatever information A. M. Kendall collected on Toy was not enough to prevent the professor from meeting the stringent membership requirements of the Old Cambridge Baptist Church.

By the following year, Toy's former student and fellow Baptist, David Lyon, had joined the Harvard faculty and was also attending the Baptist church. Toy reported to Broadus in May 1883 that Lyon had given a Sunday evening lecture at the church on "the corroboration of the O.T. from the Assyrian monuments."[91] By the following December, Toy mentioned to

---

[88] Wills, *Southern Seminary*, 132. In the letter, Kendall does query Broadus regarding Toy's views:

> There is one C. H. Toy here, Proff. of Hebrew in Harvard College, who is asking to be received as a member into our church. I am not satisfied with his views on several questions of belief.... With what I now know of this Bro. I am not prepared to give my vote to receive him, but if I am in error, I wish to be set-right. If it is your pleasure to inform me in relation to this matter you will oblige me very much and serve the cause of Christ. (A. M. Kendall to John A. Broadus, February 16, 1882, Broadus Papers, Box 9, ASC, SBTS)

There is no record of if or what Broadus replied to Kendall.

[89] OCBCA. Gratitude is expressed to Rev. Dr. Cody Sanders for permission to examine the archives of OCBC in March 2017.

[90] Derry, *Brief History of Old Cambridge Baptist Church*, 41.

[91] Crawford H. Toy to John A. Broadus, May 9, 1883, Broadus Papers, ASC, SBTS.

Broadus: "Lyon will join the Old Cambridge Bapt. Ch. in a short time. We find the pastor, Dr. Franklin Johnson, very friendly & pleasant. He doesn't approve of Lyon's critical opinions or mine, but we agree to disagree."[92]

In this same letter, Toy mentioned that the publication of his book on Old Testament quotations in the New Testament was imminent and predicted that "the book will provoke hostile criticism, but I hope will demonstrate itself to be sound in principle and method."[93] Interestingly, the book did not create a controversy in the church, at least not to the point of causing Toy to leave, since he remained a member of the congregation for several more years. But Toy's reading of the Old Testament quotations in the New Testament was apparently one of those critical opinions on which Toy and his pastor, Dr. Johnson, had, for the time being, agreed to disagree. But that uneasy alliance did not least forever.

Son of a Baptist minister, Franklin Johnson was a graduate of Colgate Theological Seminary. He continued his studies in Germany (Heidelberg, Jena, and Leipzig) and in 1869 was honored with the Doctor of Divinity degree from the University of Jena. Johnson became pastor of the Baptist church in Cambridge in 1873, a position he held until 1888. Following a stint as president of Ottawa University in Kansas, Johnson was named professor of Church History and Homiletics at the University of Chicago, where he remained until his retirement in 1908.[94] Among his several publications was *Quotations of the New Testament from the Old Considered in the Light of General Literature*.[95] Setting aside the curiosity that Johnson would publish a book on this particular topic when one of his parishioners had done the same a little more than a decade earlier, we gain a glimpse of what we can imagine were some of the disagreements between Toy and Johnson during their time together in Cambridge.

Johnson discussed Toy's (and others') interpretation of the quotation of Zechariah 12:10 ("They shall look on me whom they pierced") in John 19:37 ("They shall look upon him whom they pierced"). The author of John has changed the first-person pronoun "me" to the third-person "him." According to Johnson, "it was God who spoke through the prophet declaring that the Jews had pierced him, and John would teach us by his change of the pronoun that it was same God whom they pierced on the cross"; thus, the Zechariah

---

[92] Toy to Broadus, December 5, 1883.

[93] Toy to Broadus, December 5, 1883. See Crawford Howell Toy, *Quotations in the New Testament* (New York: Charles Scribner's Sons, 1884).

[94] John W. Moncrief, "Dr. Franklin Johnson," *The University Record*, ed. D. A. Robertson (Chicago: University of Chicago Press, 1917), 3:78–79.

[95] Franklin Johnson, *The Quotations of the New Testament from the Old Considered in the Light of General Literature* (Philadelphia: American Baptist Publication Society, 1895).

passage predicts the suffering of Christ and "equates Jehovah of the Old Testament with Christ of the New." [96] How can Jehovah be pierced? According to Johnson, "Toy would remove the difficulty by translating the passage thus: 'They shall look to me in respect to him whom they have pierced;' that is, 'the people of Jerusalem shall exhibit a kindly and powerful spirit; and, in their sorrow for their slain brethren of Judah, shall look to me, their God, for comfort." But Johnson maintained, "All these violent expedients are unnecessary."[97] Johnson offered this critique: "The exegesis of Toy is not made good, even by his own construction of the sentence. If the prophet means that the Jews shall mourn 'for their slain brethren of Judah,' how can he repeatedly and uniformly employ the singular, 'him,' for this innumerable multitude?"[98] For Johnson, the simplest reading was the one that viewed John as faithfully reproducing Zechariah's prophecy of a pierced messiah:

> The exegesis of John is based on a straightforward and natural construction of the Hebrew text, and on his perception of the divinity of Jesus; while other views [including Toy's] are induced by a certain reluctance to recognize the passage as a direct Messianic prediction, or to recognize Jehovah in Christ; or by some other supposed polemic convenience. If we consider the passage a direct prophecy of Christ, we account for every feature of it; but all other hypotheses require us to do it some violence.[99]

This is the pattern and tenor of most of Johnson's book, and where Toy departed (which was often) from Johnson's conviction that the Old Testament provides multiple, direct, messianic prophecies, Toy fell into Johnson's crosshairs.[100] It is, perhaps, worth noting that the publisher of Johnson's volume is the American Baptist Publication Society, the same society that rejected Toy's commentary on the Pastoral Epistles after he concluded Paul was not the author.[101] While such disagreements would have made for interesting conversations around the Sunday dinner table (if that ever occurred), it is noteworthy,

---

[96] Ibid., 78.

[97] Johnson, *Quotations*, 79.

[98] Ibid. Johnson also rejected the grammatical reasoning undergirding Toy's insistence that the Hebrew must be rendered "look unto" rather than "look upon," though in the end he accepts the translation of "unto" as reflecting John's intent for the passage (*Quotations*, 79–80).

[99] Johnson, *Quotations*, 82.

[100] See, e.g., Johnson's critique of Toy in the discussion of Toy's interpretation of Isaiah 7:14 in Matthew 1:23 (*Quotations*, 285). See, *inter alia*, Johnson, *Quotations*, 314–15, 340–42 (on Psalm 110 in the NT), 350–52 (on Hosea 2:23; 1:10 in Rom 9:25, 26), 355–56 (on Deut 32:21 in Rom 10:19-21), and 357–60 (on Isa 45:23 in Rom 14:11). Even Broadus does not escape Johnson's critical eye (*Quotations*, 337).

[101] See chapter 3.

finally, to observe that Toy and Johnson remained in the church together until 1888. Johnson left for Ottawa University and eventually the University of Chicago. But why did Crawford Toy leave the Old Cambridge Baptist Church?

Here is where the other part of the Toy myth comes in, and it is older than Wills's suggestion. The August 21, 1889, issue of North Carolina's *Biblical Recorder* carried this brief item: "Rev. Dr. C. H. Toy, once professor in our Theological Seminary, has been expelled from the church in Cambridge, Mass., for heresy. This is what should have been done years ago."[102] One wonders what Toy had done now to bring the judgment of a local Baptist congregation down on his head. One might suspect that Toy had a major, controversial publication appear in the months preceding the announcement in the *Biblical Recorder*. But such is not the case. *Quotations in the New Testament* appeared in 1884.[103] However much the editors of the *Biblical Recorder* wished Toy had been expelled from the Baptist church, there is incontrovertible evidence that this statement is simply untrue. In fact, up until and including 1888, C. H. Toy was listed as a "resident minster" in the records of the Boston North Baptist Association.[104]

On October 28, 1888, OCBC standing committee clerk F. H. Barbour submitted requests to the church clerk from the standing committee for "letters of dismission and recommendation" from three families to be presented to the congregation at its next business meeting. In the same minutes, Barbour recorded, "On request of Prof. C. H. Toy the committee recommends to Church to grant him a certificate of Christian character and to drop his name

---

[102] "Personal and Other Items," *Biblical Recorder*, August 21, 1889.

[103] Toy did publish an article in 1888, "The New Testament as Interpreter of the Old Testament," *The Old Testament Student* 8 (1888): 124–33. His conclusions were provocative, but hardly new: "in certain cases the New Testament interpretation of Old Testament passages is not correct. Sometimes the text is inaccurate, sometimes the exegesis" (133). Nonetheless, there are no published outcries to this article; the controversy would have emerged over the 1884 book publication, but still Toy remained at Old Cambridge Baptist Church.

[104] *The Fortieth Anniversary of the Boston North Baptist Association, held in the Central Square Baptist Church, Boston,* September 19, 1888, C. S. Scott, Clerk (Boston: Conant & Newhall, 1888), 2. David Lyon is also listed as a "resident minister" (in distinction from clergy who held pastorates in the association) (OCBCA). Toy, however, is no longer listed in the associational minutes for 1889–1890, but Lyon is still listed. Lyon's name is dropped after 1890, although he continued as an active member of OCBC. In 1909, Lyon was teaching an adult Bible class "for both sexes" (*Old Cambridge Baptist Church Bulletin,* Sunday, October 24, 1909, OCBCA). Appreciation is expressed to Andover-Newton Theological Seminary Librarian Emerita, Diana Yount, who checked the 1889–1891 minutes of the Boston North Baptist Association for references to Toy and Lyon and communicated via email correspondence on March 3, 3017.

from the Church Roll."[105] The recommendation was to be acted on the following week, and there is no reason to think the church did not uphold the committee's recommendation. It is noteworthy that the recommendation included a "certificate of Christian character" for Toy, dispelling any notion that he was forced out of the church. In fact, there was one other recommendation included in this same report for a Mr. Thomas W. Russell. The committee recommended that Russell's name be dropped from the church roll "and that the right hand of fellowship be withdrawn from him on the ground of immoral conduct."[106] So OCBC was capable of disciplining members, but such was not the case with Crawford Toy.[107]

If not exiled for teaching or publishing heresy, why did Toy leave OCBC in 1888? It is certainly plausible that Toy's evolving theology had opened an even larger chasm between him and the rest of the congregation, and he simply decided to withdraw to find a more theologically kindred communion. Against this being the primary reason for Toy's departure is the fact that David Lyon, his colleague, shared similar views to Toy (as Toy himself indicated) and yet remained a member of OCBC for the rest of his life.[108] The timing could also have been affected by the fact that the pastor, Rev. Johnson, had recently announced his resignation.[109] To be sure, as we have seen, Johnson and Toy had their disagreements, but they had managed to negotiate them in a respectful manner; they had, as Toy had noted, "agreed to disagree." There was one other event of 1888 that could have influenced at least the timing of Toy's departure from OCBC.

In the preceding May, Crawford Toy had married Nancy Inge Saunders of Norfolk, Virginia. By all accounts, Nancy Saunders Toy was an educated,

---

[105] R. H. Barbour, Standing Committee Clerk, Report to Church Clerk, October 28, 1888, OCBCA.

[106] Ibid.

[107] For examples of causes of church discipline at OCBC, see Derry, *Brief History of Old Cambridge Baptist Church*, 42.

[108] Similarities in theology, of course, do not necessarily ensure shared temperaments or sensitivities. After all, Lyon had never been ousted from a position because of his theology or critical method (though he did "lose" a teaching position at Southern—ironically, to be Toy's replacement—for his views of inspiration; see chapter 7).

[109] In a mimeographed communication dated September 1, 1888, Johnson submitted his letter of resignation to be read to the congregation on October 1; the resignation took effect the last day of October. Johnson wrote: "It is necessary for me, in this communication, to add much to that which I have already said to you in private and in public. I resign definitely the office to which you called me almost fifteen years ago. ...I shall cherish the most ardent affection for the people among whom I have labored for full half a generation, during which time not a ripple of discord has disturbed the perfect harmony of our relations" (OCBCA).

cultured, ambitious, and, in modern jargon, upwardly mobile woman. She was also not a Baptist. Nancy Saunders was the daughter of a Methodist clergy. He and Nancy's mother had spent most of their careers as administrator/teachers at institutions for female education. When Crawford and Nancy returned from their honeymoon, they held open house at their residence on Lowell Street in Cambridge for visitors.[110] It is not a stretch of the imagination to think that Nancy was drawn away from the less socially prominent Baptist congregation toward the First Parish Church of Cambridge, the Unitarian establishment church to which belonged the major personalities of Harvard and Cambridge: President and Mrs. Charles Eliot, Professor and Mrs. Francis Peabody, Professor and Mrs. James Thayer, legendary physician Dr. J. T. G. Nichols (also trustee at the Cambridge Savings Bank and for many years chair of the church's standing committee), former mayor Charles H. Saunders, and many other local dignitaries.[111] At some point after Crawford Toy secured his "Certificate of Christian Character" from OCBC, he and his new bride began attending the First Parish Church and began to find their place in the complex social life of that class-conscious New England community.

Another common element of the Toy myth is that he became a Unitarian. The First Parish Church kept detailed records during this period, and neither Crawford nor Nancy Toy is listed in its membership roll. This is an even more telling statement when one reads the prologue to the membership roll of 1896: "The following list includes not only those who are accustomed to join in the communion service, but also all those who sympathizing with the religious purpose of the church desire to share its fellowship and to unite in its work."[112] The membership roll, then, was rather expansive, including not only "members" but also persons who sympathized with the mission of First Parish, even if, for whatever reason, they chose not to formally affiliate. If "became" means that Toy joined the membership of the First Parish Church of Cambridge, there is no evidence and this is another inaccurate statement.

In fact, the best evidence we have of the Toys' presence at First Parish Church is a controversy in which Nancy became embroiled in 1891. A certain Mr. "Arthur Jones" wrote Dr. Nichols, chair of the First Parish Standing Committee, with a statement from congregants regarding "the music which I submitted to the Standing Committee...and which I withdrew temporarily

---

[110] The Toys likely traveled over the summer for their honeymoon. The *Cambridge Press* (June 16, 1888) reported they were in the Catskill mountains. For more on Nancy Toy and the Toys' relationship, see chapter 8.

[111] First Parish (Cambridge, MA) Records, 1834–1912, bMS 13/2, Membership Lists, 1868–1893, AHTL HDS.

[112] Ibid.

for the purpose of investigating certain statements" made by Nancy Toy and a "Miss Chapman." It is impossible to reconstruct the specifics of the controversy, but apparently the two women had submitted a signed statement on the topic and, at least from Jones's point of view, engaged in conduct at a business meeting in which the minister and "respectable members" of the congregation were "treated with open derision and insult" by the two women. Jones concluded with these damning words: "if the method and spirit of the ward caucus are to govern the Parish meeting and Parish Committee I think it should be known."[113] Fortunately, there are other references to Crawford Toy's involvement with the ministries of the First Parish Church.[114] The *Cambridge Tribune* reported that Professor Toy was conducting a Bible class "every Sunday noon beginning with the first Sunday in February...until further notice."[115]

Scholars state that Toy left the Baptist church and became a Unitarian. Even if we allow for the fact that the Toys attended the Unitarian church without officially affiliating with it, interpreters assert that Toy became a Unitarian as if it were obvious what that statement meant. The term has functioned in conservative evangelical circles as a kind of "deviant labelling" like "liberal." No one wants to be called a "unitarian" (or liberal). But nineteenth-century New England Unitarianism was anything but monolithic. Lydia Willsky-Ciollo has shown that New England Unitarianism at the beginning of the nineteenth century sought to characterize itself as the "church of free inquiry" while keeping its foot in the door of Christianity.[116] Their concerns did not focus on theology, even with regard to the Trinity or the concomitant issue of Jesus' divinity: "The doctrine of the Trinity was never the defining feature of New England Unitarianism. Nor were New England Unitarians even of one mind on this subject."[117]

---

[113] Arthur B. Jones to Dr. J. T. G. Nichols, March 11, 1891, First Parish (Cambridge, MA), bMS 13/2, Practical Parish Affairs, AHTL HDS. Dr. Nichols shot back with a reply on the same day: "Your letter of today enclosing the statement of certain members of the congregation in regard to music is at hand. ...Will you not write another letter simply stating the position of Mrs. Toy and Miss Chapman? I shall be very sorry to place your letter to me on file. It will be much better that your unjustifiable attack on the Standing Committee should be suppressed" (J. T. G. Nichols to Arthur B. Jones, March 11, 1891).

[114] Admittedly, these do not prove that the Toys were participating members of the congregation, since Toy also led Bible studies on a regular basis for other churches; see Diary of Crawford H. Toy, Chest of 1900, 900.11, Box 4, HUA.

[115] *Cambridge Tribune*, February 1, 1896.

[116] See Lydia Willsky-Ciollo, *American Unitarianism and the Protestant Dilemma: The Conundrum of Biblical Authority* (Lanham, MD: Lexington Books, 2015).

[117] Ibid., xviii. In fact, there was also a "biblical Unitarianism," represented by Andrew Norton (an early predecessor to Toy in the Dexter lectureship at Harvard), which continued to hold to the accuracy and authority of the Bible. In fact, Norton published a book

The driving issue, according to Willsky-Ciollo, was authority, especially when creedalism had been rejected: "What must be understood of the American Unitarians and their story of origin, is that their primary initiative, their choice of intellectual influences, and their galvanizing principle were most often about authority, or more specifically, about epistemological authority. How, they asked, do I *know* the truth and from where does it come?"[118]

For most Unitarians, the existence of God was really the only "essential" truth that one must accept to be a Christian. Other beliefs, such as the precise nature of Christ, were based on varied biblical interpretation and not critical to one's status as a Christian (and, therefore, one's salvation). Unitarian theology was unstable until the first National Convention of Unitarians in 1865, when it began to be clear that they needed to state what they believed or risk implosion. Still, even in 1888, there were few congregational options for someone like Toy who may have been looking for freedom of conscience to explore the results of his critical investigations.

Thus, the Unitarian First Parish met the social needs of C. H. and Nancy Toy, who were seeking to find their place in the social fabric of Cambridge and had the theological desire (especially of C. H. Toy) to explore religious truth unencumbered by creedal constraints. Still, it is important to remember that by participating in the Unitarian communion, Toy was nullifying President Eliot's goal in bringing him to Harvard, namely to break the Unitarian grip on the divinity school. One is tempted to surmise that Crawford Toy had his own problems with authority, whether embodied in the conservative Boyce or the liberal Eliot.

Finally, it is important also to be aware that nineteenth-century New England Unitarianism understood itself, and was understood by others, as "a definitively liberal Christian movement within Congregationalism."[119] As such, the congregations in Cambridge, despite their theological and socioeconomic differences, generally enjoyed cordial relations. One example of those relations will suffice. On January 20, 1889, just months after Toy left the Baptist church, Old Cambridge Baptist Church experienced a devastating fire that caused the sanctuary to be closed for repair for months. Both Harvard and

---

titled *The Evidences of the Genuineness of the Gospels* (Boston: American Unitarian Association, 1837).

[118] Willsky-Ciollo, *American Unitarianism*, 39. Recall the earlier discussion regarding President Charles Eliot's comments about the "religion of the future" being anti-authoritarian.

[119] Willsky-Ciollo, *American Unitarianism*, xx. Eventually, Toy would come to identify with the Unitarians "in a general way" (CH Toy to John Hill Luther. March 4, 1899. Luther-Bagby Collection, Accession #1337, Box 1, Folder 1, The Texas Collection, Baylor University). Thanks to Dr. Tracey Stout for bringing this letter to my attention.

First Parish reached out to OCBC to offer assistance. OCBC gratefully accepted First Parish's invitation to use their facilities during the restoration period. "The facilities afforded by your body and by the University promise great assistance to us in our homeless condition, and the prompt and kindly tender of your hospitality is highly appreciated."[120]

Crawford Toy was energetically and fully engaged in the various communities of which he was a part: Harvard, Cambridge/Boston, Old Cambridge Baptist Church, and (later) First Parish Church. He was, by all measures, a "good citizen" who took seriously his responsibilities to those various constituencies and discharged his duties to them to the best of his abilities—abilities which, by all accounts, were extraordinary.

---

[120] OCBC to First Parish in Cambridge, January 22, 1889, Practical Parish Affairs, AHTL HDS.

Fig. 4

David Gordon Lyon.
Andover-Harvard Theological Library, Harvard Divinity School, Harvard University

7

David Gordon Lyon:

An "Unconditioned Friendship"

On the evening of May 11, 1919, David Lyon's phone rang. On the other end was Nancy Toy, Professor Toy's wife, who informed Lyon that the condition of his Harvard colleague, Crawford Toy, had worsened and "that his end seemed to be near." On the next day, at 1:30 p.m. Crawford Howell Toy died at the age of eighty-three. Lyon went over to the Toy house on 7 Lowell Street and "spent the afternoon and part of the evening in making arrangements for the funeral." On Wednesday, May 14, David Lyon served as an honorary pall-bearer at the service held in Harvard Divinity School's Appleton Chapel, conducted by Rev. Carothers, pastor of First Parish (Unitarian) of Cambridge and assisted by Professor J. H. Ropes. Thus ended a remarkable friendship, marked by professional collaboration, humor, and personal fidelity and affection—a friendship that spanned four decades. Nearly thirty years of that friendship were spent in Cambridge where Toy and Lyon walked together the hallowed halls of Harvard.

Germany, Louisville, and the Inspiration of Scripture

Lyon's decision to study in Germany in summer 1879 has already been explored.[1] The rest of Lyon's diary for 1879 records his preparations for and travel to Germany (via London) and his early impressions of German culture, language, and religion.[2] Lyon wrote Broadus on September 1, 1879, to inform him that he had reached Leipzig, Germany, after a twelve-day voyage and four days in London, during which time he heard C. H. Spurgeon preach twice "and found his preaching all that you claim in your lecture."[3]

Lyon's diaries for 1880–1882 are missing, and there is little left of Lyon's

---

[1] See chapter 4.

[2] Lyon's diary is available from the Harvard Library online at https://iiif.lib.harvard.edu/manifests/view/drs:47567736$1i. References to the diary, unless otherwise noted, are from this source.

[3] David Gordon Lyon to John A. Broadus, September 1, 1879, Broadus Correspondence, Box 8, Folder 53, ASC, SBTS.

correspondence during his Leipzig period (and nothing thus far of any exchanges with Toy have emerged, though, as will be demonstrated, Lyon was clearly in contact with him). There do exist, however, six letters from Lyon to Broadus during the period January 1880–May 1882 that are valuable in providing information about Lyon's course of study in Leipzig as well as the invitation(s) to join the faculty of SBTS and the reasons he could not. There is, finally, a notice of his impending appointment at Harvard.[4]

On January 31, 1880, Lyon responds to a letter just received from Broadus. After lamenting the state of preaching among the Germans, who focus too much attention on "Kindertaufe" (infant baptism) and not enough on "God's holy wrath against all sin," he writes, "Our brethren fear the effects of German theology. German pulpit theology is dead orthodoxy, too dead to attract an audience, too dead to harm those who do attend."[5] He expresses regret that his going to Germany had "robbed you of assistance which we would have most cheerfully rendered," and then he asserts, "I rejoice that you now approve of my coming at the time when I did." He himself is convinced of the rightness of the decision: "After the lapse of nearly six months in Germany, I congratulate myself a thousand times on the decision which brought me here. I do not consider that my progress in acquiring the language has been in any sense remarkable, but it has at least been considerable, and I have it now at better command than perhaps would ever have been the case if I had remained in America."[6]

Lyon then turns to give an account of his studies. "Modesty will perhaps not forbid my saying that in the Syriac class, where we must translate orally, my translations into German are as good as those of the German students." The acquisition of German at this time remained "the leading and almost exclusive thought," which is "a tool whose use I must at once acquire." After two months' study with a tutor, Lyon had located "a pleasant German student and continued the language with him." His reading, too, had focused on language acquisition and consisted of reading Lessing, Schiller, and Göthe. Since the philologist Georg Curtius's lectures on Homer "did not lie exactly within my

---

[4] Lyon also writes a letter to Broadus in German, dated October 3, 1879 (see Broadus Correspondence, Box 8, File 55, ASC, SBTS). Lyon immediately regrets the act, writing in his letter of January 31, 1880, "I have often since reproached myself for writing you in German 'schrift,' for it is quite enough to ask one to read my Latin character" (Lyon to Broadus, January 31, 1880, Broadus Correspondence, Box 9, File 2, ASC, SBTS).

[5] Lyon to Broadus, January 31, 1880. Lyon goes on to criticize the "coalition of Church and State" but allows that "one must always grant that his views may be mistaken, and my criticisms may be unjust."

[6] Lyon to Broadus, January 31, 1880.

field," Lyon's Greek reading so far had been "confined to the New Testament," but he was attending the lectures of Friedrich Delitzsch (son of Franz) on Hebrew and Syriac. Those classes, he remarks, are "small, very few of the 3500 students pursuing these studies" (15 in Hebrew; 10 in Syriac). Lyon attempted to attend lectures by Franz Delitzsch on the Psalter and Old Testament Introduction but "found his German at the beginning of the semester too difficult to understand." Once a week he visited a Hebrew Society, in which after a grammatical lesson by Prof. Ryssel, students attempted oral translations of German into Hebrew (though Lyon admits he had not attempted that). He had eventually given up on lectures on New Testament Hermeneutics and the History of the Reformation "because the lecture rooms were always so badly ventilated that I could not endure the deadly air."[7] He also attended weekly lectures on the "Immortality of the Soul" and a "Companion of the Poems, Job Divina Comedia and Faust."

Lyon then takes up the topic of inspiration, which Broadus had reported was currently under discussion in South Carolina. Lyon expresses hope for a good outcome of those discussions and says that the "chief fear is that in casting doubt on old, long-prevailing opinions one seems to cast doubt on the Christian religion itself. It is only very slowly that men can safely change their views on a subject so profound as that of inspiration, even if the change brings them nearer to the truth. Meanwhile, if brethren have new light to offer, let it come, be results what they may—in the end there will be progress." The autobiographical nature of this comment will become clearer in subsequent correspondence.[8]

Lyon complains that the *Religious Herald* (denominational paper of Virginia), through which he keeps up with Baptist "affairs across the water," "never fails to vex me—it takes so much time to read it." He predicts that "Dr. Toy's promised articles will not fail to be extensively read and will produce a sensation in many an editorial sanctum." He goes on to remark on various and sundry issues related to Baptists and the seminary and then apologizes for imposing on Broadus's time with such a long letter.[9]

The next two extant letters from Lyon to Broadus were dispatched within two days of each other, May 22 and May 24, 1880. The topic of both was an apparent invitation from Broadus in a letter of April 6 for Lyon to

---

[7] Ibid. Lyon goes on to say, "The Germans do not seem to have the remotest idea of the value of pure air."

[8] Lyon to Broadus, January 31, 1880. Lyon's paragraph on this point is an autobiographical harbinger of more to come: "I believe that the strongest argument for the Bible as a record of God's salvation through Christ, is the exact correspondence of its teachings with our deeply felt spiritual needs."

[9] Lyon to Broadus, January 31, 1880.

return to Louisville for the next session (fall 1880) as a tutor in Hebrew and Greek. Lyon was delayed in receiving the letter because of a change in address and because the consul had overlooked to forward correspondence to the new address. Lyon acknowledges that in the interim "the question of employing a tutor for next session has perhaps been settled"; still, he proposes to "answer your letter as if no delay had intervened." He begins by thanking Broadus and Dr. Boyce "for the interest you take in me and the high appreciation which your proposition expresses. It is not mock modesty when I say that I do not feel myself at all entitled to such consideration." He goes on to write:

> But if your estimate be correct that my fitness for the work is greater than that of any other available young men, and if it becomes necessary to have a tutor for next session then, of course, from this point of view I should feel under obligation to accept. I love the Seminary and should be willing to do anything reasonable for its prosperity.[10]

He expresses the internal struggle he feels at the prospects of cutting his studies short: "The interference with my study of German and the Shemite languages would be very considerable, while on the other hand, the intensity of my work on Greek and Hebrew would make my knowledge of these two languages much more exact." From his view, however, "it seems to me extremely desirable to remain at least a year longer in Germany, so desirable that nothing but a case of necessity would induce me to change my original plan, and even then I should hope in the near future to return to Europe."

Apparently, Broadus had posed two questions to Lyon. To the first, as to whether Lyon will return to assume a post as Greek and Hebrew tutor, Lyon reluctantly consents, "while I should deplore the necessity of returning so soon to America, yet, if, for the present, the Seminary must have my services, I should consider it a duty to respond to the appeal."

The second question concerned whether Lyon's "present convictions would allow me to teach, as to Inspiration, in accordance with and not contrary to the opinions which prevail among intelligent American Baptists."[11] Lyon demurs, saying the question gives him "some difficulty, because I do not know what the prevalent opinions on this subject are," and with regard to the

---

[10] Lyon to Broadus, May 22, 1880, Broadus Correspondence, Box 9, File 8, ASC, SBTS.

[11] Interestingly, the language echoes the language of the Abstract of Principles, which faculty were obligated to sign indicating they would teach "in accordance with and not contrary to." Here, however, the standard is not the abstract but the prevailing opinion of "intelligent American Baptists." Later, after taking up his post at Harvard, Lyon will give an eloquent address on inerrancy and inspiration before the national meeting of American Baptists.

topic "I have been studying Inspiration somewhat, but am not yet prepared to state anything special as to my convictions. In general terms, I can say that I view the Bible as the inspired Word of God, but in the details of the subject, my opinions are not well enough matured to write anything definite." Lyon imagines, however, that given the nature of the position as a tutor in biblical languages, his views would not be disqualifying. "I suppose, however, that during the one year's tutorship my work would be such as to require no detailed teaching on the subject."[12]

Lyon ends by saying he hopes "that the matter is so settled that I remain where I am." Clearly, however, Lyon's thoughts and emotions are piqued at the prospects of returning to Southern, because two days later, on May 24, Lyon sends Broadus a brief note saying, "Two days ago I wrote you, expressing my willingness to act as tutor next session. Since then I have felt that I should have to review Greek and Hebrew very earnestly at once, if I am to teach these languages. If I must return it is therefore important for me to know at once, and so I beg you to dispatch [a telegram] at my expense, the following would be sufficient: 'D. G. Lyon, Leipzig. Yes.' A negative answer will, of course, require no dispatch."[13] We do not have Broadus's response (whether by letter or telegram), but given the fact that Lyon remained in Leipzig two more years, we nonetheless know the answer (even if we can only speculate as to the reasoning by Broadus and Boyce that led to it).

The next correspondence we have from Lyon to Broadus comes about ten months later (though we know from this current letter that Lyon had written to Broadus at least once before in the previous July and probably more frequently than that). In a letter dated March 28, 1881, Lyon indicates to Broadus that he had written Dr. Boyce (president of Southern Seminary) a week earlier expressing "my regret that our divergence of views as to inspiration hinders my accepting a position in the Seminary." Apparently, a year's time had allowed Lyon to clarify his convictions regarding inspiration. Lyon claims that "there is no position which I should more joyfully accept than the one offered," then laments: "But alas! The tears fill my eyes and sincere grief my heart as I reflect that the demand is an impossibility, for you wish a man who can assert the absolute infallibility of the Biblical writers, and that I cannot do."

Lyon then addresses again some of the concerns expressed by Broadus, chief among them the view that if one accepts that there are mistakes in the Bible it leads to the "overthrow of everything." Lyon responds, "I cannot see

---

[12] Lyon to Broadus, May 22, 1880.
[13] Lyon to Broadus, May 24, 1880, Broadus Correspondence, Box 9, File 8, ASC, SBTS.

that such consequences legitimately follow." He appeals to (some) Church Fathers and Luther whose views of inspiration were not so strict, and he then waxes eloquently:

> The divine so pervades the Scriptures as to make them the imperishable storehouse of saving knowledge. That mysterious something which draws the mind of the believing reader heavenwards is the Spirit of God living and breathing in the Word. One who has felt this drawing is immovably assured of divine things, stands on a foundation which cannot be shaken. For him the Bible ever remains God's message of salvation in Christ, and the message loses not of its value or preciousness because penned by hands which were not infallible.

In this letter, we see Lyon now relating to Broadus no longer in a student/teacher hierarchical pattern but as a peer, respectful still, but confident and eloquent regarding his own views and convictions.[14]

Given the import of the letter for Broadus's invitation to join the SBTS faculty, the comment near the end that Lyon is now studying Arabic and Assyrian and working on an inscription related to the Assyrian king, Sargon, might understandably be viewed as throwaway comments. In retrospect, the comments are no less significant given the fact that Lyon will write his dissertation on Sargon and become, in due time, a noted Assyriologist, one of the first, if not *the* first, to teach in an American school.

Lyon and the Hollis Chair of Divinity at Harvard

In May 1882, Lyon writes Broadus, "In your last letter, which I received about a year ago you assured me of your willingness to assist me if opportunity should present itself." He continues: "Little did I dream at that time that I should ever be permitted to make the request which I am to make in this letter. Soon after I became positively settled that nothing would come of our negotiations, and about the time that Dr. Boyce wrote that Baptist seminaries in the North occupy the same ground as our Sem. on the question of inspiration, I received very unexpectedly intimations that my assistance might perhaps be wanted in the Semitic department at Harvard University."[15]

Lyon then explains the appeal of the position since it would allow him to work in Hebrew and Assyrian. He also says that it is "pleasant to me to feel that we are to work in the same general direction, although we are prevented

---

[14] Lyon to Broadus, May 28, 1881. In the course of this remarkable letter, Lyon attributes "religion's death" in Germany not to a "loose view" of inspiration but rather to an "unconverted ministry, acting in connections to a church fettered by state restrictions."

[15] Lyon to Broadus May 24, 1882.

from working side by side." Lyon goes on to acknowledge that "matters are now in a fair way for my election to the Hollis Chair of Theology." Finally comes the ask: "If you will have the kindness to bear testimony to President Eliot or any member of the faculty to my faithfulness and success at the Seminary, you will place me under deep obligation."[16]

There is indirect evidence that Toy had also remained in contact with Lyon during his studies in Germany. Again, we cannot know for sure that it was Toy alone who broached the subject of Lyon coming to Harvard, but we can hardly doubt that Toy was deeply involved in the process. That an untested, young scholar would also be offered the Hollis Chair, the oldest chair at the university and one that had been vacant for more than forty years, is astounding and must have generated not a little consternation on the part of the faculty. President Eliot justified the appointment, in part, by noting that the benefactor of the chair, Thomas Hollis, had been a Baptist: "One hundred and sixty-one years after the establishment of the professorship, a member of the Baptist communion is at last elected to it."[17] Elsewhere, Eliot commented on the new vision for the Hollis Chair that Lyon's appointment represented:

> When Edward Wigglesworth was chosen in 1721 first Hollis Professor of Divinity, he became the first and only professor in Harvard College, and the statutes of the professorship assigned to him a vast range of instruction.... But when in 1882, after this ancient chair had been vacant forty-two years, the Corporation again determined to fill it, they found that the field originally assigned to the Hollis Professor had in the meantime been divided among five professors of the University, and that in the general progress of knowledge no such scholar could be expected to deal thoroughly with more than a small portion of such a field.[18]

Given Lyon's training, Eliot observed that Lyon was appointed to the Hollis Chair "with the general purpose of reinforcing the instruction in Semitic languages, Old Testament criticism and Jewish history, and so of strengthening the whole department of divinity or theology."[19]

---

[16] Ibid.

[17] *Annual Reports of the President and Treasurer of Harvard College, 1881–1882*, 28, HUA. George H. Williams observed that "in 1882, reviving the controverted Hollis Professorship of Divinity after a forty-two year eclipse, he seated in it another Southern Baptist scholar David Gordon Lyon (1852–1935), as if now to make double restitution to the chair's Baptist donor" (*The "Augustan Age,"* 125).

[18] *Annual Reports of President and Treasurer, 1881–1882*, 27–28.

[19] *Annual Reports*, 28. The dean of the divinity school, C. C. Everett, confirmed Eliot's position: "It would be impossible for any one teacher in these days to perform properly all the duties which were originally assigned to the Hollis Professor" (*Annual Reports*, 81). Williams observed:

At the June 22, 1882, meeting of the Board of Overseers, President Eliot laid the groundwork to fill the vacant Hollis Chair. The minutes record "that the President be requested to inform the Board of Overseers that it is in the interest of the Corporation to elect a Hollis Professor of Divinity."[20] A recommendation from President Eliot at the June 28, 1882, meeting of overseers to elect David Gordon Lyon as Hollis Professor of Divinity was referred to a subcommittee of three.[21] At the September 13, 1882, meeting of the Board of Overseers, the board voted "to concur with President and Fellows in electing David Gordon Lyon, Ph.D., Hollis Professor Divinity."[22] While the minutes

---

The reemergence of the Hollis Professorship for instruction in Semitic languages reflects the shift in collective scholarly interests of the Divinity Faculty under the impact of President Eliot's vision of a world-class faculty. The startling shift was no doubt all the more readily accepted by the School and the College in the general awareness that the name of the budding Assyriologist would well pass the various committees with less partisan discussion than that of, say, an Arian or an Arminian.... Moreover, the more ministerial Plummer professorship in Harvard Yard since 1855 was being held by two both scholarly and pastoral successive incumbents—Francis Greenwood Peabody and Edward Caldwell Moore in that same period (1886–1929). Thus it was that an unordained, scholarly Southern Baptist could serve serenely as Hollis Professor and then Hancock Professor, cumulatively, 1882–1922, without necessarily having had to revise his lecture notes in the unfolding forty years—the exact duration, incidentally, of the gap in the Hollis impact at Harvard. (*The "Augustan Age,"* 140–41)

As astute as Williams's observations are regarding the impact of Lyon's field of expertise in Assyriology (and the ways that field avoided protracted debates that more explicitly "theological" areas of study might elicit), it is inaccurate to describe Lyon as "unordained," since he was, in fact, an ordained Baptist minister who maintained his ministerial credentials throughout his Harvard career; see, for example, the *Boston North Association Minutes of 1888* (Boston: Conant & Newhall Printers, September 19, 1888), BX6470.B676, 1888 Book, Special Collections, ABHS, which lists Lyon as a "Resident Minister." There is no evidence that Lyon ever surrendered his ordination credentials; and, unlike Toy, Lyon remained a member of the Old Cambridge Baptist Church (OCBC) for the entirety of his residence in Cambridge. In 1919, Lyon even served as chair of the pastor search committee for OCBC and received a letter of gratitude from a Mr. Jarvis Paine who wished to express his "sincere appreciation of the successful and arduous work which you have done in the last year and a half for our church and which reached its culmination in the Installation Services last evening. Though you had a good committee I know the brunt of the work must have fallen upon you" (Jarvis Paine to David G. Lyon, October 11, 1919, HUG 1541, Papers of David Gordon Lyon, Box 3, HUA).

[20] "Minutes for June 22, 1882," *Overseer's Records*, 1871–1882, Vol. XI, HUA.

[21] "Minutes for June 28, 1882."

[22] Ibid. On that same day, Eliot wrote Lyon (already in Cambridge): "I have the pleasure to inform you that on the 26th of June last you were elected by the President and Fellows Hollis Professor of Divinity and that this election was duly confirmed by the Board

do not record any discussion of the recommendation, the vote (16-2) was not unanimous as were the other two votes regarding faculty appointments that day.[23] Years later, Lyon, in a letter to Eliot expressing gratitude for receiving an honorary D.D. degree from Harvard, alluded to opposition to his appointment as Hollis professor in 1882: "I am more than happy to be thus made a member of such an honored family. And at the same time with Dr. McK! I wonder if you thought of his attitude on the subject of my appointment nineteen years ago."[24] "Dr. McK" was Rev. Alexander McKenzie (1830–1914), 1859 Harvard graduate, pastor of the Shepherd Memorial Church in Cambridge (1867–1912), and occasional lecturer in the divinity school. McKenzie was also on the Board of Overseers in 1882 and presumably one of the two votes against Lyon. He and Lyon were the two recipients of Harvard's Honorary Doctor of Divinity Degrees in 1901.[25]

Another possible objection to Lyon's appointment as Hollis Chair (besides the fact that he was a novice professor with little teaching experience) is found in the ephemera to Lyon's 1919 diary, which included a typescript of Lyon's tribute to Toy following Toy's death. At the end of the typescript is a reference to G. F. Moore, who in the course of writing his own tribute for Toy interviewed retired President Charles Eliot. Lyon writes:

> Moore told me that he wrote this down (by dictation, I believe), shortly after the interview.... (not for publication—Incidentally, Eliot told me [Moore] a story about Lyon's Jewish ancestry, and his apprehension that the Corporation or the Overseers might object to his appointment on that ground, and added that, at a later time, when asked whether he was still an active member of the Baptist Denomination, he answered that he was, and that of all the Protestant denominations the Baptists were most like the Jews. I didn't quite see why, and Eliot replied that Lyon's explanation was that they attached the utmost importance to a rite, and that the Jews were great ritualists.) ...Copied from Moore's memorandum, Nov 14, 1919. Moore handed me the memorandum to read on Nov. 12, 1919. I had not asked him for it but he seemed eager to have me see it. I

---

of Overseers at their meeting today" (Charles Eliot to David G. Lyon, September 13, 1882, HUG 1541, Papers of David Gordon Lyon, Box 12, HUA).

[23] "Minutes for June 28, 1882." The election of Lyon (and others) was reported to the meeting of the president and fellows of Harvard College on September 26, 1882 ("Minutes of Meeting of President and Fellows," September 26, 1882, *Corporation Records*, 1880–1888, Vol. XIII, HUA).

[24] David G. Lyon to Charles Eliot, September 2, 1901, Papers of Charles W. Eliot, UAI 5.150, Box 52, HUA.

[25] See "Harvard honorary degree recipients," https://guides.library.harvard.edu/ld.php?content_id=14900437.

cannot see why, unless to see what I might have to say in regard to the foolish notion attributed to me regarding the Baptists and the Jews.[26]

The "foolish notion" to which Lyon refers appears to be the ritualistic connection between Baptists and Jews and not necessarily the idea that Lyon was of Jewish ancestry. Certainly if Eliot believed Lyon to be of Jewish ancestry, it could have been a concern of Eliot's going into the Overseers' vote, whether true or not.[27]

Lyon's Harvard Career

As already noted, the course offerings in Semitic languages increased dramatically in the 1880s under Toy and Lyon.[28] Toy's and Lyon's ambitions, however, did not end with the remarkable expansion of the Semitic languages curriculum. One of the most innovative, exciting, and ultimately complicated projects that Toy and Lyon collaborated together on was the creation of a "Semitic Fund" that eventually led to the construction of a Semitic Museum at Harvard. This interest in ancient languages and cultures fit within the immediate context of the academic study of religion at Harvard in the closing decades of the nineteenth century and the opening decades of the twentieth. Historian George H. Williams observed that

> the liberal Southern Baptist Toy and his protégé, Lyon, and their colleagues had represented the considerable range possible in the academic embrace of religion at Harvard. Now, on the morrow of the dedication of the Semitic Museum, in the quite distinguishable period from 1900 to 1922, religion as a field and a discipline...was coming to have three foci of interest and, in due course, world-class expertise in Cambridge...philosophical, psychological, and philological (also linguistic, epigraphical, and archaeological).[29]

This interest in antiquities was part of the larger Boston and American context in the late nineteenth century as well. Travel had never been easier or safer. Printed travel brochures were distributed widely. The discoveries by archaeologists (and fortune seekers) of the treasures of ancient civilizations whetted the appetite of citizens in major urban centers around the world whose museums received these cultural artifacts, looted and otherwise. Boston

---

[26] David Gordon Lyon Diary, 1919, Ephemera, HUG 1541, Papers of David Gordon Lyon, Box 3, HUA.
[27] I have not seen any acknowledgment of Lyon regarding Jewish ancestry, but admittedly, I have not read everything in his archival files.
[28] See chapter 5 for details.
[29] Williams, The "Augustan Age," 147.

wanted to be a key player.[30]

And so did Harvard. According to Lyon, he and Toy in 1887 and 1888 began conversations regarding "exploration of the ancient home of the Semites in Western Asia. We hoped to be able to win friends for such exploration and so to gather at Harvard collections of Semitic origin, which should ultimately become a Semitic Museum, furnishing material for research and illustrating Semitic history and life."[31] The initial efforts resulted in the acquisition of a few Babylonian and Assyrian inscriptions and bas-relief sculptures. With the encouragement of Lyon, Toy laid out the vision for a "Semitic Fund" in a handwritten and unpublished "manifesto," dated circa January 1, 1889:

> The desirableness of having in Harvard College a fund for the furtherance of Semitic studies is obvious. Enormous progress has been made of late in the investigation of Semitic fields. The history of Babylonia and Assyria has been reconstructed, with important results for our conception of several other sections of ancient life.... But what has been done has opened up fields even larger than those already investigated. Many questions of interest remain unanswered, great masses of material have been collected which still lie unexamined and much still awaits collection. To this work, so important for the history of civilization, Harvard College should have the best means for making its contribution.[32]

C. H. Toy lists three priorities for such a fund: (1) student scholarships "of moderate sums...to students of special ability...to undertake original investigations, under the guidance of the instructors, in the accessible materials"; (2) purchase of Hebrew, Syriac, and Arabic manuscripts (of which important ones should be published in original language and with translation); (3) "the purchase of archaeological remains from all Semitic lands, such as cuneiform tablets, cylinders and seals, Hebrew and Arabic coins," and vegetable and animal specimens.[33]

---

[30] Rita E. Freed, "The Egyptian Expedition," *MFA Highlights: Arts of Ancient Egypt*, ed. Rita E. Freed, Lawrence M. Berman, and Denise M. Doxey (Boston: MFA Publications, 2003), 25–35, here 25.

[31] David G. Lyon, "Relations of Jacob Schiff to Harvard University," 1, Typescript, HUG 1541, Papers of David Gordon Lyon, Box 16, HUA. This apparently unpublished paper of more than 60 pages was prepared by David Lyon in November 1925, after he had retired from Harvard University (1922) and during the period (1922–1932) that he served as "Honorary Curator of the museum."

[32] Crawford H. Toy, "A Semitic Fund for Harvard College," HUSMA. Appreciation is expressed to Dr. Joe Greene for permission to view the museum's archives. Dr. Greene graciously provided pdfs of all materials related to Toy and the founding of the Semitic Museum in the museum's archives.

[33] Toy, "A Semitic Fund for Harvard College."

From the beginning as Lyon indicated, the vision of the Semitic Fund included a museum. Toy concluded his vision statement: "As soon as possible, a Semitic museum should be established, opened not only to the students of Harvard College but also to all persons engaged in Semitic research. The materials for filling such a museum are abundant; they could be readily procured from the east and from Europe if the money were in hand. This collection would stimulate learned research, and it may safely be said would produce very important results for historical and archaeological science."[34]

Later that month, on January 19, 1889, Toy followed up the memo on the Semitic Fund with a brief note to Lyon: "As we have already agreed upon our general plan, I now only wish you a prosperous journey. I feel sure that the proposal to establish a Semitic fund in Harvard University will find favor with many men. Let me hear from you often as possible during your absence, and if it should seem desirable, I will join you and help push the matter in New York and elsewhere."[35]

Lyon had traveled to New York at the invitation of a former student, James Loeb, who was the brother-in-law of Jacob H. Schiff, a wealthy Jewish investment banker and philanthropist. Lyon showed some of the Babylonian artifacts already collected and, presumably drawing on Toy's vision statement, laid out "the importance and possibilities of research in Semitic lands."[36]

In Lyon's own words, "I made the acquaintance of Mr. Schiff at the home of Mr. Loeb's parents in New York, and there began one of the most intimate and inspiring friendships of my life."[37] Lyon followed up this meeting with May correspondence to President Eliot, Schiff, and Stephen Salisbury, each who supported the idea of creating a Semitic Fund and collection of materials. In October 1889, Harvard's overseers appointed a committee to investigate the viability of the plan. The original committee consisted of Andrew Peabody, chair (emeritus professor and overseer); Salisbury; and Schiff. Schiff

---

[34] Ibid.

[35] Crawford H. Toy to David G. Lyon, January 19, 1889, HUSMA. While Lyon became the public face of the museum, behind the scenes Toy continued to support Lyon's efforts. For example, in a letter to President Eliot, dated November 30, 1901, Toy indicated he did "endorse herewith Professor Lyon's report for the Semitic Museum. He asks that if you think proper, you will add a line in endorsation of his appeal. He desires to send copies of the report to a number of rich men. Possibly you may think the somewhat oratorical tone of the paper (as in its use of the expression 'sons of Harvard') more suitable for an appeal for money (as to this latter point I trust Professor Lyon's instinct) than for an official report. If so it may be slightly modified for insertion in the President's Report" (Crawford H. Toy to Charles W. Eliot, November 30, 1901, UIA 5.150, Box 68, Records of the President of Harvard University Charles William Eliot, HUA).

[36] Lyon, "Relations of Jacob H. Schiff to Harvard University," 1.

[37] Ibid.

would serve on the committee for twenty-five years, becoming chair in 1893 (with Peabody's death). The committee met in December 1889 and agreed that enlarging the collection of materials was the first order of business. Schiff pledged $10,000 for the collection, a gift that Lyon called "the real beginning of the Semitic Museum."[38]

Soon after the initial Schiff gift, the trustees of the Peabody Museum offered a gallery on its fourth floor as a temporary home for the Semitic Museum, which occupied this space from 1890 until 1903. Gifts amounting to $4,000 were used to purchase display cases for the artifacts and objects in possession of the museum. In April 1890, the Visiting Committee, at Schiff's suggestion, approved Lyon's going abroad "in the interest of the Museum." Schiff promised an annual gift of $5,000 when the initial $10,000 was "wisely expended."[39] Thus commissioned and funded, in summer 1890 Lyon traveled through London, Paris, and Berlin, looking to acquire Semitic manuscripts and antiquities from dealers.[40] He also purchased, as was the custom of the times, plaster casts of various Assyrian and Babylonian bas-relief sculptures (some of which remain on display in the museum).[41]

Following Lyon's 1890 summer tour for acquisitions, the Semitic gallery (still located in the Peabody Museum) was officially opened in a formal ceremony held on May 13, 1891. Crawford Toy spoke, explaining his understanding of the use of the term "Semitic":

The title "Semitic Museum" is justified by the unity of the material. The Semitic languages, though distinct dialects, are very closely related to one

---

[38] Lyon, 3.
[39] Ibid.
[40] As Joseph Greene has observed:

For museums, legacy collections of archaeological materials purchased from the antiquities market in the past are problematic in multiple respects. By any modern definition, they are loot: objects removed from their original contexts without regard to their find-spots (provenience), conveyed through a black market with no record of chain of title (provenance), offered openly by sellers with no rightful claim of ownership to buyers with no scruples about receiving stolen goods. Thus such legacy collections were, are, and always will be tainted to a certain extent by their origins.... The Semitic Museum at Harvard University, established in 1889, is no exception. However, the particular history of the Museum's collection and of the role played in that history by the Museum's founding curator, Harvard professor, David Gordon Lyon, make for an especially complicated legacy. ("A Complicated Legacy," 58)

Greene notes also that "none of the Museum's holdings...have ever been subject to any repatriation claims" (68).

[41] The larger portion is now in storage at the Semitic Museum.

another, the various Semitic civilizations are in important respects identical. The field however, is large in space and time. It embraces eight nations, it includes almost all of Western Asia and a part of Africa and the Mediterranean Islands and coasts; it goes back four millenniums before the beginning of our era. It includes important periods of the world's history; the long continued commercial and civilizing career of the Phoenicians, the inventors of the alphabet, who left their impress on the Greek religion, and acted as intermediaries between the East and West; the establishment of the great world-empires of Assyria and Babylon, between whose art and that of Greece there is an important relation; the rise of the first monotheistic religion, the composition of the Old Testament, with the subsequent remarkable history of the Israelite people.[42]

In his remarks, Jacob Schiff seems to share this broad cultural and linguistic understanding of the term "Semitic": "It is this that to the Semitic people mankind is indebted for its religion, the world for a great part of its culture and civilization. In Israel monotheism found its origin. In Babylon and Phoenicia were created the methods which to a considerable extent govern commerce to-day." But he goes on to assert that members of "the Jewish race" who are "the modern representatives of the Semitic people may well be proud of their origin and ancestry." And then, in words painfully prescient of events that will unfold some thirty years later, he reveals what, in part at least, must represent his personal interest in the recovery of Semitic antiquities: "Anti-Semitism in Europe, social prejudice and ostracism in free America, may for a time be rampant; posterity will with shame and disgust repudiate these passions. To combat in the meantime these unsound currents in an efficient manner, opportunities should be created for a more thorough study and a better knowledge of Semitic history and civilization, so that the world will better understand and acknowledge the debt it owes to the Semitic people."[43]

Joseph Greene has commented on the slippage in understanding of the term "Semitic" between Schiff and the Harvard professors:

> At a time when Harvard was famously white, Anglo-Saxon and Protestant, Schiff saw Lyon, a Protestant academic sympathetic to things Semitic, as an inroad into this academic bastion of New England privilege. Schiff's stated aim was that the Semitic Museum highlight the contribution of the "Semitic peoples" to Western civilization…, this at a

---

[42] "Opening of the Harvard Semitic Museum: Addresses by Pres. Eliot, Prof Toy, Curator Lyon and Mr. Jacob H. Schiff," *The American Hebrew* (May 1892): 67–70, here 67, UAI 5.150, Box 217, Folder 47.2, Records of the President of Harvard University, Charles William Eliot, HUA.

[43] "Opening of the Harvard Semitic Museum," 68.

time when "Semitic" could also be a code word for "Jewish." Lyon, by contrast, may have considered "Semitic" in more strictly linguistic terms. He was a scholar of Semitic languages and taught at Harvard in a "Semitic Department." On the variable meanings of "Semitic," Schiff and Lyon may have allowed to exist between them a degree of creative ambiguity. Lyon needed Schiff's financial support to create his "Oriental Seminar." From Lyon, Schiff sought an entrée to Harvard. Implicitly they may have agreed not to probe one another too closely on this point.[44]

With a gift of $50,000 from Schiff (that eventually reached $80,000), the Semitic Museum moved into its own three-story building (designed by Boston architect A. W. Longfellow), dedicated on February 5, 1903.[45] Toy, who was in Europe on sabbatical during the dedication, sent a letter in which he expressed his approval of the museum's mission: "Culture then, as now, was a process of give and take. In this process the Semites bore themselves bravely and with honor, borrowing freely and giving as freely."[46] At the dedication ceremony, Schiff and Eliot made pledges to one another. Schiff said,

> Mr. President, we now place this Building and its contents in the keeping of Harvard College. We commend it to the fostering care not only of yourself and of the governing bodies of this great University; but we commend it, likewise, to the good-will of all who believe that the gaining

---

[44] Greene, "A Complicated Legacy," 58. On the one hand, Schiff seems to believe that Jews were the "modern representatives of the Semitic peoples" (as cited above); on the other hand, he, according to Lyon, was not "willing that the Museum should be considered an affair of the Jews. To him it was to be of broad human interest, making its appeal regardless of race or creed. In answer to a letter from me in January 1890, suggesting that we might hope for larger success by making the Museum a Jewish enterprise, he protested in words which bordered on the undiplomatic." Schiff also often expressed his view "that the Jewish element should never predominate in numbers" on the committee and his hope that "the instruction in the Department should always prove attractive to all classes of students" (Lyon, "Relations of Jacob H. Schiff to Harvard University," 4). By refusing to allow the museum to be under the sole guardianship of Jews, Schiff was able to press his cause to combat the "unsound currents" of anti-Semitism.

[45] In January 1899, Schiff offered a gift of $25,000 if Harvard donors would match it. By June of that year, Lyon had raised subscriptions totaling $18,000 with little prospects of raising the rest. Schiff then pledged the entire $50,000 with the condition that the other $18,000 be used to enlarge the collection (Lyon, "Relations of Jacob Schiff to Harvard University," 13). In a January 1899 private letter to Lyon, President Eliot wrote, "I see clearly that this Museum and the body of instruction which it illustrates are part of an important field of knowledge too little cultivated among us Americans" (12).

[46] Cited by Lyon "Relations of Jacob Schiff to Harvard University," 18.

of a thorough knowledge of the civilization of those who have been before us means a better humanity and happier conditions for ourselves, and even more so for those who come after us.[47]

President Eliot replied that the museum "is necessarily to be a place for keeping safe sure records of the history of a great race; but we may be sure that it will also prove in the future the means of inducting our youth into new discoveries greater than any we now imagine,--discoveries as to the genesis and significance of our biblical records, and as to the development of the fundamental ideas which we owe to the Semitic peoples."[48]

It is over the issue of what constituted, in Schiff's terms, "wise" expenditures that Toy and Lyon did not always agree (though they were never in open conflict on the issue in their correspondence). In a letter dated July 28, 1890, Toy responds to a letter from Lyon sent from Paris. He comments: "If the whole outlay according to your present calculations amounts to only $2500, I should say buy photographs largely, get casts of all possible Semitic coins, and pick any manuscripts—Hebrew, Syriac, Arabic, Ethiopic or anything you feel sure of. It seems to me first that you are likely to find some cuneiform tablets and casts, & secondly that we shall have to expend a good deal in manuscripts."[49]

Thus, Lyon and Toy were largely in agreement on the need to purchase existing manuscripts and artifacts in the various venues available to them. But

---

[47] Cited by Lyon, 19.

[48] Cited by Lyon, 20. Eliot and Schiff became great friends as a result of their collaboration on the Semitic Museum. Lyon notes that after the meeting of the Semitic Fund committee in December 1889,

> Mr. Shiff [sic] was President Eliot's guest at luncheon and there began a beautiful friendship which gave great pleasure to each of these strong and far-sighted men. Each held the work and character of the other in the highest esteem. A special bond between them was their interest in the affairs of the Semitic Department, an interest manifested in many ways by Dr. Eliot, not only as President but since his retirement and up to the present time (November 1925). Whatever other reasons may have led Mr. Schiff to select Bar Harbor as one of his summer homes, the nearness of President Eliot, only a few miles away, must have been a strong additional attraction. (Lyon, "Relations of Jacob Schiff to Harvard University," 3)

For more on the Eliot/Schiff friendship and their summers together at Bar Harbor, Mount Desert Island, see Mikeal C. Parsons, "From Harvard's Semitic Museum to Mount Desert Island and Back," *Chebacco: The Magazine of the Mount Desert Island Historical Society* 20 (2019): 97–107.

[49] Crawford H. Toy to David G. Lyon, July 28, 1890, HUSMA.

as early as Lyon's first acquisitions trip to Europe in 1890, he expressed interest in excavating for artifacts as well. But Toy expressed doubt about Lyon's proposition that the mission of the museum would include not only acquiring antiquities but excavating for them as well:

> The scheme of digging of Assyria & Babylonia is an alluring one—but does Schiff understand how much it is likely to cost? We should probably have to *spend* $5000 at first *without* getting anything in return & it is doubtful whether such an undertaking would pay unless we could keep up the excavation year after year & should be firmly backed by our government…. I think we ought to provide ourselves with the necessities before undertaking an enterprise which will certainly consume all available funds. Let us first get all the tablets & manuscripts…then if Schiff wishes we can go into excavating.[50]

Apparently, Schiff did wish for the Semitic Museum to expand into excavations, or at least he was persuaded to do so by Lyon. Most of the Semitic Museum's original collection (1889–1929) resulted from purchases from antiquities dealers or gifts from individuals.[51] But while serving as annual director of the American School of Oriental Research in Palestine in 1906–1907, Lyon conducted a "salvage excavation" near the village of Samieh and deposited artifacts recovered there in the Semitic Museum.[52] Thus, Lyon began fulfilling his dream of expanding the work of the museum into field archaeology. Once again, the dream was underwritten by Jacob Schiff, who in 1905 initially authorized expenditures of another $50,000 for excavations in Samaria (which

---

[50] Ibid.

[51] Greene, "A Complicated Legacy," 58. Greene described the collection as consisting of "not only archaeological artifacts, but also manuscripts in Semitic and other Near Eastern languages (as well as Greek papyri from Egypt), ethnographic materials (costumes, jewelry, weapons, tools and other implements), specimens of natural history, contemporary photographs of peoples and places in the Near East and plaster casts of ancient Near Eastern monuments and inscriptions" (58). The purpose of the original exhibits "was intended by Lyon to create a fully rounded presentation of the ancient Semitic world: full-sized replicas to stand in for well-known ancient monuments, photographs to give museum goers a sense of 'Oriental' landscapes and peoples and contemporary Palestinian costumes and objects of everyday life that were thought (mistakenly) to fill gaps in the fragmentary material record of a vanished Biblical world" (ibid.).

[52] Green, "A Complicated Legacy," 66. See *American School of Oriental Research in Palestine Register of Students*, 9–11, for a list of students who worked with Lyon on this excavation. Appreciation is expressed to Dr. Joseph Greene for sharing a pdf of the register. See also Philip J. King, *American Archaeology in the Mideast: A History of the American Schools of Oriental Research* (Philadelphia: American Schools of Oriental Research, 1983), 38–41.

like his other gifts also grew in size), the first American excavation in Palestine.[53] An inability to secure a Turkish firman or legal mandate delayed the
excavation, which finally began in 1908 and continued intermittently through
1910.[54] Originally, George Reisner, a Harvard graduate and youthful but experienced field archaeologist and Egyptologist, was commissioned to conduct
the Samaria excavations, but previous commitments prevented him from assuming supervision of the site until 1909.[55] In the meantime, Lyon began the
work in 1908 without Reisner and with results that were mixed and that came
immediately under scrutiny. R. A. S. Macalister, who was involved in the
Gezer dig, visited Samaria during the first season and observed to the secretary
of the Palestine Exploration Fund, "Entre nous, I fear they [Lyon's team] are
making a mess of things; they have worked barely 3 months, so far as I can
make out, and have spent $50,000!"[56]

<hr/>

[53] This was actually the second of two gifts by Schiff to Harvard subsequent to his
contributions for the building of the Semitic Museum. The first was a gift of $50,000, the
interest of which was to be used for salaries of faculty and staff associated with the museum.
The implementation of this gift would later cause controversy between Lyon and the Lowell administration (see Lyon, "Relations of Jacob H. Schiff to Harvard," 24–28). This second gift was originally pledged by Schiff for excavations in Palestine and was to provide
for $10,000 per year for five years (29). By conservative calculations, Schiff would donate
a total of $275,000 to the Semitic Museum and its causes (Williams, The "Augustan Age,"
178). Others have estimated that the total contributions from Schiff to the various Harvard
initiatives in Semitics were in excess of $300,000 (Naomi Wiener Cohen, *Jacob A. Schiff: A
Study in American Jewish Leadership* [Hanover, NH: University Press of New England,
1999] 76–77).
[54] Lyon explains the various reasons for the delay in "Relations of Jacob H. Schiff to
Harvard," 33–43.
[55] Reisner was a student of Toy and Lyon, receiving his degrees (A.B., Ph.D.) in the
Semitic Department. He spent three years in Germany, learning hieroglyphs with Kurt
Sethe. He would serve as the director of the joint Harvard-Boston Museum of Fine Arts
Expedition in and around Giza, Egypt, and has been recognized as the "Father of Ameri-
can Egyptology" (Freed, "The Egyptian Expedition," 26).
[56] Cited by Thomas W. Davis, *Shifting Sands: The Rise and Fall of Biblical Archaeology*
(Oxford: Oxford University Press, 2004), 42. This judgment stands in sharp contrast to
Lyon's own assessment in a letter to Schiff on August 10, 1908: "All goes well.... You will
feel amply rewarded by the results of this year's campaign, which will excite wider interest,
I believe, than any other campaign elsewhere has done" (UAI 5.150, Box 101, Records of
the President of Harvard University, Charles William Eliot, HUA). In a sense this confirms Pére Vincent's view (reported by Macalister) that the Harvard team was "obsessed
with finding something sensation(al?)—either a big epigraphic monument, or a portrait
bust of Jezebel or a full-sized golden calf—and did not appreciate the importance of the
things they did find, nor take the trouble to examine them properly" (Davis, *Shifting Sands*,
42).

Reisner took on the Archaeological Survey of Nubia in 1907,[57] and he was unable to give his full attention to the Samaria excavation because he also assumed directorship of a joint expedition between Harvard and the Boston Museum of Fine Arts (much to the dismay of Schiff).[58] Still, Reisner managed, it seems, to bring some order to the efforts in Samaria.[59]

A number of significant discoveries were made in the Samaria excavation (especially early examples of archaic Hebrew inscribed on ostraca), but no division of finds came to the university because of the rules of excavation implemented by the Ottoman authorities.[60] In that sense, Toy's early concerns about the potential return on investments in archaeological activities proved at least partially justified.[61] In the middle of these efforts of excavation, Craw-

---

[57] Reisner worked in Egypt under the auspices of Mrs. Phoebe Hearst and in behalf of the University of California at Berkeley, which ran from 1889–1904/05. Hearst was forced to withdraw her support of the excavation because her goldmining operations had failed. Reisner was appointed head of the Harvard-Boston Expedition, which took over UC-Berkeley's work in the Giza excavation (Freed, "The Egyptian Excavation," 26–27).

[58] But not without the support of Lyon, who had been lobbying President Eliot to grant Reisner a faculty appointment at Harvard at least since 1904, asserting, "Whether at home or in the field, he would be a welcome addition to our staff, and he has unusual qualifications both in Semitics and in Egyptian" (David G. Lyon to Charles Eliot, May 6, 1904, UAI 5.150, Box 101, Records of the President of Harvard University, Charles William Eliot, HUA).

[59] Still, there were delays in publication of the results of the Samaria excavation; see Lyon, "Relations of Jacob H. Schiff to Harvard," 46–47; Ron E. Tappy, *The Archaeology of the Ostraca House at Israelite Samaria: Epigraphic Discoveries in Complicated Contexts*, Annual of The American Schools of Oriental Research 70 (Boston: American Schools of Oriental Research, 2016); Ron E. Tappy, "The Harvard Expedition to Samaria: A Story of Twists and Turns in the Opening Season of 1908," in *Buried History: Journal of the Australian Institute of Archaeology* 52 (2016): 3–30. On the 1908–1910 Harvard expedition to Samaria, see the primary and secondary resources collected at http://ocp.hul.harvard.edu/expeditions/reisner.html. The field report was finally published in 1924: George Andrew Reisner, Clarence Stanley Fisher, and David Gordon Lyon, *Harvard Excavation at Samaria, 1908–1910* (Cambridge: Harvard University Press, 1924).

[60] Greene, "A Complicated Legacy," 66. Greene reports that the lack of artifacts and materials given to the museum disappointed Schiff, though he still agreed to pay for the publication of the excavation results (66).

[61] If anything, Toy underestimated the lack of return on investing in excavation when he remarked that Schiff might spend $5,000 before "getting anything in return." As it turned out, Schiff expended well more than $50,000 (an astronomical amount for the time) with no division of finds returning to Harvard's Semitic Museum. Lyon, however, thought the ultimate purpose of archaeological exploration for a university was research: "To a great University such object can be only research, first and always. To a museum it could easily be the acquisition of specimens—as has too often been the case in the past" (David G.

ford Toy, now seventy-three years old, tendered his resignation from the faculty of Harvard in 1909, bringing to a close his nearly forty-year association with the university.[62]

A Baptist Legacy at Harvard

Freedom of conscience and religious liberty were values both David Lyon and Crawford Toy cherished from their Baptist upbringing. Those convictions were put to the test early in Lyon's tenure over the issue of Harvard's practice of compulsory chapel. President Eliot asked Lyon to lead chapel prayers in January 1885. Lyon agreed reluctantly, but recorded in his diary that he had "scruples about conducting the services."[63] Lyon spoke further with Eliot regarding his reservations about compulsory attendance at the religious services, expressing his "dislike of that element, but [I] consented to conduct the services during the month. He [Eliot] assured me that my so doing could not be understood by the students as if I advocated compulsory prayers."[64] Only a month later, in February 1885, the faculty voted 21 to 11 to request the Corporation and overseers to make attendance at chapel services voluntary.[65]

Near the end of his career, David Lyon led the resistance to President Lowell's attempt to limit the number of Jews admitted to Harvard College. Lowell apparently thought the student population had reached a "saturation point" when and if the percentage of Jewish students exceed fifteen percent.[66] Lyon's efforts against these restrictions again can be seen as an expression of his Baptist convictions regarding freedom of conscience with regard to religious beliefs. Ultimately, the Harvard faculty, led by Lyon, forced the administration to abandon its quota plan for Jewish students. The path, however,

---

Lyon to Charles Eliot, June 23, 1905, Charles William Eliot, Papers, Box 227 [1903–1909], Folder "Lyon, David Gordon," HUA). The Semitic Museum was closed to the public during the Second World War and used for Naval offices. "In the 1970s, academic activities resumed in the Semitic Museum, which is again home to the Department of Near Eastern Languages and Civilizations, and to the University's collections of Near Eastern archaeological artifacts," which "comprise over 40,000 items" (https://semitic-museum.fas.harvard.edu/about). See also Janet Tassel, "The Semitic Museum Rises Again: After forty years of neglect a revivified Harvard museum opens to the public," *Harvard Magazine* (March–April 1982): 40–46. Later, Martin Peretz detailed other difficulties encountered by the museum in a guest commentary titled "The Sabotage of The Semitic Museum," published in *The Crimson*, November 29, 1993, http://www.thecrimson.com/article/1993/11/29/the-sabotage-of-the-semitic-museum/.

[62] On Toy's resignation, see chapter 6.
[63] David Gordon Lyon Diary, January 2, 1885, HUG 1541, Box 6, Volume 3, HUA.
[64] Lyon Diary, January 3, 1885.
[65] Lyon Diary, February 10, 1885.
[66] Lyon Diary, May 9, 1922.

was not easy. On May 23, 1922, Lyon recorded in his diary that the "Fac[ulty] voted 56-44 after hot debate to draw the racial line in admitting students to Harvard." The vote, known as the Ropes vote—so-called after a fellow faculty member—did not explicitly mention the admission of Jews, but rather instructed the Committee on Admissions not only to consider academic credentials and moral character but also "to take into account the resulting proportionate size of racial and national groups in the membership of Harvard College" with an eye toward whether "their presence as members of the College will positively contribute to the general advantage of the college."[67] Lyon noted further, "In answer to my question Lowell (president) said the object [of] the vote was to limit Jews in Harvard College."[68] Lyon offered a motion that a faculty committee be appointed to find "a solution, acceptable to all parties concerned, and consistent with the liberal, democratic spirit of the University."[69]

Lyon began immediately organizing opposition to the proposal. He invited to his home "some of the Faculty opponents of racial discrimination to consider what we can still do to save the University from a false step fraught with dangers."[70] At the meeting, Lyon recorded that it "was felt the best course was to try to secure delay by the Overseers till the whole subject can have a thorough study."[71] Lyon delivered a petition calling for a re-vote, signed by thirty-one members of the faculty, to President Lowell on May 29, 1922. The meeting was held on June 2 and the often heated debate ran for more than three hours. The outcome was what Lyon desired: the anti-Jewish vote of May 23 was rescinded by a vote of 69-25.[72]

Later, David Lyon would reflect on the issue in a forty-plus-page manuscript titled "The Jew and the College," which he delivered to the Minsters' Club in Boston in January 1923. For Lyon, the efforts by Lowell, Ropes, and others to limit the numbers of Jews at Harvard needed to be placed in the larger context of intolerance that undergirded the "three-fold doctrine" of the

---

[67] Papers of David G. Lyon, HUB 1541, Box 16, Folder "Admission of Jews to Harvard, 1922–23," HUA. Official votes passed at meeting of Faculty of Arts and Sciences, May 23, 1922.

[68] Lyon Diary, May 23, 1922.

[69] Lyon Papers, HUG 1541, Box 16, Folder "Admission of Jews to Harvard, 1922–23," HUA; see also Jennifer S. Axsom, "The Catholic Baptist and the Faith of Harvard: David Gordon Lyon, 1852–1935" (final paper for Rev. Professor Peter J. Gomes, May 7, 2004).

[70] Lyon Diary, May 24, 1922.

[71] Lyon Diary, May 25, 1922.

[72] Lyon Diary, June 2, 1922.

Ku Klux Klan "to teach the negro his place, to rob the Jew from his commandeering position in business, and to drive Catholics out of politics."[73] Lyon proceeded to enumerate ten points against the policy of restricting the numbers of Jewish students given college admission. In addition to appealing to the spirit and values of "new-world democracy," Lyon also appealed to Christian principles ("Since the colleges bear in large part the name Christian, discrimination puts that name in a false light") and his own Southern heritage ("Discrimination points the road to bloodshed. If the college puts the badge of inferiority on the Jew, what may we not expect of the unreasoning mob, the lynchers, and the hooded mid-night raiders"[74]). In an earlier draft of his Ministers' Club speech, originally titled "Color, Creed, and College," Lyon positioned himself as a defender of Harvard's storied past: "Though not a son of Harvard except by adoption, I have served her so many years and entered so deeply into her spirit that I grieve as a son at any lapse, real or apparent, from her high traditions."[75]

As a result of his efforts, the Harvard Menorah Society made David Lyon an honorary member and presented him with a silver vase, bearing the inscription:

> To David Gordon Lyon
> Scholar, Teacher, and Courageous
> Upholder of Harvard Liberal Traditions
> On his
> Retirement from active Teaching
> From
> The Harvard Menorah Society
> Of which he is an honorary
> Vice-President
> Commencement
> June 1922[76]

Beyond Collegiality

Crawford Toy and David Lyon were colleagues at Harvard from the time of Lyon's appointment in 1882 until Toy's retirement in 1909. Their profes-

---

[73] David G. Lyon, "The Jew and the College," 2–3, Papers of David G. Lyon, HUG 1541, Box 16, HUA.

[74] Lyon, "The Jew and the College," 35–40 passim.

[75] David G. Lyon, "Color, Creed, and College," for the Ministers' Club, HUG 1541, Papers of David Gordon Lyon, Box 16, HUA.

[76] Lyon Diary, June 20, 1922.

sional collaborations are noteworthy but not unprecedented. What is remarkable, however, is the length and depth of their personal relationship and friendship. Lyon recalls:

> My acquaintance with Dr. Toy dates from Autumn of 1876, when I became a student at the Seminary, though I had been familiar with the report of his omnivorous reading and prodigious knowledge. I soon learned that the report was no exaggeration. In the class room he seemed to know everything about the subjects which he taught. He criticized the text-book with freedom, and sought not to fill the mind of the students with facts, though he never minimized the value of fact, but to stir up the mind to the exercise of its own powers.[77]

As we have already seen, Toy served as mentor and counselor to Lyon as he navigated his way to Germany for graduate studies after Toy's forced resignation from the seminary. Lyon comments: "Dr. Toy was for three years my favorite teacher in Seminary, and I had intended remaining a fourth year for study with him. The summer following his resignation, and as a result of it, I went to Germany to continue there the pursuit of those studies which I had begun with him."[78] Toy was also presumably instrumental in advocating Lyon's appointment to the Hollis Chair. After arriving in Cambridge in 1882, Lyon lived for six years with Toy.[79] Lyon continued to live with Toy even after 1883 when Lyon married Tosca Woehler (1855–1904), a young German he met while studying in Leipzig.[80] Only in 1888, when Crawford Toy married

---

[77] Lyon, "Toy," 6.

[78] Lyon, "Toy," 11. At this point in his tribute to Toy, Lyon cites from several letters that Toy wrote Lyon in 1879–1880 as Lyon prepared to journey to Germany for additional studies and while he was there.

[79] Lyon, "Toy," 16.

[80] Tosca often spent long stretches of time as a patient in a "sanitorium" in Arlington Heights. In a letter to President Eliot, Lyon hints that he may have to delay a planned research leave abroad:

> According to present appearance, it is not probable that I can go abroad for the next college year. On Dr. Swan's advice I had Dr. Bowles of the McLean Hospital to see Mrs. Lyon, and it is Dr. B's "opinion that she is suffering from nervous exhaustion's, and that she is not well enough to undertake the trip. There has been, I think, a slight gain during her stay of seven weeks at the Arlington Heights Sanitorium, but she feels unequal to the thought of travel." (David G. Lyon to Charles Eliot, August 3, 1900, Papers of Charles W. Eliot, UAI 5.150, Box 52, HUA)

In a letter to Eliot dated September 9, 1900, Lyon confirms that "the year abroad has now been definitely abandoned. While Mrs. Lyon seems somewhat better, she is clearly not well enough to go abroad." On January 8, 1904, she attempted suicide by jumping from

Nancy Saunders, did the Lyons move into a home of their own. Lyon reflected on that time together: "For my first six years in Cambridge it was my good fortune to live with Dr. Toy, and to have the friendship of earlier years ripen into intimacy, which I prize among my most precious memories."[81]

It is in Lyon's diaries, however, which he kept for most of his adult life, that we see the real depth of devotion and affection between the two friends. First, there is the sheer quantity of contacts between Toy and Lyon recorded in Lyon's diary. In the twenty-five years of diaries that are extant between 1882 and 1919, there are nearly 500 references to one "calling" on the other (an average of almost biweekly home visits), and an additional 125 times when Lyon had lunch, dinner, or tea with Toy. They frequently took walks together, often calling together on a colleague.[82] Beyond the quantity of exchanges are the sorts of activities in which they engaged. Not only did they meet frequently to plan courses and activities for the Semitic Department (and later the museum), but they also covered each other's classes when illness or travel caused

---

the sixth floor of the Dunvegan Apartment building on Massachusetts Avenue. She died on January 17, 1904, from massive internal injuries suffered from the fall. The *Cambridge Chronicle* carried the following story in its January 23, 1904 issue:

> Mrs. Tosca Lyon, wife of David G. Lyon, Hollis professor at the Harvard Divinity School, is dead. The death return filed at the city hall gives the cause of death "paralysis of the heart," and the secondary cause is given as "shock following a fall of 60 feet, Jan. 8, 1904." Mrs. Lyon had been suffering for some time from a mental trouble, and notwithstanding careful attention, she succeeded in eluding her nurse one day last spring. She made her way to the Harvard bridge and went along the parkway and threw herself into the river. She was rescued with difficulty and her identity was kept a secret by the police officials. Prof. and Mrs. Lyon lived at the Dunvegan, 1684 Massachusetts Avenue. It was here that Mrs. Lyon fell. Funeral services were held in Appleton Chapel at 2.30 Tuesday afternoon.

In his diary, Lyon refers to Tosca's "continued illness" (Lyon Diary, January 1, 1904). In the entry for January 8, 1904, he records that "At 12:30 called home by telephone. Tosca had had a serious fall. Found her in bed bleeding from scalp and foot. Heart action weak." He recorded that she suffered a broken arm, required stitches in her scalp, and said "It is a marvel that death was not instantaneous." On the day she died, Lyon recorded that he read Scripture to her and prayed with her. The diary entry ends, "Thus the dear heart, who has suffered so long and so painfully has been allowed to go to sleep, and now has her great desire" (January 17, 1904). On the following day, he wrote, "When dear Tosca first went my mind seemed not to comprehend what had happened. Oh, the mystery of suffering and of death!" (January 18, 1904).

[81] Lyon, "Toy," 17.

[82] Gratitude is expressed to my undergraduate assistant, Michael Barnard, for combing through Lyon's diary and compiling these statistics.

absences. They often read each other's scholarly work in pre-publication for-mat.[83] Lyon helped Toy construct an index for the second edition of *Religion of Israel*.[84] They also attended each other's lectures; Lyon even sat in on Toy's Koran class in spring 1889. Especially revealing of the nature of their relation-ship were the services Lyon provided for Toy. Some of the services were pro-fessional in nature. Lyon wrote notices of forthcoming volumes by Toy to bring them to the attention of the scholarly public.[85] Toy often suffered from a "lame" hand and was unable to answer correspondence, resorting to dictation at times; occasionally, David Lyon was Toy's amanuensis.[86] In honor of Toy's retirement in 1909, Lyon, along with George Foote Moore, edited a Fest-schrift, published in 1912; most of the contributors were affiliated with the Harvard History of Religions Club, which Toy presided over for many years and of which Lyon was also a member.[87] Other activities were more mundane. Lyon purchased materials for bookshelves for Dr. Toy and helped prepare his study for workers to lay carpet.[88] Lyon even "stopped cracks with putty in Dr. Toy's study"![89]

---

[83] For example, on May 6 and 8, 1892, Lyon read to Toy a paper he had written on inerrancy, and which he would present as "The Inerrancy of the Scriptures" (a paper read before the tenth annual session of the Baptist Congress [Philadelphia, PA, May 1882], HUG 1541, Papers of David Gordon Lyon, Box 16, HUA). Cf. Lyon's diary entry on December 10, 1893.

[84] Lyon Diary, February 10, 1883.

[85] On January 2, 4, and 31, 1891, for example, Lyon wrote a notice of Toy's *Judaism and Christianity* for *The Nation* magazine, *Christian Union*, and *Harper's*.

[86] See, for example, the diary entries for January 4 and 5, 1883.

[87] David Gordon Lyon and George Foote Moore, *Studies in the History of Religions: Presented to Crawford Howell Toy by Pupils, Colleagues, and Friends* (New York: Macmillan, 1912). Jacob Schiff covered most of the costs of publication. See Appendix 4 for the Table of Contents. On November 16, 1912, Toy wrote a note of appreciation for Lyon's contri-bution to the volume (HUG 1451, Papers of David Gordon Lyon, Box 13):

Dear Lyon

I have read with peculiar pleasure your admirable study of the consecrated women of the Hammurabi code. The facts are presented so clearly and in such coherent form, and the interpretation of them is so calm and judicious that the discussion can hardly fail to carry conviction to readers. So an interesting ques-tion of religious organization is practically settled. I must add that your English is of the best sort, ...and, as far as I observed, free from blemish. It is a great satisfaction to me to have [your] name thus associated with mine.

Aff'y yours,

CHT

[88] Lyon Diary, January 23, 24, 1885.

[89] January 30, 1885. Many of these manual services occurred while the Lyons were still living with Toy, and they are evidence of the veracity of Lyon's anecdote about "the only criticism I ever heard as to his knowledge": his laundress reported, "'Dr. Toy don't

The Toys and Lyons were frequently together on Mount Desert Island, where both couples frequently took extended summer holidays.[90] In the summers of 1889 and 1891, for example, Lyon recorded in his diary taking walks with the Toys, rowing with Crawford Toy to NE Harbor to watch a local baseball game, and playing a popular card game at the time, Casino, in the evenings with the Toys.

Lyon rarely, if ever, forgot to send Toy a note on his birthday, March 23, even when out of the country. While serving with the American School for Oriental Research in Palestine, Lyon wrote Toy: "This ought to reach you on or before March 23. It brings hearty congratulations and much love from me, with all good wishes for the day and for the new year which it begins. Above all things I wish for you good health and joy in your work."[91]

Because we do not possess Toy's diary (beyond the excerpt from 1900), we cannot know how often Toy remembered Lyon's birthday, May 24 (which was also the date of the Toys' anniversary).[92] But there is good evidence that he did, in fact, reciprocate. In the ephemera to Lyon's 1913 diary is preserved a poem by Toy in honor of Lyon's birthday:[93]

> To D.G. Lyon, on his birthday, May 24, 1913
> One and thirty years, dear Lyon,
> We have labored side by side
> To infuse Semitic learning
> Into youngsters, Harvard's pride.
> Colleagues we have been in College.
> Comrades ever in thought and aim
> Not only in pursuit of knowledge
> In much else that life may claim

---

know nothing. He don't know how to sew on a button.' In the use of tools and machinery," Lyon wrote, "he [Toy] was singularly inexpert" ("Toy," 16).

[90] The following references are taken from Lyon's 1889 Diary (August 24–September 9) and 1891 Diary (July 21–August 24). For more details, see Parsons, "From Harvard's Semitic Museum to Mount Desert Island and Back."

[91] David G. Lyon to Crawford H. Toy, February 26, 1907, Letterhead: The American School for Oriental Study and Research in Palestine, Jerusalem, HUSMA. Lyon records congratulating Toy on his birthday in 1891, 1892, 1904, 1908, 1910 (and often records having dined with the Toys in celebration of Toy's birthday). In 1906 Lyon gave a dinner in honor of C. H. Toy's seventieth birthday at Young's Hotel in Boston. He even provided a diagram detailing the seating arrangements for the dinner (March 23, 1906).

[92] On May 23, 1906, Lyon records that he bought a glass vase with silver ornament for Mrs. Toy in honor of their wedding anniversary, and had a dinner celebrating both his birthday and their anniversary at the Toys' home that year (Lyon Diary, May 24, 1906).

[93] Lyon 1913 Diary ephemera; see Appendix 3 for other examples of poetry by Toy (and Lyon).

May this birthday, which will end
One laborious fruitful year,
Begin a round of days to spend
In services that you hold most dear!
All influences of sky and earth
Combine to give you joy and rest,
To season work with helpful mirth
And Spirit's deepest highest zest!
CHT

At times, Toy treated Lyon almost paternally, especially after Tosca died. When Lyon was away on one of his site expeditions, Toy fretted about Lyon's health when he learned that Lyon had contracted a "bad cold": "I hope you will be careful to have your house properly heated & to dress warm when you go out; the weather in Palestine may be treacherous."[94] In the same letter Toy confided to Lyon that he was contemplating retirement: "I think I shall resign at the end of this College year; my object is to get leisure to finish a couple of books that I have on hand, for which I have been unable to find time. Of course I am sorry to withdraw from the Univ'y, with which my life has been so long identified, but I am anxious to put my collection of materials into shape & for that I must be freed from class-work & other college duties. This is private for the present."[95] On the other hand, Toy could be somewhat callous. In the same letter in which he revealed to Lyon his retirement plans, he concluded, "I spoke with the Pres't about Reisner who seems to be the best man for my chair; what do you think of it?" Apparently it never crossed Toy's mind that Lyon might be interested in Toy's chair.[96]

---

[94] Crawford H. Toy to David G. Lyon, February 9, 1907, HUSMA.

[95] Ibid. Toy would later decide to postpone his retirement for one year, retiring at the end of the 1908–1809 academic year. Lyon hosted a retirement dinner and arranged a Festschrift in his honor (see Appendix 4).

[96] Toy to Lyon, February 9, 1907. To be fair, Lyon did at that time hold the Hollis Chair, older and arguably more prestigious than the Hancock Chair. In January 1909, it seemed the decision of the administration to leave the chair unfilled, a view confirmed by Jacob Schiff in a letter to Lyon on January 26, 1909: "I am also indebted to you for the information you convey to me as to the Professorship now held by Prof. Toy, and I am rather sorry to learn that it is proposed to leave the position open for a time after Prof. Toy has gone. I hope to be able to discuss this with you personally more fully before long" (Jacob Schiff to David G. Lyon, January 26, 1909, HUG 1541, Papers of David Gordon Lyon, Box 13, HUA). Toy resigned his post as Hancock Professor on December 26, 1908, to take effect September 1, 1909 (Records of the President of Harvard University, Charles William Eliot, UAI 5.150. Box 68, HUA). In his diary entry for April 9, 1910, Lyon records: "Letter from President Lowell of Harvard suggesting transferring me from the Hollis to the Hancock professorship. 'I can see advantages in the change, if you would like it.'

In 1910, David Lyon married Mabel Everett Harris, and at the age of fifty-nine, he became a father to David Gordon Lyon, Jr., born in September 1911. Toy wrote Lyon a congratulatory note:

Dear Lyon,

Mrs. Toy has already telephoned our congratulations on the arrival of an heir in the Semitic Department, and I write now to express the hope that David Gordon Lyon Jr. continues to behave well. I need not say that we watch his development with the greatest interest—he is the first infant of the Department—and we hope to have favorable accounts of Mrs. Lyon. It is too soon to choose a profession for the young gentleman, but I am sure he will prove a worthy scion of the dine and a source of new life to you. As soon as possible we shall hope to have the pleasure of receiving him in our house.[97]

Three months later, Toy wrote an "ode" to and for the newborn for Christmas:

Ode to David Gordon Lyon, Junior
To our world you've come
From heaven, your home
Clouds of glory therefrom trailing.
Now have no fear
And be a dear
And dispense with useless wailing
On lucky night!
Your eyes are bright.
Lungs good and voice sonorous.
But Papa and Mama
And Grandmama
Don't half-like cries dolorous.
Rest in sleep,
Or take a peep,
At this new world you have come to.
And once in a while
Give us a smile

Replied, in part, I 'cheerfully accept your suggestion in the matter.' The Hancock Professorship of Hebrew & other Oriental Languages is a title corresponding better with my actual work" (Lyon Diary, April 9, 1910). Apparently, it never occurred to Toy to discuss Lyon's potential preference for a chair that more accurately described Lyon's expertise in Semitic languages.

[97] Crawford H. Toy to David G. Lyon, September 29, 1911, HUG 1541, Papers of David Gordon Lyon, Box 3, HUA.

And a tune that we can hum to.
Now go your way—
You cannot stay
In babydom forever.
There's work for you
To dare and do—
And fortunately you are clever.[98]

Despite the obvious care and affection the two shared for one another, there remained a hierarchical dimension to the relationship that never altered. Lyon almost always referred to Crawford Toy as "Dr. Toy," not only in correspondence with Toy and others but even in his private diary, and Toy, except in official correspondence with President Eliot and others, consistently referred to David Gordon Lyon simply as "Lyon." Lyon always the student; Toy always the professor.[99]

Lyon's care for Toy extended into Toy's retirement; his sense of responsibility more resembled that of an adopted son than a former student.[100] Crawford Toy was concerned that he would be unable to continue living in his residence at 7 Lowell Street on his professor's pension.[101] President Eliot agreed to raise a subscription of supplemental pay for Toy, a task he soon turned over to David Lyon, along with responsibilities for various repairs on the residence. For example, Eliot wrote from Asticou on Mount Desert Island June 23, 1913: "I enclose the first bill of Charles H. McClare, architect, for the changes at 7 Lowell Street, and a check to your order for the amount. Will you please pay this bill by your own check, as a friend and agent of Professor Toy? It seemed to me that your position as supervisor would naturally be

---

[98] HUG 1541, Papers of David Gordon Lyon, Box 3, Family and Personal Correspondence, HUA.

[99] In good Southern fashion and custom of the time, both Toy and Lyon always referred to the other's spouse as "Mrs."

[100] In fact, Lyon's own biological father, Dr. Isaac Lyon, had died when David Gordon was a child of seven or eight years old, and the Toys were childless. Lyon often used filial language when referring to his relationship to the university (though never in reference to Toy per se). When he received his honorary degree he remarked, "what I prize in it most is that it makes me one of the 'children of the house'" (Lyon to Eliot, September 2, 1901). In an address, "Color, Creed, and College," delivered January 25, 1923, to the Minister's Club of Boston during the controversy regarding Harvard admissions of Jews, Lyon referred to himself as "not a son of Harvard except by adoption" (Papers of David Gordon Lyon, HUG 1541, Box 16, Folder "Admission of Jews to Harvard, 1922–1923," HUA).

[101] Coolidge, "Toy," 16.

strengthened if the money went through your hands to the architect, the carpenter, and the plumber."[102]

For several years, Lyon also collected an annual supplement of $1,000 for the Toys. As Toy's health worsened, Lyon turned to his old friend, Jacob Schiff, for an increase in the supplement. Schiff was already underwriting half of the annual supplement. In 1917 (two years before Toy's death), Lyon wrote Schiff:

> President Eliot has turned over to me his part in looking after the interests of our good friend Dr. Toy. You have been accustomed to send $500 about May 1st and other friends a like amount Nov. 1st. In view of the growing infirmity of our friend, especially his blindness, making it necessary to have the constant care of an attendant, and in view of the increased cost of living, the gift last Nov. was increased to $750. There is a balance on hand which will make it possible with your 500 to do this again on May 1st. I mention this because when the philanthropy began and we were trying to devise a plan to get 1000 a year you proposed to provide half this amount as you have regularly done. I do not by any means expect you to increase your gift, already so generous, but as you have been accustomed to do as much as all the other friends combined, I thought I ought at least to let you know this new situation. You will understand me.
>
> I see Dr. and Mrs. Toy every few weeks. He is not totally blind, but is nearly so, also somewhat deaf, but his mind is clear, and his spirit calm and good.[103]

Schiff replied:

> Concerning the affairs of dear Dr. Toy, I am very sorry indeed to hear that the good man is becoming so feeble and infirm, which must be a hardship, not only for him, but also for Mrs. Toy.
>
> I am also glad you reminded me that my annual contribution of $500. is now due, and I enclose check for this, and may I ask, since you have taken over these interests from President Eliot, that you continue to remind me from year to year, but I cannot see my way to increase the amount of the contribution I am now making.[104]

---

[102] Charles Eliot to David G. Lyon, June 23, 1913, HUG 1541, Papers of David Gordon Lyon, Box 12, HUA.

[103] David G. Lyon to Jacob Schiff, April 24, 1917, Jacob H. Schiff Papers, MS 456, Box 451, Folder 3, AJA. Appreciation is expressed to Dr. Mel Hawkins for sharing a pdf of this letter as well as Schiff's response (below).

[104] Jacob Schiff to David Lyon, April 27, 1917, Jacob H. Schiff Papers, MS 456, Box 451, Folder 3 AJA.

Presumably Lyon continued this benefaction until Toy's death and perhaps beyond, attending to the needs of Mrs. Toy. His last act of friendship with Crawford Howell Toy was to write a tribute, which was published in several versions. In one version, Lyon concluded the tribute with these words:

> Dr. Toy was goodness and truth. In him was realized the ancient description of the good man, one who has clean hands and a pure heart, who has not lifted up his soul unto vanity nor sworn deceitfully. He showed us indeed how to swear to one's own heart and change not for one's profit.[105]

In preparation for the tribute, Lyon had collected materials from Crawford's brother, Walter D. Toy, who taught German at the University of North Carolina in Chapel Hill.[106] Lyon sent a copy of the tribute for which Walter Toy was grateful: "I received to-day the copies of the *Harvard Theological Review* which you kindly sent. Every member of our family will feel indebted to you for the full and sympathetic account you have given of Brother Crawford's life and work. It is admirable in every way. You have made a picture of him that will be acceptable to all who knew him. I thank you heartily."[107]

It is also Walter D. Toy who best described the affection, care, and devotion that David Lyon extended to Crawford Howell Toy from the time he was Toy's student in Greenville, South Carolina, in 1876 until he helped Mrs. Toy arrange Dr. Toy's funeral in 1919. Following the funeral, Walter Toy wrote to David Lyon, "my thoughts have been constantly fixed on Cambridge and all that that means. I have realized fully the value of your unconditioned friendship for my brother and his family."[108] Crawford Howell Toy and David Gordon Lyon—an unconditioned friendship, indeed!

---

[105] HUG Papers of David Gordon Lyon, 1919 Diary Ephemera, December 13, 1919.
[106] Walter D. Toy to David G. Lyon, May 19, 1919, HUG 1541, Papers of David Gordon Lyon, Box 16, HUA.
[107] W. Toy to Lyon, February 2, 1920.
[108] W. Toy to Lyon, May 19, 1919.

Fig. 5

Nancy Saunders Toy
passport photograph, ca. 1925.
National Archives and Records Administration

8

Nancy Saunders Toy

A "Vivid and Stimulating Personality"

Crawford Toy expressed interest in the opposite sex from near the beginning of his extant correspondence. At the close of a letter to his cousin, Morton Howell, written in 1853 (when Toy was seventeen), Toy remarks, "I can't say that I think visiting the ladies a very bad habit. I have not indulged in it to any extent myself this session; I intend to make up for lost time, during the vacation."[1]

Toy is found true to his word in his letter to Morton over summer vacation, indulging in two "bad habits." In addition to reading novels ("which bad habit I intend to drop sometime during the last week in September"), Toy confesses to "another bad habit I have contracted (isn't it a bad one?)" which is "visiting the girls. I am however very moderate and therefore feel no bad effect from it. I shall drop it too, mostly."[2]

Later in fall 1853, Toy returns to the topic of "young ladies." Toy attended a "big wedding" officiated by John Broadus, noting he and his friends "had to run about, talking to various females for about five hours, counting a sort of little interlude, supper…. I made the acquaintance of several nice ladies & on the whole enjoyed myself." Two other incidents at the wedding reveal something of Toy's youthful personality. When he realized attendees were entering the dining hall in couples, Toy confided that he "saw one young lady with whom I was acquainted, unengaged, so I made up toward her as fast as possible, and just as I got within four feet of her, I heard her introduced to a partner for supper. I backed out very quickly—then with some others, I was obliged to wait for an unknown length for the crowd to finish." He concludes the episode by noting, "I had a piece of the bride's cake, which I hid under my head one night, wrapped up in a list of names of girls; that night, though, I dreamt of nothing at-all. I have forgotten to try it again since."[3]

---

[1] Crawford H. Toy to Morton B. Howell, April 6, 1853, ASC SBTS.
[2] Toy to Howell, July 29, 1853.
[3] Toy to Howell, November 9, 1853. It was an old folk tale that if one slept with a piece of wedding cake under one's pillow, one would dream of his or her future spouse. Toy's expressed interest in the opposite sex continues in his next letter in the spring. Toy

Despite his boyish attempts to divine his future bride, Toy would not marry for another thirty-five years, at the age of fifty-two. Crawford Toy remained a bachelor during his first eight years in Cambridge until May 24, 1888, when he married the irrepressible Nancy Saunders, a young woman twenty-four years his junior but every bit his match in intellect, culture, and Southern charm.

Crawford Toy's niece, Jane Toy Coolidge, recounted the following story about her Aunt Nancy:

> One summer she invited my family to be her guests for a week at a hotel on Cape Ann and made advance reservations for rooms. When our party arrived, the manager told her that there were no rooms for us in the main hotel but that he could make us very comfortable in the annex. An inspection of the rooms was agreed on, and as we walked across the lobby, Aunt Nancy leading the procession like a ship in full sail, remarked in a loud stage whisper "I don't like to be in the annex to ANYTHING!" We were given the best rooms in the main hotel.[4]

This anecdote gives a perceptive glimpse into the personality of the woman who would be Crawford Toy's marriage partner for more than thirty years. Like many women of the nineteenth century, Nancy Saunders Toy's story is nearly effaced from the pages of history. Only because she interacted with some of the most well-known political and intellectual leaders of the early twentieth century do we know as much about her as we do.

Nancy Inge Saunders was born on July 1, 1860 (the same year Crawford Toy was rebuffed by Mary Mauldin), in Norfolk, Virginia, the youngest child of Rev. Robert Milton and Mary Jane Toomer Saunders.[5] Robert Saunders (1830–1900) was a Methodist clergy who served as teacher and principal of several different female colleges and institutes.[6] From 1859–1865, Saunders

---

notes that he took a "very nice young 'fem.' Daughter of Dr. [Socrates] Maupin, with me & enjoyed a fine promenade" at a celebration sponsored by the Jefferson Society (Toy to Howell, April 18, 1854). Dr. Maupin had recently arrived at UVA in fall 1853 as chair and professor of chemistry. Maupin's daughter was most likely Susan Grayson Maupin, who would have been fifteen at the time (Toy was eighteen).

[4] Coolidge, "Toy," 13.

[5] Mary Toomer was Robert Saunders' second wife. He and his first wife, Rebecca Hill had one child, Viola Saunders (Kinnier); cf. W. J. Young, "Rev. R. M. Saunders," *Minutes of the One Hundred and Eighteenth Session of The Virginia Annual Conference of the Methodist Episcopal Church, South, Held at Norfolk, VA, November 14-22, 1900: Memoires, Reports and Directory*, ed. Bernard F. Lipscomb (Richmond: J.W. Fergusson & Son, 1900), 37. Robert and Mary Saunders had two other children, James and William.

[6] Robert Saunders was born to Shepard and Nancy Saunders McGraw. His oldest brother, William B., was also a Methodist minister. Shepard Saunders died in 1840, and

served as president of Tuscaloosa Female College, which was under the juris-
diction of the Alabama Methodist Conference. After a year as principal of a
school in Georgia (1865–1866), Saunders and his family moved to Berlin,
Germany, where he was engaged in educational work and research.[7] During
this time, Mary was head of an institution for the training of American girls
in Berlin. They returned to the States in 1869 and, after several years of private
instruction, Saunders established the Norfolk Collegiate Institute for Young
Ladies, where he was principal and teacher of Mental and Moral Philosophy
at Norfolk Institute until 1887.[8]

Saunders was president of Mississippi Female College in Meridian, Mississippi (1888–1890) and Martin Female College in Pulaski, Tennessee
(1890–1894). From 1896 until his death in 1900, he was chaplain of the Ran-
dolph-Macon Woman's College in Lynchburg, Virginia.[9] Mary (1830–1914),
who had graduated from Wesleyan College for Women in Wilmington, Del-
aware, in 1848, taught alongside Robert at several institutions.[10] At Ran-
dolph-Macon, she served as professor of French and German until her retirement in 1907.[11] Both were popular and effective educators. Robert Saunders
was a much-loved minister:

> Brother Saunders was an admirable type of the true Christian gentle-
> man…. His work, during most of his life, brought him in closest contact
> with literature and with the new thought of this progressive age. His
> mind was ever open to new truth, but he saw in it, as if by intuition, its
> harmony with the unchanging truths of God's inspired Book…. Alt-
> hough he had been at the head of several important institutions, he filled,
> with all cheerfulness, his more humble place at the Woman's College;
> and magnified his office. Whatsoever he did, he did all in the name of

Nancy married Major W. M. McGraw in 1852 (*Southern Christian Advocate Obituaries, 1867–1878*, December 14, 1874).

[7] Young, "Rev. R. M. Saunders," 37.

[8] Ibid. See also John James Lafferty, *Sketches of the Virginia Conference, Methodist Episcopal Church, South* (Richmond, VA: Christian Advocate Office, 1880), 67.

[9] Young, "Rev. R. M. Saunders," 37.

[10] Information provided by Peg Niedholdt, archivist, Sargeant Memorial Collection, Norfolk Public Library, Norfolk, Virginia.

[11] Roberta D. Cornelius, *The History of Randoph-Macon Woman's College: From the Founding in 1891 through the Year of 1949–50* (Chapel Hill: The University of North Carolina Press, 1951), 244–45. Mary Saunders was the first woman to receive a retiring allowance from the Carnegie Foundation (*The Carnegie Foundation for the Advancement of Teaching: Ninth Annual Report of the President and of the Treasurer* [Boston: Merrymount Press, 1914], 131).

the Lord Jesus.[12]

Mrs. Saunders was described as "a superior woman, both by reason of rare endowment and wide and thorough cultivation."[13] Nancy was an 1878 graduate of the Norfolk Collegiate Institute for Young Ladies.[14] After graduation, Nancy joined her parents on the faculty of the Norfolk Institute as assistant in English and Modern Languages.[15]

We know little about Crawford Toy's courtship of Nancy Saunders. Toy and the Saunderses were in Berlin during the same period (1866–1869). Sarah Ann Strickler, a student at Albemarle Female Institute where Toy was teaching in 1866, mentions the Saunders family in connection with Toy's plans to continue his studies in Europe:

> Mr. Toy spoke to me today about going to Europe in September. Mr. and Mrs. Saunders of the South…expect to go to the old country then, and open a school for American girls at Berlin. They will take twenty young ladies, afford them the best masters in music, the languages, etc., and during the year take them traveling over the most beautiful and storied parts of Europe…. Mr. Toy is well acquainted with Mrs. Saunders and expects to go to Berlin very soon.[16]

It is possible that Toy actually lived with the Saunderses in Germany.[17]

---

[12] Young, "Rev. R. M. Saunders," 38–39. This quotation is from a very lengthy tribute by Young in this publication (released the year of Saunders's death). Certainly, interactions with his son-in-law, Crawford Toy, would have brought Saunders into "closest contact" of the "new thought of this progressive age"! See also H. W. Burton, *The History of Norfolk Virginia—A review of Important Events and Incidents which occurred from 1736 to 1877; Also a Record of Personal Reminiscences and Political, Commercial, and Curious Facts* (Norfolk, 1877 Private Schools), 263.

[13] Lafferty, *Sketches of the Virginia Conference,* 67.

[14] *Catalogue of the Norfolk Collegiate Institute for Young Ladies, Session of 1876–'77,* (Norfolk VA: Virginian Printing House, 1877), 6.

[15] *Catalogue of the Norfolk Collegiate Institute for Young Ladies, Session of 1878–'79,* (Norfolk, VA: Virginian Printing House, 1879), 2. In both catalogues, she is listed as "Nannie" Saunders; see also *The Crimson,* May 26, 1888. The Norfolk Public Library does not hold copies of the institute's catalogues for 1880–1888, but Nancy is listed as living with her parents in the 1880 Federal Census, and she was listed as living in Norfolk at the time of her marriage in 1888. My presumption is that she continued to teach at the Female Institute in Norfolk and that Crawford Toy would have visited her there during holidays and summer vacations.

[16] Strickler, "Private Diary," 195–96; cited by Hurt, "Toy," 38.

[17] Coolidge, "Toy," 7, attributes this view to a "Max Havlick" who, she claims, wrote an unpublished biography of C. H. Toy. I have not been able to identify Max Havlick or to locate the biography.

It seems safe to assume that Toy had considerable interaction with the Saunders family while in Germany; however, without additional evidence beyond this vague citation of a source citing another source, it is impossible to know if Toy actually cohabitated with the Saunderses. Nancy would have been six years old when her family moved to Berlin.

During the Civil War, Toy's parents, Amelia and Thomas, a druggist, had moved from Norfolk to Baltimore in March 1862. Following the war, his parents returned to Norfolk and the Freemason Street Baptist Church, which the elder Toy helped to found.[18] Toy returned regularly to visit his family, and presumably during those visits he saw the Saunders family and deepened his acquaintance with Nancy.[19] Jane Coolidge credits Nancy's mother with encouraging the romance:

> It seems highly probable that Mrs. Saunders gave Crawford the understanding and sympathy he needed during the period of mental storm and stress when he found himself unable to accept the literal fundamentalist faith as taught by the Baptist church, and during the time that followed when he found himself condemned as a heretic and an outcast by the church group that had been the center of his world.... What could have been more natural than for him to turn to Cousin Mollie Saunders who spoke his language, shared his beliefs, and gave him the comfort that he needed. This, I think, is what happened. Cousin Mollie was a kindred spirit and a friend in need, and Crawford never forgot it.... A clever woman who had learned worldly wisdom the hard way, Mrs. Saunders found herself, in the middle 1880s, in Portsmouth, Virginia, with a grown daughter who didn't fit into the social life of the southern town.... Crawford was settled at Harvard in a secure and respected position. He was fifty years old and needed a wife. What could be more appropriate than that Nancy should join him in the intellectual world for which she was so well suited? Mrs. Saunders was clever enough to see the advantages of such a marriage and to arrange it; it is my guess that this is what she did.[20]

Presumably, Crawford and Nancy were engaged prior to Toy's departure in fall 1887 for a year-long sabbatical, which he spent mostly in Egypt (studying spoken Arabic as well as ancient and modern Islamic culture), because little more than a month after his return, Crawford Toy and Nancy Saunders

[18] John Walters, *Norfolk Blues: The Civil War Diary of the Norfolk Light Artillery Blues* (Shippensburg, PA: Burd Street Press, 1997), 300.

[19] Unfortunately, another potential source of documentation of contact between C. H. Toy and Nancy Saunders, the diary of David Gordon Lyon, is not extant from 1886–1888. He does not mention her in the diaries of 1883 and 1885.

[20] Coolidge, "Toy," 8–9.

were married in Norfolk, Virginia, on May 24, 1888.[21] Nancy's father, Rev. Robert M. Saunders, performed the ceremony.[22] Later that year, the *Cambridge Chronicle* published the following announcement:

> Prof. and Mrs. Crawford Howell Toy of Lowell street will be at home to their friends on Thursdays from 4 to 6 during the present month. Mrs. Toy, who was Miss Saunders of Norfolk, VA, has but recently returned to Cambridge since her marriage early in the summer. The many friends who knew the charming southerner in years gone by will be glad to welcome her to her Cambridge home.[23]

The announcement is interesting because it reveals something of the Toys' efforts to find a place in Cambridge society. That same month, Crawford withdrew his membership from the Old Cambridge Baptist Church and began attending the First Parish Church, where the Harvard president and many faculty, Cambridge mayor, and legendary town doctor were all members. Clearly, the Toys intended to position themselves as near [to] the center of the social fabric of late nineteenth-century Cambridge elite as they could.[24] Their home was the focal point. Jane Toy Coolidge recalled: "Mrs. Toy's Sunday Afternoons at 7 Lowell Street became a local institution, the Cambridge equivalent of a salon. She had the gift of attracting interesting people, and of giving them the understanding appreciation that made them love her."[25] Billy Hurt, Toy's first biographer, concurred:

> Mrs. Toy's ability to make friends was her outstanding characteristic. She was also given to careful and conventional planning, but sometimes acted on impulse and in rather unexpected fashion. Mrs. Toy was remembered...as one, who while not a snobbish person, chose her friends from the "top drawer" because of her desire for the best in the intellectual and

---

[21] A brief announcement was included in *The Crimson*, May 26, 1888.

[22] Crawford Howell Toy and Nancy Inge Saunders, Document: 23 May 1888, Marriage: 24 May 1888, City of Norfolk, Hustings Court, Marriage Licenses: 1889, 1888, 1885; Microfilm #85; Norfolk, Virginia. A copy of the marriage license was provided by Peg Niedholdt, archivist, Sargeant Memorial Collection, Norfolk Public Library, Norfolk, VA.

[23] *Cambridge Chronicle*, October 13, 1888. This report also suggests that Nancy Saunders had made her presence in Cambridge known before the marriage.

[24] Nancy Saunders Toy, at various times over the next thirty years, would be a member of various social organizations, including the Cambridge Social Union, Symphony Concert Committee of Harvard, and pro-League of Nations Bureau; *Cambridge Tribune*, October 30, 1920.

[25] Coolidge, "Toy," 9.

social world of her day.[26]

Cambridge Friends: George Santayana. One of those "top drawer" friends was George Santayana (1863–1952), eminent philosopher and novelist of the early twentieth century. Santayana completed undergraduate studies at Harvard in 1886, and after two years of study in Berlin, he returned to Harvard in 1888 (the same year Nancy Saunders took up permanent residence with Crawford Toy in Cambridge). After completing his doctoral dissertation at Harvard, he joined the faculty where he taught until his resignation in 1912. At that time, he moved to Europe, where he remained until his death. The Toys and Santayana became friends during his time in Cambridge. The first reference to Nancy Toy in the collected correspondence of George Santayana is in an 1896 letter:

> I went to see Mrs. Toy the other day and was taken short, having caught cold from a sharp wind that had just sprung up. I was obliged to leave, saying I wasn't feeling well. But the law of compensation would have it that the next morning I should get a note from the lady, inviting me to come and nurse myself at her house, where she would make me very comfortable.... Of course I declined the offer, but I may actually go spend a few days there in May, while I move my things from Cambridge to Longwood, where my mother lives.[27]

Santayana kept in touch with the Toys, often arranging for copies of his publications to be sent to them.[28]

After Santayana's departure from Harvard, he and Nancy kept up a correspondence for thirty years; occasionally they saw each other in person.[29] As such, she was part of a small circle of trusted women. "So far as we know, Santayana never had a romantic relationship with a woman, though there were several women with whom he enjoyed close friendship and lifelong correspondence. Mrs. Toy, Mrs. Potter, and Mrs. Winslow fit this description."[30]

---

[26] Hurt, "Toy," 82–83.

[27] Santayana to Guy Murchie, 12 March 1896, in William G. Holzberger, ed., *The Letters of George Santayana, Book One [1868]–1909* (Cambridge: MIT Press, 2001), 1:151.

[28] See, e.g., Holzberger, *The Letters of George Santayana LGS*, 1:165, 166, 283, 318–19.

[29] Santayana mentions seeing Nancy Toy, accompanied by two young women, in Oxford in 1899 (Santayana to Boylston Adams Beal, August 7, 1899, *LGS* 1:241). Since most of the correspondence by Santayana occurred after Crawford Toy's death in 1919, and since the focus is to mine the letters for light they shed on Nancy Toy's personality, especially as it might illuminate her relationship with her husband, references to Santayana's letters in this section are selective and representative.

[30] Holzberger, *The Letters of George Santayana*, 3:xliii. Santayana viewed "women as fundamentally different from men"; furthermore, Holzberger (3:xliii) observed: "Feminists,

Nearly all the extant correspondence is from Santayana to Toy, with one exception.[31] After receiving a copy of *The Life of Reason* from Santayana, Nancy penned a thank-you note that was at once self-deprecating and revealing of her intellectual instincts and curiosity:

> I began to read in it at once and I thought to delay my thanks to you for it until I had completed reading. But I soon found that this would be to delay them too long,--for there is scarcely a page in the book which does not require reflection that hinders the rapid turning of the leaf.
>
> I wish that my opinion had the value of that of an expert in philosophical speculation, for then my estimate of the importance of your work would give you pleasure. If I were writing to a layman in philosophy like myself I should not hesitate to speak of the extraordinary range of your thought, the admirable ordering of it in a consistent system, its striking originality, and the display in it of the union of remarkable power of imagination with not less remarkable faculty of the understanding.[32]

She continued: "Now that you are away from Cambridge I know not where to look for anyone who is truly meditating on the problem of life. Contemplation is an unfamiliar practice. Nobody seems to feel the need or to say, 'So many hours must I contemplate.' The University is given over to facts and regards thoughts with suspicion.—Come back soon to redress the balance!"[33]

---

with some justification, condemn Santayana as a sexist who characterized women as inferior. S. believed that, compared to men, women are generally not as intelligent, interesting, or physically fine; men are the superior gender." Santayana never married, and many scholars have concluded that Santayana was gay or, perhaps, bisexual, though it isn't clear if he had any physical relationships with either sex. Holzberger briefly concludes that Santayana's sexual orientation was "not conventional." Having read Santayana's letters after her aunt's death, Jane Coolidge mused ("Toy," 12): "I think he was in love with her and that she was very fond of him. How fond we cannot know. We do know that she handled the situation with delicacy and tact and kept Santayana's devotion for fifty years." Santayana may well have loved Nancy Toy, but it seems unlikely that this form of love could be easily categorized with the typical terminology of "romantic" or "sexual."

[31] Of the 150 manuscript pages of correspondence, only one letter from Nancy to Santayana is (partially) preserved. These letters were recovered in Nancy Toy's apartment and given to Samuel Morrison in order to be "photostated" for the Harvard library (Coolidge, "Toy," 10–11).

[32] Nancy Toy to George Santayana, April 23, 1905, Film MSB 36. HL.

[33] Ibid.

Nancy asked Santayana to send books (by other authors) with his marginal notes, which he did.[34] At one point, after many years of doing this, Santayana mused over Nancy Toy's request to deposit marked copies of the works of Josiah Royce and others in Harvard's Widener Library:

> As to depositing the Cardoza book in the library—in the Inferno, I suppose, with my old copies of Royce, etc.—of course I am flattered and amused. Do as you think. In time the librarian himself will remove superfluous deposits to the cellar or top shelves, and meantime some candidate for an A.M. or Ph.D. may do "research" work by getting down the volume and copying a pencil note of your humble servant's! How small and accidental the learned world seems when one catches it, like this, in its witches' kitchen![35]

Santayana, arguably one of the most respected intellectuals of the first half of the twentieth century, had deep respect for Nancy Toy's intellect and literary tastes and often sought her opinions.[36] Thus, the intellectual exchange was reciprocal, if unequal. For example, Santayana sent her prepublication

---

[34] He admitted to being a bit self-conscious about inscribing notes he knew beforehand would "be seen, criticized, and perhaps repeated to the author" (Santayana to Nancy Toy, December 21, 1938, *LGS* 6:189–90).

[35] George Santayana to Nancy Toy, December 12, 1938, *LGS* 6:185. The "Inferno" referred to a restricted area of Harvard's Widener library that contained such "forbidden" works as the *Kama Sutra* and a treatise, *Why Priests Should Marry*; cf. Jan M. Ziolkowski, "Introduction," in *Obscenity: Social Control and Artistic Creation in the Middle Ages*, ed. Jan M. Ziolkowski (Leiden: Brill 1998), 12.

[36] Santayana was a student of William James and Josiah Royce and the teacher of such notables as T. S. Eliot, Robert Frost, Walter Lippmann, W. E. B. Du Bois, and Wallace Stevens. In his letters, Santayana engages Nancy Toy in a wide range of literary and philosophical topics. In a letter dated December 6, 1938, he sends her his own translation of St. Francis's "Simple Prayer," noting that it "is a beautiful prayer, and truly evangelical. Galilee and Umbria have something in common" (*LGS* 6:180–91). At one point, he wryly thanks her for "not encouraging my would-be biographer from Pennsylvania. Why not wait til I am decently dead? Or will it then be too late for the public to take any interest?" (Santayana to Nancy Toy, January 18, 1932, Film MSB 36, HL). She also seeks his opinion on a variety of topics, including issues that arose on the Harvard campus; e.g., see the discussion of whether Harvard should have a war-memorial chapel (*LGS* 4:301). Later, in 1934, Santayana responds critically to a copy of James Hardy Ropes's lectures that Toy had sent him. The critique is fascinating, and Santayana concludes: "New Testament criticism will never become straightforward and clear until two things happen together which as yet occur only separately: that the spirit and presuppositions of the critic should be thoroughly secular and scientific, and that his object should be purely religion itself; i.e., the religious feeling, imaginations, and tradition in the New Testament writers. We must substitute a scientific interest in religion for a religious interest in science; otherwise both religion and science will be muddled" (November 4, 1934, *LGS* 5:148).

chapters of his monumental novel, *The Last Puritan*, and "was pleased by her praise of the writing."[37] Nancy Toy apparently also confronted Santayana about anti-Semitic references in a letter of May 1, 1938, in which he railed against Walter Lippmann, Sidney Hook, and Irwin Edman.[38] He replied, "I had just sent you a very Jewish book when I get your letter recommending me to avoid anti-Semitism.... I ought to love the Jews, as they seem to be my only friends, intellectually, beginning with Edman."[39]

Nancy Toy had the resources to travel to Europe as late as 1925, but Santayana was already worried about her financial situation. He wrote to his friend and bookseller, Maurice Firuski, in 1924, asking if he might secure a Christmas present for his "old friend, Mrs. C.H. Toy." Santayana wrote he could "hardly find anything for her that she would not have to pay duties on if I sent it." So he asked Firuski, "I wonder if you could choose a book—something she would not be likely to buy or to read in a book-club, and that yet might interest her? All the better if a little ornamental and not cheap."[40] Within a few days, Santayana informed Firuski that he had located a suitable gift after all:

> Since my note of the other day I have come upon a book which is just the thing I should like to give for Christmas presents: "The Pleasures of Architecture" by C. & A. Williams-Ellis....
>
> If you have it on hand, and have not found anything better for Mrs. Toy, you might send it to her in my name.... But this does not cancel my request that you should choose something for Mrs. Toy for Christmas. All the better if she gets two books instead of one as they are not perishable goods.[41]

In his own hand on the fly leaf of Nancy Toy's copy of Santayana's *Sonnets and Other Verses*, Santayana composed a poem, "and a wreath of laurel," "to Nancy Toy" and dated it April 1894:

---

[37] *The Works of George Santayana*, volume 5, book 4: xxi; cf. *LGS* 4:328. In his letter of May 13, 1932, he discusses the personalities of some of the novel's characters at length (*LGS* 4:334–36).

[38] Santayana wrote, "Are the Jews going to repent of being anti's, for fear that soon there should be nothing left to be anti against? After all they have made themselves very comfortable in Christendom, and if nothing but an international proletariat remained, it would not offer them such brilliant careers as professors and prime minister and newspaper proprietors" (George Santayana to Nancy Toy, May 1, 1938, *LGS* 6:128). These remarks were made as the shadow of Nazi Germany was beginning to grow in Europe.

[39] Santayana to N. Toy, August 12, 1938, *LGS* 6:152.

[40] George Santayana to Maurice Firuski, November 29, 1924, *LGS* 3:225.

[41] Santayana to Firuski, December 5, 1924, *LGS* 3:226.

Laurel is a sacred leaf
And forbidden to be worn
Lest Apollo in his scorn
Shoot the wearer for a thief.
Yet could any human grief
Quite be uttered in a song
The dark laurel would belong
To all poets that have writ.
Let your own heart mend my wit
And my crown is not a wrong.[42]

Santayana's friendship with Nancy Toy extended across her lifetime, an uncomplicated affection between two complicated personalities.

Cambridge Acquaintances. Nancy Toy had some brief exchanges with Harvard president Charles Eliot and his assistant Jerome Greene.[43] On September 5, 1907 (?), Nancy Toy wrote President Eliot to clarify a conversation between them (probably on Mount Desert Island) regarding the date of C. H. Toy's retirement: "Mr. Toy was naturally much interested when I repeated to him our conversation some days ago. But he seemed disturbed for fear that I had given you the impression that he meant to retire next year. I reassured him as best I could but I have had it on my conscience ever since to tell you— and I know that you will understand—that it is a subject we never discuss in the family!"[44] Nancy Toy often confessed in her letters that she had lost control of her pen; apparently, this conversation with President Eliot regarding

---

[42] Quoted by Coolidge, "Toy," 11.

[43] The Toys were also friends with Professor and Mrs. William James. Although there is nothing like the substance of exchange that existed between Nancy Toy and George Santayana, clearly there was affection and admiration expressed by William James for Nancy Toy. Twice James wrote Nancy Toy expressing gratitude for her acts of kindness during an illness he and/or his family had experienced: "How much kinder one's friends are to one than one is to one's friends, especially you!" (William James to Nancy Toy, March 18, 1904, bMS 1092.9 [3819], HL). Later, he wrote regarding some unspecified act of kindness: "Dear Mrs. Toy, Am I an operatic tenor that I should be treated in this way by the bean sexe [the fair sex]? It more than compensates for being ill that one gets thereby assured of human affection" (James to N. Toy, November 9, 1909, bMS 1092.9 [3821], HL). James expressed his admiration for Nancy Toy in a letter to Crawford Toy, while James and his family were on research leave: "Pray give the love of both of us to Mrs. Toy, than whom I for one, have seen nothing more inspiring or truly satisfactory since the shores of America sank below the western horizon" (William James to Crawford Toy, May 3, 1893, bMS 1092.9 [3818], HL).

[44] Nancy Toy to Charles Eliot, September 5, 1907, Records of the President of Harvard University, Charles William Eliot, UAI 5.150, Box 68, HUA. There was continued

237

Crawford Toy's retirement plans had gotten away from her, whether beyond her own comfort level or, more likely, that of her husband.

The correspondence with Jerome Greene was initiated by Mrs. Toy, who was looking for a student who might do some housework.[45] Mr. Greene responded by suggesting that she interview a Mr. Yamaguchi, a Japanese student, looking for work: "I think I know Japanese well enough to classify Mr. Yamaguchi—on the strength of a five-minute interview—with the honest and industrious type."[46] On August 26, Nancy wrote Mr. Greene to inform him that Mr. Yagamuchi had been in contact by letter. She was amused that the letter was addressed to "Honorable professor," and stated that "his first letter was such a joy that I cannot bear to think of leading the way to less picturesque English."[47] Apparently the arrangement was a success: the 1910 census listed the household of Crawford Toy as including Nancy, Mary Saunders (mother-in-law), and two "servants": Mary Bouvier and K. Yamaguchi (age twenty-one).[48] One wonders if Crawford Toy ever reflected on the fact that fifty years after he had been commissioned as a Baptist missionary to Japan he now had a Japanese person living as a servant in his home in Cambridge.

Woodrow Wilson. In summer 1894, Crawford Toy was giving lectures at the School of Applied Ethics at Plymouth, Massachusetts, and Nancy had accompanied him there. The couple met a fellow Southerner—indeed, a fellow *Virginian*—and struck up an immediate friendship. Woodrow Wilson, a Princeton professor of jurisprudence and political economy at that time, was also giving lectures in Plymouth. He wrote briefly to his wife, Ellen, about the encounter: "I have made some delightful acquaintances,—almost friends,--here, among them at least one woman who is altogether delightful."[49]

---

confusion over the date of Toy's retirement, in part due no doubt to Toy's own conflicting opinion on the matter. Toy did finally submit his resignation to President Eliot and the Fellows of Harvard College on December 26, 1908, to take effect on September 1, 1909 (UAI 5.150, Box 68, HUA).

[45] Nancy Toy to Jerome Greene, August 15, 1908, Records of the President of Harvard University, Charles William Eliot, UAI 5.150, Box 126, HUA.

[46] Jerome Greene to Nancy Toy, August 17, 1908, UAI 5.150, Box 68, HUA.

[47] Nancy Toy to Jerome Greene, August 26, 1908, UAI 5.150, Box 126, HUA.

[48] Department of Commerce and Labor—Bureau of the Census, Thirteenth Census of the United States: 1910—Population, Cambridge, April 22, 1910. A copy of the census was provided by Peg Niedholdt, archivist, Sargeant Memorial Collection, Norfolk Public Library, Norfolk, VA.

[49] Woodrow Wilson to Ellen Axson Wilson, July 16, 1894, in Arthur S. Link, ed., *The Papers of Woodrow Wilson* (Princeton: Princeton University Press, 1966–1994), 8:615 (hereafter *PWW*). The editor's note (8:615) to this sentence reads: "She was, undoubtedly, Nancy Saunders (Mrs. Crawford Howe [sic]) Toy, wife of the Hancock Professor of Hebrew at Harvard, who was also lecturing at the School of Applied Ethics." Also: "The

There are only glimpses of contact between Wilson and the Toys in the subsequent decade, but it is reasonable to assume, given the existence of later correspondence, that they remained in contact.[50] There is one mention of Nancy Toy in Woodrow Wilson's diary of 1904. In 1902, Wilson had moved from his professorship in the Princeton law school to the presidency of the university. On Sunday, January 10, Wilson records that "Mrs. Toy, of Cambridge, came to spend the day and evening with us."[51] After dinner, Wilson states that the guests gathered there constituted a "bright, interesting circle" whose pleasure was "much added to by songs, chiefly Scottish, very naturally and sweetly sung by Mrs. Toy."[52] No further contact or correspondence between the two is preserved until 1910, when Nancy Toy writes two notes to Wilson, then still president of Princeton University, though he would relinquish the position (under pressure) to mount a successful campaign for the governorship of New Jersey.[53] The preserved correspondence between the two takes a serious uptick from August 1914 until September 1915. During that time, Toy and Wilson exchange at least twenty-five letters (thirteen by Toy and twelve by Wilson).[54] During this period, of course, the Great War (WWI) broke out (following the assassination of Archduke Ferdinand of Austria), and in the initial months, Wilson led the United States to adopt a position of

---

central theme of the Ethical Culture Society's session of 1894 at Plymouth was the labor problem. Wilson was one lecturer. Toy was one of two theologians."

[50] Presumably, correspondence between Nancy (and Crawford) Toy and Woodrow Wilson prior to the latter's election as president has been lost. What was recovered was the result of efforts by Wilson's biographer, Standerd Baker, to acquire as much correspondence to and from Wilson as possible.

[51] *PWW* 15:121.

[52] Ibid.

[53] Nancy Toy to Woodrow Wilson, May 26, 1910, and June 14, 1910. The first letter is published in *PWW* 20:475; the second is only available in manuscript form. The correspondence on microfilm was accessed at Boston College O'Neill Library in Presidential Papers microfilm, Woodrow Wilson Papers, 540 reels, E660.W66x1973 (hereafter as reel # and series #). Here the June 14, 1910, letter is found on reel 535, series 2. Technically, neither letter gives a year of composition (though both have month and day), and on both a second hand has suggested in brackets the date of 1912. The published date of 1910 is probably correct since Nancy Toy had written to request Wilson to try to convince her friend, industrialist James Ford Rhodes (1848–1927), who was convalescing from a serious illness in Cambridge, not to risk traveling to Princeton to receive an honorary L.L.D. degree. In the second letter of June 14, Toy mentions a response from Wilson, no longer extant. The request makes more sense if Wilson were still president of Princeton at the time.

[54] This is the number of extant letters; there are several instances in which referenced letters are missing from the corpus.

neutrality, a position that would ultimately be abandoned. The correspondence is also bracketed by highly personal and significant events. On the one hand, both Toy and Wilson had experienced significant personal losses in summer 1914. Nancy Toy's mother, Mary Jane Saunders, died on July 23, 1914, at the age of eighty-four. Woodrow Wilson's wife, Ellen Axson Wilson, died on August 6, 1914, at the age of forty-four. On the other side, Wilson's engagement to Edith Galt became public news in October 1915 (they would marry on December 18, 1915). In between, Nancy Toy and Woodrow Wilson exchanged letters that ranged over topics from shared grief over their losses to issues of politics and government. The letters were often long—Nancy's letters averaged seven handwritten pages and 750 words, while Wilson responded with typed letters, averaging three and a half pages and 500 words. The total words exchanged between them during this fourteen-month period is well more than 15,000 words. Beyond the quantity of the correspondence (remarkable, given that one of the correspondents was president of the United States!), is the quality of their content. The language was friendly, often familiar, sometimes intimate. When their letters have been examined, it has almost always been from the perspective of what the exchanges reveal regarding the personality and character of Woodrow Wilson. That is reasonable; he was, after all, the president of the United States. I wish, rather, to examine the correspondence for what it reveals about the personality and character of Nancy Toy, as a way to provide additional context for understanding her relationship with Crawford Toy (a relationship that has left few historical traces). Nancy Saunders Toy was an educated and literate woman with a keen, at times wicked, sense of humor and a desire, as we have seen, to have "top shelf" friends. The president of the United States would sit atop most any shelf one might construct. At one point she acknowledges as much to Wilson:

> I wish you could know what your letters mean to Mr. Toy and to me. But even your political opponents give you credit for reading people's thoughts, and perhaps you know already that besides the joy of simple *human* friendship, the friendship of the President of the United States makes me very proud.[55]

Literary Citations and Allusions. In her correspondence with Woodrow Wilson, Nancy Toy employs her education in languages and literature to draw a number of literary allusions and citations. At various times, she cites or alludes to Horace, Shakespeare, William Wordsworth, Matthew Arnold, Alfred Lord Tennyson, and Rudyard Kipling. In many cases, she is drawing comparison between the literary citation and Wilson himself. For example,

---

[55] Nancy Toy to Woodrow Wilson, December 6, 1914, reel 535, series 2.

she cites Matthew Arnold's poem about Shakespeare in which Arnold describes the Bard as "self-schooled, self-scanned, self-honor'd, self-secure." Toy continues, "and I thought of you."[56] Elsewhere, she quotes Horace, *Ode* 1.2, "Te duce, Caesar" to suggest that Wilson's friends will follow wherever he leads: "where you are philosophical, we your friends are—where you are political, we are."[57] At least once, she confesses to thinking of Wilson while reading to her husband. On Washington's birthday (February 22) she writes, "I have just been reading aloud to Mr. Toy 'The Happy Warrior' to celebrate the day and the man. But I could think as I read of nobody but you."[58] She then goes on to quote these lines from "The Happy Warrior":

> Who, doomed to go in company with Pain,
> And Fear, and Bloodshed, miserable train!
> Turns his necessity to glorious gain;
> In face of these doth exercise a power
> Which is our human nature's highest dower:
> Controls them and subdues, transmutes, bereaves
> Of their bad influence, and their good receives:
> By objects, which might force the soul to abate
> Her feeling, rendered more compassionate;
> Is placable—because occasions rise
> So often that demand such sacrifice;
> More skilful in self-knowledge, even more pure,
> As tempted more; more able to endure,
> As more exposed to suffering and distress;
> Thence, also, more alive to tenderness.[59]

Wilson responds, obviously flattered:

> It was generous of you to think of any part of Wordsworth's Happy Warrior as applying to me. I seem to myself so unheroic a figure (just a man who intends right things and looks for them every day with a steady mind, uncommon in nothing except that it is at his command when he wishes, as the result of long discipline) and with none but common tools to work with. If there is anything that can infuse the heroic into me it is the trust and confidence of those whom I honour and who know the

[56] N. Toy to Wilson, October 25, 1914, reel 535, series 2.
[57] N. Toy to Wilson, January 13, 1915, reel 535, series 2. Translation: "Lead on, O Caesar!"
[58] N. Toy to Wilson, February 22, 1915, reel 535, series 2.
[59] Ibid. Toy is quoting from William Wordsworth, "Character of the Happy Warrior" (1807).

right from the wrong. Any heroism I may be vouchsafed will come from the outside, not from within.[60]

At other times, Nancy Toy alludes to literary references to present her view on current circumstances in which Wilson finds himself. Quoting Tennyson (again without naming him), she writes, "It is a strange world you are inhabiting now—'so many worlds, so much to do' and you standing like 'a pillar steadfast in the storm', with your own foundations swept all away."[61] She cites and then modifies Shakespeare to make the point that now is an opportune time for Wilson to serve as president: "If one has to be President, wouldn't you choose just this time of all others with all its terrible decisions, its fresh crisis for every day, its thrilling possibilities 'from the nettle danger to pluck the flower' not 'safety' so much as victory over a thousand foes of a thousand kinds?"[62] She also compares her mother and Wilson's wife (both deceased) with Thomas Mowbray, Duke of Norfolk, a character in Shakespeare's *Richard II*, who had died in exile while fighting in the Holy Crusades:

> When I came home from church this morning, I glanced at the Shakespeare which Mr. Toy had left open on his table at Richard II, and my eye fell on those touching words about the Duke of Norfolk:
>
> "And there at Venice; gave his body to that pleasant country's earth,
> And his pure soul unto his captain Christ under whose colours he had fought so long".
> Didn't our loved ones fight always under the colours of their captain Christ? And isn't it a comfort to know that they did?[63]

In another letter she references Rudyard Kipling to characterize Wilson's success with a difficult Congress: "I congratulate you in good American that *'the tumult and the shouting'* of the 10 months old Congress *has died away*, leaving behind such an honorable record of unswervingness of purpose and a close attention to business. History will write large the records of the 'partnership'— but nobody—not even you yourself—can know its records on your heart and

---

[60] Wilson to N. Toy, March 7, 1915, reel 535, series 14, no. 73.

[61] N. Toy to Wilson, January 13, 1915, reel 535, series 2. Toy is citing Tennyson, *In Memoriam* Canto 113 (1850).

[62] N. Toy to Wilson, Washington's Birthday [February 22], 1915, reel 535, series 2. She is citing Shakespeare, *Henry IV*, part 1, act 2, scene 3: "From this nettle, danger, we pluck this flower, safety."

[63] N. Toy to Wilson, December 6, 1914, reel 535, series 2. The citation is from *Richard II*, act 4, scene 1.

brain and soul."[64]

Nancy Toy effortlessly uses foreign language phrases to make a point, often humorously. During the first few months of the European conflict, which came to be known as the "First World War," Wilson resolved to remain neutral, despite the urgings of powerful figures (including Harvard president Charles Eliot).[65] Nancy wrote, "Ich gratuliere—or if it isn't 'neutral' to 'sprechen Deutsch', I congratulate you in good American."[66] Elsewhere, in her effort to speak against the Shipping Bill of 1915, which Wilson favors, she begins her letter, "My dear Mr. President—I am not afraid of lèse-majesté. I am too oppressed. You will say 'It wearies me', and it wearies *me* too."[67] In a more comforting vein, Toy sends Wilson birthday greetings asking him "to try to realize how young you are today. I know you don't want to. I know you wish it were not so. I know that the *joie de vivre* has gone."[68]

She also makes effective use of humor. This often comes in the form of anecdotes she tells or that have been told to her. She tells of hearing an effective sermon by a Chicago Baptist in College Chapel on the text from James 1: "So speak ye and so do as men that are to be judged by a law of liberty." She relates a story told by the minister, which the audience (and she) found compelling:

> I watched the students actually *listening* as he told them about the 40 prisoners released a year ago from the Illinois State prison, the 40 who stood at the head of the good conduct roll and the first to try the honor system initiated by the Legislature. As they came out from the shadow of the prison walls into the broad sunshine of the highway, they were followed by the shouts of the hundreds left behind them: "Make good, boys, make good, and give us a chance." And they did make good. A reporter left his coat in their camp with his watch and twenty dollars. A

---

[64] N. Toy to Wilson, October 25, 1914. Citing Rudyard Kipling, *Recessional* (1897). Emphasis added.

[65] Woodrow Wilson to Nancy Toy, December 14, 1914:

Many weeks ago, when the war had just begun, Mr. Eliot wrote me a long and earnest letter arguing that we should actively join the Allies against Germany. I was amazed and distressed then, because I so sincerely respect Mr. Eliot and had thought that he might be so confidently counted on to serve always as part of the ballast of the nation, and utter what would be its sober second thought; but that shock has passed. The speeches he makes now add nothing. They come to me like a thing already discounted, an experience that is past and has faded a bit. I school myself to *look on* as impersonally as possible. (*PWW* 31:454–56)

[66] N. Toy to Wilson, October 25, 1914, reel 535, series 2.
[67] N. Toy to Wilson, January 22, 1915, reel 535, series 2.
[68] N. Toy to Wilson, Christmas Day, 1914, reel 535, series 2.

notorious Chicago burglar took it to their head man: "See here, boss, that chap ought to be more careful—there are a lot of outsiders 'round here'," he said.

She then reports that the minister ended his sermon with this question: "Without the restraining power of religion or of society what would you personally be like today? What would you do with your law of liberty?" On the way home Nancy posed the preacher's question to a friend accompanied by her niece whom she encountered on the street: "What would you do with your law of liberty?" Nancy writes to Woodrow, "'Oh, I don't know about myself,' she answered frivolously and disloyally, 'but I know my husband would eat with his knife.' 'Uncle Charles does now,' said his undutiful niece."[69]

At one point Wilson had given a shorthand version of a speech he was scheduled to deliver in Indianapolis for Nancy Toy to preview.[70] She comments on its content and then adds, "the little curlicue which I have picked out as 'Woodrow chuckles' spies at me defiantly and I should have rubbed my hand softly over its face could I have guessed its meaning."[71]

In another instance, she relates another story: "I have cut out your picture with Master Frank in your arms and pinned it to my curtains. Over it, in the Boston Post, were in moderate head-lines: 'The President with his grandson.' In immoderate headlines, cheek by jowl, in the next column, was the startling announcement: 'Hurls baby from the window—leaps to his own death.' It turned out to be a poor ex-rider of a circus."[72]

---

[69] N. Toy to Wilson, December 6, 1914, reel 535, series 2. In a later letter, outside our immediate purview, Nancy Toy relates a story told her about then Harvard president Lowell and a Bishop Lawrence. Lawrence asked Lowell: "'How did it happen and when that Princeton got into the same talk with Harvard and Yale? For a long time Princeton was spoken of with Brown and Williams but now—' Pres. Lowell interrupted him by putting a significant forefinger right under Bishop Lawrence's lips: 'Wilson!' he said" (N. Toy to Wilson, July 2, 1922, reel 535, series 9).

[70] This probably occurred during her visit to the White House, January 2–6, 1915.

[71] N. Toy to Wilson, January 13, 1915, *PWW* 32:537. The editor's note (538 n.2) explains that the "curlicue" is the "symbol in Graham shorthand for humor. It looks like a beehive." In a letter written in 1922, when she was working to raise money for the Woodrow Wilson Foundation, Nancy Toy wrote to Wilson: "Never have I enjoyed anything more than the scribbling of the past two weeks (I wonder if I haven't written your name almost as many times as you have!), the delightfulness of the fight (for isn't the pen *smitier* than the sword!), the sudden glimpses of what it all is about" (13, 1922, "The Zero Hour," *PWW* 67:526–27; here 527).

[72] N. Toy to Wilson, February 6, 1915, reel 535, series 2.

Her letters had their own literary, at times lyrical, quality.[73] Wilson commented several times on what he called the "rare quality" of Toy's letters: "Your letters have the rare quality of making me feel, after reading them, as if I had really seen you and had a talk with you of many things. I wish that I could return the visit by writing a like vivid-epistle, with the person in it who wrote it!"[74] Writing "vivid-epistles" was apparently characteristic of most of her letter writing. Her brother-in-law, Walter Toy, recognized this quality, though less charitably than Wilson, when he quipped, "Nancy writes her letters for publication!"[75]

Political and Social Issues. Another interesting feature of Nancy Toy's letters to Woodrow Wilson are the places in which she engages in discussion of, and occasionally debate over, political and social issues. She was a keen observer of current events and usually held an opinion that conformed to Wilson's policies or position—but not always. Her willingness to disagree with, or at least demur from, the president's policy is seen most clearly after her visit to the White House in January 1915.

Nancy Toy visited the White House from January 2–6, 1915—her ailing husband, Crawford Toy, did not accompany her. She kept a diary of her four-day visit to Washington, D.C.[76] She described her initial encounter with the president in the White House Red Room:

> The President came in followed by Dr. Grayson. He looked better than I have ever seen him physically and acknowledged later in a reply to a question from Helen that he had never felt better in his life. But in his talk and manner the old buoyancy had gone and I missed it during my whole visit. Also there was more formality beneath the unvarying friendliness of voice and manner. Was it, as John Hay said about Roosevelt, "the Kingly shadow falling upon him"? Or what is more likely, the schooling in self-control which Mrs. Wilson's death has forced upon him?[77]

---

[73] Though to be sure, one of the less attractive features of her letters is her penchant to drop names of other "top shelf" persons. In the correspondence with Wilson, she mentions at one point or another encounters with Adolf Harnack (German theologian), Felix Frankfurter (later Supreme Court Justice), Bertrand Russell (philosopher from whom she had received a "sweet" letter), and Harvard president Charles Eliot, among others.

[74] Wilson to N. Toy, December 12, 1914, *PWW* 31:454–56; here 454. See also Wilson to N. Toy, October 15, 1914. *PWW* 31:157.

[75] Coolidge, "Toy," 13. Little did Walter Toy know that some of her letters were, indeed, destined for publication!

[76] *PWW* 32:7–10, 12–13, 21–22.

[77] Diary of Nancy Toy, January 2, 1915, *PWW* 32:7.

Two particular events recorded in the diary have captured the attention of Woodrow Wilson scholars. On January 3, Nancy Toy attended church services at Central Presbyterian Church with the president and his eldest daughter Margaret Wilson. In the afternoon she went with the president and Helen (Helen Wilson Bones, Wilson's cousin and de facto White House hostess since the death of his first wife, Ellen) on a "2 ½ hours motor ride." Her diary entry records what has become one of the most famous of Wilson's definitions of his own faith:

> He talked much about Mrs. Wilson, about my mother and about religion. This began with a question from Helen—did I not enjoy Dr. Fitch's sermons very much? I said I had heard him only once and then he aroused my opposition by declaring that in this break-down of civilization, these hugenesses of suffering, life would not be worth living did we not believe that God was behind everything and working out his living. I do not believe that and still I think life is worth living, I added. The P. took up my challenge. His views are those of Dr. Fitch's. "My life would not be worth living," he declared, "if it were not for the driving power of religion, for *faith*, pure and simple. I have seen all my life the arguments against it without ever having been moved by them." "Did you never have a religious Sturm und Drang period?" I asked. "No, never for a moment have I had one doubt about my religious beliefs. There are people who *believe* only so far as they *understand*—that seems to me presumptuous and sets their understanding as the standard of the universe. Why shouldn't Helen's dog, Hamisch here set up his understanding as a standard! I am sorry for such people."[78]

Wilson biographers recognize this statement as reflective of Wilson's deeply held Presbyterian convictions regarding divine sovereignty. Biographer Edwin Weinstein has concluded from this diary entry that Nancy Toy did not believe in a "personal God."[79] While that reading is possible, it seems more likely that Nancy Toy rejected belief in an omnipotent God or (given her Methodist and Arminian upbringing) in Wilson's staunchly Presbyterian view of Providence. That is, she could believe in a personal Deity without necessarily subscribing to a Calvinistic view of divine destiny.

There is also this curious entry regarding Wilson's view on the women's suffrage movement.

---

[78] Diary of Nancy Toy, January 3, 1915, *PWW* 32:8–9.

[79] Edwin A. Weinstein, *Woodrow Wilson: A Medical and Psychological Biography* (Princeton: Princeton University Press, 1981), 263. Weinstein (261) did acknowledge that "Mrs. Toy was an educated, independent-minded woman, interested in national affairs, with whom Wilson could discuss both his emotional and political problems."

At breakfast this morning the President announced that he was to receive a deputation of Suffragists after luncheon. "Suffrage for women," he said, "will make absolutely no change in politics—it is the home that will be disastrously affected. Somebody has to make the home and who is going to do it if the women don't?" The Suffragists came and went without a crumb of comfort, and I said my goodbyes and went with too many crumbs of comfort.[80]

Wilson addressed a delegation of nearly one hundred women that day and remarked:

I certainly am one of those who admire the tenacity and the skill and the address with which you try to promote the matter that you are interested in. But I, ladies, am tied to a conviction, which I have had all my life, that changes of this sort ought to be brought about state by state. If it were not a matter of female suffrage...I would hold the same opinion. ...therefore, I would be without excuse to my own constitutional principles if I lent my support to this very important movement for an amendment to the Constitution of the United States.[81]

Most Wilson scholars think his views on women's suffrage evolved from the time of the 1912 campaign (when he opposed the movement) to his open support in1919 when Congress passed Amendment 19.[82] Recently, though, one scholar has suggested that Nancy Toy's account of those breakfast remarks might not have been entirely accurate:

So did Wilson really say at breakfast, on the morning before his meeting with the Democratic women, that "suffrage for women will make absolutely no change in politics—it is the home that will be disastrously affected. Somebody has to make home and who is going to do it if the women don't?" His houseguest, Nancy Saunders Toy, recorded those words in her diary, adding with pleasure that the "suffragists came and went without a crumb of comfort," thus revealing where she stood on the issue. But we wonder if, while Wilson was chewing his toast, Toy herself had not opined on the disastrous effects of woman suffrage and the president had graciously nodded and affirmed that hers was, indeed, a valuable perspective. We wonder because the Democratic women had not

---

[80] Diary of Nancy Toy, January 6, 1915, *PWW* 32:21–22.

[81] *PWW* 32:22.

[82] For a survey of Wilson scholars on this topic, see Barbara J. Steinson, "Wilson and Woman Suffrage," *in A Companion to Woodrow Wilson*, ed. Ross A. Kennedy (New York: Wiley-Blackwell, 2013), 343–63.

actually left the White House without a "crumb of comfort."[83]

Certainly, Nancy was capable of shaping a story to serve her own ends. Admittedly, we do not (yet) have any writing in which she explicitly expresses her views on women's right to vote. Still, her progressive stance on most social issues on which she did state an opinion, along with the fact that she was well educated and both her parents had devoted their careers to female higher education (not to mention her husband's participation in, and advocacy for, women's education), it seems unlikely that she was projecting her own views onto Wilson at this point.[84] There is, of course, the additional fact that Wilson was known to be opposed to the amendment (allegedly, as he claims in his remarks to the women's delegation gathered that day, on constitutional grounds), despite the fact that he lived with a White House full of strong, articulate women. Finally, Nancy Toy did not miss many opportunities for rhetorical flourish in her letters, as here with her contrast between the "crumbs of comfort" with which she had left the White House in contrast to the delegation of Suffragists.

Following her visit to the White House, one of the political issues that most continued to vex her, and one of the few over which she openly disagreed with the president, was the "Shipping Bill" of 1915.[85] The Shipping Bill,

---

[83] Victoria Bissell Brown, "Did Woodrow Wilson's Gender Politics Matter?" *Reconsidering Woodrow Wilson: Progressivism, Internationalism, War, and Peace*, ed. John Milton Cooper, Jr. (Baltimore: Johns Hopkins University Press, 2008), 125–64; here 141.

[84] Indirect support of the view of the Toys' support for women's suffrage can be found in Crawford Toy's support of Samuel June Barrows's failed bid to be President McKinley's nomination for Librarian of Congress. Barrows, a Baptist minister, Harvard Divinity School graduate, former state congressman, and reformer, was a strong advocate of Native American rights and women's right to vote. On January 26, 1899, Crawford Toy had written Barrows, in the midst of his campaign for Librarian (after losing a bid for reelection to the Massachusetts State legislature): "I take pleasure in sending my modest addition to your support, with my best wishes for your success. Mrs. Toy joins me in kindest greetings" (bMS Am 1807 [511], HL).

[85] Another (less important) topic on which Toy takes Wilson to task is Wilson's infatuation with the political landscape of the Western states and their inhabitants (whom he extolled in his November 9, 1914, letter to Toy just after the general election). Nancy Toy observed:

These Western folk have a strange spell over you, Mr. President—you know and said that I resent it. It is, I think, because you idealize their spirit. It may be, however, that you truly realize it. But one of these days when we are seventy or thereabouts, I wish we could we could meet sometime at a corner by the fireside and see if the spell still holds. I myself frankly prefer the Easterners. The refusal of the West to "gird up", like T.R.'s, bores me. But I am ready for a fight as are all your Eastern friends, and you find when the time comes that our loins are

which Wilson supported, would have empowered the U.S. government to purchase and operate merchant ships. Wilson thought the shortage of U.S. merchant ships would lead to an increase in freight rates and would put the U.S. at a distinct disadvantage in the international markets, particularly with regard to the sale of the South's only "marketable crop, cotton."[86] "Wilson hoped the ship purchase bill would free the United States from its reliance on the foreign carrying trade."[87] In addition to raising objections from private business owners who feared government-owned ships would produce unfair competition, others were concerned that the bill would result in the purchase of German ocean liners, which would create conflict with England, Germany's opponent in the emerging conflict. As a result, Senator Lodge proposed an amendment to the bill that would prohibit the government from purchasing German vessels, but Wilson refused to accept those changes. Among the opponents to the bill was Harvard president Charles Eliot, who wrote to President Wilson on several occasions to express his opposition: "You recognize that the Bill makes it possible for the Administration to do foolish things. Is not the passage, under pressure from the Administration, of a Bill which contains such possibilities a bad precedent? Suppose that another Roosevelt should become President of the United States?"[88] Eliot ended with a candid admission:

> I ought to confess that my interest in your disposition of the Shipping Bill is intensified by my belief that your relation to the Shipping Bill up to this date seems likely to make a breach in the Democratic party, to contribute to the alienation from you of the great mass of the business men of the country, and to make probable the return of the Republican party to power in 1916. These results all seem to me calamitous.[89]

That was February 15, 1915. By then, Nancy Toy had already entered the fray. First, on January 21, 1915, she wrote Helen Wilson Bones, asking her to mark "Yes" or "No" on a half sheet that she had enclosed whether or not the president wished to see opinions she had collected on the Shipping

---

girded up as securely as the apparently more brawny ones of the West. (Nancy Toy to Woodrow Wilson, January 13, 1915, reel 535, series 2)

[86] Wilson expresses this concern in a letter to Nancy Toy, October 15, 1914, *PWW* 31:157–58; here 158.

[87] M. Ryan Floyd, *Abandoning American Neutrality: Woodrow Wilson and the Beginning of the Great War, August 1914–December 1915* (Basingstoke: Palgrave-Macmillan, 2013), 90.

[88] Charles Eliot to Woodrow Wilson, February 15, 1915, *PWW* 32:244–45; here 245.

[89] Ibid.

Bill.[90] She was apparently doubtful, or at least self-conscious, of her strategy. She ended her brief note to Bones: "Don't think me a goose!"[91]

Unwilling or unable to await Bones's response, she wrote Wilson the next day: "I am overwhelmed with such a sense of disaster that write to you I must, not to the President but to our old friend, Mr. Wilson, without waiting for your consent via Helen. If you had heard all that I have heard these last two days, you wouldn't blame me."[92] She then employs a strategy that she has used previously in her letters to Wilson and that she will use again: she reports what others are saying. She mentions that Mr. Rhodes "gives me leave to quote him as saying that if the Administration buys those German ships, it will place the country in serious danger of a war with England."[93] She continues:

> Three other men, *our* kind, are gravely anxious, and O Mr. President, think of my overhearing this in a box-shop yesterday! As I came up, one man was saying, "Well, every man has his Waterloo, and this Bill is going to be Wilson's. It's going to ruin him—that he won't care particularly about—but he will care if it ruins the Democratic Party and puts his country in jeopardy." "It will be an awful tragedy," said the other man.[94]

These warnings sound a bell similar to that rung by Eliot. Toy ends with an indirect appeal for Wilson to consider "fresh evidence": "Ah well, I know 'the Court' has decided this case, but when there is fresh evidence, there can be another trial before the Supreme Court of a fresher mind—can't there?— and why shouldn't a mind be fresher with breezes from all sides blowing?"[95]

Wilson responds to Toy's letter with the same seriousness and substance with which he will answer Eliot:

> As for the shipping bill, it does, as you perceive, permit us to commit blunders, fatal blunders, if we are so stupid or so blind; but it is not a blunder in itself, and, if we use ordinary sense and prudence, it need lead us into no dangers. ...the shipping interests do not want this bill. They will do nothing themselves without a subsidy, unless, that is, they are given government money out of the taxes to use as they think best for themselves; if they cannot get that, and of course they cannot, they do not mean to let the development take place, because the control of ocean carriage and of ocean rates will pass out of their hands. We are fighting

---

[90] Nancy Toy to Helen Bones, January 21, 1915, reel 535, series 2.

[91] Ibid.

[92] Nancy Toy to Woodrow Wilson, January 22, 1915, reel 535, series 2.

[93] Ibid.

[94] Ibid.

[95] Ibid.

as a matter of fact the most formidable (covert) lobby that has stood against us yet in anything we have attempted; and we shall see the fight to a finish; trying, when we have won, to act like men who know very familiarly the dangers of what they are about to undertake. It pleases me that you should be so generously distressed at the possibility of our doing what will lead to disaster or even danger; but those who speak to you of these risks have a very poor opinion of our practical sense, and are unconsciously misled by what the press represent, for their own purposes, as the main object of the measure when it is not its object at all. One would suppose that this was a bill to authorize the government to buy German ships. There would be just as stiff a fight against it, and from the same quarters, if it merely conferred the power to build ships.[96]

He ends on an apologetic note: "The path is indeed strewn with difficulties at every turn...but of one thing I am resolved, to break the control of special interests over this government and this people. Pardon the seriousness of this letter. These are critical things in which much is wrapped up."[97]

In a subsequent letter of January 28, 1915 (no longer extant), Toy apparently expressed remorse over her letter and for sharing criticisms of Wilson's policies. He responded:

They are exceedingly critical; but so much the better, if they are fair. There is no harm done in their speaking out their minds or my hearing what they say. It is the necessary tonic and test of men in public life. No, no! Please don't worry about that! I want to be told exactly what is in your mind; and I shall always understand exactly the spirit in which you utter it. Even if it hurts, it will not wound my heart. Things are desperately hard here, but there is no sense in trying to make them soft; for they cannot be. A man must eat meat.[98]

In her next letter, Nancy Toy continues to express misgivings: "Your grave, generous letters have made me writhe a poor woman that wants to crawl away out of the sight of every man, and most of all out of yours."[99] She falls back into the mode and tone of most of her letters, a tone of unrestrained praise of Wilson, his character, and his actions (recall her comparisons of Wilson to Horace's Caesar, Arnold's Shakespeare, and Wordsworth's "Happy Warrior"). Citing a phrase from Wilson's letter of January 31, she gushes: "'The path is strewn with difficulties'...and it is *your* path on *our way* in your blazing the trail for us, brushing off the cobwebs, warning us of the stumps

---

[96] Woodrow Wilson to Nancy Toy, January 31, 1915, reel 535, series 14, no. 73.
[97] Ibid.
[98] Wilson to N. Toy, February 4, 1915, reel 535, series 14, no. 73.
[99] N. Toy to Wilson, February 6, 1915, reel 535, series 14, no. 73.

and throwing aside the fallen branches. ...It is too much! Forgive! Forgive! I wish you knew how our hearts go out to you, how we thank God that the country has you for its Chief and we have you for a friend."[100]

It is that friendship to which she often returns. Already we have seen her refer to "our old friend, Mr. Wilson."[101] This is a common refrain: "My dear Mr. President—though I feel so much more like saying 'my dear Mr. Wilson', for it is about *him* I have just been talking with Mr. Eliot."[102] Her letter of July 15, 1915, from their summer vacation spot in Seal Harbor, sounds this theme in a light, frivolous manner: "This has been such a Wilson day. May I tell you about it?"[103]

More often than not, however, especially in the correspondence at the beginning of the period, the bond holding the friendship together at a personal level is sealed by shared grief—Nancy over the loss of her beloved mother, and Wilson over the loss of his beloved wife. In fact, in the first letter during this period from the hand of Wilson, he writes:

> How selfish I have been, how absorbed in my own anxieties, how thoughtless of you and yours! For five months, nearly, I saw my dear one go slowly, slowly down the hill, a great fear growing darker and darker in my heart, the burden more and more nearly intolerable to my heart, while I tried to command myself for the great tasks which *had* to be performed, and performed with a clear head and an attentive conscience, if I was to be faithful to the trust a great nation had imposed upon me; and while I staggered to keep my feet I heard of your great loss, of the death of the wonderful lady whom you had made me admire and even love by the glimpses you gave me of her wonderful mind and great heart; I knew what it meant to you, and yet I was dumb! It was as if I *could* not speak. It was as if, should I speak to you at all about the fears that had come true to *you* my own fear would overcome me. I feared to open the floodgates in my own soul. Or else my own grief overtopped everything. I do not know. It seemed to me that I stood looking at you, and was unable to speak, trusted that you would somehow see in my eyes what I was not able to utter. But I see now how selfish that was, and beg that you will forgive me! How were you to know what I was *thinking* of you, or how my heart went out to you in your loss? How were you to know that, too, made the world a little darker for me?[104]

---

[100] Ibid.

[101] N. Toy to Wilson, January 22, 1915, reel 535, series 2.

[102] N. Toy to Wilson, August 28, 1914, reel 535, series 2. See also Toy to Wilson, 25 October 1914.

[103] N. Toy to Wilson, July 17, 1915, *PWW* 33:517–18; here 517.

[104] Wilson to N. Toy, September 6, 1914, *PWW* 31:4–5; here 4.

Nancy Toy also addresses the losses both experienced: "Today I have been thinking so much of your and yours—this sixth day of the month which I try always to make a little different from other days as I do the twenty-third."[105] She then told Wilson, "I took my courage in both hands this afternoon and read…my dear mother's letters before burning them."[106] In a poignant passage, which must have been bittersweet to Wilson, she reports finding a note she had written to herself after a visit to the Wilsons in Princeton:

> I found one that I had written on the train going from Princeton to Washington two years ago: "Mrs. Wilson came to the station with me herself", & wrote, "how kind of her! Indeed there emanates from her more than from any other person I know an indescribable atmosphere of nobility, sweetness and winningness. Nobody could *feel* mean or little, much less *say* anything mean or little in her presence."[107]

Wilson responds to this passage: "I am deeply grateful to you for the glimpses you give me of your dear mother and of my own lost sweetheart from the old letters you have been reading and from your diary. You know the kind of ministrations I need!"[108]

At points the language of friendship shifts into a rhetoric of familiarity and intimacy that are, at first glance, jarring. Nancy Toy, describing the ways illness had overtaken her household, writes, "We have been having a perfect orgy of illness without the fun that is supposed to go with *orgying*."[109] Wilson's language is not so provocative, but its familiarity is striking: "Your letters are always the most welcome things the postman could bring."[110] "Your letters give me a great deal of pleasure."[111] "All of this discourse means only that your letters are a delight!"[112] "The generous, affectionate friendship which shows itself so finely in every line you write cheers and sustains me more than you know."[113]

For Christmas 1914, Nancy Toy sent Wilson a Scottish spoon carved from animal bone, along with a ditty she had composed:

---

[105] N. Toy to Wilson, December 6, 1914, reel 535, series 2. Toy's mother had died on July 23 and Ellen Wilson on August 6, both in 1914.

[106] N. Toy to Wilson, December 6, 1914, reel 535, series 2.

[107] Ibid.

[108] Wilson to N. Toy, December 12, 1914, *PWW* 31:454–56; here 454.

[109] N. Toy to Wilson, February 6, 1915, reel 535, series 2. (Emphasis in original.)

[110] Wilson to N. Toy, February 4, 1915, reel 535, series 14, no. 73.

[111] March 7, 1915.

[112] November 9, 1914, *PWW* 31:289–91; here 289.

[113] October 15, 1914, *PWW* 31:157–58; here 157.

Porridge is a goodly think,
Smacks of Scotland's "banks and braes"
Be it added to its praise—
Smacks of health and strengthening,
Yet if gusto we would bring,
We must fetch from "Bonney Doon"
The really, truly old bone spoon.
(The only thing to use, on dit),*
Let your own heart mend my writ—
And here's the end—a timely boon!
*Pronounced as English. This *ought* to be ten lines of seven syllables—I *couldn't* make it! N.T.[114]

Now it was Wilson's turn to gush:

Dearest Friend,

The horn spoon pleases me deeply. I am Scots very deep down in me, and porridge in a horn spoon seems to me like a thing of (minor) religion. I had broken the only one I ever had, and shall rejoice in this one, the more because you thought of it and sent it. And the lines I relish greatly. They are not only of the right flavor themselves, but they speak of a lightness of heart in the writer (if only for the nonce) which makes me happy.[115]

Though they do not (usually) transgress expected social interactions, the letters do reflect a level of familiarity and affection that might give the modern reader pause; that is, unless one is familiar with President Wilson's habits of correspondence. One historian observed:

The other nonfamily members with whom Wilson maintained *frank, intimate relations* were his physician, Dr. Cary T. Grayson, with whom he rarely discussed affairs of state, and three women, with whom he did. They were Mary Allen Hulbert (formerly Mrs. Peck), with whom he had had a brief love affair in 1909 or 1910; Nancy Saunders Toy; and Edith Giddings Reid. Of these women, Mrs. Toy and Mrs. Reid occasionally visited Wilson in the White House. Wilson maintained relations with them and Mrs. Hulbert mainly through frequent, revealing letters.[116]

---

[114] N. Toy to Wilson, Christmas 1914, *PWW* 31:532.
[115] Wilson to N. Toy, December 26, 1914. *PWW* 31:532.
[116] John Milton Cooper, *The Warrior and the Priest: Woodrow Wilson and Theodore Roosevelt* (Cambridge, MA: The Belknap Press of Harvard University Press, 1983), 398 (emphasis added). In a similar vein, John Mulder (*Woodrow Wilson: The Years of Preparation*

On the one hand, this larger context reveals that Wilson's relationship with Toy was not unique (among his other relationships with women). On the other hand, knowledge of these other "friendships," especially with Mary Hulbert, with whom it was widely believed Wilson had an affair, casts a darker hue on certain aspects of the Toy-Wilson correspondence because Wilson arranged for Toy to meet Hulbert and encouraged Toy to help her in a variety of ways.

Wilson first tentatively raises the possibility of the two women meeting in his December 12, 1914, letter to Toy in a rather awkward transition from discoursing about friendship to a specific request:

> Human friendship means an infinite deal to me; and I find my thoughts going out to my friends now as never before, trying to make a circle of them close about me no matter how far away in space they may be, and no matter whether they all know one another or not. I wonder if you feel free to make new acquaintances or not now, or free to seek people out at all? I have a friend now living at 49 Gloucester St. in Boston whom I wish very much you might know. She has had a hard life, chiefly hard because it denied her access to the things she really loved and was meant to live by and compelled her to be (or to play at being until she all but became) a woman of the world, so that her surface hardened and became artificial while her nature was of the woods, of hearty unconventional friendships, and of everything that is sweet and beautiful: a born democrat. Her name is Mary A. Hulbert. She lives with a son about whose health and conduct she is constantly anxious; and she has very few friends in Boston. I met her in Bermuda. I would put real pleasure in her way if I could: therefore I am wondering if I might some time be instrumental in sending you to her.[117]

Wilson now triangulates Nancy Toy into his web of friendships in much

---

[Princeton: Princeton University Press, 1978], 246) explained that Wilson's first wife had permitted, even encouraged, these relationships:

> Ellen Wilson had encouraged Wilson's friendships with women who were particularly vivacious and intellectually stimulating, including Edith Gittings Reid, Henrietta Ricketts, Jenny Davidson Hibben, and Nancy Saunders Toy. Ellen felt that she was "too grave" or "too sober" and said of herself, "I am not gamesome." "Since he has married a wife who is not gay," she told her cousin Florence Hoyt, "I must provide for him friends who are." Wilson himself believed that all his best friends were women, and in his letters to Ellen he frequently noted the pretty women he met or the ones he found singularly "conversable."

[117] Woodrow Wilson to Nancy Toy, December 12, 1914, *PWW* 31:454–56; here 455–56.

the same way as he did when he wrote Edith in 1894 about making the acquaintance of a "delightful" young woman, Nancy Saunders Toy. We do not know if Nancy Toy was aware, or suspicious, of the exact nature of Wilson's prior relationship with Hulbert; we do know from her letters that she was eager to fulfill Wilson's request that she reach out to Hulbert. After making her acquaintance, Toy describes Hulbert as having a "breezy, refreshing, delightful personality" that "is going to adjust itself and refuse to go under."[118] In his letter of December 23, Wilson thanks Toy: "It was very sweet of you to have Mrs. Hulbert out to take tea with you. I hope you liked her. She has just written me how intensely she enjoyed it, poor lonely lady."[119] His next step is to explain Hulbert's dire situation.

> But what prompts this letter about her is the news I have just received from her of complete and all but overwhelming misfortune. Just before she went over to Cambridge to take tea with you her son had told her of his complete dissipation of his fortune! It was not a large one. On the contrary, it was small, only enough to keep them in moderate comfort. He was trying to make it big, and did not know what he was about! The result is, that they are penniless, and he has very little capacity for earning a living.[120]

Wilson then muses, "I have been wondering this: could anybody you know in Boston guide me to helping her to earn a living?" He explains that Hulbert is an interior decorator with "extraordinary taste and knowledge" of furniture, house furnishing, and china. Wilson reassures Toy, "If I am imposing on you, my dear friend, or suggesting anything that it is impossible for you to give me guidance in, I know that you will feel free to tell me so."[121] Again, Nancy does not question how Wilson acquired his knowledge regarding Mary Hulbert's expertise; rather, she thanks Wilson for "taking me into your confidence," and she immediately sets to work. Having already introduced Hulbert to Mrs. Charles Eliot (spouse of the Harvard president) who had "cottoned" decisively, she contacted the owner of a large department store in Boston and an architect to inquire about employment possibilities for Hulbert.[122] Four days after the Christmas letter, she reports that while the store owner did not seem interested, the architect is "sure he can help," and Toy advises Wilson to contact him immediately. She also informs Wilson that she told the architect

---

[118] N. Toy to Wilson, Christmas Day, 1914, reel 535, series 2.

[119] Wilson to N. Toy, December 23, 1914, *PWW* 31:515–16; here 515.

[120] Wilson to N. Toy, December 23, 1914, *PWW* 31:515.

[121] Ibid.

[122] N. Toy to Wilson, Christmas Day, 1914, reel 535, series 2.

that her "name mustn't come up in the matter."[123] Later, she arranges for Hulbert to have Mr. Toy's ticket to the symphony orchestra, and offers to help find a publisher for her cookbook.[124] The last reference to Hulbert in the Toy-Wilson correspondence comes in February 1915, and Nancy Toy is now a bit more circumspect about intervening directly into Hulbert's affairs:

> And just a word about Mrs. Hulbert before I say goodbye. She and her son came to luncheon with us before he went away and she seemed jubilant over having disposed of 9 mahogany tables at 1.50 apiece, adding that she had lots and lots of this salable furniture. A few days ago I telephoned to her that I had been ill enough to have a trained nurse and for that reason hadn't been able to see her, but Channing Toy, our nephew, who is now the Advertising Manager of the Atlantic Monthly, thought he had found a publisher for her cook-book. She then told me she had just had a check for $50 for some contribution to some magazine and that she was going very soon to the Hot Springs. So this does relieve your anxiety about her pecuniarily—doesn't it? or, at least temporarily. *Putting myself in her place (not always the wisest procedure), I think she would rather decide for herself what she is fitted to do.* And so I have not mentioned to her any knowledge that I haven't got from her of her life and needs.[125]

In this note, Toy both relieves herself of the responsibility of finding employment for Hulbert, since the reported news should remove Wilson's anxiety about her financial situation, and distances herself from Wilson's request that she (Toy) play the role of *deus ex machina* in presuming that she and Wilson know what Hulbert is "best fitted to do."[126] By June 1915, Hulbert had moved to Los Angeles to join her son there.[127] And by fall 1915, correspondence between Wilson and Toy had begun to taper off. The last extant letter by Nancy Toy is the "Wilson Day" letter. That was no doubt due, largely, to the growing romance between Wilson and Edith Galt. It is striking that the last correspondence from the Toy family to Wilson comes not from

[123] N. Toy to Wilson, December 29, 1914, reel 535, series 2. This is not the first time Nancy has sought to keep secret her role in a plot hatched between the two of them; see N. Toy to Wilson, May 26, 1910 and June 14, 1910, reel 535, series 2.

[124] N. Toy to Wilson, January 13, 1915, reel 535, series 2.

[125] N. Toy to Wilson, Washington's Birthday [February 22, 1915], reel 535, series 2. Emphasis added.

[126] Nancy Toy used the phrase *deus ex machina* to describe her clandestine part in trying to convince her ailing friend, Mr. Rhodes, not to attend Princeton to receive an honorary doctorate; see Nancy Toy to Woodrow Wilson, May 26, 1910, *PWW* 20:475.

[127] Barry Hankins, *Woodrow Wilson: Ruling Elder, Spiritual President* (Oxford: Oxford University Press, 2016), 179. For more on the relationship between Wilson and Hulbert, see pp. 164–86.

Nancy but from Crawford Howell Toy, who sent a brief telegram on the public announcement of Wilson's engagement to Galt. It reads in its entirety: "My wife and I wish to send to you and to Mrs. Galt heartiest congratulations and sincerest good wishes. C.H. Toy."[128] Wilson's response is only slightly longer and addressed, of course, to "My dearest Professor Toy":

> The telegraphic message which Mrs. Toy and you were gracious enough to send me on October seventh gave me very deep pleasure. It was very delightful to have you think of me in such terms and you may be sure that no message I received gave me deeper gratification.
> With warmest regards to you both,
>
> Cordially and sincerely yours,
> Woodrow Wilson[129]

As far as we know, this brings to an end the extant correspondence between Nancy Toy and Woodrow Wilson for the remainder of his presidency.[130] The correspondence will resume after Wilson leaves office in 1921 and Nancy Toy becomes involved with the Cambridge branch of the Woodrow Wilson Foundation. By that point, both had endured life-changing events. Wilson was left partially paralyzed from a stroke suffered in 1919, and Nancy Toy was now a sixty-year-old widow. She remains exuberant in her praise of Wilson, but his language is definitely more formal. No longer is she "my dear friend" or "dearest friend"; now she is "Dear Mrs. Toy."[131] Apparently Edith Wilson had reeled in Wilson; his pen is more or less under her control. The lone exception appears to be the last extant letter from Wilson to Toy, April 5, 1922, in which he addresses her as "My dear Friend," and references a recent visit Toy apparently made to the Wilsons' home. He does not mention Mrs. Wilson in his closing of "with warmest regard," and the last

---

[128] Telegram, Crawford H. Toy to Woodrow Wilson, October 7, 1915, reel 535, series 2.

[129] Woodrow Wilson to Crawford H. Toy, October 19, 1915, reel 535, series 2.

[130] Wilson did send a brief note of thanks to both Toys in November 1916, though the reason for it is not clear (the letter from the Toys is missing). Wilson's last letter to Nancy was on June 16, 1915, a month before Nancy's "Wilson day" letter on July 17, 1915.

[131] Woodrow Wilson to Nancy Toy, January 13, 1922, *PWW* 67:520, in response to a birthday greeting sent by Toy in behalf of the Woodrow Wilson Foundation. He does observe (520), "What made it [the greeting] all the more delightful to me was that it seemed to speak in your own voice and to be in effect a personal message." But he is quick to add that "Mrs. Wilson joins me in warmest regards." See also Wilson to N. Toy, January 19, 1922, *PWW* 67:531; Wilson to N. Toy, February 13, 1922, *PWW* 67:543. Hankins, *Woodrow Wilson*, 182, notes that correspondence with Hulbert also "nearly disappears from the record" around this same time.

exhortation recorded by Woodrow Wilson to Nancy Toy in the extant correspondence is this: "Please give my respects to all friends and make a face at my enemies for me."[132]

After Woodrow Wilson died in 1924, Nancy Toy wrote Edith Wilson a touching note of condolence: "I have thought of him so much, my dear Mrs. Wilson, since knowing that his illness had taken a serious turn that now when he is at rest, I can think of only you and say over and over to myself 'Well done, good and faithful servant!' I see you hovering over him, cutting up his food, pouring out his tonic, stroking his hand, and always before me in radiant beauty."[133]

Nancy Saunders Toy: A Portrait

What portrait of Nancy Saunders Toy emerges from her correspondence? She is above all an educated woman, well versed in ancient and modern literature, especially poetry (and she kept various quotations ready at hand—see below). She knew foreign languages—or at least foreign phrases. And she made relevant application of both. She could be impetuous in conversation and in letter. She had to retract a conversation regarding C. H. Toy's retirement that she had conveyed to President Charles Eliot, and she regretted writing candidly to President Wilson regarding the Shipping Bill. She had a keen sense of humor and wrote in effusive, flattering, and sometimes somewhat gratuitous language to her corresponding partner (almost always a male in the extant corpus). Her letters were familiar, sometimes intimate, in ways that might surprise a modern audience. Combined with what we know of her social life from newspaper reports and reflections of family members, Nancy Toy was also a socially ambitious woman who desired to move in the upper register of Cambridge/Boston society, if not beyond. Her niece, Jane Toy Coolidge, has observed:

> Nancy Toy was a charming person. ...I have seen her enter a group of young people and assume, as though by royal prerogative, command of the conversation, taking charge of it with such consummate skill that the group (and it was a distinguished group of people, including two Harvard deans and their wives) hung on her words, enjoying every one of them. She had given advance thought to what she planned to talk about, chosing [sic] subjects of interest to her companions, and mapping out her procedure, including, I am sure, some of the apparently spontaneous re-

---

[132] Wilson to N. Toy, April 5, 1922, reel 535, series 14, no. 73.

[133] Nancy Toy to Edith Wilson, February 4, 1924, reel 507, series 9, vol. 7, p. 175, University of Texas Special Collections.

marks that delighted her audience. This had been her practice throughout her career as a hostess. She kept a notebook of apt and interesting
quotations which she used skillfully. She prepared herself for each occasion so that nothing was left to chance. And it worked.[134]

One also wonders if the strong personality that shines through these stories and letters did not at times annoy or even threaten those with whom she
interacted, especially men. Nancy Toy had friendships with men of extraordinary intellect and influence. Once again, Jane Coolidge has commented in an
insightful way:

> Nancy was educated beyond the limits of its polite society; she had a
> sophisticated viewpoint, acquired in Europe, and an awareness of intel-
> lectual values alien to the community. She was not a beauty (though she
> was attractive) and there was neither money nor position to back her. I
> think her education must have frightened away the boys, for Aunt Nancy
> once told me that she had never been invited to a dance in her life. She
> just didn't fit into the Portsmouth picture.[135]

One wonders if the cutting remarks that occasionally surface in the comments of her interlocutors comes in part as a result of Nancy Toy's refusal to
conform to late nineteenth and early twentieth century social norms for "ladies" of a certain social class. George Santayana recorded an early impression
of Nancy Toy: "Mrs. Toy is a very good friend of mine: her attentions are of
the kind that make one feel a little flattered and a little grateful and a little
annoyed. You know the kind I mean, don't you?—the kind your friends are
apt to impose upon you.[136] Santayana describes "Mrs. Toy" as a "good friend"
but notes her attentions leave one with a mix of feelings—flattered, grateful,
and annoyed! Woodrow Wilson had recorded a backhanded compliment in
his diary after Nancy visited him and Mrs. Wilson in Princeton in 1904: "Mrs.
Toy, of Cambridge, came to spend the day and evening with us.—as alert and
full of (half artful) charm as ever."[137] Yet, as we have seen, and as Jane Coolidge has observed, Wilson "wrote to her as to an intellectual equal and a val-
ued friend."[138] Certainly personality types can be grating without regard to
gender or social standing, but one cannot help but wonder if a man, with the
same level of intellect, wit, charm, and ambition as Nancy, would have been
described by his peers in the same ways.

---

[134] Coolidge, "Toy," 9.

[135] Ibid.

[136] George Santayana to Guy Murchie, March 12, 1896, *The Letters of George Santayana*, 1:151.

[137] Wilson Diary, January 11, 1904, *PWW* 15:121.

[138] Coolidge, "Toy," 13.

Nancy and Crawford Toy

So how does this portrait square with what we know of Nancy Toy and her relationship to Crawford Toy? By 1890, Crawford and Nancy Toy, along with her mother, Mrs. Saunders, had begun taking summer vacations on Mount Desert Island. The Glencove Hotel at Seal Harbor was a favorite resort.[139] In 1894, Nancy accompanied Toy on his research leave. He wrote David Lyon from Paris: "Nannie and I are trying to go carefully over the Louvre, & to get a taste of the College du France & the Sorbonne. There is so much to do that the days pass quickly; I am already beginning to think with regret that we must soon leave Paris. We have seen Berenson and Fullerton and Mr. Clemens (Mark Twain)."[140] This is the only extant reference to Crawford Toy's use of "Nannie" as a term of endearment for Nancy Toy (a nickname by which she was known since her days at Norfolk Collegiate Institute for Young Ladies). Elsewhere Toy consistently refers to her as "Mrs. Toy"; perhaps the relaxed atmosphere of a research leave in Paris had loosened his pen a bit![141]

Crawford Toy's March 1900 diary[142] gives a few tantalizing glimpses of their relationship some twelve years after they were married.[143] One may presume this month is more or less representative of the kinds of activities in which they engaged and with what frequency.[144] Several times during this month, the Toys were either hosts or guests at dinner parties. In fact, in the very first entry (Thursday, March 1, 1900), Toy indicates that he and Mrs. Toy had entertained several guests for dinner, including George Santayana.

---

[139] Crawford H. Toy to David G. Lyon, July 28, 1890, Glencove House, Seal Harbor; cf. Toy to Lyon, June 21, 1906, Harvard Semitic Museum Archives.

[140] Crawford H. Toy to David G. Lyon, December 11, 1894, HUG 1541, Papers of David Gordon Lyon Box 13, HUA.

[141] It is interesting to compare this note of Toy, who was now fifty-eight years old, with his reflections as "European correspondent" for the *Religious Herald* some twenty years earlier (cf. chapter 2).

[142] Members of staff and students were asked to contribute materials as part of a time capsule initiative at Harvard. Librarian William Coolidge solicited items from the Harvard community intended to give a snapshot of everyday life at Harvard in March, 1900 and placed them in a wooden chest that served as a time capsule. Toy contributed his diary of March 1900. The chest was opened in 1960 and promptly forgotten. In 1999 its contents were rehoused in various archival holdings. See Chest of 1900, 900.11, Box 4, HUA.

[143] Toy records on March 19 that a telegram arrived from Mr. Saunders, Nancy's father, reporting that Mrs. Saunders had taken a fall and requested that Nancy travel to Lynchburg, VA, to be with them: "I went down immediately and made the arrangements, & returned after my lectures & took my wife into the...train." Nancy Toy did not return until March 30, so we have only slightly less than three weeks of interaction between them.

[144] Their summer activities, often spent at Seal Harbor, Mount Desert Island, or other resort areas, would have reflected a different rhythm, no doubt.

Talk, Toy asserts, was "pleasant" and ranged from the Second Boer War (while admiring the "pluck of the Boers," guests agreed in hoping that "England would win speedily and completely") to a discussion of Josiah Royce's "The World and the Individual."[145] Later that evening, guests from New York returned to Boston for the night, and Nancy Toy attended the Symphony Concert in Harvard's Sanders Theater, accompanied by Santayana to whom Toy had surrendered his ticket. A week later on March 8, the Toys hosted another dinner party, with five guests in attendance. Once again, dinner conversation revolved around the English/Boer conflict (the Transvaal, as Toy referred to it), and again "the general opinion was in favor of the English in the Transvaal." Toy further recorded that Harvard Law professor J. B. Thayer had recently returned from Washington, where he had been asked by President McKinley to join the Philippines Commission to make recommendations regarding the restructuring the current political system (Thayer declined for reasons of health). Given Nancy's keen interest in politics, evident from her later correspondence with Woodrow Wilson, there is every reason to believe that she entered these discussions fully and well informed.[146]

On the next evening, Friday, March 9, the Toys received a note at 6:00 p.m. from a Mrs. Hopkinson "saying that two of her guests (for dinner party) had just folded her & asking my wife & me to come & fill up the table; of course, we went." Talk that evening included the "recent decision of Committee not to allow smoking in Brooks House—an unfortunate decision."[147] Within the next two weeks, the Toys hosted dinner guests on March 11, 17,

---

[145] Originally delivered by Royce as the 1898 Gifford Lectures at the University of Aberdeen and published in 1899. Royce had come to Harvard from Berkeley in 1882 as a sabbatical replacement for William James, becoming a fulltime faculty member in 1884 and remaining there until his death in 1916 (at age sixty).

[146] Toy Diary, March 8, 1900, HUA. Toy goes on to comment on one guest in particular, E. H. Strobel, Bemis Professor of International Law at Harvard since 1897. Before that, Strobel had a distinguished career as a diplomat, serving as Secretary of the United States Legation in Madrid, Spain (1885–1890); Third Assistant Secretary of State (1893–1894); and Minister Plenipotentiary to Ecuador and Chile (1894–1897). Strobel, Toy observed, "is a good dinner-guest, simple unaffected, with definite opinions,--full of anecdotes of his diplomatic life." Toy also related a story told by Thayer of "the man who takes care of his house at Bar Harbor; being askt of what Mr. Thayer was professor, he replied, 'oh, he's professor of the whole damn thing'."

[147] Toy Diary, March 9, 1900, HUA. Not only did Crawford Toy smoke (a pipe; see Lyon, "Toy," 17), but Nancy also smoked, according to her niece (Coolidge, "Toy," 13): "Aunt Nancy smoked. She must have started it in Europe, but however that may be, she did it steadily, publicly, and without apology, during the years when women just didn't smoke in polite society. She smoked daintily and gracefully, like a great lady, using in the years when I knew her, a little holder made of twisted wire with a ring in which the cigarette was inserted and a separate handle at the side."

and 18.[148] At the March 18 dinner, the conversation ranged from recent plays to "the Church of Christ Scientist (Mrs. Eddy's Church)."[149] On the day Nancy returned from Lynchburg (March 30), they were guests at the home of a Mrs. Whitman, who was hosting a dinner in honor of a guest lecturer. The most exciting event of that evening was the ride in the electric trolley: "We had seats in the electric car going & returning—a rare privilege."[150] All told, Nancy and Crawford Toy (together or separately) were hosts or guests at meals on nine of the nineteen days that Nancy was in Cambridge.

The Toys, together or separately, also frequented musical performances and lectures, either in Cambridge or Boston. Concerts included the already mentioned Symphony Concert in Sanders Theater (Nancy on March 1), Chamber Concert (Crawford on March 13), Beethoven Concerto in Cambridge (both, March 15), Beethoven Concerto, Boston (Nancy, same as March 15). In addition, Crawford Toy had dinners on March 16 ("Dinner Club") and March 17 (History of Religions Club dinner), both at the Colonial Club.[151] The Toys also attended the First Parish Church (Unitarian) on several Sundays during the month. In addition, Crawford Toy spoke at the Unitarian church in Boston on Sunday afternoons, March 11, 18, and 25.[152] Obviously, they had a full social life, both together and apart!

The few evenings when they were not out also reveal some interesting glimpses into the Toys' relationship. On several occasions Toy reports that he and Nancy enjoyed a game of Casino, a popular parlor card game in the late nineteenth and early twentieth centuries.[153] Often, they would read to each other. On March 3, Nancy gave to him a "résumé" of the *Transcript* (a local Boston newspaper). On March 4, Crawford read to Nancy an essay from *Poetry & Religion* (1900) by George Santayana, a dinner guest at their home only

---

[148] On all three Sundays (4, 11, 18) in March (before Nancy left to be with her mother), the Toys entertained dinner guests. This supports Jane Coolidge's assertion that most Sundays saw house guests at 7 Lowell Street ("Toy," 7).

[149] Toy Diary, March 18, 1900, HUA.

[150] Toy Diary, March 30, 1900, HUA.

[151] According to Toy, both George Foote Moore (then president of Andover Theological Seminary and later colleague at Harvard) and his brother E. C. Moore attended the dinner. Apparently, G. F. Moore spent the night and attended church services with the Toys on the following day. At dinner on Sunday evening, Moore "spoke of his plans for reorganizing Andover Sem'y so as to get it out of the clutches of the creed—this done, the Sem'y might be brought to Cambridge" (Toy Diary, March 18, 1900, HUA).

[152] Toy was recovering from a cold on March 4 and did not lecture at First Church Boston on that date.

[153] He mentions playing Casino with Nancy on March 3, 7, and 31. The game was also popular during summer vacation periods on Mount Desert Island. For a description of the rules of Casino, see https://www.britannica.com/topic/casino-card-game.

three evenings before: "The essay is an acute & interesting criticism of 'mysticism' (that is, the attempt to transcend the limitations of human thought)."[154] The conversations between the two no doubt often revolved around politics of the day, as they did at dinner parties they hosted or attended. At one point Crawford Toy recorded: "She [Nancy] finds it hard to understand why so many people are hostile to England in the Transvaal war. I suggested that it was simply a point of view & without difference of opinion life would not be worth living."[155] While Crawford nowhere in the diary displays the disdain that Santayana and Wilson record, there is nonetheless a hint of condescension in this entry.

Like Nancy (whose humor shines through her correspondence), Crawford Toy has already been shown to possess a dry wit, from his early UVA letters to cousin "Mote" Howell to the lyrics he composed (some of which are preserved in the ephemera of David Lyon's diary).[156] No doubt he appreciated Nancy's keen wit as he did in others. In the March 28 entry to his diary, Toy records the following story heard at tea with General and Mrs. Loring of Boston:

> Miss Annie Fuller told story of young lady driving with her aunt in New York, she sitting by Nathan P. Willis, & her aunt by Mr. Campbell—...her careful aunt passed her a note, saying: "talk less to Mr. Willis & more to the lady on your right", to which she replied in pencil:

> Do not try my dear Aunt my actions to trammel
> Let me strain at a Nat, while you swallow a Campbell.[157]

Most of Nancy Toy's extant references to her husband occur in correspondence with Woodrow Wilson and reflect conversations between them about the president. In October 1914, just months after the death of his first wife, Wilson released a proclamation of gratitude in advance of Thanksgiving. Nancy Toy reported, "Just now I have read Mr. Toy your Thanksgiving Proclamation—'what class that will bring to thousands of lives,' he said, 'but it must have been hard for him to write it.'"[158] In a passage cited earlier, when

---

[154] Toy Diary, March 4, 1900, HUA.

[155] Toy Diary, March 3, 1900, HUA.

[156] This is counter to Jane Coolidge's assessment that "in none of his writings that I have seen is there evidence that a sense of humor was among his gifts" ("Toy," 6).

[157] Toy Diary, March 28, 1900, HUA. Ever the linguist, Toy could not resist proposing an emendation to the rhyme: "Witty but would perhaps be better to say *strain out* (as the expression stands in New Testament)."

[158] Nancy Toy to Woodrow Wilson, October 25, 1914, reel 535, series 2.

Nancy admits that "the friendship of the President of the United States makes me very proud," she continues, "I wonder if it does Mr. Toy? He never would confess it!"[159] The Toys also speculated on what the Wilson family discussed:

> "I wonder what they talk about, family and guest," I said curiously to Mr. Toy. "Something restful and frivolous, I hope," he answered emphatically, "do you realize that no President was ever confronted by such a situation as is our President now?"[160]

By the time of this exchange between Nancy Toy and Woodrow Wilson in 1914–1915, Crawford Toy's health was severely failing, and many of Nancy's references to him are in connection with that. After her visit to the White House, she reported to Wilson, "Our doctor…came to see Mr. Toy who has been suffering Job-wise since my return and declined more skillful treatment than that I could give him. But today I summoned the doctor, a shrewd man of 60, the best surgeon in the State."[161] In a letter from May 1915, Nancy reveals the apparent cause of Crawford Toy's near blindness: "It is harder and harder to leave Mr. Toy. The cataracts are slowly growing and it is horrible to see him clutch at things now when he walks…. But a nice nurse takes my place for the week who reads aloud and writes for him satisfactorily."[162] Nancy also wrote for and read to Crawford, who despite his diminishing eyesight maintained his sense of humor: "I am reading to Mr. Toy the American Statesmen series—'the series for discrediting Southern statesmen,' he calls it."[163]

What emerges from these brief notices is a couple who, despite the difference in their ages, seems compatible in their political leanings, their religious convictions, their affection for music and culture, and their apparent love of socializing (especially with well-connected individuals, of which there

---

[159] N. Toy to Wilson, December 6, 1914, reel 535, series 2.

[160] N. Toy to Wilson, July 17, 1915, *PWW* 33:517–18.

[161] N. Toy to Wilson, January 13, 1915, reel 535, series 2.

[162] N. Toy to Wilson, May 5, 1915, reel 535, series 2.

[163] N. Toy to Wilson, July 17, 1915, *PWW* 33:517–18. Nancy Toy frequently took dictation for her husband. Sometimes this is noted in the letter itself, as in the last extant letter known to me—a letter to Barrett Wendell, dated 14 January, acknowledging Wendell's retirement as chair of Harvard's English Department—marked "Dictated" at the top of the letterhead and ending with "by N.T." under Toy's name (Harvard Houghton Library, bMS 1907.1, Folder 1293; cf. Toy's birthday wishes to William Thayer, also "dictated" to "N.T."; bMS Am 1081 [1783], HL). Even without such markings, Nancy's flourished handwriting, so distinct from Crawford's minute script, makes distinguishing her hand from his quite easy.

was no shortage in Cambridge in those days!).[164] Jane Coolidge observed: "She [Nancy] made his home a serene and gracious one, gave him sympathetic understanding in his work and brought into his life the pleasure of companionship with many interesting people who felt the spell of her charm. She gave him loving care in his old age and survived him by twenty-three years."[165]

Though neither is likely to have described theirs as a "match made in heaven," nor was it a marriage of convenience. Here were two formidable intellects whose passion for finer things drew them time and time again away from their individual pursuits back together in the home they created for themselves and others on 7 Lowell Street and to their beloved summer vacation spot at Seal Harbor. To be sure, Nancy Toy maintained familiar, at times even intimate, correspondences with influential men, apparently with the knowledge of her husband. What many might consider an "unconventional marriage" seems to have worked for them for more than thirty years.

The Demise of Nancy Toy

Crawford Toy was gravely concerned about maintaining his standard of living, and especially his home, into retirement.[166] Apparently he expressed those concerns to Harvard president Charles Eliot, who engaged David Lyon's support to raise a supplemental subscription from friends and colleagues.[167] Toy was able to live out his remaining days of retirement from 1909 to his death in 1919 in the home on Lowell, but Nancy Saunders Toy was not so fortunate. In the immediate years following her husband's death, Nancy Toy had the means to travel to Europe. But according to George Santayana, these trips were less than successful. He reported on her European trip in 1925 to his nephew George Sturgis: "I was going to Switzerland to see Mrs Toy (who has suddenly invaded Europe), but Mrs Toy has grown homesick and doesn't know what she will do or where she will be."[168] By June 2, 1925, Santayana reported: "Poor Mrs. Toy, scarcely arrived in England, was so very homesick, bored, and ill, that she went back directly to blessed Boston! This is the second time that has happened, and I think I know the reason, but it is too psychological and complicated for a letter."[169]

---

[164] If Nancy were prone to "name-dropping," this brief sampling of Crawford Toy's diary would suggest he was no less inclined in that direction!

[165] Coolidge, "Toy," 7.

[166] Coolidge, "Toy," 16.

[167] On this, see chapter 7.

[168] George Santayana to George Sturgis, May 14, 1925, *PGS* 3:247.

[169] George Santayana to Charles Augustus Strong, June 2, 1925, *PGS* 3:298.

Eventually forced to leave her home after Crawford's death, Nancy Toy took up residence in several different apartments in Cambridge.[170] In 1936, Santayana was so concerned about Nancy's finances that he took steps to raise funds for her. He wrote to his nephew, George Sturgis:

> My old and dear friend Mrs. Toy has been at death's door, having had an operation for stone, but has recovered enough to return home, but with two nurses. She has a very inadequate income, and I have written to friends at Cambridge (from whom this news has come) suggesting that we raise a subscription to defray Mrs. Toy's extraordinary expenses. I may therefore telegraph to you at any moment asking you to send, perhaps $1,000 to somebody in Cambridge.[171]

Her financial situation continued to grow dire, and, by 1939, Nancy (age seventy-nine) decided to move back to Portsmouth, Virginia, hoping to make her home with some cousins. Nancy arrived in Virginia only to find her relatives could not accommodate her because of an ailing daughter. After a few weeks in a hotel, Nancy returned to Cambridge and settled into her own apartment. George Sturgis recounted to his uncle, George Santayana, a meeting he had with her in May 1939, just before she left for Virginia:

> Dear Uncle George:
> I had the pleasure of meeting your friend, Mrs. Toy, the other morning. She wrote me the other day, and said that she was planning to leave soon for her old home in Virginia so that she could "die in the same place she was born." ...She seems in excellent health, and I haven't a doubt but that she has many years of life still ahead of her. I found her most charming and gracious, and I enjoyed meeting her very much because I had always heard of her and knew she was such a good friend of yours. She struck me as being very young in spirit because she is seriously contem-

---

[170] In addition to her last apartment on Garden Street, according to locations given in correspondence with George Santayana, Nancy Toy also resided at 8 Craigie Circle and Ware Hall. It did not help, of course, that the entire country was in the grips of a Depression. Santayana noted that he "was rather alarmed to hear that your business man said discouraging things about the future," but he commends Toy on being thus far undeterred and "giving dinner parties and ready to give more" (George Santayana to Nancy Toy, May 13, 1932, *LGS* 4:334).

[171] George Santayana to George Sturgis, May 19, 1936, *LGS* 5:337. Subsequent letters reported that Nancy's condition was much improved (5:348) and that Cambridge friends had raised the needed funds; thus, Santayana instructed his nephew to hold the $1,000 "to tide her over her difficulties" if needed. This suggests that no money was sent (5:358).

plating traveling to Virginia by airplane. I like to see her youthful enthusiasm for a modern mode of travel, from which many elderly persons instinctively shy away.[172]

Sturgis was right about Nancy Toy's intention to fly to Virginia on an airplane ("in itself an adventure for one of her years").[173] But it would turn out that Sturgis was wrong to think that Nancy Toy had "many years of life still ahead of her." By now, she was living on $100 a month and had nearly exhausted all of her savings.[174] Santayana had detected a change in Nancy Toy's disposition from a letter she wrote him in November, 1938: "Your note of Nov. 25 is not like your usual letters, but sad, as if you were not well. I know you hate conventional inquiries or good wishes about health; they are *sous-entendu* among old friends. And your mood may have changed now, so that the old note might jar."[175] Nancy Toy presumably wrote Santayana shortly after George Sturgis's visit. Santayana responded, "The depressing tone of your last letter would have alarmed me had I not received the enclosed about the same time from my nephew."[176] Certain warning signals were beginning to sound. They continued into fall 1939. Santayana observed that Nancy Toy's most recent letter had "the tragic feelings of a person condemned to exile." But that was a feeling with which Santayana could not identify: "It is impossible for me to be sympathetic on that subject, since I am hardened to exile, and like it. If I had not always been an exile, I could never have had a good time."[177]

Twice, Nancy Toy had attempted to relocate to Virginia but was unable to make the move permanent. Santayana reflected on the significance of her aborted moves:

---

[172] George Sturgis to George Santayana, May 25, 1939, manuscript, film MSB 36, HL.

[173] Coolidge, "Toy," 14. Apparently, Nancy had been planning a return home for some time. On August 12, 1938, George Santayana wrote to Nancy Toy: "It is news indeed that you are going back to Virginia to live in the house in which you were born. To me, that would be a great relief from the pressure of society; but you love society and society loves you, and I hope your arrangements are such that you can return to Cambridge, if you find your old home too remote from the intellectual world" (*LGS* 6:153).

[174] Coolidge, "Toy," 14.

[175] George Santayana to Nancy Toy, December 12, 1938, *LGS* 6:185.

[176] Santayana to N. Toy, June 6, 1939, *LGS* 6:246. Santayana had enclosed his nephew's letter to Nancy, which accounts for its presence in the collection of correspondence in Nancy Toy's possession at the time of her death, and now on microfilm in Harvard's Houghton Library (even though the editor of *LGS* indicates the letter is "unlocated").

[177] Santayana to N. Toy, October 10, 1939, *LGS* 6:276.

Why haven't I written to you for so long?—I think it is because your return to Cambridge puzzled me; not in itself, who might not prefer Cambridge to any other focus of light and virtue? But Cambridge being so admirable, and you so accustomed to life there, and so important a part of it, you must have had grave reasons for thinking of leaving it. You had been to your friends in Virginia before, you could make comparisons; and once having taken flight (literally as well as rhetorically) it seems strange that you should give up your plan. No doubt, it is not really strange. You rather choose the ills you had, than fly to others you are less used to. And I see you have the old address, probably the same apartment, and we can dismiss the excursion to Virginia as a troubled dream.[178]

On June 12, 1941, Nancy Saunders Toy leapt to her death from her fifth-story apartment window. The *Cambridge Tribune* carried a brief, but chilling, notice on June 20:

Mrs. Nancy Toy, 71, widow of a Harvard professor, was killed Thursday when she plunged five stories from a screenless window in her apartment at Garden St., Cambridge. Her body was found in a passageway under the window by two Belmont milkmen, Howard Stacy and Robert Aird. They called Dr. John Rockwell of Garden Street, and he reported to police that she was dead. Dr. David Dow, medical examiner, arrived a few moments later and ordered the body removed to a local funeral home. Kenneth Robbins, janitor in the apartment, told authorities that Mrs. Toy had asked him to remove the screen about three weeks ago.[179]

Like her husband, Nancy Toy was cremated. Unlike Crawford Toy, there was no one to spread her cremated ashes at Seal Harbor. Mount Auburn Cemetery Research Docent, Stephen Pinkerton, reported:

---

[178] Santayana to N. Toy, January 24, 1940, *LGS* 6:324. In March, Santayana received word that Nancy Toy had an accident. "Today I receive Miss Hopkinson's letter about your accident and its unhappy consequences. Your ill luck always calls forth your courage, and your courage carries you through until all seems well again, and then comes a fresh stroke of ill luck. That is because you love too much. ...I don't love life, and here I am enjoying life almost uninterruptedly, in spite of old age with its little ailments, in spite of solitude, and in spite of the alarms and inconveniences of the troubled times. I ought to love life and you ought to hate it, but *la raison n'est pas ce qui règle l'amour* whether of life or of anything else" (Santayana to N. Toy, April 2, 1940, *LGS* 6:349). Apparently Nancy Toy recovered from her accident and wrote Santayana on July 25 that she was now going to dinner parties (see Santayana to N. Toy, August 8, 1940, *LGS* 6:391).
[179] *Cambridge Tribune* 63/21: June 20, 1941. The paper account is mistaken on Toy's age; she was less than a month shy of her eighty-first birthday (July 1).

Nancy Toy's official burial record notes her date and place of death as June 12, 1941, Cambridge, MA. Her age was 80 years, 11 months, 10 days. The cause of death was listed as "Crush of chest with other injuries, jumped from 5th story window." According to her cremation record, her body was incinerated at 4:10 pm on June 14, 1941, after a short service at Bigelow Chapel. The cremation was ordered by her executor E. Willard Phippen of Cambridge Trust Co., Cambridge, MA. The record includes a comment that she had "no relations." Her cremated remains were then "placed in a copper cylinder and interred in the Rec Tomb," which referred to the old receiving tomb on Greenbrier Path.

Cemetery practice at that time was to retain unclaimed remains in the old receiving tomb until there was no longer room for them (or later, when the tomb was closed) and then to re-inter them in various "memorial grounds" around the Cemetery. In the absence of any indication in the records that her remains were retrieved or shipped elsewhere, I think they are probably still here, but at an unspecified location. It would be nice to think they were scattered at Seal Harbor, but there appear to have been no relatives to carry that out.[180]

George Sturgis informed Santayana of the deaths of Nancy Toy and Herbert Lyman.[181] Writing from Italy, Santayana responded twice: "The death of Mrs. Toy is sad, but only as all death is sad. Her health was insecure, she was very brave about it, but at eighty (she must have been about eighty, though she would never confess her age), the future holds nothing new, except more illness and incapacities."[182] And again:

> Today I received yours of June 16, with notices of the deaths of Mrs. Toy and of Herbert Lyman. The latter died (and lived) just as one should according to commonsense standards, doing honest business and dying

---

[180] Email from Stephen Pinkerton, docent, Mount Auburn Cemetery Research Department, June 21, 2018. It is sad to think that Nancy Toy died destitute and alone and that her cremated remains are now at an "unspecified location." Cremations were not as common in the first half of the nineteenth century as today. Pinkerton reported that the first cremation took place at Mount Auburn on April 18, 1900. Crawford Toy was number 4,644, and Nancy Toy was number 15,897. "Mount Auburn's was one of only a handful of crematoria in the Northeast. It served a wider population than just metro-Boston, and not all of the cremated remains were buried here. It was not uncommon for bodies to be brought down from northern New England for cremation and shipment of the ashes for burial or scattering farther away in the Midwest or the West Coast" (email correspondence, June 21, 2018).

[181] Herbert Lyman (1864–1941) was a fellow Harvard graduate with Santayana (1886) and a member of prominent Boston family.

[182] George Santayana to George Sturgis, June 17, 1941, *LGS* 7:43.

in perfect health. Mrs. Toy suffered more, physically and morally, as most women do, and I am not surprised that she should wish to die, there was nothing but illness for her to look forward to; but the method of it was rather tragic and unseemly. She had no religious comforts or scruples; but she had never, to my knowledge, been hysterical or desperate. It is too bad.[183]

A decade later, Santayana had occasion to reflect more deeply on the possible reasons for Nancy's suicide. Responding to a letter from Miriam Stuart Thayer, daughter of Harvard Divinity School professor Joseph Henry Thayer, he reminisced:

> Your name and your letter instantly turned my thoughts to Mrs. Toy, who so often and so affectionately used to speak of you. Her letters in her later years, and what I heard about her, which was very little, left a rather sad impression, as if her health and spirits suffered in solitude from the absence of the duties and pleasures of her former life. This was not a matter on which I could speak sympathetically, solitude being for me a sort of liberty realized.[184]

A combination of being financially destitute and feeling "the absence of duties and pleasures" of a life that was previously full with social engagements and intellectually stimulating discussions, along with various ailments that come with age, made it "easy to see how she could not face the future. But…[the suicide] was in a moment of unbearable pain when she was not herself."[185] Whatever the reasons, the life of Nancy Saunders Toy came to a sad ending, an ending that much sadder because she had been such a "vivid and stimulating personality,"[186] a veritable force of nature whose life with Crawford Howell Toy, however unconventional, had been rich and full.

---

[183] Santayana to Sturgis, July 2, 1941, *LGS* 7:44–45. Given what we have seen from Nancy's correspondence, it is probably not accurate to say Nancy Toy had "no religious comforts or scruples," though Santayana may not have been privy to them.

[184] George Santayana to Miriam Thayer Richards, February 7, 1952, *LGS* 8:417.

[185] Coolidge, "Toy," 14.

[186] Ibid.: "Like all who knew her, I am grateful to Aunt Nancy for enriching my life by contact with a vivid and stimulating personality."

CONCLUSION

9

CRAWFORD HOWELL TOY: A "TRANSLUCENT SOUL"

He [Toy] thought strange the prediction made in conversation that within twenty years he would utterly discard all belief in the supernatural as an element of Scripture,—a prediction founded upon knowledge of his logical consistency and boldness, and already in a much shorter time fulfilled, to judge from his latest works. Some of us are persuaded that if any man adopts the evolutionary reconstruction of Old Testament history and literature, and does not reach a like attitude as regards the supernatural, it is simply *because he is prevented by temperament or environment*, from carrying things to their logical results.... Some of his attached former pupils and other friends thought that there was no necessity for losing him, and that his views are not really in any high degree objectionable, and began vehement remonstrances in private or in the newspapers. This proceeded in a very many cases from sympathy with his opinions; in most cases from lack of acquaintance with the real nature of those opinions and *their necessary outcome*.[1]

John Broadus's prediction that Crawford Toy would one day discard "all belief in the supernatural as an element of Scripture," written in 1893, might strike one as a *vāticinium ex ēventū* ("prophecy after the event") since by then Toy had published several books (especially *Judaism and Christianity* in 1890) that had been vigorously criticized in some quarters as too "rationalistic." Broadus's prediction may be more prescient than even he could have imagined and perhaps for reasons he would be reluctant to embrace. Exiled from SBTS, Toy was untethered from the confessional community that had nurtured him from childhood and to which he had fierce loyalty, commitments that continued even into his early years at Harvard. If Broadus is correct in his assertion that only "temperament or environment" could have prevented what was, in his eyes, Toy's radical turn toward anti-supernatural rationalism, then those responsible for removing Toy from his environment at SBTS were at least partially responsible for whatever departure from orthodoxy Toy may have taken.[2]

---

[1] Broadus, *Memoir*, 262–63 (my emphasis).
[2] W. O. Carver made the same tentative observation when he mused: "Whether by patience and fraternal conference Dr. Toy might have been led into a deeper and more comprehensive understanding of the principles of progress must remain an open question"

W.O. Carver argued that "the openings which came to Dr. Toy for the pursuit of scholarship in his field led him into an environment wholly conducive to the secularistic interpretation of the history of religions in what was already an essentially humanistic environment."[3] Historical evidence points strongly in the direction that Boyce and Broadus were at the center of the events that transpired to remove Toy from the faculty of The Southern Baptist Theological Seminary and from his vocational calling to train ministers who were mostly and naturally inclined to be politically, culturally, and religiously conservative. In other words, if Broadus is right, then those most concerned about Toy's theological orthodoxy—and their contemporary theological heirs—are those most responsible for his "heresies."

Justifying Toy's Departure

Efforts to vindicate the trustees' decision to accept Toy's resignation by shifting the "blame" entirely to Toy go right back to Broadus, who described Toy's views as having their "necessary outcome" regarding his later rejection of orthodox views regarding inspiration, biblical authority, supernaturalism, etc. W. O. Carver also took the tack of arguing that it was Toy's later views that vindicated the trustees' decision in 1879. Carver concluded, "Under all the circumstances he ultimately justified the action of the Seminary Board in dismissing him."[4] The "orthodoxy" or acceptability of Toy's views at the time of his forced resignation are left unexamined in this version of the seminary's vindication of itself. According to this logic, the "bitter fruits" of Toy's rationalistic teaching and scholarship at Harvard proved the wisdom of cutting his SBTS roots.

("Recollections and Information from Other Sources Concerning the Southern Baptist Theological Seminary," unpublished typescript, 27–28, MSS 922.6173 C256r, SBTS archives).

[3] Carver, "Recollections and Information," 28.

[4] Ibid. Carver continued: "He came at some stage to identify himself with a Unitarian church, conforming to the Unitarian domination of the Harvard atmosphere and community. He took less and less interest in organized religion and is said in the latter years of his life to have membership in no church and rarely to have attended worship in any." As we saw in chapter 6, Carver's description is not exactly accurate. There is no evidence Toy ever joined a Unitarian church, although he did, with Mrs. Toy, regularly attend the unitarian First Parish Church in Cambridge, perhaps a combination of accommodating his wife's (and his own) desires to socialize with the social elites of the community as well as his own commitment to worship in an explicitly non-creedal context (which he perhaps had at one time hoped to find in his Baptist community). There is also no evidence that Toy left organized religion, and if in his latter years he rarely attended worship, it was no doubt due mostly to health concerns and his diminishing eyesight that eventually left him virtually blind.

Recently, conservative scholars have not been content with the view that Toy's later activities confirmed the earlier decision to terminate his seminary service. Paul House, for example, has argued that Toy was unaware of "the significance of his own hermeneutical system" and that this "unawareness led not only to his adoption of theological views that diverged from conservative Christianity, but from Trinitarian Christianity itself."[5] Furthermore, House argues that Toy's methodology was set by the time of his SBTS faculty address and "did not change substantially after 1869. All that remained by then was for him to follow the logical path his methodology suggested."[6] In that address, according to House, Toy proposed a "two-sphere" hermeneutic that stressed "the need for both the internal and external principles, but it is clear that he divides the two, assigning each separate tasks, and without stating how they are to be integrated or what the interpreter should do if the data seems not to cohere."[7] For House, Toy's method is inadequate because it "offers no statement on either historical or doctrinal accuracy."[8] To justify his claim that Toy's articulation of his method does not significantly change between the time of his 1869 address until his 1879 resignation, House must deal with Toy's statement in his 1869 address in which he asserts "a fundamental principle of our Hermeneutics must be that the Bible, its real assertions being known, is in every iota of its substance absolutely and infallibly true."[9] While most interpreters have understood that Toy's view changed in the interim of his resignation letter (in which he manifestly does not use the term "infallible"), House admits that the context of the passage is "a bit ambiguous" but concludes that Toy "means the Bible's true spiritual, not historical statement." How does House know this? Because "later events bear out this reading of the passage."[10] In this sense, House's view, however much he tries to guise it in an interpretation of Toy's 1869 address, is no different than Broadus's or Carver's appeal to Toy's later writings.

House is insistent that the seeds of Toy's two-sphere hermeneutic that divided and separated concern for the external, objective historical and scientific facts from inward, spiritual, and psychological truth would lead ultimately to such views in *Judaism and Christianity*. According to House, those views, which were decried as overly rationalistic and anti-supernatural in 1890, were

---

[5] Paul House, "Crawford Howell Toy and the Weight of Hermeneutics," *Southern Baptist Journal of Theology* 3 (1999): 28–39; here 29.

[6] House, "Toy and the Weight of Hermeneutics," 29.

[7] House, "Toy and the Weight of Hermeneutics," 30.

[8] Ibid.

[9] Toy, *The Claims of Biblical Interpretation on Baptists*, 44.

[10] House, "Toy and the Weight of Hermeneutics," 31.

present in 1869. House maintains this point, despite the fact that Toy's colleagues and founders of the seminary assumed "his view of inspiration was the same as theirs, a conclusion still drawn by most historians."[11] On the one hand, House implies that Toy's method led him to change his views (rather than vice versa), suggesting the two-sphere method had an inevitable outcome,[12] and, on the other, he concludes that "not everyone who holds Toy's interpretative methodology comes to his conclusions, though they must make a decision of where to stop short of his theological beliefs."[13]

Thomas Nettles, another traditionalist who ultimately condones the trustees' actions in accepting Toy's resignation, admits the possibility of House's interpretation of Toy's 1869 faculty address, but offers another interpretation:

> While House believed that no fundamental change occurred in Toy's understanding of the relation of the external to the internal principles, it is possible to view Toy's struggle as precisely the opposite. Toy sought, in fact, to develop an interpretive scheme that would assume perfect coherence between the external and internal principles. In the imperfect state of biblical interpretations in the past, it has often been true, given the internal witness of the Spirit, that overall spiritual impressions were more accurate than individual biblical interpretations. Here Toy labored to warn against the illusion of establishing religious convictions built on impressions formed in absence of biblical data.... Toy's designation of an internal principle of hermeneutics would have sounded no alarm since he described it in historic Reformed concepts. It did not seem Kantian but Calvinistic.[14]

---

[11] House, "Toy and the Weight of Hermeneutics," 35.

[12] House, "Toy and the Weight of Hermeneutics," 27. In contrast, Hurd ("Confronting an Intellectual Revolution," 14) has observed that Toy's "beliefs were an unstable mixture of Baptist traditionalism, moderate German biblical interpretive theory, and fragments of philosophical idealism. The mixture was unstable, but this hardly made the future direction of his thought inevitable."

[13] House, "Toy and the Weight of Hermeneutics," 37–38. House (36) is critical of Toy's later refusal (in his 1879 letter of resignation) to extend the text's "true assertions" to "matters of authorship, date, historical veracity, or comments that could be ascertained to disagree with scientific claims." Yet House is unable or unwilling to state what the interpreter should do when such matters arise in his or her analysis of the text. Thus, House is vulnerable to Toy's critique of those who use *a priori* reasoning to assert the text's veracity in all matters.

[14] Nettles, *Boyce*, 342. Nettles also cited as evidence for his interpretation of Toy an article Toy published in the *Baptist Quarterly* during 1869, while he was teaching at Furman, in which Toy roundly criticized the position of F. C. Baur; cf. Crawford H. Toy, "The Tübingen School," *Baptist Quarterly* 3 (1869): 210-35.

Nettles examines Toy's example of Augustine in his inaugural lecture, concluding that "Toy's purpose in this extended treatment of Augustine is clear. Even the most spiritual and orthodox writers cannot be excused from building theology on the exact meaning of the biblical text.... A theological conviction free of textual fetters is a matter of mere opinion and not faith."[15]

So what moved Toy from the traditional position he expressed in 1869 to less conventional interpretations that caused the crisis of 1879? According to Nettles, it was the series of questions that modern science of the mid- and late-nineteenth century was pressing on religion. And Toy was not the only Baptist affected by these questions. Toy's Southern Seminary colleagues "had struggled with the issue of biblical authority and interpretation in light of the rapid advances in science that seemed to challenge the biblical text."[16] The difference for Toy was that he was no longer able to harmonize external principle with internal principle because modern science had convinced Toy that the external claims of the biblical text were not infallible.[17] Toy was left with the claim that it was the internal spiritual or theological truth that mattered—in the case of creation, that God was the author of the created order and all which that confession entailed theologically. Nettles's account of the evolution of Toy's thought seems to match what evidence we have, as well as Toy's own testimony.[18] Thus, while the "crisis in the interpretation of Genesis thus affected all" of the SBTS faculty, "Toy's treatment [in his 1869 address] did not reveal an abiding insidious principle of destruction always present in his hermeneutic."[19] Despite this rather generous interpretation of Toy on the part of a conservative interpreter, Nettles still concludes by bemoaning Toy as an example of one in whom "even the greatest vigilance and most determined confessional commitment could not hold back the pressure toward embracing modernity."[20]

In his 1879 letter of resignation, Toy continued to speak of the external and internal aspects of Scripture but also described it in Christological terms:

---

[15] Nettles, *Boyce*, 344.

[16] Nettles, *Boyce*, 346. Nettles (346–48) gives specific examples in which Boyce and Manly engaged vigorously and took seriously questions regarding, for example, the implications of conclusions reached by modern geology for the dating of the creation of the earth.

[17] Nettles, *Boyce*, 348–49. Toy himself had acknowledged as much regarding the Genesis account of creation in six twenty-four-hour days versus the conclusions reached by geology and evolutionary science; see chapter 3.

[18] See chapter 3.

[19] Nettles, *Boyce*, 348.

[20] Nettles, *Boyce*, 355. In contrast, Nettles (355) praised Boyce for displaying a "clear resolution to encourage orthodoxy and cut off error wherever he found it."

"I believe that the Bible is wholly divine and wholly human."[21] Greg Wills argued that Toy "intended this schema to bridge the human and divine elements of scripture, but it drove them apart. And as it did, it drove him away from traditional interpretations of the Bible and away from Southern Baptist views."[22] Thus, Toy was guilty of erecting a "kind of Nestorian division between the human and divine elements in scripture."[23] Cut loose from its divine nature, the accuracy of the human element of scripture now "had no bearing on the truth of the spiritual elements."[24] According to Wills, matters grew even worse for Toy.

Crawford Toy was friends with, and an admirer of, his Harvard colleague, William James.[25] In 1907 Toy wrote to James, after reading his newly published book on pragmatism:[26]

> The book has cleared up some things for me. It has helped to free me from the obsession of metaphysical speculation, as Paul's doctrine of faith freed him from bondage to works. And, what is more important, it has given me a more satisfying conception of "truth". My own categories have been simply the "verifiable" and the "unverifiable". The latter I rejected for myself, though I admitted vaguely the right of others to hold things that seemed to me irrational if they found them helpful. I see now more clearly the real ground of my scarcely formulated view. And if I find myself ready to accept the doctrine that "truth" is not a static and stagnant thing, but a thing that we are constantly creating for ourselves. My faith has long been hedonistic, utilitarian, and your Lectures have extended it and given it a firmer basis. By the way, when you "take the bull by the horns" and say that our act creates the world's salvation you have the support, to a certain extent, of the New Testament, which not [only] declares that we are coworkers with God, but also exhorts the believer to fill out in his own person what remains of the sufferings of Christ.[27]

---

[21] Toy, Letter of Resignation, 2. See chapter 3.

[22] Wills, *Southern Seminary*, 114–15. Wills (114) agrees with Nettles that Toy's loss of the conviction that the Bible is infallibly true in its external, historical elements caused the irreparable rift between Scripture's human and divine aspects.

[23] Wills, *Southern Seminary*, 114; see also 129. Nestorianism was a fifth-century heresy that allegedly posited a sharp division between the two natures of Christ, human and divine.

[24] Wills, *Southern Seminary*, 114.

[25] Toy and James attended each other's lectures, read each other's works, and exchanged occasional letters; for the extant correspondence between James and Crawford and Nancy Toy, see William James Papers, Hou b MS Am 1092.9, HL.

[26] James, *Pragmatism*.

[27] Crawford H. Toy to William James, July 22, 1907, William James Papers, HL.

Based on his interpretation of aspects of Toy's letter, Wills accuses Toy of becoming a "philosophical pragmatist" and by the end of his life having "advanced beyond Unitarianism and perhaps beyond theism."[28] Wills treats pragmatism as he does "unitarian" and "liberal," assuming meanings for those terms without exploring them in their literary and historical contexts.[29] Rather than seeing Toy's remarks as evidence that he has left even theism behind, it is possible to see that Toy is here relinquishing not his theistic beliefs but rather a rigid historicism that had trapped him into a narrow definition of truth in terms of verifiability or falsifiability; in other words, James had led Toy to question the very premise of the "scientific" nature of biblical higher criticism, which had informed his scholarship and teaching from the beginning of his career.[30] It would be interesting to know how Toy's new insights into pragmatism might have affected, for example, his earlier analysis of science and religion.[31]

Inerrantists are not immune to their own set of critiques, also using Christological or incarnational idiom. Charles Talbert, himself a Baptist scholar, describes his relationship to Scripture as that of a "spiritual friend."[32]

---

[28] Wills, *Southern Seminary*, 132, 133.

[29] Wills seems to assume that adopting epistemological non-foundationalism entails embracing also an anti-metaphysical realism (see, e.g., Richard Rorty, *Philosophy and the Mirror of Nature* [Princeton: Princeton University Press, 1979]). But Baptist evangelical scholars such as Stanley Grenz (among many others) have shown the possibility of pursuing metaphysical truth through non-foundational avenues; see Grenz, *Beyond Foundationalism: Shaping Theology in a Postmodern Context* (Louisville: Westminster/John Knox, 2001). Later, Wills (*Southern Seminary*, 238–39) explores the influence of James on E. Y. Mullins. Here, Wills's sweeping generalizations ignore the impact of pragmatism's resurgence in the form of non-foundationalism that include Christian theologians such as Cornell West (see Richard J. Bernstein, "The Resurgence of Pragmatism," *Social Research* 59 [1992]: 813–40).

[30] That there is no reason to suspect Toy's newly found "pragmatism" had caused him to abandon his religious, theistic beliefs can be deduced from the sentence preceding the cited passage, when Toy says that "Mrs. Saunders is pleased that Pragmatism admits the possible validity of theism as a working hypothesis." It is likely that Toy shared this view with his mother-in-law. Admittedly the evidence is too scant to draw hard conclusions either way.

[31] Pragmatic philosophy seems to have had no influence in one of his last essays, "The Higher Criticism," *Christian Register* 89 (1910): 455–57, in which he dismantles H. M. Weiner's apologetic defense of Mosaic authorship of the Pentateuch. On the other hand, Toy does list James's books and essays as reference works on "Works on the Nature of Religion," in *Introduction to the History of Religions*, 587.

[32] Charles H. Talbert, "The Bible as Spiritual Friend, *PRSt* 13 (1986): 55–64. The essay was originally delivered as the presidential address of the National Association of Baptist Professors of Religion in 1985. It was reprinted in Mikeal C. Parsons and Richard

Talbert takes aim at inerrantists of the Chicago Statement variety, who claimed, "We deny that the humble, human form of Scripture entails errancy any more than the humanity of Christ, even in His humiliation entails sin."[33] Advocates of such a view, according to Talbert, would be forced to conclude, for example, that when Jesus accepted Mosaic authorship of the Law (Mark 10:4–5; John 5:45–47; 7:19), Christian interpreters must also conclude that Moses is author of the Pentateuch. According to Talbert this view presumes that "when Jesus speaks, in the area of matters of [historical] fact, it is God the Son speaking."[34]

Such a proposition, however, Talbert asserts, does not reflect Nicene orthodoxy (Christ is fully human *and* fully divine). It is, rather, more like the heresy of Monophysitism, in which the humanity of Christ was real but "so subordinated that the ultimate reality was the divine."[35] The problem with biblical inerrancy is, according to Talbert, "a massive confusion about the relationship between finitude and sin."[36] "Fallibility," according to Talbert, "is not the result of sin but the natural by-product of human finitude....Our finitude, moreover, is not something that is evil but something good, because it was created by God.... For Jesus to have been a man of his own time in his knowledge of matters of fact would not have subverted either his divinity or his sinlessness but instead would have guaranteed his full humanity, including finitude, even the finitude of limited knowledge in matters of fact."[37] Talbert then makes a comparison with the Bible with which Crawford Toy (at least in 1879) would have resonated: "Christological orthodoxy, therefore argues for a distinction between matters of fact and matters of religion [Toy might say spiritual matters]...in the Bible as a whole."[38]

Walsh, *"A Temple Not Made with Hands": Essays in Honor of Naymond H. Keathley* (Eugene, OR: Pickwick Publications, 2018), 205–15. References here are to this most recent reprint.

[33] 1978 Chicago Statement on Inerrancy reported in *Christianity Today*, 17 December 1982, 47.

[34] Talbert, "Bible as Spiritual Friend," 213.

[35] Ibid. Talbert (213) additionally claimed inerrancy might also resemble Apollinarianism, which also functionally denied Christ's humanity.

[36] Talbert, "Bible as Spiritual Friend," 214.

[37] Ibid.

[38] Talbert, "Bible as Spiritual Friend," 214–15. Interestingly, Talbert cites the article on Scripture in Southern Seminary's Abstract of Principle in favor of his view of the human finitude of the Bible: "The Scriptures of the Old and New Testaments were given by inspiration of God and are the only sufficient, certain and authoritative rule of all *saving* knowledge, faith and obedience" (211). The emphasis is Talbert's and underscores his point that the Bible is reliably, even infallibly, true in its soteriological message. This saving message for Talbert is irreducibly a relational one; hence the use of "spiritual friend" to describe the essential nature of the Bible.

By 1899, Toy's views had evolved beyond traditional Christian doctrine. In response to an inquiry by John Hill Luther (retired president of Baylor Female College), Toy gave a "short outline of my course of thought." He traced the gradual development of his views regarding the authority and "supernatural element" of Scripture. His studies at Southern led him to conclude that the value of Genesis was not to be found in its science but rather in its recognition of "one God only as creator." After arriving at Harvard, he

> examined anew the statements of O.T. & N.T. The result was that I was convinced that the science of the Bible is just that of its time & people, that its morality is a… human product not superior to the best products of other peoples (though I attach great importance to its doctrine of love), and that its religious conceptions, which are of different characters (some good & some not good) are traceable to the thought of the time & are not of final authority. Thus the distinctively church-ideas (the Trinity, the fall of man, the atonement & c.) ceased to have any but an historical interest for me. My present position is that God utters himself in all the universe—most clearly in man, & in gifted men like Jesus of Nazareth, Paul of Tarsus, Buddha, Socrates—and that religion is the union of the soul with God regarded as the moral ideal—he alone is truly religious who lives & acts in conscious sympathy with the moral order of the world.[39]

Had he remained within the Baptist fold, no doubt Crawford Toy would have continued to pursue the progressive agenda set out by higher criticism. And perhaps he would have ended up in the same place, theologically, that he did after a decade or so at Harvard. But that is not necessarily the case, and it is not necessarily a bad thing—creating a rival tradition of interpretation in dialogue with more traditional views. Furthermore, the community so quick to condemn Toy as a heretic, which is also responsible for removing him from the community, has been painfully slow to acknowledge the racism that has undergirded the institution from its founding and continued through the "Lost Cause" ideology embedded in its second generation of faculty, most notably with John Sampey. What counts as more heretical—denying the inerrancy of Scripture or perpetuating structural and institutional racism? What would have been the result had the seminary been able or willing to raise its umbrella so as to include the views held by Toy in 1879?

Conversely, what would have been the result if Toy had been able to moderate the expression of his views, as Boyce and Broadus requested? While I am convinced, as I have said, that those responsible for his departure from the seminary (and their theological heirs) bear significant responsibility for whatever theological aberrations they think he held, Toy also has some accountability as

---

[39] Citations are from CH Toy to John Hill Luther. March 4, 1899. Luther-Bagby Collection, Baylor University.

well, a point Toy would have readily accepted.[40] After all, Broadus said one's view may be constrained by "environment" (e.g., institutional context) or "temperament." By all accounts, Toy carried himself as a Southern gentleman and scholar. His views were measured and thoroughly researched. But there is also evidence to suggest that Crawford Toy was more than a little stubborn, perhaps at times bordering on arrogance. After all, how else might one earn the nickname "Great and Mighty"? What would have happened if "Great and Mighty" Crawford Toy had been more able to accept figures of authority and abide within certain established expectations?[41] Toy had a pattern of difficulty with authority, whether Boyce's insistence that Toy avoid pursuing certain views in class (only to have Toy unable to honor that request) or Eliot's expectation that with Toy he had broken the Unitarian stranglehold on the Harvard Divinity School faculty (only to have Toy begin attending a Unitarian congregation—Eliot's First Parish in Cambridge, no less—just a decade after joining the faculty).

Toy's Baptist Legacy

Greg Wills has pronounced that Toy's "efforts to enlighten Southern Baptists largely failed."[42] But Wills also admitted that "a new generation of educated minsters drew encouragement from Toy's teachings and adopted the new liberal

---

[40] In a letter congratulating Broadus on the publication of the biography of Boyce, Toy wrote, "You are quite right in describing my withdrawal as a necessary result of important differences of opinion. Such separations are sometimes inevitable, but they need not interfere with general friendly cooperation" (Crawford H. Toy to John A. Broadus, May 20, 1893, ASC SBTS).

[41] The evidence of Toy's difficulty with authority stands in contrast with his theoretical understanding of the need for "perfect sympathy and perfect unity of action" necessary for a university to function effectively: "The relation between governors and governed is always a delicate one—it cannot be both potent and happy without a considerable exercise of moral imagination, without the capacity in each party to put itself in the place of the other. Failing this capacity, there is apt to result undue severity on one side and rebellion and fraud on the other. We may hope that the harsher aspects of the relation no longer exist among us, but there must be unfortunate results so long as there is not social and scholarly unity. Everything that fosters separation in this regard is morally injurious to all concerned—everything that promotes sympathetic and hearty cooperation is morally beneficial" ("Ethical Influences in University Life," 148). Mutual accountability between governors and governed (whether faculty and students or administrators and faculty) is balanced by the necessity of free and honest pursuit of the truth. Perhaps reflecting on his own personal experience, Toy counseled: "Freedom to say precisely and fully what one thinks removes a great part of the temptation to prevarication and concealment. It increases the sense of personal responsibility, and thus ministers to the growth of that deep inward truthfulness which is the glory of a university teacher" (154).

[42] Wills, *Southern Seminary*, 148.

view of inspiration."[43] Others have also recognized Toy's lasting effects on Southern Seminary, if not on the denomination as a whole. W. O. Carver wrote in 1954 that Toy's views "would today not be regarded as sufficiently revolutionary to call for drastic action."[44] William Mueller agreed: "Today the critical views which Dr. Toy espoused in the seventies are receiving a hearing in the classes of Southern Seminary without, however, being made into shibboleths."[45] Roy Honeycutt, Southern Seminary president (1982–1993) concurred: "Despite the fact that Crawford Howell Toy was forced to resign from the faculty in 1879 and later abandoned his heritage, his ideals continued to provide an impetus to open inquiry and dedicated scholarship."[46]

Like many before him, from, among others, Baptist founder John Smyth to Roger Williams to those who followed, such as John Claypool, Crawford Toy eventually left the Baptist fold. And though his theological pilgrimage led him beyond the horizon of most Baptists and even most orthodox, trinitarian Christians,[47] aspects of Toy's Baptist heritage remained with him long after he left the Old Cambridge Baptist Church. His progressive theological views, as we have already seen, were carried on by his former student and colleague, David Lyon, who remained an active member of OCBC until his death.[48] Toy and

---

[43] Ibid. It was the rooting out of those "liberal views" at Southern that Wills chronicles in his last chapter, "R. Albert Mohler and the Remaking of Southern Seminary" (511–47).

[44] Carver, "Recollections and Information," 27. That many of Toy's views are now commonplace is true and not true. Views regarding servant songs of Isaiah as having Israel as primary referent are standard (allowing for the view that early Christians also saw fulfillment in Christ). Likewise, all but the most strident fundamentalists now view Genesis as presenting theological truths with no claims as to scientific explanation for origins of life. But not everything has continued. Toy's view of evolutionary development of religion in general from primitive to advanced and from particularistic Judaism to universal Christianity is now largely discredited. Much of the sea change in latter view was due to work of Toy's colleague, George Foot Moore.

[45] William A. Mueller, *A History of Southern Baptist Theological Seminary* (Nashville: Broadman, 1959), 142.

[46] Roy L. Honeycutt, "Heritage Creating Hope: The Pilgrimage of The Southern Baptist Theological Seminary," *Review and Expositor* 81 (1984): 367–91; here 379. Honeycutt (379) singled out two of Toy's contributions: "his appreciation for the positive contributions of studies in the evolution of man and his implementation of the historical-critical study of the Bible." Of course, the "impetus" to "open inquiry" is thwarted if it results in the loss of employment, as in Toy's case.

[47] A. H. Newman, *A History of the Baptist Churches in the United States*, sixth edition (Philadelphia: American Baptist Publication Society, 1915), 519, claimed that by the end of his life, Toy preferred the label "Theist" to "Christian" to describe his religious beliefs.

[48] The history of progressive Baptists in the eighteenth through early twentieth centuries is still not well known; see, however, E. Glenn Hinson, "Southern Baptists and the Liberal Tradition in Biblical Interpretation, 1845–1945," *Baptist History and Heritage* 19 (1984): 16–20. Hinson singles out Toy and William L. Poteat as examples. For an excellent introduction on representatives of progressive Baptists in the twentieth century, see David L.

Lyon shared similar views regarding the nature of Scripture (as evidenced by the strong resonances between Toy's resignation letter and Lyon's correspondence with Broadus and his address before the Baptist congress in Philadelphia) and religious freedom (as evidenced by their commitment to dismantle compulsory chapel attendance at Harvard).[49] But Toy's Baptist legacy while at Harvard is not confined to what he shared with David Lyon. Toy's assertion of the right of the individual to dissent is articulated in a 1905 article titled "The Church and the Individual." Toy maintained that "dissidents [may] prefer to remain in a church and assert the right of individual interpretation of creeds and articles of faith."[50] In his last published book, Toy describes the Constantinian "Fall" of the early church in words only a Baptist, or heir of the radical Reformation, could use:

> In the beginning it [the church] was thoroughly individualistic and volun-
> tary. It had no connection with the State, was not a *religio licta*; its adher-
> ents joined it solely out of preference for its doctrines; its activity was
> wholly religious.... The introduction of infant baptism (toward the end of
> the second century) and the adoption of Christianity as the religion of the
> State by Constantine went far to make membership in the Church an ac-
> cident of birth or of political position...it was a religion but not a church.[51]

Apparently, Crawford Toy's Baptist DNA, in terms of his commitment to the separation of church and state, religious liberty, and freedom of conscience, never changed.

A "Translucent Soul"

What then are we to make of Crawford Howell Toy, the man, the scholar, and the teacher? On a personal level, Toy was a remarkable person who was surrounded by equally extraordinary personalities—Charles Eliot, David Lyon, Nancy Saunders Toy, to name a few. He was a person of integrity, honesty, and

---

Stricklin, *A Genealogy of Dissent: Southern Baptist Protest in the Twentieth Century* (Lexington, KY: University Press of Kentucky, 2000). Toy differs from the Baptist progressives of the twentieth century not only in terms of issues (race and gender for the twentieth century; higher criticism for the nineteenth) but also in the fact that Toy was not a social activist. In his quiet way, however, by allowing females into his classes and lectures and teaching at Radcliffe College on a regular basis, Toy did champion women's rights to education.

[49] See chapter 7.

[50] Crawford H. Toy, "The Church and the Individual," *The International Quarterly* 12 (October 1, 1905): 293–311; here 301–302. Toy's view here can be linked with the Baptist version of the priesthood of the believer and soul competency.

[51] Toy, *Introduction to the History of Religions*, 547.

loyalty. As a scholar, Toy published a number of significant articles and monographs, and he and Lyon, along with William Raney Harper at the University of Chicago and Paul Haupt at Johns Hopkins University, laid the groundwork for the establishment of the study of Ancient Near Eastern languages and cultures in America. In that sense, he exceeded the dream he expressed to John Broadus in 1881: "I don't doubt that if I live, I shall be able to do something for Semitic study in N. England and perhaps in a wider region."[52] As a teacher, he was praised for being articulate, organized, and committed to his students. Indeed, from the Albemarle Female Institute to Furman College to Southern Seminary and finally at Harvard, Professor Toy engendered a deep sense of loyalty and admiration among his students.

Per his request, Crawford Howell Toy was cremated at the Mount Auburn Cemetery Crematorium on May 14, 1919. After the memorial service in Harvard's Appleton Chapel, Nancy Toy and Crawford's brother, Walter, traveled to Seal Harbor and spread his cremated ashes in the sea off the shoreline of his beloved summer home.[53]

At the end of the day, a biographer must be satisfied with presenting the known details of the subject as fully and frankly as possible. It is beyond the call of duty to pronounce the subject either "hero" or "heretic." Such is surely the case with Crawford Howell Toy. Toy's student, colleague, confidante, and friend, David Lyon, realized that also. Lyon's concluding words to his eulogy for Toy seem a fitting ending here as well:

> A student of his of nearly half a century ago writing recently about him called him "a translucent soul". As such he lived among us, and as such he fared forth into the unseen. But such a man must fare well in any realm, seen or unseen. In his behalf we may say with Whittier:

> "I know not where His islands lift
> Whir fronded palms in air;
> I only know I cannot drift
> Beyond His love and care."[54]

---

[52] Crawford H. Toy to John A. Broadus, June 4, 1881, Broadus Papers, SBTS.

[53] Jane Coolidge, "Toy," 1. There was some confusion regarding Toy's final resting place since the local paper reported that Toy had been buried in Mount Auburn Cemetery (see *Cambridge Tribune* 42/12 [May 17, 1919]). Toy's cremation was corroborated by Regina Harrison, executive assistant of the Mount Auburn Cemetery, in an email dated March 8, 2017, in which she stated: "After looking in our records, it appears that Crawford Howell Toy was cremated here…, but that he was not buried here." Thus, there is no reason now to doubt Jane Coolidge's report of the scattering of Toy's cremated remains off the coast of Seal Harbor.

[54] Lyon, "Minute on Crawford Howell Toy," December 13, 1919, Harvard Biblical Club, HUA.

Fig. 6

Charlotte "Lottie" Moon.
Virginia Missionary Union, used by permission of WMU, SBC

EXCURSUS

Exploring the Toy-Moon Myth[1]

The Myth—Part 1: A Proposal Rejected?

It was a serious world into which she [Lottie Moon] stepped from the schoolroom. War was on, war that was to tear the fair land of Virginia into bloody shreds for four long years.... Yet not so serious were the times that youth was all forgot. For down to Viewmont in that troubled June the young professor came a-wooing.... Though war drums might sound in all the valleys of Virginia, it was peaceful here at Viewmont in June of 1861.... After the custom of the day in courtship, the young professor was also a guest in the home.

It would be a most excellent match, that of this distinguished young scholar and the cultured, gifted daughter of an old Virginia family.... The call to the defense of his state had been answered by the young man. He would leave Viewmont to begin his duties as a Chaplain in the Confederate Army and be in active service during the days of battle to come.

This was rather to the advantage of the young man's suit. With Virginia women all astir with zeal to aid and inspire their men, with all the excitement of war and the apprehension of its dangers in the air, with June at its loveliest,—truly a maid's heart would be cold indeed not to stir at the touch of love....

There was one last talk, as the young man and Lottie Moon walked among the roses in the silver moonlight, when the decision was given. Perhaps because of some as yet faintly glowing purpose in her heart, perhaps simply because she could not be sure she loved him, she said "no" to the love he offered her, and turned aside from all the fascination of the life amid the scholarly atmosphere of universities that would be hers

---

[1] By "myth" I do not mean to suggest *a priori* that the story of the romantic relationship between C.H. Toy and Lottie Moon is purely fiction, but rather that historical facts (whatever they may be) were combined, synthesized, and embellished to create a powerful alchemy and a foundational story crucial for narrating the story and successes of late nineteenth and early twentieth centuries Southern Baptist missions—embodied in the person of Charlotte "Lottie" Moon—in the mid-twentieth century. That story is primarily one of the sacrifice of missionary Lottie Moon; an additional benefit of the story (from the traditionalists' point of view) has been the further ostracizing of Crawford Toy from the SBC establishment.

at his side.

The next morning the young man bade the household farewell, to ride gallantly away from Viewmont to his duty in the battle lines then forming. Polly Anna, who read in the faces of her two friends the answer Lottie had given, ran out to the garden, where pansies were blooming in purple and gold splendor. Gathering a handful of these she gave them to him as he was leaving.

"Take these, my friend, they are all in the heart's ease I can find for you,"—and the young man rode away with Polly Anna's pansies in his buttonhole.

So love came, and went—to await a fairer time for his call to her heart again.[2]

Most readers, especially Baptist ones of a certain age, who are even vaguely familiar with Crawford Toy will have heard that Toy was engaged to Lottie Moon, who ended the relationship because of theological differences. Some will also be acquainted with the account given above of an earlier romance in which Moon rejected a marriage proposal from Toy in June 1861. Familiarity with the story is due primarily to the pervasive influence of the story (with other "events" that precede and follow) described above by Lottie Moon's first biographer, Una Roberts Lawrence.[3]

---

[2] Una Roberts Lawrence, *Lottie Moon* (Nashville: Sunday School Board, 1927), 49–51, passim. By 1976, this work had gone through 23 printings and sold more than 50,000 copies (see Irwin T. Hyatt, Jr. *Our Ordered Lives Confess: Three Nineteenth-Century American Missionaries in East Shantung* [Cambridge, MA: Harvard University Press, 1976], 127). Although Lawrence "coyly avoids naming the man," Toy's name is found in her research notes (Una Roberts Lawrence Papers, SBTS; cited in Hyatt, *Our Ordered Lives*, 266 n. 18). For a critical review of Lawrence's biography, see Alan Neely, "Saints Who Sometimes Were: Utilizing Missionary Hagiography," *Missiology: An International Review* 27 (1999): 441–57.

[3] Literature—pamphlets, children's lessons, etc.—on Lottie Moon produced by the SBC Woman's Missionary Union in the next several decades was heavily influenced by the account of Lawrence, often repeating this story in condensed fashion; see, e.g., "Biographical Sketch of Lottie Moon," "Big Love Heart—A brief biographical sketch of Lottie Moon," and "The Romance of Lottie Moon," *Baptist Intermediate Union Quarterly*, March 30, 1941, 30–31, Lottie Moon, Baptist History File, SBHLA. Lawrence served as Young People's secretary for the WMU from 1920–1926 (at the time of the writing of Moon's biography) and later as Home Mission Board Study Editor (1926–1947). Hyatt, *Our Ordered Lives*, 127–29, reviews the history of the Moon story as it subsequently developed. One play, "Her Lengthened Shadow" (1964), explores the purported 1861 romance between Moon and Toy (whose character is named Reverend Mr. Fleming). When Moon rejects Rev. Fleming (Toy), he laments:

Maid of Viewmont—'ere we part

The Toy-Moon story has been relegated to an excursus in this current work because, regardless of the particular shape of the relationship between Crawford Toy and Lottie Moon, that relationship played no significant part in the life story of Crawford Toy. However, since the broken engagement with Lottie Moon is one of the two most well-known "facts" of the Toy legacy (in addition to leaving SBTS because of his "heretical" views), it is necessary to explore that tale here. Below we trace what we know and what we do not know regarding the relationship of Crawford Toy with Lottie Moon in the late 1850s and early 1860s, independent of the account given by Una Lawrence.

Unraveling the Proposal Myth

Charlotte "Lottie" Moon was a student of Toy's at the Albemarle Female Institute. Moon was a member of the second class who entered in 1857. She was, by all accounts, an outstanding pupil. One of her Albemarle instructors, unnamed, later made this tribute in the *Biblical Recorder*:

> Miss Moon came to the school at Charlottesville with very good preparation as to attainments, and with unusual preparation as to natural abilities. Thus her career as a student was marked by distinguished success. She never failed to pass every examination that she attempted, and usually she was highest in the class. It would be hard to say in what studies she most excelled. The writer, who had the pleasure of reading many of her examination papers, remembers her superlatively fine work in Latin, history, literature, and moral philosophy. He thinks that her strength lay especially in the direction of the languages and Belles Lettres studies. The Greek language was not included in the graduating course; but Miss Moon, entering on the work with her usual industry and intelligence, became a very good Greek scholar. Since that day, the writer has not heard young ladies read with fluency and appreciation the plays of Euripides and Sophocles.... It is not insidious to say that, in the judgment of many who had opportunity to know, she was the most scholarly of all

---

Give, oh give me back my heart!
Or, since that has left my breast,
Keep it now, and take the rest!
Hear my vow before I go
'Zoe moy sas agapo.'
Later in China, Moon confesses that "the temptation is great," but the professor holds views that "do not square with God's Word." She rejects her suitor a second time, confessing "My cross is loneliness," and she recites Byrant's "To a Waterfowl" (cited in Hyatt, *Our Ordered Lives*, 128–29).

the graduates of that school.[4]

Some have been inclined, not without good reason, to attribute this quotation and other accolades like it to C. H. Toy.[5] Following Lawrence's lead, earlier writers accepted that there was a developing romance between Toy and Moon that resulted in a rejected marriage proposal in 1861.[6] There is, as we shall see, no evidence of a romantic relationship in this period.

Of course, it "was not unheard of for Albemarle Female Institute's professors to show attentions to young women," and girls "were known to develop serious crushes on the eligible Professor Toy."[7] Sarah Ann Strickler [Fife] wrote in her diary about meeting Toy for the first time, as a student during Toy's second stint at AFI: "I was presented today, to my most worshipful masters Rev. H. H. Harris and Rev. C. H. Toy (an unmarried man); both said to be very smart, especially the latter who is so extremely dignified and exquisite that the girls stand in awe of him."[8] Toy himself joked with his cousin, Morton Howell, about attention from women accounting for a missing photograph of the two of them: "Either you or I have made an impression on some heart, most probably female, & our Daguerreotype [photograph] is gone. Can't you come up at the end of the session, if only for a day & Wood will retake us."[9]

Around this same time, in an 1860 letter to John Broadus, Toy did make reference to a romantic interest, but it was not Lottie Moon. It was rather a "'new' from G'ville" who "presents no news." We then learn that the "new" is apparently a new love interest who has been in correspondence with him: "Her last letter breathes a beautiful spirit of holy devotion and holy desire. I cannot read her letters without being stimulated & lifted up into a higher atmosphere of Christian feelings & at the same time humbled at the view it gives me of my own inferiority in piety. But God is Ruler in heaven & earth–."[10]

The next extant letter to Broadus (September 12, 1860) follows a similar

---

[4] *Biblical Recorder*, January 17, 1877; cf. Allen, *New Lottie Moon*, 33. It is possible that Toy was the author of this anonymous encomium, but nothing in the article suggests anything other than a teacher who is justifiably proud of his star pupil.

[5] Allen, *New Lottie Moon*, 33.

[6] Hurt, "Crawford Howell Toy," 23; Jane Toy Coolidge, "Crawford Howell Toy: 1836–1919," 3, unpublished manuscript, WMU Archives, Birmingham, AL.

[7] Allen, *New Lottie Moon*, 33.

[8] Sarah Ann Strickler [Fife], "Private Diary of Sarah Ann Strickler [Fife]," SCU, VA; cited by Hurt, "Toy," 37.

[9] Crawford H. Toy to Morton B. Howell, May 16, 1857, ASC, SBTS.

[10] Crawford H. Toy to John A. Broadus, July 27, 1860, ASC, SBTS.

pattern.[11] Toy rehearses his various church speaking engagements, bemoans his lack of oratory skills, shares the comings and goings of mutual acquaintances, and, finally, returns to news of his "new" whose name we now learn is "Miss Mary"; we learn also that the mother is staunchly opposed to Toy's courting of Miss Mary. Toy tells Broadus:

> I think you may by all means call on Miss Mary, but only collectively, not individually. The condition of things is as before, but rather more so. I received yesterday a letter from her mother, expressing a desire that I should not come to G'ville, stating that it would not be to my interests. I have not yet determined, but I think I shall go. I would like to know your opinion. Her opposition is very bitter & quite openly expressed.[12]
>
> For this reason I think you had better call on the family at first, & you may happen to meet Miss Mary somewhere.[13]

In a letter dated October 13, 1860, Toy reveals that he did indeed decide to visit "Miss Mary," her mother's objections notwithstanding. He writes:

> As to the object of my visit I can say nothing definite. Of the correspondence I am quite sure. You know that the decision is to be put off. I have, however now, not much fear as to the result. I have no doubt of her faithfulness, & her mother cannot always maintain her opposition. The difficulties in the way are just what we foresaw, but they are not so great. I think the opposition is now confined to Mrs. M. & the Judge and that of the latter is only conditional—I am better satisfied than I have been before.

Apparently, Toy badly overestimated his ability to overcome the opposition of Miss Mary's parents to his romantic overtures. In a letter some months later, he writes to Broadus: "Perhaps you know that my relations with Miss M. are at an end, & that my place has already been filled (apparently.) I confess it seems strange to me. But I do not blame her or him at all. I hope to number them both among my dearest friends. I don't know whether any publicity has been given to it or not. I relapse into my old self, with nothing earthly to occupy me but studies."[14]

---

[11] In addition to the pattern discussed in the text, Toy also, rather comically, having detailed his digestive problems in the July 27 letter, writes at the beginning of this one that I "am glad to be able to report myself about as usual—with the same general tendency in my gastronomic apparatus to be ill at ease & the same invincible propensity in my palate & masticating parts to give it opportunity of being so."

[12] The nature of the opposition is nowhere stated; perhaps it is resistance on the mother's part to seeing her daughter marry a missionary and move to a distant place.

[13] Toy to Broadus, September 12, 1860, ASC, SBTS.

[14] Toy to Broadus, January 31, 1861, ASC, SBTS.

"Miss Mary" was Mary Mauldin of Greenville, South Carolina. She was an 1858 graduate of the Greenville Baptist Female College.[15] The young man who filled Toy's place was J. A. Chambliss, a fellow student at SBTS who would become a prominent pastor in the convention. In his October 23, 1861, letter to Broadus, Toy identified Chambliss.

> Chambliss has written me of the date of his marriage, & I have congratulated him. Throughout he has acted as a Christian gentleman should do, & I have assured him that my regard & love for him was not diminished. But I am convinced of the fickleness (I don't mean to use a harsh term,) of the female sex. Their wounds of the heart are easily cured. And we ought not to find fault with a weakness wh. nature is responsible for, and wh. is given for a wise purpose. I think they will be happy & useful, & I pray that they may be, both having qualities highly estimable & useful.[16]

According to Lawrence, Toy proposed to Moon in June 1861. Between July 1860 and October 1861, however, the correspondence between Toy and Broadus demonstrates that Toy was clearly still processing the rejection by "Miss Mary," and there is nothing that indicates his affections had turned toward Lottie Moon (or any other person) at this point.[17] Furthermore, we have already established that Toy did not join the confederacy until April 1862 and was not appointed as a chaplain until six months later.[18] Thus, the chronology and details outlined by Lawrence at the beginning of this Excursus simply do not conform with the available evidence.

Chambliss and Mauldin were married in October 1861; they had five children. If the couple did not fulfill Toy's expressed hope that they would remain among his "dearest friends," at least it can be said that he had a loyal ally in Chambliss. J. A. Chambliss was one of two trustees who voted not to

---

[15] Judith Townsend Bainbridge, *Academy and College: The History of the Woman's College of Furman* University (Macon: MUP, 2001), 48.

[16] Crawford H. Toy to John A. Broadus, October 23, 1861, ASC, SBTS. Catherine Allen (*New Lottie Moon*, 42 fn. 29) correctly identified Chambliss as the one who "won" Miss Mary. She tentatively and mistakenly identified Miss Mary as Mary Boatwright. At any rate, Toy's failed romance with Mary Mauldin during 1860–1861 should put to rest any suggestions that Toy and Lottie Moon were romantically involved at this time (contra Lawrence and Hurt).

[17] Given the extent to which Toy had involved Broadus in his personal life in this period, it seems improbable that Toy, should he have actually proposed to Toy in June 1861, would have failed to mention that to Broadus at any point during this time.

[18] See chapter 2.

accept Toy's resignation from Southern Seminary in 1879.[19]

Regina Sullivan has suggested that there is another trace of a relationship between Toy and Moon in a letter Lottie Moon's mother wrote to her in 1869. In the letter, she asked Lottie, "Do you recollect writing a confidential letter last summer to a gent, just before you went to the springs? Well he has written a long letter to me, his explanation for not fulfilling his engagement is quite *satisfactory* to *me*."[20] Sullivan comments, "Moon and Toy may have become involved in 1868, when Toy returned to the United States from Berlin. A letter between Moon and her mother suggests Moon had a love interest around this time."[21] Catherine Allen, on the other hand, thinks the "gent" may have been interested in Lottie's younger sister, Colie, whom Anna Moon has mentioned in the immediate context: "I doubt that a possible suitor of Lottie's would have corresponded with Mrs. Moon, since Lottie was her own woman and nearly 30. On the other hand, Colie was a dependent and a suitor or employer would have had to speak with her mother."[22]

There is little solid evidence of any love interests by Toy during his years at Southern Seminary, either in Greenville or in Louisville.[23] There is, however, a passing reference in W. H. Whitsitt's correspondence to his fiancée, Florence Wallace, to Toy's having been engaged to Miss Carrie Davis, the niece by marriage of James Furman and a close friend of Whitsitt's sister Maggie. Carrie Davis had excused herself from a dinner Whitsitt had arranged with Daniel Henry Chamberlain, then governor of South Carolina, and which Toy was scheduled to attend: "she and Dr. Toy (who were once engaged to be married) were not on speaking terms."[24] At one point, Whitsitt expressed

---

[19] Hurt, "Toy," 64.

[20] Anna Moon to Lottie Moon, January 7, 1869, Lottie Moon Personal Correspondence, SBHLA.

[21] Regina D. Sullivan, *Lottie Moon: A Southern Baptist Missionary to China in History and Legend* (Baton Rouge, LA: LSU Press, 2011), 54–55.

[22] Catherine Allen, email correspondence, July 10, 2018. For different reasons, then, neither Sullivan nor Allen thinks another suitor of Moon is in mind here. Lawrence apparently was unaware of this correspondence between Moon and her mother.

[23] Toy's admiration of and interest in the opposite sex continued, even during the war. While he was teaching in Alabama near the war's end, Toy wrote to Broadus that Tuscaloosa was distinguished by its "attractive ladies, who are especially fatal to young unmarried Virginians" (C. H. Toy to John A. Broadus, October 19, 1865, Woman's Missionary Union Archives, Birmingham, AL).

[24] W. H. Whitsitt to Florence Wallace, October 29, 1875, in *Mirror*. Based on Whitehead's practice of appending editorial comments before letters (rather than within them), it would appear that the parenthetical note is from the hand of Whitsitt himself. Miss Wallace was from Woodford County, Kentucky, and presumably did not know Miss Davis personally, hence Whitsitt's parenthetical explanation. Apparently (and somewhat curiously) there was also a brief romance (at least from Davis's point of view) between her

his wish that Toy could find "a good lady who would take care of him." After several days of nursing Toy, who was suffering from bronchitis, his fellow bachelor roommate W. H. Whitsitt reflected on the "sad" situation of a sick single man: "I have had hands and heart full on account of the illness of Dr. Toy. To speak the truth a bachelor's chamber is the saddest spot in the world when illness & distress invade it. 'There is lack of woman's nursing, there is dearth of woman's tears.'[25] I do wish he would marry some good lady, who would take care of him, now that a constitution which once was regarded impregnable appears to be unequal to the shocks and changes of Kentucky climate."[26]

There have been skeptics of Lawrence's account, practically from the beginning. Notable among these is Charles E. Maddry, who served as the executive secretary of the Southern Baptist Foreign Mission Board from 1933–1944. In *Christ's Expendables*, Maddry recounts the Lottie Moon story. About the alleged Toy-Moon affair, he wrote: "There is a vague and unconfirmed tradition coming down from that glamorous time [1861] that there was a budding romance between the brilliant and attractive young graduate of the [Albemarle Female] Institute and a young ministerial student who was an honor graduate of the University of Virginia." After recounting Lawrence's version of the June 1861 proposal, he concluded, "The romance, *if such ever existed*, was crowded out during the terrible years of fratricidal strife and the tragic years of Reconstruction which followed."[27] Given the evidence marshalled

---

and David Lyon, then Toy's student in Louisville and later his colleague. In his diary of 1878–1879, Lyon mentioned going to various church and social functions with Carrie Davis, who was then living with John Broadus and his family. On the night before he left Louisville on his way, eventually, to Germany, he stopped by the Broadus house to say goodbye. Davis refused to come downstairs to bid farewell because she did not "feel well." A few days later, Lyon received a letter from Davis in which she scolded him for his indifferent actions toward her before he left and then closed "her letter with professions of love and subscribing herself, 'Faithfully yours, CTD.'" Lyon recorded that he told her in his response that he "liked her as much as ever but it was a like and had not thoughts of a possible marriage in the future." He then quoted from his reply: "The past is dead. You will recall the agreement, friends forever, devoted friends, but friends only" (Diary of David Lyon, July 22, 1879, HUA).

[25] This line is from a poem, "Bingen on the Rhine," by Caroline Elizabeth Sarah Sheridan Norton (1808–1877), about a German soldier dying in Algiers and comforted by a comrade. Stephen Crane would later quote the same lines in his war novel, *The Red Badge of Courage* (1895).

[26] W. H Whitsitt to Florence Wallace, December 17, 1878, in *Mirror*.

[27] Charles E. Maddry, *Christ's Expendables* (Nashville: Broadman, 1949), 31, 32 (my emphasis). Maddry's description of Moon as an "attractive young graduate" has a different nuance than the portrayal of Lawrence, who also says that Moon was "attractive" but "never

here, it is safe to conclude that such a romance between Toy and Moon simply did not exist in 1861. At most, we have evidence of a teacher who appreciated the intellectual powers of a remarkable student.

The Myth—Part 2: An Engagement Broken?

According to some scholars, the friendship between Crawford Toy and Lottie Moon, which had begun during her student days at Albemarle Female Institute, may have taken a romantic turn in the late 1870s. Quite possibly, there was contact between Toy and Moon when she returned from China (where she had been doing mission work since 1873) to Virginia in 1876 with her sister, Edmonia, who had become quite physically ill and emotionally vulnerable during the time in China.[28] Lottie Moon remained in Virginia until October 1877, when she returned to China; her sister Edmonia ("Eddie") remained in Virginia.[29]

Una Lawrence presents this version of the 1870s romance between Toy and Moon that culminated in another broken engagement. She writes that in 1877, several of Lottie Moon's appeals for financial assistance for the mission in China were published in the *Religious Herald*:

> In these letters…there crept now and then a note of loneliness, which was but natural. To one reader there was a personal appeal in this wistful evidence of the courage it took to lay out plans for a life forever apart from loved ones. So there went from Virginia to old Tengchow a letter bearing friendly greetings from the friend of schooldays, the young professor, now a distinguished teacher in a great college. The years between that June time of shadowed gayety at Viewmont had brought many experiences to him. Soon after the war he had gone to study in the great universities of Germany. There he had won laurels of scholarship that made him much sought on his return. No one had as yet taken the place in his heart, however, that he had once given to the blue-eyed Lottie Moon.
>
> The letter was answered and all the pleasure of a touch with the old atmosphere of study and happy discussion of subjects absorbingly interesting was brought to the home at the Little Cross Roads.

---

considered a beauty" (*Lottie Moon*, 47). Her distinctive features, according to Lawrence (43), were her "dominant personality" and "keen wit, often merciless."

[28] See Lottie Moon to H. A. Tupper, March 22, 1880, Lottie Moon Correspondence File, SBHLA.

[29] Edmonia Moon remained in the U.S.; she took her own life in 1909 (Catherine B. Allen, "The Legacy of Lottie Moon," *International Bulletin of Missionary Research* 17 [1993]: 146–52; here 151).

Just at that time the controversy over the theories of Darwin, which had been raging in Great Britain and on the Continent for twenty years, began seriously to disturb American scholars…. In Germany the brilliant mind of the young professor had been deeply interested in all the fascinating possibilities of this new and revolutionary theory. He had been a deep student of Old Testament literature, and when the opportunity came for him to take a professorship in this subject in a seminary, he accepted, with his thinking along the line of Darwinian theory still in a state of uncertainty. In his classroom he advanced some of his ideas of reconciliation of the new hypothesis with the Genesis account of creation and the new ideas of the German scholars on history and inspiration of Old Testament. A great stir was made over the matter and he resigned to accept a professorship in the greatest American university of his day. In harmony with his changed views, he left the Baptist denomination and united with a Unitarian congregation.

In the meantime, Mrs. [Martha] Crawford, on furlough in Virginia, visited a dear friend of Lottie Moon's and confided to her the delightful bit of news that Miss Moon was to be married to her old lover of her schooldays. The only part of the wedding plans yet undecided at the time Mrs. Crawford had left China was the question of whether they would settle in Japan, where he wished to go as a missionary, or come to her field in Tengchow.

Down to the home of Lottie's brother, Isaac Moon, there came a letter from the sister, saying that she was returning in the spring to be married. She wished to be married from her brother's home. She mentioned in that letter that it was not yet decided whether they would live in Japan or China.

The young professor himself talked the matter over with Dr. Tupper, Secretary of the Board. That he told this dear friend of Miss Moon's of his attachment through the years to her we know from a letter which Dr. Tupper wrote, containing a bit of gentle teasing about the delightful secret….

Lawrence then indicated that Lottie Moon read the accounts surrounding the theological controversy swirling around the "young professor" (Toy) in the Baptist papers and began researching the matter for herself.

That she studied the question from his viewpoint is quite evident from the marginal notes in the scientific works in her library. She had practically all the notable works that came out of that first controversy on Darwinian theories. Her notes show unmistakably that she came to the conclusion that it was an untenable position, and certainly it could

not be so harmonized with the Word of God as to make one who believed it a "good workman" on a frontier of the Kingdom.

We do not know just what brought the crisis, but we do know that
in the spring when the little sister-in-law was expecting a letter telling
when she would arrive, there came a letter from Lottie Moon saying that
there would be no marriage. We know, too, that in after years she said
to a beloved relative who had been so bold as to ask her if she ever had a
love affair:

"Yes, but God had first claim on my life, and since the two con-
flicted, there could be no question about the result."

So love came and went, and life went again as usual in the house at
the Little Cross Roads.[30]

As with the purported romance in the 1860s, there is no extant correspondence between Toy and Moon during this period, but unlike the 1860s
episode, there is indirect evidence of some contact. The use of phonetic
spelling by Lottie Moon in correspondence with Henry Tupper in late 1879
is one bit of evidence that she was in communication with Toy during that
time and had also come under the influence of his phonetic spelling, much as
W. H. Whitsitt had. In a postscript to a letter to Tupper written on September 8, she wrote: "Hav yu eny rules for speling in the Fr. J? I ask bekaus I hav
adopted the fonetic style of speling. But I shal not have to spel that way, if
your compositor snubs me by putting my letters in type in the old way. Please
let me kno."[31]

Elsewhere, Moon had responded to Tupper, apparently referring to Toy
as "our mutual friend": "What you say of our mutual friend is very pleasing to
me. You are right in supposing that I 'think very highly of him.'"[32] Later in
1880, she would again affirm Tupper's positive assessment of Toy, this time

---

[30] Lawrence, *Lottie Moon*, 91–96, passim. Lawrence has compressed the chronology
to the point it is difficult to discern what year she thinks the broken engagement occurred,
and there is no corroborating evidence that Lottie Moon had informed her family of an
impending wedding. Among other inaccuracies, there is no evidence that Crawford Toy
ever entertained the prospects of missionary service after his initial commitment in 1860,
and certainly not in the aftermath of his leaving Southern Seminary. Mrs. T. P. Crawford's
role in the whole affair, however, is one worth pondering; see below.

[31] Moon to Tupper, September 8, 1879, Lottie Moon Correspondence 1877–1887,
SBHLA. See also her use of phonetic spelling in her letter to Tupper on September 21,
1879, which she ends with this note: "Don't yu admir this nü speling?" (SBHLA). On
Whitsitt's use of phonetic spelling in correspondence, see chapter 4.

[32] Lottie Moon to H. A. Tupper, March 22, 1880, Lottie Moon Correspondence
1877–1887, SBHLA. Moon adds a postscript (with modified phonetic spelling): "This is
not ment for the public. L.M."

with a mixture of phonetic spelling: "Yu say sum veri nice things about 'our mutual friend' in which I agree. But I fancy he wd be both amused and amazed at the amount of 'humility' yu ascribe to him. I trust he haz a bright future before him at Harvard.... This is 'unofficial' please."[33] In a letter to Tupper on June 14, 1880, Moon provided the clearest indication that she and Toy had been corresponding with each other. She informed Tupper that she had information about George Eager, a student at Southern Seminary, who was preparing for missionary service: "I happen to know through a mutual friend (Dr. Toy in fact) that Mr. Eager remained in America this year because he wished to discharge a debt contracted in his education."[34]

The "Toy Myth" presumes that the two were engaged and that Moon broke off the engagement because she could not tolerate his theological liberalism, perhaps as a result of his resignation from SBTS. Others have suggested that the rejection of two of Toy's students, T. P. Bell and John Stout, for missionary service in 1881[35] was the precipitating event that influenced Moon's decision to end her courtship with Toy.[36] H. A. Tupper wrote to Moon during this time: "You see by the papers that they [Stout and Bell] are not to go to China. This is a dreadful disappointment. But you will say, 'Is it not your own fault?' Now, my sweet sister, don't turn on the friend seeking your good offices. I know your love for Dr. Toy, which cannot be greater than mine for I love him with the love of a woman. But let me say that the Board does not hold to the view imparted to it...plenary verbal inspiration...(Stout) and Bell are among the noblest among the noble."[37]

The news of the failed appointments of Stout and Bell were devastating to the Chinese mission. T. P. Crawford, a fellow missionary in China with whom Moon had increasing tensions, reported in late 1881, after Bell and Stout had been refused appointment to China by the Foreign Mission Board, that he had consulted "with Miss Moon over the situation and what was best to be done." Crawford then dramatically claimed that Lottie Moon

> informed us that her stay with us was going to be short.... What could all this mean? We soon found out the secret. She [Moon] has been in- vited to take the Professor of Hebrew's chair in the University of Harvard

---

[33] Moon to Tupper, September 11, 1880, LMLF; cited by Allen, *The New Lottie Moon Story*, 137.

[34] Moon to Tupper, June 14, 1880, Lottie Moon Correspondence 1877–1887, SBHLA.

[35] See chapter 4.

[36] According to Allen ("The Legacy of Lottie Moon," 149), however, Moon supported the FMB appointment of Bell to the Chinese mission in Tengchow.

[37] Tupper to Moon, July 13, 1881, Copy Book, FMB; cited by Allen, *The New Lottie Moon Story*, 138.

and she had accepted the invitation, Dr. Toy vacating on her arrival. The call was urgent and she must go at an early day. What next you will ask![38]

Later in the same letter, Crawford reports that after "full discussion and consideration of the various questions and difficulties before us, it was decided that Miss Moon would remain till Spring," after she had heard from Tupper. It is difficult to know what to make of Crawford's muddled comment. Was he seeking to taint Lottie Moon by association with the recently disgraced Toy?[39] Or was he boasting that someone from his mission post had been appointed to a prestigious university like Harvard?[40] In either scenario, Crawford was certainly concerned about the diminishing missionary force in China that would be further depleted with Moon's departure.[41]

---

[38] T. P. Crawford to H. A. Tupper, September 1881, T. P. Crawford Letter File, Jenkins Library and Archives, IMB.

[39] As Allen points out (*New Lottie Moon Story*, 138): "Crawford must surely have misunderstood the situation, as neither Harvard nor its associated women's school, Radcliffe, was to have women faculty for another forty years. Mrs. Crawford was probably more accurate when she told a friend of Miss Moon's, upon arrival in Richmond, that Lottie would be going to Harvard as Toy's wife." The passage is rendered more ambiguous when one acknowledges the difficulty of deciphering the word rendered here "vacating" (suggesting Toy was ceding his chair to Moon?!), which might also be "vacationing" (implying an impending wedding/honeymoon?). Neither makes much sense, in part because Crawford's logic is so tortured! Crawford was present at the 1879 SBC convention when Toy's resignation was accepted.

[40] Carol Vaughn Cross has suggested:

I think the Sept 1881 letter to Tupper was a bit of his ego suggesting that someone from their mission station would be going to Harvard in some capacity near Toy (he didn't have to agree with the intellectuals to want to be engaged with them, which was evident in China). T.P. Crawford using or exaggerating the idea of Moon's uncertainty as leverage for more missionaries doesn't necessarily mean there was or wasn't an engagement. Maybe Moon thought they were engaged. Maybe TPC overheard or misheard conversations between Moon and MFC. Maybe *he* made it all up just to get more missionaries and brag about an association with an intellectual like CT, and the KY paper randomly got wind of TPC's letter to Tupper. (Email correspondence with Carol Vaughn Cross, June 11, 2018; quoted with permission)

[41] Carol Vaughn Cross again observed:

It makes sense that TPC would use the possibility of Moon's uncertain future in China for leverage to get more missionaries asap. TPC's lines about Moon (Sept 1881) give a dramatic flair to TPC's point that thanks to the loss of Bell and Stout he could possibly be all alone as the sole SBC missionary in 1882. His plea seemed to have worked: two young men arrived in early 1882 while MFC was in

It is also possible that Martha Crawford, as noted by Lawrence, was responsible for spreading the rumor of Moon's engagement. Martha Crawford had returned stateside in late 1881 and began a speaking tour with Sallie Ford in 1882: "That tour was an important part of the myth-making of the SBC's history regarding race, sex, and missions. Martha Crawford and Sallie Ford participated in the postbellum SBC inventing its 'noble missions' history of 'race uplift' (deflecting from slavery) and the part to be played by unmarried women like Moon."[42]

Whatever its source—whether T. P. Crawford, or Martha Crawford, or some other person ("a friend in Richmond?")—the June 1, 1882, edition of the Kentucky denominational paper, the *Western Recorder*, carried this brief notice: "The distinguished Oriental scholar, Prof. C.H. Toy, formerly of the Southern Baptist Theological Seminary, is shortly to be married to a young lady who has been a missionary to China."[43] Moon did not return to the States at any point in 1882, and, of course, there was no wedding. It is also noteworthy that the wedding announcement occurred *after* Toy's resignation and *after* the rejection of his two former students for missionary service because they shared theological views similar to Toy's. If there were an engagement, it was broken well after the events often pointed to as determinative in Moon rejecting both Toy and his theological liberalism.

There did circulate in the extended Toy family a story regarding Toy and Moon. Jessie Johnson Harris, daughter of Crawford Toy's sister Julia Anna Toy Johnson, wrote about the relationship of Lottie Moon with both her mother and her uncle:[44]

---

the U. S., and Moon stayed on at her own work. She could have left when Halcomb and Pruitt arrived, but she didn't. She kept doing her own mission and didn't interact with the men much until Martha Crawford got back. (Carol Vaughn Cross, email correspondence, June 11, 2018)

[42] Carol Vaughn Cross, email correspondence, June 11, 2018.

[43] The engagement announcement was also carried in the Mississippi *Baptist Record* (June 8, 1882) a week later, presumably a reprint of the *Western Recorder* announcement and not, therefore, independent witness to the impending event.

[44] The friendship between Lottie Moon and Julia Toy Johnson is well documented. In *The Heathen Helper*, a publication designed to promote the work of the WMU, Julia Johnson published recollections of her schooldays with Moon at AFI: "On a certain Monday morning...we were puzzling over some difficult Greek passages. Lottie said, 'Jule, I was in better business than this yesterday (Sunday) lying on a hay stack reading Shakespeare.'" Johnson continued that she considered "pressing the subject of personal religion, but I had not the courage to do it" (*The Heathen Helper*, May 1888, cited by Sullivan, *Lottie Moon*, 23–24).

At one time Miss Lottie was engaged to Julie's brother Crawford. I have been told that religious differences caused this relationship to be broken, but this never changed the love and devotion of my mother [for Moon]. In those days handsome Autograph Albums were quite the thing for young ladies and young gentlemen. In my mother's Album, Miss Lottie wrote the following in Latin, but I'm giving the translation—Virgil Lines 584-587, Bk. II:

"While rivers shall run into the sea, while clouds shall move around the convex summits of the mountains, while the vault of the sky shall sustain the stars; always thy honor and thy name and thy praises shall continue with me whatever lands may call me."

—Aeneas speaking to Queen Dido—
Albemarle Female Institute—Lottie Moon
June 3, 1858

This seems prophetic as Lottie Moon went as a missionary to China and was there many, many years. During this time she kept in touch with my mother through letters.[45]

A similar comment is found elsewhere in John Lipscomb Johnson's autobiography: "Two stories about him have come down to the family. [The first is that Toy]…is said to have had a romance which was not consummated with Lottie Moon of missionary fame."[46]

---

[45] Jessie Johnson Harris, "My Mother, Julia Anna Toy Johnson," Appendix A in *Autobiographical Notes*, 349. This memoir was written at the invitation of the editors (also family members) of Johnson's autobiography and would have been composed in the 1950s; is the source of the report of the broken engagement Harris's mother (Toy's sister) or someone else? The use of the passive voice in this context is curious. Certainly, we learn more about the friendship between Moon and Julia Toy Johnson from this passage than about Crawford Toy and Lottie Moon. Later in the memoir (354), Harris compares her mother to C. H. Toy: "Hers was a highly-developed mind, very much on the order of her brother Crawford who at that time was a professor of Greek and Sanskrit in Harvard University."

[46] Johnson, *Autobiographical Notes*, 119. John Johnson was married to Crawford Toy's sister, Julia. This quotation is in brackets and was provided as an editorial comment by Johnson's grandson, Cecil Johnson, as part of the publication process in the mid-1950s (*Autobiographical Notes*, 388). Una Roberts Lawrence published her biography of Lottie Moon in 1927. Thus, it is impossible to establish the origins of this family story: does it go back to John Lipscomb Johnson himself, or was it a story picked up through Lawrence (or some other rumor venue)? The other story of Johnson family lore was that Crawford Toy had been asked by the Taft Administration to translate a communication written in an "obscure dialect." Ironically, there is no mention of the Wilson Administration, with whom Toy (and his wife) had much closer relations (see chapter 8).

Disentangling the Engagement Myth

The gaps in the evidence make solving the Toy-Moon puzzle exceedingly difficult for the alleged romance during the 1877–1882 period. Lottie Moon's correspondence with H. A. Tupper breaks off in 1881, as does Martha Crawford's diary. Also missing for this time period are the diaries of David Lyon, who was likely to mention any impending engagement for Toy with Lottie Moon, as he did for Toy and Nancy Saunders, at the March 1888 meeting of the Harvard Biblical Club.[47] Significantly, in none of the minutes of the Harvard Biblical Club for 1881–1882 is mention made of an engagement by its president, Crawford Toy. Toy himself never mentions Lottie Moon in the extant correspondence, not even in letters to Broadus in late 1881, just months prior to the time the engagement announcement appeared in the *Western Recorder* and Mississippi *Baptist Record*. We can plot evaluations of the evidence along a spectrum from a maximalist to a minimalist perspective.

Una Lawrence represents the maximalist view. She had Toy and Moon engaged in an "on again off again" romance that stretched from 1861 until the early 1880s. Had she known about Anna Moon's letter to Lottie mentioning another mysterious "engagement," no doubt she would have included that bit of "evidence" as well. Lawrence's maximalist view proved very influential over the years.[48] But as we showed in the previous section, an early romance is untenable based on the records now available.

On the minimalist end of the spectrum are those who question whether there was an engagement at all. Certainly, the lack of any mention of Moon in the extant Toy corpus is an obstacle, especially in the correspondence between Toy and Broadus in late 1881, when one might have expected Toy to confide in Broadus about an impending wedding. Thus, there remains the possibility that the engagement itself never happened. Catherine Allen suggests that T. P. Crawford is the one who "pretended to tattle to Tupper at the Foreign Mission Board that Lottie was going to Harvard. …he was trying to

---

[47] March 3, 1888, Harvard Biblical Club, vol. 1, Jan. 1881–May 1897, HUD 3211, Box 2, Records of the Harvard Biblical Club, HUA. On the Harvard Biblical Club, see chapter 6. While a student at SBTS, Lyon recorded in his diary that he had attended a Missionary Society meeting on New Year's Day 1879 in which a letter from "Miss Lottie Moon" was read. Lyon gave no indication that he knew of any relationship between Toy and Moon (Diary of David Lyon, January 1, 1879, HUA). Lyon's silence on the matter does not constitute evidence, but it does contribute to the developing picture.

[48] In addition to various popular denominational writings, Billy Hurt, whose unpublished SBTS dissertation represents the first Toy biography, also accepted Lawrence's account (with some hesitation).

taint Lottie's standing at home in the U.S."[49] Crawford may also have been the source for the engagement announcement in the *Western Recorder*: "Gossip. No doubt mongered by T. P. Crawford, native of Kentucky with a perpetual base there from which he could agitate."[50]

On the other hand, it is possible that the account of a broken engagement was embellished by "friends" of Lottie Moon who meant to bolster her reputation not tarnish it. Martha Crawford or even Henry Tupper might have encouraged the story of the engagement knowing nothing would ever come of it.[51] But for what purpose? Carol Vaughn Cross has speculated:

> An "official" romantic connection and *broken romance* of Moon to Toy was useful for two if not three reasons: 1) she had allegedly "rejected" him and his views (I don't think that it was true she rejected all of his views, although she didn't necessarily embrace all of them, either); 2) the story of a sacrificed romantic relationship for the cause of Christ/the FMB was too good not to tell and use for PR; and 3) it gave Moon an official hetero romance she otherwise *never* had.[52]

Speculations about Lottie Moon's sexual orientation (to use modern terminology) are not new. Irwin Hyatt raised the possibility in 1976:

> Anyone who wants to can find abundant atonement, and a certain amount of sex frustration, in the purplish prose of Una Lawrence's Lottie Moon. By reproducing an apparently unique "love letter" to a young female missionary, for instance—and by identifying it with the "tender, loving, confiding Lottie Moon whom few people ever knew"—she creates in a non-Southern Baptist mind the impression that Miss Moon's

---

[49] Email from Catherine B. Allen, January 19, 2018; quoted with permission. Allen goes on to observe, "Another later attempt was made by some of his [Crawford's] female apostles in Georgia to bring charges that Lottie was teaching contrary to orthodox beliefs. So, Crawford remained her de facto enemy to the end."

[50] Email from Allen.

[51] In either of these scenarios, the silence of C. H. Toy regarding the alleged engagement (about which he surely knew, given his continued contacts with the Baptist world through the early 1880s) would have been his greatest gift to Lottie Moon.

[52] Carol Vaughn Cross, email correspondence, June 12, 2018. Dr. Cross is author of "Missionary Returns and Cultural Conversions in Alabama and Shandong: The Latter Years of Madam Gao (Martha Foster Crawford)," in *North American Foreign Missions, 1810–1914: Theology, Theory, and Policy*, ed. Wilbert R. Shenk (Grand Rapids: Eerdmans, 2004), 243–60. Under the supervision of J. Wayne Flynt, she wrote her dissertation, "'Living in the Lives of Men': A Southern Baptist Woman's Missionary Journey from Alabama to Shandong, 1830–1909" (Ph.D. dissertation, University of Auburn, 1998).

"innermost feelings" were homosexual.[53]

The letter to which Hyatt refers is cited in Lawrence's biography of Lottie Moon. It reads in full:

> My own precious Fan,
> Many greetings have I met since landing in China and especially many most cordial and affectionate in Shantung, but none have sent such a glow of happiness as your dear letter, received at breakfast this morning. You brave, noble, unselfish darling! My trust in you has not failed. I relied implicitly upon your promise that whether I lived or died, you would push the work at Pingtu. Right nobly have you kept your word. It was our Lord's work, and you were only too glad and thankful to do it for his sake. Yet I cannot forget how you upheld my weary hands and cheered my sometimes almost fainting spirit during that first winter in Pingtu together. Do you wonder, then, my precious darling, that I turn to you with all and more than all the old time love and that if you are "homesick" for me, I am longing with intense desire to look upon your dear face again? In China, you are my dearest and you know that I do not speak lightly words of affection. When I truly love, as I love you, it is with my whole heart.
> Yes, come to me, dear child, in the early spring. I had thought of doing some much needed work in this region before going to Pingtu. You may help me in this and then in the summer I can go with you to Pingtu.
>   Lottie Moon
> Postscript. This is a love letter, so you must regard it as for yourself alone, for I am naturally very shy of expressing much of my own feelings to anyone.[54]

In an otherwise laudatory review of Hyatt's work on Moon, Alan Neely takes Hyatt to task for this reading of Moon: "It should be obvious to any reader that she [Lawrence] saw nothing inappropriate or sexually suggestive in the missive. The fact is—before our current preoccupation with peoples'

---

[53] Irwin T. Hyatt, *Our Ordered Lives Confess: Three Nineteenth-Century American Missionaries in East Shantung* (Cambridge, MA: Harvard University Press, 1976), 133.

[54] Quoted in Lawrence, *Lottie Moon*, 193–94. Fannie Knight joined the mission in 1889 and was the first missionary to China funded by the Christmas foreign missions offering, urged by Lottie Moon. In 1893/94, she joined T. P. Crawford's "Gospel Mission" movement; see Adrian J. Lamkin, "The Gospel Mission Movement within the Southern Baptist Convention" (Ph.D. dissertation, Southern Baptist Theological Seminary, Louisville, KY, 1979), 151–52.

sexual orientation—women and men often used sentimental and florid language in correspondence to express deep feelings of friendship and affection."[55] It is difficult not to read Moon's words through a post-Freudian psychosexual lens, but Neely is certainly correct that the language used between correspondents of the same sex in the nineteenth century could be much more intimate than today without any suggestion of a sexual relationship.[56] This point has been underscored by the groundbreaking work of Carroll Smith-Rosenberg, who has argued that historians might evaluate female friendships more effectively though a psychosocial methodology, that is, by looking at these friendships "as they existed in a larger world of social relations and social values."[57] Thus, it would be instructive to place correspondence such as that above between Moon and Knight within the web of female relationships that Lottie Moon experienced, with her mother, sisters Edmonia and Colie, classmates like Julia Toy (Johnson) and Sarah Ann Strickler (Fife), and mission colleagues Martha Crawford and Sally Holmes. If Lottie Moon were a kind of apprentice to the older Crawford, she served as a kind of mentor to the younger Knight, and such intimate language was not anomalous.

On the other hand, these female bonds, as Smith-Rosenberg notes, "were often physical as well as emotional. An undeniably romantic and even sensual note frequently marked female relationships."[58] Moon's postscript to

---

[55] Neely, "Saints Who Sometimes Were," 448. Obviously, Lawrence saw no impropriety in the letter; it was beyond the realm of what was possible for Lawrence to imagine at the time.

[56] One need only think of H. A. Tupper's declaration to Moon that he loved Toy "with the love of a woman" (H. A. Tupper to Lottie Moon, July 13, 1881). Neely ("Saints Who Sometimes Were," 455) cites the example of the relationship between missionary Jessie Ankeny and her Chinese teacher Ding ("Eleanor") Miduang, as an example of an intimate relationship without "any sexual feelings."

[57] Carroll Smith-Rosenberg, "The Female World of Love and Ritual: Relations between Women in Nineteenth-Century America," *Signs* 1 (1975): 1–29; here 2–3. Smith-Rosenberg points out that the typical psychosexual reading of these same-sex friendships presumes a kind of psychopathology, e.g., attempting to explain the "abnormalities" of those relationships. Smith-Rosenberg's work was the subject of a retrospective review, "Women's History in the New Millennium: Carroll Smith-Rosenberg's 'The Female World of Love and Ritual' after Twenty-Five Years," in the *Journal of Women's History* 12/3 (2000): 6–248. See also Sharon Marcus, *Between Women: Friendship, Desire, and Marriage in Victorian England* (Princeton: Princeton University Press, 2007), who described the complexities of female friendships in the nineteenth century, especially in Victorian England. I am grateful to Dr. Betsy Flowers for bringing these sources to my attention.

[58] Smith-Rosenberg, "Love and Ritual," 24. The author of the book from which Neely takes his example of female friendship is not quite as definitive as Neely in describing the "non-sexual" nature of the relationship: "Ankeny's frequent letters home documented the attentiveness, antics, and charm of her teacher, …and described a unique relationship

Knight certainly moves in this direction.[59] Furthermore, it was in the mid-nineteenth century that interest in same-sex expression began to capture the imagination and attention in both academic and more popular venues. Nineteenth-century "sexologists" coined the term "inverted" women to describe persons with "male souls in female bodies" who demonstrated masculine characteristics and social behaviors, at times including, but not limited to, physical expressions of affection for the same sex.[60] Whether or not Lottie Moon was such an "inverted" woman (to use the terminology of the day) who manifested traditionally masculine attributes, the story of a broken engagement, even with a religious heretic, was a useful tool to the SBC establishment having to address concerns that emerged concerning its single female missionaries, especially those like Lottie Moon who aggressively advocated for more leadership roles for women in foreign missionary service.[61] The sacrifice of romantic love for religious vocation was a crucial element in the SBC myth-making.

Recently, Lottie Moon scholars, skeptical of the 1861 proposal, have adopted a mediating position between maximalist and minimalist perspectives, accepting the purported broken engagement of 1879–1882. There is certainly more evidence of contact between Crawford Toy and Lottie Moon, especially in the correspondence between Moon and Tupper at this time and in subsequent collective memories among Toy's family. And there is, of course, the published engagement announcement in the *Western Recorder*.[62] For those who do accept the notion of a broken engagement, there remains the question as to why. Again, Lawrence's view that Lottie Moon broke the engagement because of theological differences with the more liberal Toy has

---

that approximated the dynamics of a fond turn-of-the-century marriage" (Jane Hunter, *Gospel of Gentility: American Women Missionaries in Turn-of-the-Century China* [New Haven, CT: Yale University Press, 1984], 198.

[59] In 1897, Fannie Knight married fellow "Gospel Mission" missionary, W. D. King, and, tragically, died in childbirth; email correspondence with Catherine Allen, August 3, 2018; Lamkin, "Gospel Mission," 164.

[60] This view was developed by Richard von Krafft-Ebing and Karl Heinrich Ulrichs in the 1860s; see Christine Lafazanos, "The Female Sexual Invert: A Threat to Sexologists' World View," *Footnotes* 1 (2006): 71–77; George Chauncey, Jr., "From Sexual Inversion to Homosexuality: The Changing Medical Conceptualization of Female 'Deviance,'" in *Passion and Power*, ed. Kathy Peiss and Christina Simmons (Philadelphia: Temple University, 1989). I am grateful to Dr. Carol Vaughn Cross for pointing me in the direction of the nineteenth-century discussions regarding "inverted" women.

[61] Sullivan, *Lottie Moon*, 58–60.

[62] It is conceivable that Moon thought, based on her correspondence with Toy and anxious to escape the ever-worsening conditions of the China mission, that an engagement/marriage proposal from Toy was imminent when Toy himself entertained no such notion.

persisted over time, especially among more conservative interpreters.[63] Available evidence, however, points in another direction. The announced engagement occurred more than three years after Toy's resignation. By then, Lottie Moon would have been familiar with the reasons for the resignation. She was also supportive of the appointment of Bell and Stout as missionaries, even though the Foreign Mission Board had rejected them on the grounds that their views of inspiration resembled those of their teacher, C. H. Toy. Whatever caused the broken engagement in 1882, theological differences would not seem to be on the list of most likely reasons.

More reasonable is the proposal that the determining factor was Moon's own sense of calling to the mission field. In October 1881, Lottie Moon was distressed by the news that no new missionary appointments were on the horizon, and, with the retirement of Sally Holmes and the imminent return of Martha Crawford to the States in December 1881, she faced the prospects of serving alone with T. P. Crawford for the foreseeable future. The possibility of joining Toy in Cambridge, either as his replacement or associate (T. P. Crawford) or as his wife (Martha Crawford) must have appealed to her. Remaining in the mission until spring gave her time to reflect and adjust to her new reality. Returning to the States in order to join Toy would mean abandoning her post in China; that may simply have been a sacrifice she was unwilling to make, regardless of C. H. Toy's theology of Scripture.[64] Her early biographer reported that "when asked about her romantic attachments, she responded that she had once been forced to make a choice between God and love, and she had chosen God."[65] Whatever the nature of love shared between Toy and Moon, in this mediating view, Moon did, indeed, choose God.

Lottie Moon has had profound influence on the Southern Baptist collective psyche. As Hyatt observed:

> Miss Moon carries gracefully a load of baggage that has lain ecumenically in almost every white southern mind. Born to a "small empire of beauty and culture," she was dispossessed by outside forces and left to shift for

---

[63] See Mohler and Criswell in chapter 1; also see the more cautious Jerry Rankin, *A Journey of Faith and Sacrifice: Retracing the Steps of Lottie Moon* (Birmingham, AL; New Hope, 1996), 44–45.

[64] Sullivan (*Lottie Moon*, 56) seems to favor this view. Catherine B. Allen, *Lottie Moon* biographer, surmised: "I can imagine that there probably were times when Lottie might have fanaticized about Toy; he had been her much-admired professor and sometime correspondent. There would have been an intellectual affinity. However, calling and work came first with her. I don't think she had any theological argument with him. She defended mission appointees like Stout, Bell, Halcomb and perhaps other missionaries who liked Toy" (email from Catherine B. Allen, January 19, 2018; quoted with permission).

[65] Lawrence, *Lottie Moon*, 96.

herself. Her only chance for happy normality (Professor Toy) would have required acceptance of disquieting ideas, plus personal alienation from the people who meant most to her. Taking up her cross of loneliness, she thus bore faithful witness to correct ideas until she died, a sacrifice to more causes than the average reader can comfortably handle. The Lottie Moon story is very much the whole white south's traditional story of itself—full of grace, good intentions, and tragic luck, and somehow a little closer to God. One further notes that the years of greatest expansion in the Lottie Moon business—the fabulous fifties and sixties, with all their promoting of Miss Moon the southern lady—were also years of increasing civil rights activism, white resistance, and heightened (in some ways) sectional awareness in the south.[66]

Unless and until more documentation is forthcoming, we shall never know the reasons the 1882 engagement between Crawford Toy and Lottie Moon was broken or if there were ever even an engagement to begin with. If there were some kind of romantic involvement, it would seem to have been very much one-sided. Even so, the Lottie Moon story does not need Crawford Toy. Even without the story of a failed romance to underscore Lottie Moon's devotion to her vocation, her essential biography remains a remarkable and influential chapter in the history of missions,[67] and however important the supposed romantic relationship may have been to the subsequent

---

[66] Hyatt, *Our Ordered Lives*, 132. On the various ways the Lottie Moon story has been utilized, see Elizabeth Flowers, "The Contested Legacy of Lottie Moon: Southern Baptists, Women, and Partisan Protestantism," *Fides et Historia* 43/1 (2011): 15–40.

[67] In fact, the Lottie Mon model provided the model for future SBC missions. Up until the conservative takeover of the Southern Baptist Convention in the 1980s, one-third of all SBC foreign missionaries were single women. As Catherine Allen remarked,

In the same period, far more than half of all the money was controlled exclusively by the Woman's Missionary Union. Not only was this female-based system of missions protective of (if not prejudiced in favor of) women missionaries derived from the Lottie Moon model, but there was also a definite strategic intention: to reach women with the gospel within the cultural isolation that was (and is) reality for many "unreached" women in cultures where the dominant religion is decidedly anti-female. If men were also reached along the way, fine. But women could not be overlooked. In Lottie's time, and under her pen and under the editorship of her Presbyterian friend Anna Safford, the "Woman's Mission to Woman" concept was framed and carried out with enormous success. There is a vast body of literature outside the SBC that documents and supports this development, and most of it inevitably gets around to laud for Lottie Moon—without any consideration at all of Crawford Howell Toy. (January 19, 2018, email.)

"Lottie Moon business," that relationship plays no role whatsoever in any of the documents available for reconstructing the life and times of Crawford Howell Toy.[68]

---

[68] It remains unclear how much weight to give to the Toy family testimony regarding a Toy-Moon engagement. For example, Mrs. X. O. Steele, great-niece of Crawford Toy, wrote, "I never heard any doubt expressed that Dr. Crawford Toy was the young man to whom Miss Moon was engaged. There definitely was an engagement prior to the Civil War. I had never heard of a second engagement" (Julia Frances Lipsey Steele to Catherine Allen, November 10, 1978, LM-Toy File, WMU Archives). If the evidence garnered here has established anything, it is that an antebellum Toy-Moon engagement, the very thing Mrs. Steele was certain of, was highly improbable (even Lawrence does not claim an engagement before the Civil War, only a rejected proposal).

APPENDIX 1

Crawford Toy's "Sketch of My Religious Life"

Sketch of My Religious Life

My paternal ancestors were Swedish and Scotch. I have heard of not more than one individual of the name, (Toy,) in the U.S., who was not connected immediately with our family. My maternal ancestors, (Rogers,) were English. Both these families were, for the most part, Methodist. My father's mother, (a Morton,) was, however, Baptist, and he was educated in that faith. My parents are both natives of the city of Norfolk, in Virginia, and there I was born, March 23d, 1836, and named, after Rev. Dr. Howell, who married my father's sister, Crawford Howell.

My boyhood passed quietly. A trip to Nashville, when I was about 3 years old, and a sojourn there of a year, was the event of that period of my life. I grew up, as most town boys do, learnt to read early, when I was about 4 years old, and was mostly occupied with books. All the while my religious education was carefully attended to. My father's ideas of observance of the Sabbath, and similar things, were string. I was never allowed to go to the circus or theatre, and was expected to be regular in attendance at the Sunday School. Sunday afternoon, just after dinner, we children used to recite a lesson to my father, from a Scripton Question Book, or from the Bible, or Biblical Antiquities, or with the youngest, he would read or tell them Scripture stories, on which he would afterwards question them. This Sunday afternoon exercise, kept up for many years, and graduated to our capacity, we found and find very profitable. It not only kept us from idleness between dinner and the prayer meeting, but stored our minds with knowledge of Bible-facts and -doctrines. I learnt many texts and passages of Scripture, came to be familiar with the order of books, and experience now the advantage of that training.

I had from time to time, many religious impressions, as every religiously educated boy must have. At one time, when I was 11 or 12 years old, I set myself seriously to mend my ways. I retired for prayer and reading the Bible. I read diligently a little book called "Guide to the Saviour." I was anxious to be good, but my evil temper would triumph over my good resolutions, fortified, though these were, by reading and prayer, and I gave up the attempt.

My parents were members of the 'Cumberland St Church.' In May, 1848, a member of the brethren, deeming it advisable to establish a new interest, formed the church now called 'The Freemason St Church,' and at first occupied the old Oddfellows' Hall. Bro. J. B. Taylor preached for them some months. In June of that year, Rev. T. G. Jones was elected pastor and agreed to take charge of the church in the following Fall. Meantime, bro. A. B. Cabaniss, then a theological student, now a missionary to China, supplied the pulpit, and lived in my father's house. In the Fall, Mr. Jones came, and the Church invited bro. J. S. Reynoldson, widely known and loved as a fervent and efficient evangelist, to assist brother J. in conducting a series of meetings. During the meeting I became interested, went forward and asked the prayer of the church, and finally professed conversion, more, however, by Mr. R's persuasion than by my own conviction. My feelings had not been deeply stirred, as, indeed, my temperament, did not admit. It was, throughout, conviction of duty that urged me on. As I had no overpowering sense of sin, so there was no burst of light and joy. I cannot well describe my state of mind at the time. I wish I could recall it. But, I took stand as a professor of religion— took part in prayer meeting, was regular in my devotions, etc., but did not offer myself for baptism. Gradually my interest abated, my hope, never very bright, grew less and less, till a year or so from my profession, I had a conversation with Mr. Jones, and we agreed that it would not be well for me to ask for baptism. After this, I gave up my religious profession. Looking back now, I can see that I acted precipitately in the first case; I was not sufficiently cared for. But I do not know whether my conversion was real or not. I fell into sin afterwards, but so have many Christians. I lost sight of Christ, and was utterly without religious hope, or enjoyment. I continued to be outwardly respectful to religion, and even devout. I was always a regular attendant on the prayermeetings of the church, where my father commonly led, and I joined in the hymns with as much zeal as anyone. I was not happy. My conscience continually urged on me the claims of religion, and I quaked inwardly at many a sermon, and hoped vaguely that I should be a Christian at some time. So, till I went to college, October 1852. I was nothing but a boy, had never been away from home, and was thrown alone into the temptations of a great university. It was the University of Va to which I went. But here my previous education, which had provided me with fixed principles, and my temperament, which was not excitable, proved, under Providence, my safeguard. At college I was a regular in the discharge of religious duties, went to church, prayermeeting, and S. School, and towards the close of the session, I again experienced a hope that my sin was forgiven. But this lasted for a short while only. It was not till the next session that I came to have a permanent religious hope. About April, 1854, there commenced a season of revival in college. It was very quiet. There were sermons in the Chapel Sunday, and part of the time, special meetings in the Presbyterian and Baptist Churches in Charlottesville, about a mile from which the University is situated. Dr. Hoge and others preached in the former, and Dr. Jeter and Cumberland George in the latter. The students held quiet prayermeetings among themselves, and Dr. Rice, of the Presbyterian Ch. did much good by the conversations which he held with them in private. Many interesting cases of conversion occurred. After much doubt and trouble, I offered myself to the ch in Charlottesville for baptism, and was received. After this, for months, I was subject to the most harassing doubts. Bro. J. A. Broadus was my advisor and guide throughout this period. I often wished myself out of the church, felt that I was acting the hypocrite, and had little peace of mind. By bro. B's advice, I retained my place as a church-member. In a case of alternating doubt and hope, when one is conscious of sincerity of intention, it is no hypocrisy to stand before the world a professed Christian. For a long time every public act that involved a profession of religion cut like a dagger into my soul. But gradually my faith and hope became steadier. I took part in the public worship more freely. And I have been enabled to maintain my profession ever since, often with much trembling, sometimes almost in despair, but never for a long time unable to look to Christ as my salvation. Several times the subject of the ministry was brought specially to my attention, and I gave it thought and prayed in relation to it. After years of reflection I came to the conclusion, and my friends on whose judgment I most relied, concurred with me, that I was not adapted to the work. My temperament, habits of thought and study, and oratory, (or lack of oratory,) seemed to promise rather a life of study and instruction. Accordingly I had determined to go to Europe in the summer of 1859, and spend some years there in preparation for teaching Languages, and especially the Sanscrit, which I wished to have the satisfaction of introducing into my native State. I looked forward to the trip with great delight. The treasures of art, architecture, Painting and Music, would open to me a world of enjoyment. The historical attractions, the scenery, and everything that the Old World offers to youthful imagination, often passed before me. But this was not to be. My plans were completely changed by a missionary Sermon preached by bro. John A. Broadus, in the regular course of his ministry, about February, 1859. The possibility of my being a missionary first presented itself to me. Before I had thought of it, but very vaguely, and very far off. Now it took hold on me. I reflected on it for months, consulted with my friends, and finally offered myself to the Board as missionary to Japan, or wherever else they should think expedient. I did not at first think of preaching. It was missionary work and not properly preaching that I felt called to. But it was necessary to have a better acquaintance with the Bible than I possessed. I must be acquainted with that system of truth which I was to teach to the heathen. I embraced the opportunity afforded by the opening of the So. Bapt. Theolog. Seminary. And it seemed proper that I should go out as an ordained minister of the gospel. So I found myself, what I had not looked to for a long time, a student of Theology, and endeavoring to preach. I go out now to make a brief trial, and then to depart to my life work.

C. H. Toy
So. Bapt. Theolog. Sem.
Greenville, So. Ca.
May 24th, 1860

[Transcribed by Jason Fowler on January 27, 2003, from a handwritten document in a collection of T. T. Eaton's papers in the archives of the Southern Baptist Theological Seminary.[1] This document appears to be in Toy's own hand. The document may have been a prerequisite to his ordination or his examination by the Foreign Mission Board. How Eaton obtained it is unknown.]

[1] Fowler's transcription has been corrected in comparison with the handwritten manuscript. Most of the corrections are simple matters of preserving abbreviations in the ms, which Fowler, for the sake of clarity, spelled out. The abbreviations, however, are clear enough as they stand. Gratitude is expressed to Dr. Adam Winter, SBTS Archivist, for permission to reproduce here this previously unpublished document.

APPENDIX 2

CRAWFORD TOY'S LETTER OF RESIGNATION

To the Board of Trustees of the Southern Baptist Theological Seminary,
Dear brethren:

It having lately become apparent to me that my views of Inspiration differ considerably from those of the body of my brethren, I ask leave to lay my opinions on that subject before you and submit them to your judgement.

At the outset I may say that I fully accept the first article of the Fundamental Principles of the Seminary: "The Scriptures of the Old and New Testaments were given by the inspiration of God, and are the only sufficient, certain, and authoritative rule of all saving knowledge and obedience", and that I have always taught and now do teach in accordance with and not contrary to it.

It is in the details of the subject that my divergence from the prevailing view in the Denomination occurs. This divergence has gradually increased in connection to my studies, from year to year till it has become perceptible to myself and to others.

In looking for light on Inspiration, my resort has been and is to the Scriptures themselves alone, and I rest myself wholly on their testimony. It seems to me that while they declare the *fact* of divine inspiration they say nothing of the *manner* of its action: we are told that men spake from God, borne along by the Holy Ghost, and that all Scripture is given by inspiration of God, and is profitable for doctrine, for reproof, for correction, for instruction in righteousness, that the man of God may be complete, thoroughly furnished for every good work. The object of the Scriptures is here said to be an ethical, spiritual one--they were given man for his guidance and edification in religion, as our Lord also says: Sanctify them in truth: Thy word is truth.

As nothing is said of the mode of operation of the divine Spirit, of the manner in which the divine saving truth is impressed on the mind, of the relation of the divine influence to the ordinary workings of the human intellect, we must as to these points consult the books of the Bible themselves and examine the facts. Against facts no theory can stand, and I prefer therefore to have no theory, but to submit myself to the actual words of Holy Scripture.

As the result of my examination I believe that the Bible is wholly divine and wholly human. The Scripture is the truth of God communicated by Him to the human soul, appropriated by it and given out with free human energy as the sincere, real conviction of the soul. To undertake to say a priori what must be the outward form of God's revelation of himself to man, seems to me presumptuous. If rationalism be the decision of religious questions by human reason, then it appears to me rationalistic to say that a divine revelation must conform to certain outward conditions, to insist, for example, that it must be written in a certain style, or that it must teach certain things in Geography or Astronomy or similar matters.

I hold all a priori reasoning here to be out of place, and all theories based on it to be worthless. Such procedure seems to me to be out of keeping with the simple, reverent spirit appropriate to him who comes to search into the truth of God.

For this reason, I am forced to disregard the theories of some pious men as Fichte and Wordsworth, who have proceeded in this a priori way, and to keep myself to the facts given in the Bible itself.

These facts make on me the impression that the Scripture-writers are men who have received messages from God and utter them under purely free human conditions. The inspired man speaks his own language, not another man's, and writes under the conditions of his own age, not under those of some other age. His personality, his individuality has the freest play, all under the control of the guiding divine spirit. In illustration of what I mean, I refer to 1 Cor. 1:14-15, where Paul first says he had baptized nobody at Corinth but Crispus and Gaius, then a while after, remembering himself adds that he had also baptized the household of Stephanus, and finally coming to doubt his memory, declares that he doesn't know whether he had baptized any other person. Here, if we indulge in arithmetical criticism, is a flat contradiction; but if we see simply the free play of the writer's mind, under the ordinary conditions of human thought, there is no difficulty. And if anyone asks me how this perfectly free thought consists with divine guidance, I answer that I can tell no more than how supernatural, divine power co-exists with free action of the soul in conversion, or how I exist at all or how, in general, the finite and the infinite can co-exist.

I find that the geography, astronomy, and other physical science of the Sacred Writers was that of their times. It is not that of our times—it is not that which seems to us correct. But it has nothing to do with their message of religious truth from God. I do not feel authorized to impose on divine revelation the condition that it shall accord with modern geography and geology, nor to say that I will not accept it except on this condition. It seems to me that geography has nothing to do with religion. The message is not less divine to me because it is given in Hebrew and not in English, or because it is set in the framework of a primitive and incorrect geology. When the Psalmist says (Ps. 121:6): "The sun shall not smite thee by day, nor the moon by night", it does not matter to me whether the moon is injurious or not at night, for the obvious religious thought is independent of this outward form.

Or, when discrepancies or inaccuracies occur in historical narrative, this does not even invalidate the documents as historical records, much less does it affect them as expressions of religious truths. I am slow to admit discrepancies and inaccuracies; but if they show themselves, I refer them to the human conditions of the writer, believing that his merely intellectual status, the mere amount of information possessed by him does not affect his spiritual relation to God, or the validity of his message as spiritual truth. If our heavenly Father sends a message by the stammering tongue of a man, I will not reject the message because of the stammering.

My position is the same when I find political details have not fallen out in accordance with the form in which the prophets clothe their religious exhortations. If Hosea looked for captivity of Ephraim in Egypt (Hos. 9:3), or Isaiah for political friendship between Assyria, Egypt, and Israel (Isa. 19:23-25), that is the mere clothing of their real thought. The prophet uttered everlasting truths which are embodied and fulfilled in Jesus Christ, and with which the geographical and political details have no essential connection. To them Israel is the centre and hope of the world, and the prospective possessor of all prosperity; and the spiritual gist of their teachings has been perpetuated in Christ, while the merely outward has passed away.

The prophets and priests were not only preachers of religion, but writers of religious history. The early history of Israel was for a long time not committed to writing, but handed down by oral tradition, under which process it was subject to a more or less free expansion. In this expanded form it was received at a comparatively late time by the Prophets and Priests, who put it into shape, and made it the vehicle of religious truth. All historical writing in Israel that has come down to us was of the nature of a sermon; it was composed not so much for the sake of facts but for the lessons they taught. The idea of scientific history did not then exist – it was all pragmatic, that is, written for the purpose of inculcating a truth. The traditional history is treated by the pious of Israel in the spirit of profound trust in God and regard for his law. I can no more demand historical science in the Scriptures than in geological science. I regard them both as being outside the domain of religion.

The same thing I hold in respect to the Levitical law, which grew up, as it seems to me, from generation to generation on a Mosaic basis, and could thus be called Mosaic.

In one word, I regard the Old Testament as the record of the whole circle of the experiences of Israel, the people whom God chose to be, the depository of his truth, all whose life he so guided as to bring out of its lessons for men's instruction, which he then caused to be written down for preservation. The nation lived out its life in a free, human way, yet under divine guidance, and its Prophets, Priests, and Psalmists recorded this spiritual, religious history under the condition of their times. The divine truth is presented in a framework of relatively unessential things, as Christ in his Parables introduced accessories merely for the purpose of bringing out a principle, so that the Parable of the Ten Virgins, for example, may properly be said to be the framework or vehicle of religious truth. As a whole, the Parable may in a sense be called a religious teaching, but, speaking more precisely, we should say that a part of it is such teaching, or that the teaching is contained in it.

What I have said of the outward form of the Old Testament applies, as I think, to the outward form of the New Testament. I will not lightly see a historical or other inaccuracy in the Gospels or the Acts; but if I find such, they do not for me affect the divine teaching of these books. The centre of the New Testament is Christ himself. Salvation is in Him, and a historical error cannot affect the fact of his existence and his teachings. The Apostles wrote out of their personal convictions of the reality of the truth of Christ. If Paul makes a slip of memory, as in the case above cited, that cannot affect his spiritual relation to Christ and to the Father, nor detract from his power as an inspired man. If his numerical statements do not always agree with those of the Old Testament (as in Gal. 3:17 compared with Ex. 12:40), that seems to me a matter of no consequence. If the New Testament writers sometimes quote the Old Testament in the Greek Version, which does not correctly render the Hebrew (as in Heb. 10:5 quoted from Ps. 40:6), that does not affect the main thought or the religious teaching. And it may be that in some cases my principles of exegesis lead me to a different interpretation of the Old Testament passage from that which I find of some New Testament writer (as in Ps. 40:6 above mentioned); but this again I look on as an incidental thing of which the true religious teaching is independent. [See insert below.] In these men the spirit of God dwelt, and out of their writings comes a divine power; recognizing in them a divine element, I cannot reject it because of what seems to me outward or non-spiritual limitation. I do not condition divine action, but accept it in the form in which I find it.

As to criticism (questions of date and authorship) and exegesis, these stand by themselves, and have nothing to do with Inspiration. The prophecy in Isa. 40-66 is not less inspired if it be assigned to the period of the Babylonian Exile and the "Servant of Jehovah" be regarded as referring primarily to Israel. These are questions of interpretation and historical research in which, as it seems to me, the largest liberty must be allowed. If some of the Psalms should be put in the Maccabean Period (B.C. 160), this is no reason for doubting their inspiration. God could act as easily on men in the year B.C. 160 as in B.C. 400 or B.C. 700.

It is proper to add that the above statement of my views of Inspiration is the fullest that I have ever expressed. Some things I have not thought it expedient to state to my classes in the Seminary. At the same time I regard these views as helpful for Bible-study; if at first they seem strange, I am convinced that they will appear more natural with further strict study of the text.

I beg leave to repeat that I am guided wholly by what seems to me the correct interpretation of the Scriptures themselves. If an error in my interpretation is pointed out, I shall straightaway give it up. I cannot accept a priori reasoning, but I stake everything on the words of the Bible. And this course I believe to be for the furtherance of the truth of God.

And now in conclusion I wish to say distinctly and strongly that I consider the view above given to be not only lawful for me to teach as Professor in the Seminary, but one that will bring aid and firm standing-ground to many a perplexed mind, and establish the truth of God on a surer foundation.

But, that I may relieve the Board of all embarrassment in the matter, I respectfully tender my resignation as Professor in the Southern Bapt. Theological Seminary.

Respectfully submitted,

May, 1879.   C. H. Toy

[Insert on p. 6 of Manuscript]

I should add that in the majority of cases I hold that the New Testament quotations correctly represent the sense of the Old Testament, and that there is always a true spiritual feeling controlling them. I think that Peter's discourse in Acts 2nd gives the true spiritual sense of the passage in Joel, and so many references of the Old Testament passages to Christ throughout the New Testament. It ought also to be noticed that the ancient ideas of quotations were different from ours. Ancient writers cite in a general way from memory for illustration, and permit themselves without remark such alterations as a modern writer would think it necessary to call attention to. This is to be regarded as a difference of habit arising from the difference of the times. The freeness of quotation of the Scripture-writers does not, for example, affect their general honesty and truthfulness, nor their spiritual train of thought, nor their spiritual authority. It is only a human condition of the divine truth they utter.[1]

---

[1] Original in SBTS Archives.

APPENDIX 3

POETRY OF CRAWFORD TOY AND DAVID LYON

C. H. Toy often celebrated Lyon's birthday by penning poems in his honor. In the 1898 ephemera of Lyon's diary is this poem by Toy:

> To D. G. Lyon on his birthday, May 24, 1898
> Down time's vista as I gaze
> All my senses in a maze
> Visions set my soul ablaze.
> In a might field of green
> Deep inset in dazzling sheen
> Gorgeous buildings meet my een.
> Oriental splendors rise
> Radiant to the arching skies
> Destined for the truly wise
> On floors and walls are tablets rare,
> Nimrod and Sargon – all are there –
> Long line of worthy names and fair.
> Yours be the lot to realize
> On some new birthday this grand prize –
> No smaller joy before you lies.
>
> CHT

The next year, Toy penned another poem in honor of Lyon's birthday and the prospects for the Semitic Museum that the new connections to Jacob Schiff promised:

> A Wish
> May '88 and '89
> Bring all these things to thee and thine!
> May Semitic study flourish
> And fair Harvard bravely nourish
> Love of the cuneiform—
> Crowds of eager students storm
> The golden gates of Babylon!

May some mighty cultural surge
Schiff's eyes from film premier purge
And soon before your gladdened eye
A fair museum quickly rise,
Well stocked with tablets, seals and gems,
Manuscripts and books of items
And all material archaeologic
To suit the student Semitologic.

And may the life at home be bright
With study and all other delight.
When the hurly-burly done
And the year is over and gone
May you begin the long vacation
with a fanciful inspiration!
CH Toy

To D.G. Lyon
May 24, 1889
And again in the ephemera to the 1912 diary:

To D.G. Lyon, on his birthday, May 24, 1912
The years roll on apace,
Hither and thither we're burled,
New tasks are set us in the race
To keep up with the world.
But nor change of place nor of Task
Can change the constant mind
Content to do and only ask
That nobler it can find.
May coming days bring fresh delight,
Fulness of love and peace,
Spirit to see and seize the night,
And joy without success(?)!
CHT

Incidentally, Toy was not the only one who had fancied himself something of a poet. David Lyon penned a poem for Schiff in honor of Schiff's seventieth birthday on January 10, 1917.[1] There are three drafts of the poem in Lyon's papers.[2] The final (and much shorter) version (which was submitted to the *New York Times*) reads:

> To Jacob Henry Schiff
> January 10, 1917
> I
> The days of our years are threescore years and ten, Ps 90:10
> They shall still bring forth fruit in old age, Ps 92:14
> "Three score and ten," the plaintive strain
> Sung by the bard of old
> Perchance fourscore, of labor full
> And sorrow manifold.
>
> Is this the sum of life? Then why
> Pursue the joyless tale?
> Bring down the curtains, quench the lights,
> And let the night prevail.
>
> II
> Another bard in happier mood,
> With hope dispels our fears:
> He sings of trees that bring forth fruit
> Despite the rolling years.
>
> What though the eye grow dim, the hand
> Here cunning less employ,
> The frame be bowed! The heart may still
> Exult in hope and joy.
>
> III
> Age measures life with eyes serene,
> With judgment calm and true,
> Casts lower hopes and aims aside,
> The noblest to pursue.
>
> With age comes wisdom, strength and poise

---

[1] Crawford Toy also reported that David Lyon had written a poem in honor of President Charles Eliot's birthday in 1900. Lyon had arranged for the *Crimson* to print the poem and tributes to Eliot by three others (Toy Diary, March 20, 1900, HUA).

[2] HUG 1541, Papers of David Gordon Lyon, Box 3, Diary Ephemera, 1917.

Beyond the ken of youth,
With love of justice, right, and peace,
And deeper love of truth.

IV
The man who threescore years and ten
Has bravely borne his part
In great affairs and bear it still,
With steady hand and heart,

Whose quiet mien, and earnest way,
Sagacious, tranquil mind
Accord so well with heart intent
To serve and bless mankind,--

To him how many hearts today
Send greetings of good cheer,
With wishes for a life serene
Through many a coming year.
David G. Lyon
Cambridge, Mass

David Lyon's love of poetry apparently passed to his son, David Jr. Several poems by the young Lyon are preserved in the diary ephemera. Among them are these two written when David Jr. was about ten years old:[3]

A Child's Own Prayer—D.G.L. Jr.
Oh Lord we thank Thee this day,
For all the kind things Thou hast done for us,
We ask of Thee O Lord one blessing,
And that is to make us good, kind, and useful to other people,
We also pray that Thou wilt bless the poor, the sick, and the sinful,
For they need help.
May the grace of our Lord Jesus Christ be with us all. Amen
Ca. Feb 20, 1922

The Moon
Slowly the dusk is settling down,
Softly, softly over the town,

---

[3] HUG 1541, Box 3.

And just as the day fades into
the night,
Far off in the east appears
Something bright.
'Tis the moon, the moon of the
Skies,
Yes far beyond me the great
moon lies.
Beautiful moon, silvery moon,
Out of the firmament thou was
Hewn,
God set a-whirling thy silver
Tinged ball,
He was thy maker, and He made all.
David G. Lyon, Jr.
March 26, 1922

APPENDIX 4

CRAWFORD TOY FESTSCHRIFT

---

[1] This is the original table of contents from the Crawford Howell Toy Festschrift compiled and edited by] David Lyon and George Foot Moore (*Studies in the History of Religions* [New York: The Macmillan Company, 1912]).

BIBLIOGRAPHY

ARCHIVAL MATERIAL (unpublished materials, with abbreviations)

ABHS: American Baptist Historical Society, Atlanta, GA

AHTL HDS: Andover-Harvard Theological Library, Harvard Divinity School, Cambridge, MA

AJA: American Jewish Archives, Cincinnati, OH

ANTS: Andover Newton Theological School, Newton, MA

ASC, SBTS: Archives and Special Collections, James P. Boyce Centennial Library, The Southern Baptist Theological Seminary, Louisville, KY

HL: Houghton Library, Harvard University, Cambridge, MA

HUA: Harvard University Archives

HUSMA: Harvard University Semitic Museum Archives, Cambridge, MA

JMLA: Jenkins Memorial Library and Archives, International Mission Board, Richmond, VA

L-S-C, SCL: Papers of the Families, South Carolina Library, University of South Carolina

OCBCA: Old Cambridge Baptist Church Archives, Cambridge, MA

Presidential Paper Microfilm, Woodrow Wilson Papers, 540 Reels, O'Neill Library, Boston College, Boston MA

SBHLA: Southern Baptist Historical Library and Archives, Nashville, TN

SCUVA: Special Collections, University of Virginia Library, Charlottesville, VA

Sargeant Memorial Collection, Norfolk Public Library, Norfolk, VA

VBHS: Virginia Baptist Historical Society, Richmond, VA

WMU Archives Woman's Missionary Union Archives, Birmingham, AL

CITED NEWSPAPERS AND DENOMINATIONAL PAPERS

Baptist Battle Flag
Baptist Courier
Baptist Immediate Union Quarterly
Biblical Recorder
The Baptist Reflector
Cambridge Chronicle
Cambridge Tribune
The Christian Index
Christian Intelligencer
Daily Dispatch (Richmond, VA)
Harvard Crimson
The Journal and the Messenger
Religious Herald
Texas Baptist Herald
The Watchman
The Western Recorder

PUBLISHED WORKS OF CRAWFORD HOWELL TOY
Books (and Reviews)
1869. *The Claims of Biblical Interpretation on Baptists*. New York: Lange & Hillman.
1882. *The History of the Religion of Israel: An Old Testament Primer*. Boston: Unitarian
Sunday School Society. Reviewed in *The Hebrew Student* 2 (1883): 328–29.
1884. *Quotations in the New Testament*. New York: Charles Scribner's Sons. Reviewed in:
Christian Union, May 28, 1885, 21.
The Expositor 3/2 (1885): 142–48 (Warfield).
New York Evangelist, March 20, 1884, 1.
Unity: Freedom, Fellowship and Character in Religion 11 (1884): 74 (G.L.C.).
Zion's Herald, March 5, 1884, 74.
1890. *Judaism and Christianity: A Sketch of the Progress of Thought from Old Testament to
New Testament*. Boston: Little, Brown, and Company. Reviewed in:
The Andover Review 16 (1891): 311–14 (Smith).
The Critic: A Weekly Review of Literature and the Arts, n.d.
Magazine of Christian Literature (May 1891): 116–17 (Moore).
The Monist 2 (1891): 123–24.
The Old and New Testament Student 12 (1891): 367–73 (Lyon).
The Unitarian Review 35 (April 1891): 325.
1899a. *The Book of the Prophet Ezekiel: A New English Translation, with Explanatory Notes*.
Edited by Paul Haupt. Polychrome Edition. New York: Dodd, Mead, Co. Re-
viewed in:
Expository Times 11 (1900): 225 (Tasker).
London Quarterly Review (1900): 358–59 (Tasker).
Orientalistische Litteratur-Zeitung 12 (1900): 455–56 (Giesebrecht).
1899b. *A Critical and Exegetical Commentary on the Book Proverbs*. ICC. New York:
Charles Scribner's Sons. Reviewed in:
The American Journal of Theology 4/4 (1900): 825–28 (Peters).
The Athenaeum, May 12, 1900, 589.
The Biblical World 16/5 (1900): 379–81 (McCurdy).
The Bookman (January 1900): 124.
The Methodist Review 49 (1900): 462–63.
Theologische Literaturzeitung 11 (1901): 284–87 (Beer).
1913. *Introduction to the History of Religions*. Edited by Jastrow Morris, Jr. Vol. 4. Hand-
books on the History of Religions Series. Boston: The Athenaeum Press. Reviewed
in:
American Anthropologist 18 (1916): 277–78 (Goddard).
Anthropos 20 (1925): 365–68 (Schmidt).
Bibliotheca Sacra 71 (1914): 168–69.
Harvard Theological Review 7 (1914): 441–46 (Webster).
Journal of Religion 32 (1952): 74–75 (Wach).

CITED ARTICLES AND ESSAYS
1869. "The Tübingen School." *Baptist Quarterly* 3:210–35.
1877a. "On Hebrew Verb-Etymology." *Transactions of the American Philological Association* 7:50–72.

1877b. "On the Nominal Basis of the Hebrew Verb." *Proceedings of the American Philological Association* 8:29–30.

1878. "The Yoruban Language." *Transactions of the American Philological Association* 9:19–38.

1879. "Critical Notes." *Sunday School Times*, April 19, 1879.

1880a. "The Outward Form of Divine Revelation." *Religious Herald*, January 22, 1880.

1880b. "Inspiration and Criticism." *Religious Herald*, February 5, 1880.

1880c. "The Historical Books of the Bible." *Religious Herald*, March 11, 1880.

1880d. "A Bit of Personal Experience." *Religious Herald*, April 1, 1880.

1880e. "Destruction for Reconstruction." *Religious Herald*, April 22, 1880.

1880f. "Genesis and Geology." *Religious Herald*, May 6, 1880.

1881. "The Babylonian Element in Ezekiel." *Journal of Biblical Literature* 1:59–66.

1886. "The Present Position of Pentateuch Criticism." *Unitarian Review* 24:47–68.

1888. "The New Testament as Interpreter of the Old Testament." *The Old Testament Student* 8:124–33.

1890. "Evil Spirits in the Bible." *Journal of Biblical Literature* 9:17–30.

1893. "Myths and Legends as Vehicles of Religious Teaching." *Christian Register* 72:404–405.

1896. "Text-Critical Notes on Ezekiel." *Journal of Biblical Literature* 15:54–58.

1898. "Esther as Babylonian Goddess." *New World* 7:130–44.

1899a. "The Relation between Magic and Religion." *Journal of the American Oriental Society* 20:327–31.

1899b. "Taboo and Morality." *Journal of the American Oriental Society* 20:151–56.

1900a. "Charles Carroll Everett." *New World* 9:714.

1900b. "The Sacred Books of the Old Testament, Ezekiel." *The Expository Times* 11:225.

1902. "Creator Gods." *Journal of the American Oriental Society* 23:20–37.

1904. "Recent Discussion of Totemism." *Journal of the American Oriental Society* 25:146–61.

1905a. "An Early Form of Animal Sacrifice." *Journal of the American Oriental Society* 26:137–44.

1905b. "The Church and the Individual." *The International Quarterly* 12:292–311.

1905c. "Mexican Human Sacrifice." *Journal of American Folk-Lore* 18:173–81.

1906. "Ethical Influence in University Life." *International Journal of Ethics* 16:145–57.

1910. "The Higher Criticism." *Christian Register* 89:455–57.

OTHER ARTICLES AND ESSAYS BY TOY[1]

1879a. "Modal Development of the Shemitic Verb." *Transactions of the American Philological Association* 10:5–25.

1879b. "On the Shemitic Derived Stems." *Proceedings of the American Philological Association* 10:22.

1880a. "The Study of the Semitic Languages." *Proceedings of the American Philological Association* 11:10–13.

---

[1] This list is by no means exhaustive. For other works by Toy, see the Bibliography prepared by Harry Wolfson in Lyon and Moore, *Studies in the History of Religions*, 367–73, and Hurt, "Toy," 320–31.

1880b. The Hebrew Verb-termination *un.*" *Proceedings of the American Philological Association* 11:18–34.

1880c. "Remarks on J. G. Müller's Semitic Theory." *Journal of the American Oriental Society* 10:lxxii–lxxiii.

1880d. "The Study of Arabic." *Harvard Register* 1:212–13.

1881. "On the Home of the Primitive Semitic Race." *Transactions of the American Philological Association* 12:26–51.

1882. "The Semitic Personal Pronouns." *Proceedings of the American Philological Association* 13:x–xii.

1883. "Recent Progress among the Baptists." *Christian Register* 62:292.

1884. "The Date of the Korah Psalms." *Journal of Biblical Literature* 4:80–92.

1885a. "On Noun-Inflections in the Sabean." *Journal of the American Oriental Society* 11:xxiv–xxxi.

1885b. "Remarks on Guyard's Theory of Semitic Internal Plurals." *Journal of the American Oriental Society* 11:lix–lx.

1885c. "Notice of F. Delitzsch's Views as the Alleged Site of Eden." *Journal of the American Oriental Society* 11:lxxii–lxxiii.

1885d. "On the Kushites." *Journal of the American Oriental Society* 11:cviii–cix.

1885e. "The Masoretic Vowel System." *Hebraica* 1:137–44.

1885f. "The Revised Old Testament." *Christian Register* 64:468, 500, 516–17, 549–50.

1885g. "The Date of Deuteronomy." *Unitarian Review* 23:97–118.

1885h. "The New Philology." *Science* 6:366–68.

1886a. "On the Asaph Psalms." *Journal of Biblical Literature* 6:73–85.

1886b. "On Maccabean Pslams." *Unitarian Review* 25:47–68.

1886c. "The Older Arabic Poetry." *Harvard Monthly* 1:135–48.

1887a. "Kuenen's Critical Work." *Christian Register* 66:117.

1887b. "Rise of Hebrew Psalm-Writing." *Journal of Biblical Literature* 7:47–60.

1887c. "Modern Biblical Criticism." *Unitarian Review* 28:354–59.

1889a. "The Thousand and One Nights." *Atlantic Monthly* 63:756–63.

1889b. "The Lokman Legend." *Journal of the American Oriental Society* 13:clxxii–clxxvii.

1890a. "On Some Phonetic Peculiarities of Cairo Arabic." *Journal of the American Oriental Society* 14:cxii–cxiv.

1890b. "Ethics and Religion." *Popular Science Monthly* 36:727–44.

1890c. "That it might be Fulfilled." *The Unitarian* 5:284–85.

1891a. "Analysis of Genesis ii, iii." *Journal of Biblical Literature* 10:1–19.

1891b. "Relation of Jesus to Christianity." *Christian Register* 70:168–69.

1891c. "The Religious Element in Ethical Codes." *International Journal of Ethics* 1:289–311.

1892. "Abraham Keunen." *The New World* 1:64–68.

1893. "Israel in Egypt." *The New World* 2:121–41.

1896. "The Pre-Prophetic Religion of Israel." *The New World* 5:123–42.

1897a. "Accadian-Babylonian and Assyrian Literature." *Library of the World's Best Literature* 1:51–83.

1897b. "The Old Testament and the Jewish Apocrypha." *Library of the World's Best Literature* 27:10775–10818.

1899a. "The King in Jewish Post-Exilian Writings." *Journal of Biblical Literature* 18:156–66.

1899b. "The Earliest Form of the Sabbath." *Journal of Biblical Literature* 18:190–94.

1899c. "The Relation between Magic and Religion." *Journal of the American Oriental Society* 20:327–31.

1900. "Pope Leo XIII (The Dudleian Lecture for 1899)." *Christian Register* 79:65–69.

1902. "Remarks on the Hebrew Text of Ben-Sira." *Journal of the American Oriental Society* 23:38–43.

1905. "The Triumph of Yahwism." *Journal of Biblical Literature* 24:91–106.

1907a. "The Queen of Sheba." *Journal of American Folk-Lore* 20:207–12.

1907b. "Survey of Recent Literature of the Old Testament." *Harvard Theological Review* 1:377–81.

1910. "Pan-Babylonianism." *Harvard Theological Review* 3:47–84.

1912. "The Islam of the Koran." *Harvard Theological Review* 5:474–514.

OTHER CITED WORKS

Abbott, Lyman. "The Evolution of Christianity." *New World* 1 (1892): 1–18.

Ahlstrom, Sidney E. "The Scottish Philosophy and American Theology." *Church History* 24 (1955): 257–72.

Allen, Catherine B. *New Lottie Moon Story*. Nashville, TN: Broadman Press, 1980.

———. "The Legacy of Lottie Moon." *International Bulletin of Missionary Research* 17 (1993): 146–52.

Allen, Garrick V. "Scriptural Allusions in the Book of Revelation and the Contours of Textual Research 1900–2014: Retrospect and Prospects." *Currents in Biblical Research* 14/3 (2016): 319–39.

Allen, Leslie C. *Ezekiel 20–48*. WBC 29. Dallas, TX: Word, 1990.

———. "The Structure and Intention of Ezekiel I." *Vetus Testamentum* 43 (1993): 145–61.

Announcement of the Summer School of Theology. Eleventh Session.—July 7-22, 1909. Subject: Present Religious Conditions and Prospects. Cambridge, MA: Harvard University, 1909.

Announcement of the Summer School of Theology. Tenth Session.—July 1-18, 1908. Subject: The Relation of Christianity to Other Religions. Cambridge, MA: Harvard University, 1908.

Aubert, Annette G. *The German Roots of Nineteenth Century American Theology*. Oxford: Oxford University Press, 2013.

Axsom, Jennifer S. "The Catholic Baptist and the Faith of Harvard: David Gordon Lyon, 1852–1935." Final Paper for Rev. Professor Peter J. Gomes, Harvard Divinity School, 2004.

Bainbridge, Judith Townsend. *Academy and College: The History of the Woman's College of Furman University*. Macon, GA: Mercer University Press, 2001.

Balla, Peter. "2 Corinthians." In *Commentary on the New Testament Use of the Old Testament*, edited by G. K. Beale and D. A. Carson. Grand Rapids: Baker Academic, 2009.

Barilan, Y. Michael. "The Vision of Vegetarianism and Peace: Rabbi Kook on the Ethical Treatment of Animals." *History of Human Science* 17/4 (2004): 69–101.

Barth, Karl. *Protestant Theology in the Nineteenth Century: Its Background and History*. Translated by Brian Cozens and John Bowden. New Edition. Grand Rapids: Eerdman's, 2002.

Barton, George. *The Religions of the World*. 2nd ed. Universtiy of Chicago Publications in

Religious Education. Chicago: University of Chicago Press, 1919.

Beetham, Christopher A. *Echoes of Scripture in the Letter of Paul to the Colossians.* BibInt 96. Leiden: Brill, 2008.

Bernard, L. L. "The Sociological Interpretation of Religion." *Journal of Religion* 18 (1938): 1–18.

Bernstein, Richard J. "The Resurgence of Pragmatism." *Social Research* 59 (1992): 813–40.

Bertoluci, Jose M. "The Son of the Morning and the Guardian Cherub in the Context of the Controversy Between Good and Evil." ThD Diss, Berrien Springs, MI: Andrews University, 1985.

Black, John Sutherland, and George Chrystal. *The Life of William Robertson Smith.* London: Adam and Charles Black, 1912.

Bledsoe, Albert Taylor. *An Essay on Liberty and Slavery.* Philadelphia: J. B. Lippincott & Co, 1856.

Böck, Barbara. "Proverbs 30:18-19 in the Light of Ancient Mesopotamian Cunieform Texts." *Sefarad* 69/2 (2009): 263–79.

Bodi, Daniel. *The Book of Ezekiel and the Poem of Erra.* OBO 104. Göttingen: Vandenhoeck & Ruprecht, 1991.

Broadus, John Albert. *A Gentleman and a Scholar: Memoir of James P. Boyce.* Birmingham, AL: Solid Ground Christian Books, 2004; from the 1893 edition by A.C. Armstrong and Son, New York, NY.

Brown, C. C. "Letter to the Seminary Magazine." *The Seminary Magazine*, March 1889.

Brown, Victoria Bissell, "Did Woodrow Wilson's Gender Politics Matter?" *Reconsidering Woodrow Wilson: Progressivism, Internationalism, War, and Peace*, ed. John Milton Cooper, Jr. (Baltimore: Johns Hopkins University Press, 2008), 125–64.

Buell, Denise K., and Caroline J. Hodge. "The Politics of Interpretation: The Rhetoric of Race and Ethnicity in Paul." *Journal of Biblical Literature* 123 (2004): 235–51.

Burton, H. W. *The History of Norfolk Virginia-A Review of Important Events and Incidents Which Occurred from 1736 to 1877; Also a Record of Personal Reminiscences and Political, Commercial, and Curious Facts.* Norfolk, VA: Private Schools, 1877.

Byington, Edwin. "Letter from Rev. Edwin Byington." In *Congregationalist and Christian World*, n.d.

Carman, John B., and Kathryn Dodgson, eds. *Community and Colloquy.* Cambridge: Center for the Study of World Religions, Harvard Divinity School, 2006.

Catalogue of the Norfolk Collegiate Institute for Young Ladies, Session of 1878-'79. Norfolk, VA: Virginian Printing House, 1877.

Cathcart II, William, ed. "Toy, Crawford H." *The Baptist Encyclopedia.* Philadelphia: Louis H. Everts, 1881.

Chambliss, J. A. "Reminiscences of the First Two Sessions." *The Seminary Magazine*, 1898.

Chauncey, Jr., George. "From Sexual Inversion to Homosexuality: The Changing Medical Conceptualization of Female 'Deviance.'" In *Passion and Power*, edited by Kathy Peiss and Christinna Simmons. Philadelphia: Temple University, 1989.

Christianity Today. "1978 Chicago Statement," December 17, 1982.

Clayton, John Powell. "Crawford Howell Toy of Virginia." *The Baptist Quarterly* 24 (1971).

Clopton, S. C. "Reminiscences of My Life at the Seminary." *The Seminary Magazine*,

February 1892.

Cohen, Naomi Wiener. *Jacob A. Schiff: A Study in American Jewish Leadership*. Hanover, NH: University Press of New England, 1999.

Conant, Thomas J. *Proverbs*. New York: Sheldon & Co, 1872.

"Contemporary Literature." *Presbyterian Quarterly and Princeton Review* 1/1 (1872): 181–200.

Cook, Harvey Toliver. *The Life and Work of James Clement Furman*. Greenville, SC: n.p., 1926.

Cornelius, Roberta D. *The History of Randoph-Macon Woman's College: From the Founding in 1891 Through the Year of 1949-50*. Chapel Hill: The University of North Carolina Press, 1951.

Coski, Ruth Ann. "John Singleton Mosby (1833-1916)." *Encyclopedia Virginia*, n.d. https://www.encyclopediavirginia.org/Mosby_John_Singleton_1833-1916#start_entry.

Cox, James L. *An Introduction to the Phenomenology of Religion*. London: Continuum, 2010.

Cox, Joseph P. "A Study of the Life and Word of Basil Manly, Jr." Unpublished dissertation, Louisville, KY: Southern Baptist Theological Seminary, 1954.

Crew, Jr., R. Thomas, and Benjamin H. Trask. *Grimes' Batter, Grandy's Battery and Huger's Batter Virginia Artillery*. The Virginia Regimental Histories Series. Lynchburg, VA: H.E. Howard, 1995.

Criswell, W. A. "Whether We Live or Die (SBC)." 1985. https://www.wacriswell.com/sermons/1985/whether-we-live-or-die-sbc/.

Cross, Carol Vaughn. "'Living in the Lives of Men': A Southern Baptist Woman's Missionary Journey from Alabama to Shandong, 1830–1909." Ph.D. dissertation, Auburn, AL: University of Auburn, 1998.

———. "Missionary Returns and Cultural Conversions in Alabama and Shandong: The Latter Years of Madam Gao Martha Foster Crawford." In *North American Foreign Missions, 1810–1914: Theology, Theory, and Policy*, edited by Wilbert R. Shenk, 243–60. Grand Rapids: Eerdmans, 2004.

Daniel, Robert Norman. *Furman University: A History*. Greenville, SC: Furman University, 1951.

Davis, Thomas W. *Shifting Sands: The Rise and Fall of Biblical Archaeology*. Oxford: Oxford University Press, 2004.

Delitzsch, Franz. *Wise King—Royal Fool: Semiotics, Satire and Proverbs 1–9*. JSOTSup 399. London: T & T Clark, 2004.

Derry, Cecil Thayer. *A Brief History of the Old Cambridge Baptist Church 1844–1944*. Cambridge, MA: The Cosmos Press, 1944.

Dill, J. S. *Lest We Forget: Baptist Preachers of Yesterday That I Knew*. Nashville, TN: Broadman Press, 1938.

Divinity School of Harvard University: Summer School of Theology. Seventh Session: The Bible. July 5-21, 1905. Cambrigde, MA: Harvard University, 1905.

Divinity School of Harvard University. Summer School of Theology. Sixth Session. July 5-21, 1904. Cambridge, MA: Harvard University, 1904.

Dorrien, Gary. *Social Ethics in the Making: Interpreting an American Tradition*. Oxford: Wiley-Blackwell, 2011.

Duncan, Pope A. "Crawford Howell Toy: Heresy at Louisville." In *American Religious*

Heretics: Formal and Informal Trials, edited by George H. Shriver, 56-88. Nashville: Abingdon, 1966.

Ehorn, Seth M. "The Citation of Psalm 68(67).19 in Ephesians 4.8 within the Context of Early Christian Uses of the Psalms." Ph.D. dissertation, Edinburgh, Scotland: University of Edinburgh, 2014.

Ellis, E. Earle. "Quotations in the NT." In *International Standard Bible Encyclopedia*. Grand Rapids, MI: Eerdmans, 1989.

Erdmann, Christian Friedrich David. *The Books of Samuel*. Translated by Crawford H. Toy and John Albert Broadus. New York: Charles Scribner's Sons, 1877.

Estep, William R. *Whole Gospel—Whole World: The Foreign Mission Board of the Southern Baptist Convention 1845–1995*. Nashville, TN: Broadman and Holman, 1994.

Everett, Charles Carroll. "The Historic and Ideal Christ." *New World* 1 (1892): 14–29.

Finsterbusch, Karin. *Weisung Für Israel: Studien Zu Religiösem Lehren Und Lernen Im Deuteronomium Und in Seinem Umfeld*. FAT 1/44. Tübingen: Mohr Siebeck, 2012.

Flowers, Elizabeth. "The Contested Legacy of Lottie Moon: Southern Baptists, Women, and Partisan Protestantism." *Fides et Historia* 43/1 (2011): 15–40.

Floyd, M. Ryan. *Abandoning American Neutrality: Woodrow Wilson and the Beginning of the Great War, August 1914-December 1915*. Basingstoke: Palgrave-Macmillan, 2013.

"Four Professors Retire." *The Harvard Graduates Magazine* 17 (1909): 622–26.

Foster, Stephen. "My Old Home Kentucky, Good Night!" 1853.

Fox, Michael V. "The Pedagogy of Proverbs 2." *Journal of Biblical Literature* 113 (1994): 223–43.

_____. "Who Can Learn? A Dispute in Ancient Pedagogy." In *Wisdom, You Are My Sister: Studies in Honor of Roland E. Murphy on the Occasion of His Eightieth Birthday*, edited by Michael L. Barré and Ronald E. Murphy, 62–77. Washington, DC: Catholic Biblical Association, 1997.

Freed, Rita E. "The Egyptian Expedition." In *MFA Highlights: Arts of Ancient Egypt*, edited by Rita E. Freed, Lawrence M. Berman, and Denise M. Doxey, 25–35. Boston: MFA Publications, 2003.

Gardner, Robert G. *A Decade of Debate and Division: Georgia Baptists and the Formation of the Southern Baptist Convention*. Macon, GA: Mercer University Press, 1995.

Giese, Ronald L. Jr., "'Iron Sharpens Iron' as a Negative Image: Challenging the Common Interpretation of Proverbs 27:17." *Journal of Biblical Literature* 135 (2016): 61–76.

Gladd, Benjamin. *Revealing the Mysterion: The Use of Mystery in Daniel and Second Temple Judaism with Its Bearing on First Corinthians*. BZNW 160. Berlin: De Gruyter, 2008.

Greene, Joseph. "A Complicated Legacy: The Original Collections of the Semitic Museum." *Journal of Eastern Mediterranean Archaeology & Heritage Studies* 5/1 (2017): 57–69.

Grenz, Stanley. *Beyond Foundationalism: Shaping Theology in a Postmodern Context*. Louisville, KY: Westminster/John Knox Press, 2001.

Griffiths, R. Marie. "Sexing Religions." In *The Cambridge Companion to Religious Studies*, edited by Robert A. Orsi, 338–59. Cambridge: Cambridge University Press, 2012.

Hankins, Barry. *Woodrow Wilson: Ruling Elder, Spiritual President*. Oxford: Oxford University Press, 2016.

Harris, Jessie Johnson. "My Mother, Julia Ann Toy Johnson." In *Autobiographical Notes*, 347. Printed privately. 1958.

Hart, D. G. *The University Gets Religion: Religious Studies in American Higher Education*. Baltimore, MD: Johns Hopkins University Press, 1999.

Hays, Richard B. *Echoes of Scripture in the Letters of Paul*. New Haven: Yale University Press, 1993.

Heim, Knut Martin. *Poetic Imagination in Proverbs: Variant Repetitions and the Nature of Poetry*. BBRSup 4. Winona Lake, IN: Eisenbrauns, 2013.

Hincks, Edward Y. "Review of Johnson's The Quotations of the New Testament from the Old." *The New World: A Quarterly Review of Religion, Ethics, and Theology*. 1897.

Hinson, E. Glenn. "Southern Baptists and the Liberal Tradition in Biblical Interpretation, 1845–1945." *Baptist History and Heritage* 19 (1984): 16–20.

Hodges, George. "Censured Saints." *Atlantic Monthly*, April 1913.

Holzberger, William G., ed. *The Letters of George Santayana*. 8 vols. Cambridge, MA: MIT Press, 2001–2008.

Honeycutt, Roy L. "Heritage Creating Hope: The Pilgrimage of The Southern Baptist Theological Seminary." *Review and Expositor* 81 (1984): 367–91.

House, Paul. "Crawford Howell Toy and the Weight of Hermeneutics." *Southern Baptist Journal of Theology* 3 (1999): 28–39.

Howell, Morton B. "The Howells and the Toys." In *Autobiographical Notes*, edited by Lipscomb Johnson, 365–66. Privately printed. 1958.

Howell, R. B. C. *The Early Baptists of Virginia*. Philadelphia: The Bible and Publication Society, 1857.

Hughes, Jr., Nathaniel Cheairs. *Yale's Confederates: A Biographical Dictionary*. Knoxville: The University of Tennessee, 2008.

Hurd, Stephen. "Confronting an Intellectual Revolution: The Southern Baptists and the Toy Controversy." M.A. thesis, Nashville, TN: Vanderbilt University, 1987.

Hurt, Billy G. "Crawford Howell Toy: Old Testament Interpeter." Dissertation, Louisville, KY: Southern Baptist Theological Seminary, 1965.

Hyatt, Irwin T. *Our Ordered Lives Confess: Three Nineteenth-Century American Missionaries in East Shantung*. Cambridge, MA: Harvard University Press, 1976.

Isenberg, Nancy. *White Trash: The 400-Year Untold History of Class in America*. New York: Penguin Books, 2016.

James, William. *Pragmatism: A New Name for Some Old Ways of Thinking*. New York: Longman and Green and Co., 1907.

Jankowski, Paul. *Shades of Indignation: Political Scandals in France, Past, and Present*. New York: Berghahn, 2007.

Jarausch, Konrad H. "American Students in Germany 1815–1914: The Structure of German and U.S. Matriculates at Göttingen University." In *German Influences on Education in the United States to 1917*, edited by Henry Geitz, Jürgen Heideking, and Jurgen Herbst, 195–211. New York: Cambridge University Press, 1995.

Jeffers, M. D. "Reminiscences of My Seminary Life." *The Seminary Magazine*, January 1892.

Johnson, Franklin. *The Quotations of the New Testament from the Old Considered in the Light of General References*. Philadelphia: American Baptist Publication Society, 1895.

Johnson, John Lipscomb. *Autobiographical Notes*. Privately published. 1958.

Johnstone, William. "Introduction." In *William Robertson Smith: Essays in Reassessment*, edited by William Johnstone, 19–20. Sheffield: Sheffield Academic Press, 1995.

Jones, J. William. *Christ in the Camp: Religion in Lee's Army*. Richmond, VA: B.F. Johnson, 1887.

———. "Recollections of the First Session of the Seminary." *The Seminary Magazine*, October 1891.

Jones, Reuben. *A History of the Virginia Portsmouth Baptist Association*. Raleigh, NC: Edwards, Broughton & Company, 1881.

Kassis, Riad Aziz. *The Book of Proverbs and Arabic Proverbial Works*. VTSup 74. Leiden: Brill, 1999.

Keefer, Arthur. "A Shift in Perspective: The Intended Audience and a Coherent Reading of Proverbs 1:1-7." *Journal of Biblical Literature* 136 (2017): 103–16.

Kimball, Charles. *Jesus' Exposition of the Old Testament in Luke's Gospel*. JSNTSup 94. Sheffield: JSOT Press, 1994.

King, Philip J. *American Archaeology in the Mideast: A History of the American Schools of Oriental Research*. Philadelphia: American Schools of Oriental Research, 1983.

Knowles, Michael. *Jeremiah in Matthew's Gospel: The Rejected Prophet Motif in Matthean Redaction*. JSNTSup 62. Sheffield: Sheffield Academic Press, 1993.

LaFantasie, Glenn W., ed. *The Correspondence of Roger Williams*. 2 vols. Hanover, NH: University Press of New England, 1988.

Lafazanos, Christine. "The Female Sexual Invert: A Threat to Sexologists' World View." *Footnotes* 1 (2006): 71–77.

Lafferty, John James. *Sketches of the Virginia Conference, Methodist Episcopal Church, South*. Richmond, VA: Christian Advocate Office, 1880.

Lamkin, Adrian J. "The Gospel Mission Movement within the Southern Baptist Convention." Ph.D. dissertation, Louisville, KY: Southern Baptist Theological Seminary, 1979.

Lawrence, Una Roberts. *Lottie Moon*. Nashville, TN: Sunday School Board, 1927.

Leeman, William P. "George Bancroft's Civil War: Slavery, Abraham Lincoln, and the Course of History." *The New England Quarterly* 81 (2008): 462–88.

Lenzi, Alan. "Proverbs 8:22-31: Three Perspectives on Its Composition." *Journal of Biblical Literature* 125 (2006): 687–714.

Link, Arthur, et al., eds. *The Papers of Woodrow Wilson*. 69 vols. Princeton: Princeton University Press, 1966.

Lucas, Ernest. *Proverbs*. Two Horizons. Grand Rapids: Eerdmans, 2015.

Lyon, David. "Crawford Howell Toy." *Harvard Theological Review* 13/1 (1920): 1–22.

———, and George F. Moore. *Studies in the History of Religions*. New York: Macmillan and Co., 1912.

Lyons, Michael A. "'A Barley Cake' (Ezek 4:12a): Syntax and Redaction." *Journal of Northwest Semitic Languages* 40 (2014): 79–92.

Lyu, Sun Myung. *Righteousness in the Book of Proverbs*. FAT 2/55. Tübingen: Mohr Siebeck, 2012.

Maddry, Charles E. *Christ's Expendables*. Nashville, TN: Broadman, 1949.

Manly, Jr., Basil. *The Bible Doctrine of Inspiration Explained and Vindicated*. New York: A.C. Armstrong 1888.

Marcus, Sharon. *Between Women: Friendship, Desire, and Marriage in Victorian England*.

Princeton: Princeton University Press, 2007.

Marty, Martin, and Scott Appleby. *The Fundamentalist Project*. Chicago: Chicago University Press, 1994.

McGlothlin, W. J. *Baptist Beginnings in Education: A History of Furman University*. Nashville, TN: Sunday School Board, 1926.

McKim, Randolph. *The Soul of Lee by One of His Soldiers*. New York: Longmans, Green, and Co., 1918. https://leefamilyarchive.org/reference/books/mckim/09.html.

McMichael, Mandy E. "'We Must Go out of This Union': The Two Secessions of Basil Manly Sr." *Baptist History and Heritage* 52/2 (2017): 8–19.

Meek, James A. *The Gentile Mission in Old Testament Citations in Acts: Text, Hermeneutic, and Purpose*. LNTS 385. London: T & T Clark, 2008.

Mencken, H. L. *Treatise on the Gods*. 2nd ed. New York: Knopf, 1946.

Merriam, Edmund F. *A History of American Baptist Missions*. Philadelphia: American Baptist Publication Society, 1900.

Mohler, Albert. "Heresy Is Not Heroic—Is Crawford Howell Toy a Baptist Hero?" n.d. https://albertmohler.com/2010/01/13/heresy-is-not-heroic-is-crawford-howell-toy-a-baptist-hero/.

Moncrief, John W. "Dr. Franklin Johnson." In *The University Record*, volume 3, edited by D.A. Robertson. Chicago: University of Chicago Press, 1917. 78–79.

Moore, Christopher. "Apostle of the Confederacy: J. William Jones and the Question of Ecumenism and Denominational Identity in the Development of Lost Cause Mythology." Dissertation, Waco, TX: Baylor University, 2016.

Moore, George F. "An Appreciation of Professor Toy." *American Journal of Semitic Languages and Literatures* 36 (1919): 1–17.

———. "Christian Writers on Judaism." *Harvard Theological Review* 14 (1921): 197–254.

Moore-Jumonville, Robert. *The Hermeneutics of Historical Distance: Mapping the Terrain of American Biblical Criticism, 1880–1914*. Lanham, MD: University Press of America, 2002.

Mueller, William A. *A History of Southerb Baptist Theological Seminary*. Nashville, TN: Broadman, 1959.

Munson, John W. *Reminiscences of a Mosby Guerrilla*. New York: Moffat, Yard, and Co., 1906.

Murphy, John. *The Origins and History of Religions*. Manchester: Manchester University Press, 1952.

Neely, Alan. "Saints Who Sometimes Were: Utilizing Missionary Hagiography." *Missiology: An International Review* 27 (1999): 441–57.

Nettles, Thomas J. *James Petigru Boyce: A Southern Baptist Statesman*. Phillipsburg, NJ: P&R Publications, 2009.

Newman, A. H. *A History of the Baptist Churches in the United States*. 6th ed. Philadelphia: American Baptist Publication Society, 1915.

Norton, Andrew. *The Evidences of the Genuineness of the Gospels*. Boston: American Unitarian Association, 1837.

Norton, Caroline Elizabeth Sarah Sheridan. "Bingen on the Rhine," n.d.

Odell, Margaret S. *Ezekiel*. SHBC 16. Macon, GA: Smyth & Helwys, 2005.

Olshausen, Hermann. *Biblischer Commentar Über Sämmtliche Schriften Des Neuen Testaments Zunächst Für Prediger Und Studirende*. Königsberg: A.W. Unzer, 1854.

————.*Biblical Commentary on the New Testament, Adapted Especially for Preachers and Students*. Translated by David Fosdick. New York: Sheldon & Co., 1860.

Owsley, Harriet Chappell. "The Morton B. Howell Papers." *Tennessee Historical Quarterly* 25/3 (1966): 287–309.

Parsons, Mikeal C. "From Harvard's Semitic Museum to Mount Desert Island and Back." *Chebacco: The Magazine of the Mount Desert Island Historical Society* 20 (2019): 97–107.

————, and Richard Walsh, eds. *A Temple Not Made With Hands: Essays in Honor of Naymond H. Keathley*. n.d.

Peabody, Francis G. "Voluntary Worship, 1886–1929." In *The Development of Harvard University Since the Inauguration of President Eliot: 1869-1929*, edited by Samuel Eliot Morison, li–lviii. Cambridge, MA: Published by the University, 1930.

Pemberton, Glenn D. "The Rhetoric of the Father in Proverbs 1-9." *Journal for the Study of the Old Testament* 30 (2005): 63–82.

Peretz, Martin. "The Sabotage of The Semitic Museum." *The Harvard Crimson*, November 29, 1993. http://www.thecrimson.com/article/1993/11/29/the-sabotage-of-the-semitic-museum/.

Peterson, Brian Neil. *Ezekiel in Context: Ezekiel's Message Understood in Its Historical Setting of Covenant Curses and Ancient Near Eastern Mythological Motifs*. PTMS 182. Eugene, OR: Pickwick, 2012.

Pollard, Edward. *The Lost Cause: A New Southern History of the War of the Confederates*. New York: E.B. Treat, 1867.

Powery, Emerson B. *Jesus Reads Scripture: The Function of Jesus' Use of Scripture in the Synoptic Gospels*. BibInt 63. Leiden: Brill., 2003.

"Preface." *Jewish Encyclopedia*. http://www.jewishencyclopedia.com/preface. n.d.

Reisner, George Andrew, Clarence Stanley Fisher, and David G. Lyon. *Harvard Excavation at Samaria, 1908-1910*. Cambridge: Harvard University Press, 1924.

Robertson, A. T. *Life and Letters of John Albert Broadus*. Philadelphia: American Baptist Publication Society, 1909.

Ropes, James Hardy. "Theological Education at Harvard." *Harvard Alumni Bulletin* 17/15 (1915).

Rorty, Richard. *Philosophy and the Mirror of Nature*. Princeton: Princeton University Press, 1979.

Royce, Josiah. "Professor Everett as a Metaphysician." *New World* 9 (1900): 726–41.

Rupp, Leila J., Molly McGarry, Kanchana Natarajan, Dasa Francikova, Tania Navarro Swain, and Karin Lützen. "Women's History in the New Millennium: Carroll Smith-Rosenberg's 'The Female World of Love and Ritual' after Twenty-Five Years." *Journal of Women's History* 12/3 (2000): 6–248.

Ryland, Charles H. "Recollections of the First Year." *Southern Baptist Theological Seminary Boyce Digital Library E-Text Collection*, n.d. Accessed February 1, 2018.

Ryland, Garnet. *The Baptists of Virginia*. Richmond: The Virginia Baptist Board of Missions and Education, 1955.

Saiman, Chaim N. "Talmud Study, Ethics and Social Policy: A Case Study in the Laws of Wage-Payment as an Argument for Leo-Lamdanut." *Villanova University School of Law Public Law and Legal Theory Working Paper No. 2016-1024*, 2014.

"Sampey and Lee." http://archives.sbts.edu/the-history-of-the-sbts/our-lore/sampey-and-lee/. n.d.

Sanders, E. P. *Paul and Palestinian Judaism: A Comparison of Patterns of Religion*. Philadelphia: Fortress Press, 1977.

Sandoval, Timothy. "Revisiting The Prologue of Proverbs." *Journal of Biblical Literature* 126 (2007): 455–73.

Santayana, George. *The Last Puritan: A Memoir in the Form of a Novel*. 5 vols. New York: Charles Scribner's Sons, 1964.

Saunders, Ernest W. *Searching the Scriptures: A History of the Society of Biblical Literature, 1880–1980*. Chico, CA: Society of Biblical Literature, 1982.

Scharnhorst, Gary, and Denise D. Knight. "Charlotte Perkins Gilman's Library: A Reconstruction." *Resources of American Literary Study* 23/2 (1997): 181–219.

Schechter, Solomon. "The Law and Recent Criticism." *Jewish Quarterly Review* 3 (1891): 754–66.

Schmidt, Jr., Donald Lee. "An Examination of Selected Uses of the Psalms of David in John and Acts in Light of Traditional Typology." Ph.D. dissertation, Fort Worth, TX: Southwestern Baptist Theological Seminary, 2014.

Schwartz, Shuly Rubin. *The Emergence of Jewish Scholarship in America: The Publication of the Jewish Encyclopedia*. Vol. 13. Monographs of the Hebrew Union College. Cincinatti: Hebrew Union College Press, 1991.

Scott, C. S. *The Fortieth Anniversary of the Boston North Baptist Association, Held in the Central Square Baptist Church, Boston*. Boston: Conant & Newhall, 1888.

Seaburg, Alan. "Earl Morse Wilbur." *Dictionary of Unitarian and Universalist Biography*, n.d. Online. Accessed August 21, 2018. http://uudb.org/articles/earlmorsewilbur.html.

Shurden, Walter B. *Not a Silent People: Controversies That Have Shaped Southern Baptists*. Macon, GA: Smyth & Helwys, 1995.

Smend, Rudolf. "William Robertson Smith and Julius Wellhausen." In *William Robertson Smith: Essays in Reassessment*, edited by William Johnstone, 226–42. JSOT. Sheffield: Sheffield Academic Press, 1995.

———. "The Interpretation of Wisdom in Nineteenth-Century Scholarship." In *Wisdom in Ancient Israel: Essays in Honor of J. A. Emerton*, edited by John Day, R.P. Gordon, and H. G. M. Williamson, 257–68. Cambridge: Cambridge University Press, 1998.

Smith-Rosenberg, Carroll. "The Female World of Love and Ritual: Relations between Women in Nineteenth-Century America." *Signs* 1 (1975): 1–29.

Snell, Daniel C. *Twice-Told Proverbs and the Composition of the Book of Proverbs*. Winona Lake, IN: Eisenbrauns, 1993.

Soares, George M. *The Formula Quotations in the Infancy Narrative of Matthew: An Enquiry Into the Tradition History of Mt 1–2*. AnBib 63. Rome: Pontifical Biblical Institute, 1976.

Spears, Richard. *Forbidden American English*. Chicago, IL: Passport Books, 1990.

Stanley, Christopher D. *Paul and the Language of Scripture: Citation Technique in the Pauline Epistles and Contemporary Literature*. SNTSMS 69. Cambridge: Cambridge University Press, 1992.

———. "Paul and Scripture: Charting the Course." In *As It Is Written: Studying Paul's Use of Scripture*, edited by Stanley E. Porter and Christopher D. Stanley, 3–14. SBLSymS 50. Leiden: Brill, 2008.

"Statistics." n.d. https://iiif.lib.harvard.edu/manifests/view/drs:47567736$1i).

Steinmann, Andrew E. "Three Things...Four Things...Seven Things: The Coherence of Proverbs 30:11-33 and the Unity of Proverbs 30." *Hebrew Studies* 42 (2001): 59–66.

Steinson, Barbara J. "Wilson and Woman Suffrage." In *A Companion to Woodrow Wilson*, edited by Ross A. Kennedy, 343–63. New York: Wiley-Blackwell, 2013.

Stricklin, David L. *A Genealogy of Dissent: Southern Baptist Protest in the Twentieth Century.* Lexington, KY: University Press of Kentucky, 2000.

Sullivan, Regina. *Lottie Moon: A Southern Baptist Missionary to China in History and Legend.* Baton Rouge, LA: LSU Press, 2011.

Sutton, Jerry. *The Baptist Reformation: The Conservative Resurgence in the Southern Baptist Convention.* Nashville: Broadman and Holman, 2000.

Talbert, Charles H. "The Bible as Spiritual Friend." *Perspectives in Religious Studies* 13 (1986): 55–64.

Tappy, Ron E. *The Archaeology of the Ostraca House at Israelite Samaria: Epigraphic Discoveries in Complicated Contexts.* Annual of The American Schools of Oriental Research 70. Boston: American Schools of Oriental Research, 2016.

———. "The Harvard Expedition to Samaria: A Story of Twists and Turns in the Opening Season of 1908." *Buried History. Journal of the Australian Institute of Archaeology* 52 (2016): 3–30.

Tassel, Janet. "The Semitic Museum Rises Again: After Forty Years of Neglect a Revivified Harvard Museum Opens to the Public." *Harvard Magazine,* April 1982.

Taylor, George Braxton. *Virginia Baptist Ministers.* Lynchburg, VA: J.P. Bell Company, 1912.

The Carnegie Foundation for the Advancement of Teaching: Ninth Annual Report of the President and of the Treasurer. Boston: Merrymount Press, 1914.

Thomas, Ella Marshall. *History of Freemason St. Baptist Church.* Norfolk, VA: Hampton Roads Paper Company, Inc., 1917.

Venter, Pieter. "Review of James Alfred Loader 'Proverbs 1-9." *HTS Teologiese Studies/Theological Studies* 72/4 (2018): 1–8.

Vere, M. Schele de. *Outlines of Comparative Philology, with a Sketch of the Languages of Europe, Arranged upon Philologic Principles; and a Brief History of the Art of Writing.* New York: G.P. Putnam & Co., 1853.

Vetne, Reimar. "The Influence and Use of Daniel in the Synoptic Gospels." PhD Diss, St. Andrews, Scotland: St Andrews University, 2011.

Wach, Joachim. "Introduction to the History of Religions." *Journal of Religion* 32 (n.d.): 74–75.

Walters, John. *Norfolk Blues: The Civil War Diary of the Norfolk Light Artillery Blues.* Shippenburg, PA: Burd Street Press, 1997.

Waltke, Bruce K. *The Book of Proverbs Chapters 1–15.* NICOT. Grand Rapids: Eerdmans, 2004.

Warner, Charles Dudley. *A Library of the World's Best Literature XLV: Synopses of Famous Books & General Index.* New York: Cosimo, 2009.

Waters, Guy Prentiss. *The End of Deuteronomy in the Epistles of Paul.* WUNT 2/221. Tübingen: Mohr Siebeck, 2006.

Weaver, C. Douglas. *Baptists and the Holy Spirit: Interactions with the Holiness Pentecostal-Charismatic Traditions.* Waco, TX: Baylor University Press, 2019.

Weinstein, Edwin A. *Woodrow Wilson: A Medical and Psychological Biography.* Princeton:

Princeton University Press, 1981.

White, Andrew Dickson. *A History of the Warfare of Science with Theology in Christendom.* New York: Braziller, 1955.

Whybray, R. N. *The Book of Proverbs: A Survey of Modern Study, History of Biblical Interpretation 1.* Leiden: Brill, 1995.

Wilbur, Earle Morse. *A History of Unitarianism.* 2 vols. Boston: Beacon Press, 1945.

"William Holmes McGuffey: American Educator." *Online Britannica*, n.d. https://www.britannica.com/biography/William-Holmes-McGuffey.

Williams, George H. *Divinings: Religion at Harvard: From Its Origins in New England Ecclesiastical History to the 175th Anniversary of The Harvard Divinity School, 1636–1992.* Edited by Rodney L. Peterson. Vol 1. Göttingen: Vandenhoeck & Ruprecht with The Boston Theological Institute, Newton, MA, 2014.

Wills, Gregory. *Southern Baptist Theological Seminary, 1859–2009.* Oxford: Oxford University Press, 2009.

Willsky-Ciollo, Lydia. *American Unitarianism and the Protestant Dilemma: The Conundrum of Biblical Authority.* Lanham, MD: Lexington Books, 2015.

Wong, Ka Leung. "A Note On Ezekiel VIII 6." *Vetus Testamentum* 51 (2001): 396–400.

Young, W. J. "Rev. R.M. Saunders." In *Minutes of the One Hundred and Eighteenth Session of The Virginia Annual Conference of the Methodist Episcopal Church, South, Held at Norfolk, VA, November 14-22, 1900: Memoires, Reports and Directory*, edited by Benard F. Lipscomb. Richmond, VA: J.W. Fergusson & Son, 1900.

Ziolkowski, Jan M., ed. *Obscenity: Social Control and Artistic Creation in the Middle Ages.* Leiden: Brill, 1998.

INDEX

88, 90n.7, 91, 93, 94, 99, 101, 102,
103, 104, 105, 106, 107, 110,
111n.95–96, 117, 118n.122, 119,
126, 127, 128n.8, 139, 161n.1, 164,
175, 176, 177, 181, 182n.80, 183,
184, 185, 186n.100, 195, 196, 197,
198, 199, 200, 227, 275, 276, 277,
283, 284, 292, 293, 294, 295n.23,
296n.24, 304, 315
Broadway Baptist Church (Louisville),
182
Brown, A. B., 27
Brown, C. C., 63n.37, 98n.40
Brown, J. E., 75n.88, 86, 87
Brown, Victoria Bissell, 248n.83
Brown University, 85, 183, 244n.69
Buell, Denise K., 148n.117
Burton, H. W., 230n.12
Byington, Edwin, 131n.19
Calkins, Raymond, 136, 137, 138n.44–
48, 153
Cambridge University, 117n.117
Carman, John B., 159n.189, 171n.35
Carnegie Foundation, 181, 229n.11
Cartledge, Tony, 3
Carver, W. O., 106, 275n.2, 276–277,
285
Cathart II, William, 18n.35, 35n.95
Central Presbyterian Church (Wash-
ington, D. C.), 246
Chambliss, J. A., 25, 26, 77n.100,
78n.100, 79n.107, 80, 92n.13, 294,
295
Charlottesville Baptist Church (Char-
lottesville, VA), 15, 18, 25, 29, 315
Chauncey, Jr., George, 308n.60
Chrystal, George, 113n.107,
116n.114&116–117, 117n.118–
119
Cincinnati College, 17
Clayton, John Powell, ixn.2, 91n.8
Clopton, S. C., 63n.37–38
Cohen, Naomi Wiener, 212n.53
Colgate Theological Seminary, 185
Conant, Thomas J., 102
Cook, Harvey Toliver, 58n.9,
108n.79&81

Coolidge, Jane Toy, 110n.92, 181n.79,
223n.101, 228, 230n.17, 231–232,
234n.30, 237n.42, 245n.75, 259–
260, 262n.147, 263n.148,
264n.156, 266, 268n.173–174, 271,
287n.53, 292n.6
Cornelius, Roberta D., 229n.11
Coski, Ruth Ann, 16n.26
Cox, James L., 101n.56
Cox, Joseph P., 159n.189
Crawford, Martha, 298, 299n.30, 302,
304–305, 307, 309
Crawford, T. P., 299n.30, 300–302,
304–305, 306n.54, 309
Crew, Jr., R. Thomas, 40n.113
Criswell, W. A., 4, 309n.63
Cross, Carol Ann Vaughn, xvi,
301n.40–41, 301n.41–42, 305n.52,
308n.60
Cumberland Street Baptist Church
(Norfolk, VA), 35, 39, 314
Daniel, Robert Norman, 108n.78&80,
109n.82–83
Dargan, J. O. B., 94
Darwin, Charles, 60, 298
Davis, Thomas W., 212n.56
Davis, Carrie, 66, 295, 296n.24
Delitzsch, Franz, 153n.154, 197, 334
Derry, Cecil Thayer, 183n.86, 184n.90,
188n.107
Dill, J. S., 41n.116, 61n.30, 63n.37
Dodgson, Kathryn, 159n.189, 171n.35
Dorner, Isaac August, 51, 171
Dorrien, Gary, 114n.109,
121n.130&137
Duncan, Pope A., 51n.150, 80n.111,
111n.98, 112n.101
Eaton, T. T., 12n.11, 68n.61, 94, 316
Eaton (E. T. R.), Josephine, 71, 72
Ehorn, Seth M., 145n.89
Eliot, Charles W., xi, xiii, xiv, 5, 112–
122, 125–126, 128, 132, 134, 170,
175, 177–180, 181n.75–78, 189,
191, 201–204, 206, 209, 210,
213n.58, 214, 217n.80, 223–224,
232, 237, 238n.44, 243, 245n.73,

179n.67, 182, 184, 185, 187n.104,
188, 193, 195–225, 231n.19, 261,
264, 266, 285, 286, 287, 296n.24,
304, 323–326, 329, 332
Lyon, Mabel Everett (Harris), 222
Lyon, Tosca (Woehler), 217, 218, 220,
221
Lyon, Jr., David G., 222, 326, 327
Lyons, Michael A., 151n.142
Lyu, Sun Myung, 153n.157
Maddry, Charles E., 296
Manly, Jr., Basil, 25, 28n.67, 33,
34n.92, 37, 63, 67, 79n.107,
84n.121, 86, 89, 96n.31, 99–101,
279n.16
Marcus, Sharon, 307n.57
Martin Female College (Pulaski, TN),
229
Marty, Martin, 132n.25
Mauldin, Mary, 228, 293–294
McCurdy, J. F., 154, 332
McGlothlin, W. J., 108n.79–80, 109
McGuffey, William Holmes, 17, 18,
19
McKim, Randolph, 40n.115
McMichael, Mandy E., xvi, 36n.98, 37
Mead, C. M., 162, 163
Meek, James A., 145n.89
Mencken, H. L., 158
Merriam, Edmund F., 29n.72
Merrill, Selah, 162, 166
Midwestern Baptist Seminary, 4
Mississippi Baptist Convention, 57
Mississippi Female College (Meridian,
MS), 229
Mohler, R. Albert, 3, 309
Moncrief, John W., 185n.94
Moon, Anna, 295, 304
Moon, Colie, 295, 307
Moon, Charlotte "Lottie", xi, xiv, xvi,
xvii, 3, 20–21, 288–311
Moon, Edmonia, 297, 307
Moore, Christopher, xvi, 29n.73,
37n.103
Moore, George F., 19n.39, 39n.111–
112, 40n.114, 41n.117, 51n.148,
60n.26, 63n.39, 64n.46, 72n.80,

74n.87, 110n.91, 117n.120, 118,
129, 130, 134, 135n.32, 139n.53,
141, 143n.74&77, 144, 145, 148,
149, 150, 151, 152n.144, 153, 156,
157, 159, 168, 170, 171n.36, 173,
174, 178n.62, 179, 203, 219,
263n.151, 285n.44, 329, 332,
333n.1
Moore, E. C., 179, 202n.19
Moore-Jumonville, Robert, 141
Morgan, Morris, 168, 169
Mosby, John Singleton, 16
Mount Desert Island, 210n.48, 220,
223, 237, 261, 263n.153
Mount Pleasant College, 77
Mueller, William A., 285
Munson, John W., 16n.25
Murphy, John, 158
Neely, Alan, 290n.2, 306, 307,
Nettles, Thomas J., 70n.67, 278–279,
280n.22
New Church Seminary (Boston), 162
Newell, William, 168, 169
Newman, A. H., 285n.47
Nichols, J. T. G., 189, 190n.113
Nock, Arthur Darby, 159
Norfolk Academy, 13
Norfolk Collegiate Institute for Young
Ladies, 229, 230, 261
Norton, Andrew, 190n.117, 191n.117
Norton, Caroline Elizabeth Sarah
Sheridan, 296n.25
Odell, Margaret S., 152
Ohio University, 17
Old Cambridge Baptist Church
(OCBC) in Cambridge, MA, xiv,
xv, xvii, 145n.87, 160, 162n.5,
177n.58, 182–185, 187–188, 189,
191–192, 202n.19, 232, 285
Olshausen, Hermann, 48, 49, 50
Orne, Jr., John, 162
Ottawa University (Kansas), 185, 187
Owsley, Harriet Chappell, 13
Pacific Unitarian School for Ministry,
136
Paine, F. O., 162
Palmer, George Herbert, 171

Woman's Missionary Union, xiv,
    290n.3, 310n.67, 331
Wong, Ka Leung, 151n.142
World War I, 132, 239, 243
Worrell, A. S., 77
Wriglit, John, 168, 169
Yale College [University], 39, 85n.123,
    138n.44, 178n.65, 244n.69, 329
Young, W. J., 228n.5, 229n.7&9,
    230n.12
Young, Edward J., 5, 114n.109, 117,
    120n.128, 125, 126
Ziolkowski, Jan M., 235n.35